THE PROMISE
OF SOCIOLOGY

THE PROMISE
OF SOCIOLOGY

IIIIIIIIIIIIIIIIIIIIIIIIIIIIIIIIIIIIIIIIIIII

THE CLASSICAL
TRADITION AND
CONTEMPORARY
SOCIOLOGICAL
THINKING

ROB BEAMISH

University of Toronto Press

LIBRARY AND ARCHIVES CANADA CATALOGUING IN PUBLICATION

Beamish, Rob B. (Rob Barker), 1949–
    The promise of sociology : the classical tradition and contemporary sociological
thinking / Rob Beamish.

Includes bibliographical references and index.
Issued also in electronic format.
ISBN 978-1-4426-0187-1 (pbk.)

    1. Sociology—Textbooks. 2. Sociology—Philosophy—Textbooks.
3. Culture—Textbooks. I. Title.

HM586.B42 2010   301   C2010-903465-1

We welcome comments and suggestions regarding any aspect of our publications
—please feel free to contact us at news@utphighereducation.com or visit our
internet site at www.utphighereducation.com.

North America
5201 Dufferin Street
Toronto, Ontario, Canada, M3H 5T8

2250 Military Road
Tonawanda, New York, USA, 14150

ORDERS PHONE: 1-800-565-9523
ORDERS FAX: 1-800-221-9985
ORDERS E-MAIL: utpbooks@utpress.utoronto.ca

UK, Ireland, and continental Europe
NBN International
Estover Road, Plymouth, PL6 7PY, UK
ORDERS PHONE: 44 (0) 1752 202301
ORDERS FAX: 44 (0) 1752 202333
ORDERS E-MAIL: enquiries@nbninternational.com

The University of Toronto Press acknowledges the financial support for its
publishing activities of the Government of Canada through the Book Publishing
Industry Development Program (BPIDP).

Printed in Canada

Typesetting by Em Dash Design

To the students

CONTENTS

PREFACE

Among the first courses I taught was the introduction to sociology at the University of Toronto in 1980. With the exception of the six years I spent as Associate Dean (Studies) at Queen's University (1995–2001) and a year developing a program in human health, I have taught introductory sociology on a regular basis for over two decades. In the early years, I used standard introductory texts and then switched to several more focused books that I supplemented and drew together with my lectures. I never taught the same course twice, making changes every year as I tried to meet my own goals as an instructor while striving to meet the wants and expectations that each cohort of students expressed in course assessments. With more than twenty years behind me, I felt it was time to fashion a text that introduced students to sociology based upon what I had learned practicing the craft of sociology, gleaned from my experiences in the lecture hall, believed was most important for first year students to learn about the discipline, and took into account students' abilities to grasp what is, in fact, a very complex subject. This book draws upon the wisdom and experiences I have gained over my academic career, and I hope it will help first year students today begin a journey that I and others have found so challenging and fulfilling.

Three key principles inform this text. The first stems from the advice a senior colleague gave me in 1980 and students over the years have continually reinforced: never underestimate the abilities of your students. Although many think the education system has been "dumbed down" to meet the expectations of the proverbial lowest common denominator, my experiences as an instructor have suggested that today's students are highly capable and are looking for intellectual challenges. If an instructor sets low expectations, most students will do what is needed to meet the mark. If students are challenged with higher expectations, most will rise to the challenge and often exceed it. While some students grumble that the course was harder than they had anticipated, far more take the time to thank me for giving them the opportunity to genuinely expand their knowledge and to challenge their stocks of everyday knowledge. Most of all, the results that I read in term papers and examinations indicate that today's students possess some formidable skills, and university instructors should be obliged to let students demonstrate their abilities and build upon them.

The second principle was to keep socio-historical context as a key element. The easiest students to teach are those who are entering the postsecondary education system later in life or returning to it as "mature students." Students who have a wealth of life experiences behind them grasp sociology and the sociological frame of reference quickly and easily because they can see from their own lives how one's social location at a particular point in time influences one's perception of the world fundamentally.

The corollary is that younger students, with far fewer life experiences and much less appreciation for historical time, have more difficulty grasping the main features of sociology. As a result, there is a temptation to focus exclusively on the contemporary and the popular, on what is familiar, so that students will find immediate relevance and interest in sociology. But I have never found that a good teaching strategy.

Good sociology requires the examination of how people's immediate experiences (their personal biographies) intersect with the history of the social structure. And one cannot adequately grasp the immediate without knowing what happened before. As a result, I continually strive to place every topic, issue, and problem within a broader socio-historical context. This means my course is inescapably informed by social history—more to the point, it is structured so that students must begin to appreciate social history because it is so critical to good sociology.

Almost every issue I cover begins with a context that predates the year in which the majority of my students were born. At first, some find it frustrating: who cares what happened in 1968? But, as they proceed through the course, what is almost intuitive to the mature student becomes automatic for younger students as well. Social context becomes not only meaningful but a powerful departure point for how students examine their immediate, everyday life experiences. Not only does 1968 become relevant, but 1776, 1789, 1848, 1912, 1945, 1989, 2009, and numerous other signposts become highly meaningful as the context for a fuller understanding of today's world.

Despite the resistance and impatience of youth, holding firm on the importance of socio-historical context is a principle that has paid many dividends
over my two decades in the lecture hall.

My final principle is to enjoy the freedom sociology brings to human life.
I do not know how often students think of enjoyment, freedom, and sociology in the same sentence, but they all belong together. Sometimes sociology is work, sometimes it represents an obstacle to taking the day or night
off from study, but, in the end, and in the process of learning about the social
world, sociology should bring excitement, satisfaction, and accomplishment—all feelings that one can enjoy. The most enjoyable experience, however, is freedom—the freedom to explore, discover, and learn; the freedom
to disagree, dispute, and reject. Sociology provides a framework that facilitates all of these freedoms and their enjoyment.

Rules are almost always associated with constraint—something is ruled
out. But rules also enable. Without the rules of language, people could not
communicate; without the informal rules of social interaction, we would
never know how to proceed in social situations. Sociology is the same.

The sociological frame of reference rules out some forms of knowledge
and inquiry. Sociology, for example, rejects mysticism as a form of explanation; it rejects tradition as the sole basis for legitimate action. As the discussion of Max Weber in the text emphasizes, sociologists must adhere to
some very specific rules and criteria to achieve the goals of genuine, scholarly
inquiry. But, as much as those rules constrain, they also enable. Sociology's
rules enable those who employ the sociological frame of reference to explore
the world in a very open, systematic, and critical fashion. Enjoying the freedom sociology offers is the final principle I always keep in mind as I introduce students to what Auguste Comte called "the queen of the sciences."

Although many friends and colleagues have contributed over the years
to what emerges in this book, there are three groups of people, in particular, whom I want to recognize and thank.

Bill Munn, a long-serving tutor-marker for the correspondence section
of introductory sociology at Queen's University, and Christina Salavantis,
the Teaching-Assistant Coordinator for the Department of Sociology at
Queen's, were central to the development of this text and my current introductory course. Reading this book meticulously from beginning to end in
various drafts over the last five years, Christina and Bill helped improve its
form, style, content, and coverage in ways that leave me deeply in their debt.

I want to thank the anonymous reviewers of an earlier draft of this text,
Anne Brackenbury for her skill and dedication in bringing this project to fruition, Karen Taylor for her careful attention to detail and fine aesthetic sense
of the English language, and Anna Del Col and her team for producing the

cover image for this book. The reviewers' positive comments were encouraging and motivating while their critique provided an important "outsider" perspective that has resulted in several fundamental improvements to the text. I wish to extend my profound thanks to them for the attentive and detailed professional feedback they provided—I hope they recognize all the places where their thoughts have added to the substance of the discussions that follow. Anne's belief in the project has been central to the final form it has taken today. She took a risk in supporting an introductory text that differs significantly from the norm, and her confidence that others will find this book stimulating and useful bolstered my own belief in the project. I deeply appreciate all she has done to make this text available to a much wider audience than it has enjoyed over the past few years. Karen's contributions went well beyond ensuring that this was a clean, clear, tight text. The suggestions she offered on the basis of her own knowledge and genuine interest in the material covered, along with her wonderful feel for words, added immeasurably to the text that has gone to publication. Anna had the almost impossible task of producing a cover design that would capture the essential themes of *The Promise of Sociology*. While a book should never be judged by its cover (alone), I cannot imagine a better first impression of what lies inside than the image Anna and her team produced. Working with the team Anne assembled at the Higher Education division of the University of Toronto Press has been a distinct pleasure.

Finally, I want to thank my family—especially Nada—for their unfailing support of this project and all of the countless hours I spend in lecture preparation, many of which I could have spent at home with them. I am truly fortunate to have a partner and family who value the university's educational mission as much as I do and who share my belief that the students I teach are part of an extended family and are an integral part of my life. For Weber, scholarship was a vocation; for me, teaching is no less a calling. So I am truly fortunate to have a family that is so fully supportive of my commitment to that dimension of my life-world.

Despite these debts, I want to dedicate this book to the students—past, present, and future—who have followed or will one day read the arguments and ideas presented in this text. It is my firm hope that they, too, will discover not only the liberating freedom and passion that Karl Marx, Émile Durkheim, Max Weber, C. Wright Mills, and ensuing generations of sociologists have found in the systematic study of the social worlds within which they lived but also the same sense of commitment to making the world safer, more equitable, and far more intrinsically rewarding than has ever been the case before.

Rob Beamish, Kingston

INTRODUCTION

Sociology should be one of the most interesting, challenging, and intellectually liberating courses of study that a student can pursue. Sociologists focus on a broad range of issues that cover everything from the most mundane aspects of people's everyday lives through to concerns about globalization, the concentration of international power, war and famine, and the social processes that degrade the environment—the ways humans produce, consume, and generate and dispose of waste.

Good sociology provides a much-needed corrective to the taken-for-granted understandings people have about the world around them. It seeks to provide more comprehensive knowledge about issues that affect individuals, groups, local communities, countries, regions of the world, or the global population as a whole. Sociological analyses can help policy makers and everyday women and men change their own lives and the lives of others. Learning to think sociologically can be a life-altering experience, but it is not easy to become a good sociologist.

In the same way that an Olympic sprinter dedicates hour upon hour to heavy training for a decade or more in order to cover 100 metres in one one-hundredth of a second less than the record, students must complete a lengthy, sometimes difficult, and frequently solitary learning process before they are ready to change the world through a sophisticated sociological understanding of the problems they seek to address. An introductory sociology course and an introductory text are just two resources that will assist students in this long and occasionally arduous but ultimately exciting and highly rewarding journey.

There are times when studying sociology is work; there are times when it is fascinating and others when it is totally empowering. Becoming a good sociologist requires learning a certain vocabulary and building specific skills; the process of gaining and refining both is easier for some than for others. Similarly, some terms, ideas, or skills are mastered quickly while others require time, concerted effort, and the will to understand the complexities of sociology and social life. It is, however, the total package that counts, and the rewards for mastering the terminology, skills, and knowledge required to become a good sociologist are deeply satisfying at a personal level and of significant consequence at an interpersonal and broader social level.

THE SOCIOLOGICAL FRAME OF REFERENCE

To help students begin the sociological journey, I have written this book to meet four main objectives. The first is to introduce students to what C. Wright Mills (1959) calls "the sociological imagination." Even though each person is a highly knowledgeable, sophisticated human agent who draws upon a vast wealth of social knowledge, that does not mean people think sociologically. On the contrary, even though many feel they have an almost intuitive familiarity with sociology, the everyday stocks of knowledge they use in their daily activities are significantly different from the theories and methods that sociologists routinely employ to understand society critically.

An exploration of how one thinks sociologically is the first and foremost task facing students and their instructor in an introductory course. In many respects, this entire book is designed to introduce students to the sociological frame of reference and to help them refine and consolidate that particular perspective as they cover the material presented in each chapter. In contrast to the quick overview provided in most introductory texts, a full chapter of this book is dedicated to exploring the sociological imagination in detail, so this way of thinking can serve as a firm foundation for students throughout their university studies as well as in their lives as citizens of the world.

The second objective for every introductory text and instructor is to provide students with a focused introduction to the discipline. Unfortunately, no introductory course or text can cover everything; they are always selective. In making difficult choices, an instructor and the author of a text must try to ensure that the core areas and issues are covered while also providing students with a meaningful range of the areas of inquiry that sociologists undertake.

There is also the question of breadth of coverage versus depth of analysis. One can cover a broad range of issues without going into too much detail or one can tackle a narrower range of material in greater depth. Unfortunately, there is not a perfect balancing point because some students will prefer broader coverage while others want greater depth; in a large class, it is impossible to meet the desires of every student. At the same time, instructors' opinions on what the correct balance is will vary.

The Promise of Sociology is written to stand alone as an introduction to modern sociological thinking and the classical tradition. But it can also be used in conjunction with one of the many introductory readers in sociology to give students a broader understanding of the discipline and of the key issues sociologists tackle. Irrespective of how the book is used, it presents more material than a student new to sociology can fully internalize during a first year course. Becoming a sociologist takes time. Claude Henri de Rouvroy, comte de Saint-Simon; Auguste Comte; Karl Marx; Émile Durkheim; and Max Weber—to name five thinkers relevant to sociology—did not make great contributions to the discipline until they had read and amassed considerable knowledge. And their quest for knowledge was not always easy and pleasurable. Scholarship is demanding work—it is time consuming and labour intensive.

Writing to his daughter Jenny in 1867 after publishing the first volume of *Das Kapital*, Marx remarks on some of the frustrations and disappointments that scholars face:

> You are surely convinced, my dear child, that I love books a great deal because I must annoy you with how much time I spend with them. But you would be wrong. I am a machine, condemned to devour them and then throw them, in an altered form, on the dung hill of history. (Quoted in Marx and Engels 1999:2)

Here is a very personal glimpse into the demanding and, at times, disheartening life of a committed scholar; it is also a sentiment that many students feel during their studies—"There is just too much to know, too much to read!" is a frustration and fear that every student, instructor, and scholar feels at one time or another.

The reality is that becoming a sociologist takes time, concentration, and a good deal of critical reading and sifting. No one expects a first year student to devour books at the same rate as Marx or Weber, but reading widely— reading with discipline every day—is the first step towards gaining a fully rewarding university education. The old adage that completing even the longest journey requires putting one foot in front of the other over and over again is true for scholars as much as it is for explorers—consistent effort over time brings the greatest rewards for both.

Sociology as a Passion

The text's third objective is to convey the passion that sociologists feel for their discipline. It is not easy to project passion in an introductory text—particularly because students learn better when they are calmly focused on the ideas and concepts before them rather than emotionally stimulated, agitated, and even provoked by that material. Most often, instructors are more successful in transmitting their passion for sociology through their lectures, but there are ways in which this text tries to stimulate a passion for sociology.

Mills, Marx, Durkheim, and Weber—all featured in this text—wanted to do more than simply understand the world in a systematic manner; they also wanted to change it. Sociology is not an "academic" discipline in the negative "ivory tower" sense of the word. From its emergence as a discipline, sociology has been used by conservatives, reformers, and revolutionaries to support particular social and political goals. Sociology is a discipline of and for change.

Sociological passion is also represented in the texture of some of the material and arguments included in this book. Some might think it unnecessary to quote so extensively from different sociologists' works or to include so many terms in the original French or German, but engaging directly with original sources places students in contact with thinkers' texts and ideas as they are developed. The direct engagement and dialogue between students and texts is the epitome of higher learning. At the same time, as each new generation of students wrestles with the meaning of classical texts, these writings are given new life and renewed significance. As a 17-year-old university student at the University of Bonn, Marx understood Hegel's *Philosophy of Right* very differently than did some of his professors or other established university authorities. Marx's fresh reading of Hegel, along with all-night sessions with members of the Trier Tavern Club, changed the way Marx and some of his fellow students thought about the world around them. This radical critique of classical texts should not remain confined to the nineteenth century—students today should engage passionately with classical texts from the perspective of the present as they seek to improve the world in which they live.

Citizens of the World

This text's final objective is to further the same goal that animated Mills's sociology. In *The Sociological Imagination,* Mills (1959) points out that ordinary men and women "often feel that their private lives are a series of traps" (p. 3). They feel constrained by "the private orbits in which they live; their visions and their powers are limited to the close-up scenes of job, family, neighbourhood" (Mills 1959:3). In other aspects of their lives, ordinary men and women feel they are merely spectators. "What they need, and what they feel they need," Mills (1959) argues, "is a quality of mind that will help them to use information and to develop reason in order to achieve lucid summaries of what is going on in the world and what may be happening within themselves" (p. 5). What they need, Mills continues, is the sociological imagination to "understand the larger historical scene" and how it directly affects them and the lives of people around them.

Not every student who takes an introductory course in sociology or reads an introductory text will become a sociologist. But they all become citizens of the world. So they all need to be able to observe, analyse, and judge social actions and social relations. Mills discusses these and other benefits of sociology at the end of his introduction to *Images of Man: The Classic Tradition in Sociological Thinking*:

> Reading sociology should increase our awareness of the imperial reach of social worlds into the intimacies of our very self. Such awareness, of course, is the cultural goal of all learning as well as of much art. For all humanistic disciplines, if properly cultivated, help us to transcend the moral sloth and the intellectual rigidities that constitute most of everyday life in every society of which we know.
>
> Sociological reflection is only one way of carrying on this cultural struggle, but surely today it is among the most direct of ways. Through such reflection, we become aware of our own "common sense" as being itself a social phenomenon to be examined and understood. One cuts beneath it, locating it within a particular nation or class or race at a particular period of history.... Classic sociology contains an enormous variety of conception, value, and method, and its relevance to the life-ways of the individual and to the ways of history-making in our epoch is obvious and immediate. This is why it is central to contemporary cultural work, and among the most valuable legacies of Western civilization. (Mills 1960:17)

The Promise of Sociology will help students who read it carefully, critically, and reflectively begin to cultivate sociology's unique awareness and insights, so they can better understand and shape the contemporary world. It is an extremely ambitious objective, but it is also a small, reasonable, and realistic one. Why? Mills (1960) notes that the sociological frame of reference can begin with "the acquisition of a vocabulary that is adequate for clear social reflection":

> Such a vocabulary need not be very extensive. In fact, I should say that only some twenty or so pivotal terms are essential. (P. 17)

This text suggests some words that a student might include in a vocabulary "adequate for clear social reflection." Determining their adequacy and considering others is something that students and their instructors may choose to explore together further.

AN OVERVIEW OF THE TEXT

Following this introduction, *The Promise of Sociology* focuses directly on the students who will be reading this book. Drawing upon several sources, including the Beloit College Mindset List and Michael Wesch's *YouTube* video "A Vision of Students Today," Chapter 1 presents students and their instructors with a collective portrait of "the Millennials" as a generation. Heavily reliant upon digital information and deeply embedded in electronic culture, today's first year students feel keenly the tensions and contradictions between the information sources they have relied upon and used throughout their lives and those that still dominate postsecondary education. The chapter closes with a discussion of the tenets of a liberal education and of the inspiration it may hold for students as they engage with the postsecondary educational experience.

Although inspirational, Thomas Arnold's notion that culture is sweetness and light, encompassing the best that has been said and thought about the world, is hardly an action plan. It does not provide much to help people critically understand the world and change it—that challenge is addressed in Chapter 2.

Chapter 2 takes students directly into the heart of this text as they encounter and explore the richness of Mills's conception of the "sociological imagination"—a perspective that draws directly from the roots of the discipline and has now served a couple of generations of sociologists extremely well. To animate this concept, the chapter focuses on Alfred Hitchcock's (1960) *Psycho,* a movie that overlaps in many interesting ways with *The Sociological Imagination.* The discussion uses the film to demonstrate the key dimensions of the quality of mind that Mills termed "the sociological imagination." At the same time, the chapter outlines a number of the important sociological themes and issues within *Psycho* and examines how a sociological understanding of the movie itself, the audiences that viewed it, and the social bases for its themes produce a rich appreciation of the movie as far more than a horror film.

The six chapters that constitute Part II—"The Classical Tradition"—introduce students to the three dominant macrosociological perspectives of classical sociology as they were developed by Marx, Durkheim, and Weber. There are three fundamental reasons for the depth and breadth of focus given to these three thinkers. First, their thought was shaped by the events and social circumstances that fundamentally changed the lives of humanity around the globe—they lived through a period of change that Karl Polanyi (1944) has aptly called "the great transformation." Writing during the emergence and early consolidation of industrial capitalism and the epoch of modernity, Marx, Durkheim, and Weber directly witnessed the profound changes that were taking place in England and western Europe. And they could draw important contrasts between their social worlds and earlier social formations while memories and interpretations of recently past times were still vivid and avidly debated by scholars, politicians, and people in the street (Giddens 1971, 1976). In short, all three thinkers wrote during a period that was highly conducive to developing the sociological frame of reference, and each of them did so with tremendous depth and insight.

Second, Marx, Durkheim, and Weber are complex, synthetic thinkers. Although introductory texts traditionally provide summary overviews of their work, a student can better grasp and understand their perspectives when given the opportunity to explore their ideas at some length. Although the precise details may fade from memory over time, the overall framework will remain vivid and alive when a student has the opportunity to work through some of the complexity of their perspectives rather than trying to memorize simplified summaries of Marx, Durkheim, or Weber "in a box."

Finally, the work of each of these early sociological thinkers was central to the development of sociology in the period after World War II. Their ideas shaped the discipline when it was becoming most influential in people's lives and firmly established within higher education. At the same time, even as postmodernist perspectives grow in influence, Marx, Durkheim, and Weber remain key reference points (and foils) for those engaged in sociological thought today.

The writings of Marx, discussed in Chapter 3 and Chapter 4, and of Durkheim, presented in Chapter 5 and Chapter 6, have features in common. But each scholar's work constitutes a unique perspective within the classical tradition. (Some might say these two perspectives are diametrically opposed, although the analysis presented here differs from that position.) While Durkheim stresses people's socially constructed consciousness as the main source of social constraint, Marx emphasizes the social relations of production within which people produce and tend to reproduce their lives as the departure point for understanding how people's full human potential is left unrealized. Durkheim tends to focus on the integrating aspects of societies while Marx seeks to highlight the often invisible but inescapably important tensions and contradictions in different social formations. Both

Marx and Durkheim address the ongoing presence of social change, and both think their work can contribute to the improvement of people's lives.

Weber's work also engages in very important ways with that of Marx and Durkheim. As the discussion in Chapter 7 indicates, Weber's emphasis upon sociology as the comprehensive study of social action contrasts with Durkheim's work, which was heavily influenced by the positivist tradition within French social thought, in general, and the legacy of Saint-Simon and Comte, in particular. At the same time, however, Durkheim's approach to sociology was influenced by German sociological thought, and there are important aspects of his work that complement or reinforce some of Weber's fundamental conceptions and perceptions of social life.

With respect to Marx, Weber is sometimes regarded as having overturned much of Marx's critique of capitalist society. However, Weber is best understood as engaging in a debate with Marx's legacy (including various distortions of Marx's positions by his successors) and as complementing critical aspects of Marx's contributions to sociology. Writing during the first two decades of the twentieth century and dealing, in particular, with the realities of German social and political life in the period between World War I and World War II, Weber faced many social and political challenges. These challenges, as the material in Chapter 8 demonstrates, helped to make his contributions to sociology among the most significant and enduring, even though a school of Weberian sociology never developed during or after his lifetime.

Part III—"Sociology and Contemporary Culture"—draws upon the ideas developed in the first two parts of the book to examine, in Chapter 9, the critical reservations a number of sociologists and public intellectuals have expressed about mass culture as stultifying entertainment. In Chapter 10, however, the text explores the manner in which popular culture can and often does achieve many, if not all, of the objectives that the critics find within high culture. By examining the intersection of culture and social structure, the chapter indicates the social forces that allow for cultural heterogeneity, social critique, and critical exploration of human meaning. Although any of a number of popular culture figures or artists could have served as the focal point for the analysis, Bob Dylan is selected partly because of his longevity—over Dylan's almost 50-year musical career, instructors and students alike have listened to Dylan's music in all its different forms. Mainly, however, Dylan is an excellent choice because of the link he provides between the early roots of popular culture in North America, its exponential growth in the period after World War II, and its current transformation in the digital age of e-culture. The discussion of popular culture and Dylan illustrates the ways in which sociology can take us beyond our ordinary stocks of everyday knowledge to a much deeper appreciation of how social life is shaped and conditions the present and future.

Chapter 11 brings the material covered in the text to a conclusion. It draws the key ideas together while also pointing to how students might develop their sociological imagination further and to the issues upon which they might concentrate.

PART ONE

WHY THINK
SOCIOLOGICALLY?

THE MILLENNIALS, KNOWLEDGE, AND CULTURE

When an instructor in a first year course first enters the lecture hall, she or he usually looks out on a large lecture theatre, about two-thirds full, with students still flowing in looking for places to sit—choosing, as much as possible, to avoid the first couple of rows. At one level, year after year, the students look the same: they are young; filled with energy, enthusiasm, and vitality; either engaged in animated conversation or searching for a familiar face in the great expanse of the lecture hall. At the same time, no matter how much they try to mask it, the students are nervous and begin to feel a growing sense of trepidation as the room fills, the conversational volume rises, and the instructor makes her or his final preparations before beginning the lecture.

Despite superficial similarities, today's students are not at all like the undergraduates with whom the instructor—even a very young one—attended university. Their high-school experience was different, the work world that they anticipate entering holds considerable uncertainty, and, most important, the everyday culture within which today's students have grown up and matured differs fundamentally from that of their instructor.

For just over a decade, Beloit College in Beloit, Wisconsin has produced—and trademarked—"The Beloit College Mindset List." It can serve as a useful one-way mirror for instructors and students as they prepare for their first encounter. This list lets an instructor look through the mirror to observe unobtrusively the students she or he will teach and to reflect upon them, while the students who look at the list will see themselves reflected back, not as individuals but as a generational cohort. They can know how others perceive them collectively and consider how much, as individuals, they fit the overall profile.

This chapter opens with a general portrait of first year students as a whole.[1] It then focuses on some of the social forces that have influenced the life experiences and expectations of students entering postsecondary education and considers how that background has (or has not) prepared students to engage with the university experience fully and profitably. This part of the chapter presents some contrasts between first year students' high-school preparation and the expectations of university instructors, the types of knowledge professors emphasize, and the traditional expectations associated with postsecondary education.

The final section of the chapter examines the tenets of "a liberal education"—what does it involve? Why do some critics feel that the system no longer prepares students for a genuinely liberal education and, indeed, no longer even supports such an objective? What does this circumstance mean for students entering university today, and how can they realize some of the most important objectives inherent in a traditional, liberal education?

THE "MILLENNIALS" IN PROFILE

The Beloit College Mindset List is an interesting idea—even an inspired one. The list provides a stimulating and sometimes humorous broad pan over the collective biography of the students entering postsecondary institutions each year. Although the list's generalizations do not apply to all students beginning postsecondary education in the United States and Canada, it does "identify the worldview of 18-year-olds" and captures the important "experiences and event horizons" that have had an impact on the cohort of students entering higher education each fall (Beloit College 2008). For the class that entered universities in September 2009, Beloit (2009) noted the following quick essentials:

> As millions of students head off to college this fall, most will continue to experience the economic anxiety that marked their first two years of life

---

1 There are two important points to note. First, this sketch is an *overall* sketch of students entering higher education; not every student reflects all of the characteristics noted. However, there are identifiable traits of this generation of students that constitute an overall profile of the cohort. Second, the discussion is not designed to blame or praise students, teachers, parents, or others for the profile that is presented—the objective is simply to establish a general profile, to examine critically why it includes particular traits and not others, and to suggest some of the implications this has for first year university students and their instructors.

just as it has marked their last two years of high school. Fears of the middle class—including their parents—about retirement and health care have been a part of their lives. Now however, they can turn to technology and text a friend: "Momdad still worried bout stocks. urs 2? PAW PCM."

Members of the class of 2013 won't be surprised when they can charge a latté on their cell phone and curl up in the corner to read a textbook on an electronic screen. The migration of once independent media—radio, TV, videos and CDs—to the computer has never amazed them. They have grown up in a politically correct universe in which multi-culturalism has been a given. It is a world organized around globalization, with McDonald's everywhere on the planet. Carter and Reagan are as distant to them as Truman and Eisenhower were to their parents. Tattoos, once thought "lower class," are, to them, quite chic. Everybody knows the news before the evening news comes on.

Thus the class of 2013 heads off to college as tolerant, global, and technologically hip … and with another new host of *The Tonight Show* [briefly].

Drawing from this and earlier Beloit lists, scholarly research, and some popular commentaries on the current generation of students entering colleges and universities in the recent past, this chapter will provide a profile of contemporary postsecondary students. As one begins to grasp that profile, it is readily apparent how different today's students are from their counterparts in the early 1950s or from their Baby Boomer parents born between the end of World War II and 1960, who streamed, en masse, into postsecondary institutions throughout the 1960s and 1970s.

Most of the students now entering colleges and universities were born after 1990; they are part of what is variously identified as Generation Y, Echo Boomers, the Boomlet, Nexters, the Nintendo Generation, the Digital Generation, or the Net Generation, although those who constitute the cohort overwhelmingly informed Peter Jennings, through abcnews.com, that they prefer to be identified as the Millennials (Howe and Strauss 2000:6–12).

The Millennials, born between 1982 and the present, follow Generation X, born between 1961 and 1981 (Howe and Strauss 2000:15).[2] Depending on one's focus, the generations can be broken into smaller cohorts—Generation X,

---

2 It was Canadian writer Douglas Coupland's 1991 novel *Generation X: Tales for an Accelerated Culture* that first identified the generation of Americans and Canadians who entered adulthood in the 1980s as "Generation X." The novel chronicles the lives of Dag, Andy, and Claire, who have moved into small bungalows in Palm Springs, California to escape the over-commercialized world in which they have grown up. Their stories show that members of their generation are not only restricted to low paying work in the service sector (the term "McJob" is coined by Andy) but also live in a culturally desolate world and have few prospects of an intrinsically fulfilling future. The beginning of the Millennial cohort is set at 1982 because its first members came of age—turned 18—at the millennium.

demarcated between 1960 and 1966, is seen as part of the Baby Boom and is followed by the Baby Bust (1967–79) and the Baby-Boom Echo (1980–95), which is the group under focus here (Foot 1996:18–25). Based on the differences that distinguish one cohort from another, the Millennials merit their own designation within the Baby-Boom Echo generation.

In North America, the Millennials will be as large a cohort as the Baby Boomers and perhaps larger. They will have the same type of generational impact as their Boomer parents. Viewed from a distance, as we pan across the Millennials, what are this generation's most relevant features?

The Millennials entering postsecondary institutions in the twenty-first century tend to come from small, close families; they see their parents positively and seem to share their values and worldview. No generation has experienced the same level of parental involvement, supervision, advocacy, and planning as the Millennials—childcare, school selection, enrichment opportunities, extracurricular activities, test coaches, and personal safety have all been carefully considered. The Millennials lives have been thoroughly planned and organized—and very closely monitored.

Although "helicopter parents" have served as vital, positive influences, their hovering has had its costs.[3] Despite their high self-esteem, the Millennials rely heavily on adults for direction, reassurance, and confirmation. They have difficulty budgeting their time on their own, and they have a sense of self-entitlement that makes it difficult for them to be self-reflective and self-critical.

At the same time, students entering postsecondary education in the new millennium have had to wrestle with conflicting images of who they are and what is expected from them. Time and again, they have heard "be smart" or "you're special." But, in the next breath, they were told that they must be inclusive and tolerant of everyone—no one is special; everyone is essentially the same.

The students entering higher education this century have faced constant pressure to achieve, both now and in the long term, but also to serve the community. Was all of their volunteer work simply to get ahead, or was it tied to a broader social commitment and a set of fundamental, humanitarian values?

The Millennials are the first to grow up surrounded by digital media— cyberspace has always been there, and they could turn to virtual reality when the real thing was too grim or difficult. This cohort may use "Google" as a verb more frequently than it does "to be."

For today's students, television is a distant second to the computer. Almost all of them own at least one and use it to download, view, and share

---

3 See Côté and Allahar (2007:138–46) for a sympathetic account of helicopter parents.

movies, television programs, and music videos and to gain access to all the other entertainment forms they want. More students will tote laptop computers around campus than science and math majors of the 1950s and 1960s wore holstered slide rules and carried tin boxes with 2H pencils and ten-piece geometry sets—and there is a far less "browner" stigma attached to their brightly decaled laptops or notebooks.

The Millennials constantly "text" (another verb the generation has always used) "1 n othr." Whenever students of this generation need "411," they go instantly to digital technology—Google, Wikipedia, and texting friends. These students constantly multi-task in their leisure time and while doing school work—watching a music video, playing solitaire, downloading a television program, and Googling information for a research assignment while checking or sending text messages is part of their frenetic life-world.

Students currently entering postsecondary education have always had CDs, and, although vinyl is making a comeback, most of them rely on digital forms of music. If these students have seen a 78-rpm record, it was probably in a museum of technology. Few have ever owned their own record player, and, if they did, it was certainly not a portable like those the Boomers carted from room to room in their teens. Most students in the freshman class have never seen a television set with only 13 channels let alone a functioning black and white, and they have always had cable and never lived without a remote.

Star Trek (1966–9), *M*A*S*H** (1972–83), and *The Muppet Show* (1976–81) have always been in reruns for the Millennials, and, although *Star Trek: The Next Generation* (1987–94) and *Seinfeld* (1989–98) originally played during the early years of their lives, the Millennials have only appreciated them outside of prime time. On the other hand, Homer, Marge, Bart, Lisa, and Maggie have been with these students forever. Indeed, *The Simpsons* (1989–present) serve as one of their primary sources of history—particularly the history of popular culture. Along those lines, Woodstock is a bird, a reunion, or part of a *Simpsons'* episode, but it is not a cultural touchstone for the Millennials.

Because of their direct and immediate access to so much information, the Millennials are politically aware but less sceptical than their parents at a similar age. Part of the reason is the way information reaches them—it is bits of disconnected information rather than systematic news located within a broader context (Postman 1988, 1995). Another reason is the relationship that the Millennials had—at least initially —to "their generation's war."

In the immediate aftermath of 9/11 (a term that has one, universal meaning), the Millennials saw and heard the words "hero" and "heroism" more often than any generation previously; the broadcast media and Internet were saturated with images of police and firefighters—people from all walks of life—acting "heroically." At the same time, broadcast and digital media focused on terrorism, terrorists, and the "direct threat of terror" allegedly facing the citizenry of Canada and the United States. The result was a rapid and powerful resurgence of patriotism. Unlike the Viet Cong of the Vietnam War, members of al-Qaeda attacked the United States directly, and numerous Americans felt it was their patriotic duty to respond or, in the case of Canadians, provide protection for those whom al-Qaeda were suppressing, controlling, and denying proper freedom. The media message was so consistent and overwhelming that few were sceptical about the appropriate response—everything seemed so self-evident.[4]

The sense of individualism and of the power of the individual is extremely high among the Millennials. Not only have all the Millennials continually heard how much they, as individuals, control their own destinies but also the notion of individual heroism in the post-9/11 period reinforced the belief that individuals and individual initiative influence outcomes. The election of Barack Obama as president of the United States in 2008 and his message of "Yes we can!" further underscored the belief that individuals make their own history, irrespective of the conditions they inherit.

University students in the twenty-first century have, on the whole, a weaker sense of history than their Boomer parents. The difference is partly because of changes in emphasis in secondary school curricula as well as the approach to educating this particular generation. Of at least equal importance is the way the current generation of students consumes information.

Although the Millennials were actively encouraged to read at a younger age than their parents and were read to far more than the Boomers, from a larger and richer body of engaging children's literature, they read less, and more superficially, than their parents did as postsecondary students. Students now in the postsecondary education system grew up always pressed for time in fully scheduled lives; they have had information bombarding them instantly and continuously; and they have felt pressured to be connected to their peers (sometimes around the globe). As this group of students moved into their teens, multi-tasking had become a survival strategy: with so much "requiring" attention, difficulty in establishing priorities, and no time to reflect and consider, the Millennials tried to do everything at top speed. As a result, they frequently did things superficially, and Nike's "just do it" changed from a branding slogan to part of the Millennials' inner being.

With so many demands, so little time, and an education that overwhelmingly emphasized the process of learning rather than learning outcomes,

---

4 It is important to remember that, in the first years of full American involvement in the Vietnam War, public support was also overwhelmingly on the side of military intervention, and the White House and Pentagon promised a short war with a decisive outcome that would be favourable to the interests of the democratic West.

Millennials have gaps in their knowledge that the Boomers find astonishing. Not only have John Diefenbaker, Lester B. Pearson, Dwight D. Eisenhower, John F. Kennedy, Vladimir Lenin, Leon Trotsky, Joseph Stalin, Nikita Khrushchev, Leonid Brezhnev, Andrei Sakharov, Mao Zedong, Emperor Hirohito, Winston Churchill, Glenn Gould, Andy Warhol, Huey Newton, Orson Welles, Abbie Hoffman (the Yippie not the Canadian runner), Richard Burton, Elvis Presley, John Lennon, and John Belushi always been dead for this generation, but many Millennials could not pair faces to those names, with the exception of the last three. While some of the students entering postsecondary education in the new millennium will have "heard of them," few would be able to say why they were important. More to the point—fewer still would think they matter as more than curiosities or answers to questions on the television game show *Are You Smarter Than a 5th Grader?* (2007).

Globally, the current generation of students has grown up in a single superpower world, and Russia has always had a multi-party political system. The Berlin Wall fell before most students entering postsecondary education in 2009 were born; they have known only one Germany. Tiananmen Square is an Olympic Games venue, not the scene of student protest and a massacre.

On a positive note, in their lifetime, apartheid has never existed as official South African policy, and Nelson Mandela has always been free and a force in that country. First year students will encounter roughly equal numbers of female and male professors in the classroom, women's studies programs have always existed during their lives, and women have always been judges, political leaders, CEOs in large corporations, police officers, astronauts, soldiers, and firefighters.

YouTube—"A Vision of Students Today"

Although some Millennials will have read about themselves on the Beloit Mindset site, more will have seen themselves in a medium with which they can more directly relate—Michael Wesch's (2007a) YouTube post, "A Vision of Students Today."[5] Wesch, "in collaboration with 200 other students" in his well-enrolled "Introduction to Cultural Anthropology" course at Kansas State University, created the video to reflect critically on today's university students by drawing upon the strengths of digital technologies and the cyber world (see Oberg 2007; Wesch 2008b). The video is an important

---

5 Wesch (2008b) is a "multiple award-winning teacher," who has won a *Wired* Magazine Rave Award and the John Culkin Award for Outstanding Media Praxis. His work has been featured by *The Chronicle of Higher Education*, and he is the coordinator for the "Peer Review of Teaching Project" at Kansas State University. The data and themes presented in the video represent the averaged responses of 131 students to a survey Wesch and his class conducted (Wesch 2008a).

contribution to an analysis of the contradictions and tensions the Millennials will feel within institutions of higher learning and merits close attention.[6]

The video begins with the door opening into a large lecture theatre; the camera enters, and a 1967 quotation from Marshall McLuhan appears overlaying a series of camera shots of the seats in the lecture hall, shots taken from different locations. The viewer is given 16 seconds to read the 32 words—about the rate at which a grade four student reads (Tindal, Hasbrouck, and Jones 2005). Here is the text:

> Today's child is bewildered when he enters the 19th century environment that still characterizes the educational establishment where information is scarce but ordered and structured by fragmented classified patterns, subjects, and schedules. (Quoted in Wesch 2007a)

Wesch's main point is the apparent disjunction that exists between the way information is treated by the educational establishment and the expectations of contemporary students. It is not clear if he has used the quotation because McLuhan (1964), who noted almost half a century ago that "the medium *is* the message [emphasis added]," was so perceptive or if Wesch is trying to indicate that a problem in existence almost 50 years ago remains not only relevant today but even more pressing because the media have changed as have the messages in the new cyber-world context. Most likely, Wesch intended both. This video and its complement, "Information R/evolution," clearly establish the different information realities that exist in two cultures—the print-based and often regionally specific culture of the Boomers and the hyper-real, digitally based, cyber-world culture of the Millennials (Wesch 2007b).

The bulk of "A Vision of Students Today" is a self-assessment of the Millennials' main characteristics. Individual students use different media—notes on pieces of paper or the pages of notebooks, text on laptop screens, comments scribbled on a machine-readable data card for a multiple-choice exam—to establish a collective profile that complements the material already presented in this chapter.

The viewer learns that classes are large and students tend to remain anonymous to their professors; students complete only half their course readings and feel that "only 26% are relevant to … life." Students buy expensive texts

---

6 The video also demonstrates how much technology and its fluidity affect Millennials. A 2009 YouTube posting, coordinated by the instructor in an English 101 class at Clark College and offered in response to Wesch's video, indicates how, in less than two years, texting has almost replaced email—a cell phone text notes "I send 6930 text messages per month." The students also note that they spend "a lot of time on the go, but the going is more technological than intellectual." They hope, despite their reliance on technology, "to break the mold" (mclainlove 2009).

they never open and pay hefty tuition for classes they seldom attend. A student today will read only 8 books in one year but consume 2,300 web pages and almost 1,300 Facebook profiles; she or he will produce 42 pages for class papers and assignments but generate over 500 pages of email.

Time matters—although it is also clear where the Millennials place their priorities. The next sequence shows that today's student spends 7 hours sleeping, 1.5 watching television, 3.5 online, 2.5 listening to music, 2 on a cell phone, 3 in class, 2 working in a part-time job, 3 studying, and 2 eating—for a total of 26.5 hours per day. "I am a multi-tasker," reads one sign. "(I have to be)."

The students note their debts but also recognize their privilege. Holding up a multiple-choice response card with 19 wrong out of 50, a student claims on the back of the card that "filling this out won't help me get there"; then, on another card, we see the words "or deal with," and these words are surrounded by arrows pointing to other cards referencing more than a dozen global problems different students have identified. "I did not create the problems," a student indicates, "but they are my problems."

"Some have suggested that technology can save us," the video notes; then it follows with "Some have suggested that technology alone can save us." But the next images challenge the second statement as well as the first. "I Facebook through most of my classes," and "I bring my laptop to class, but I'm not working on class stuff." The video ends with Wesch demonstrating the limitations of the erasable chalkboard as an educational tool in comparison with today's hypermedia, but this occurs after the following inaccurate quotation appears on the screen:

> The inventor of the system deserves to be ranked among the best contributors to learning and science, if not the greatest benefactors of mankind.
> Josiah F. Bumstead 1841[7]

What Wesch has left out of Bumstead's assessment of the invention of the erasable chalkboard is the word "blackboard" itself: so what "system" is Wesch critiquing or praising? He has brought the video full circle—the medium is the message and today's students are at the cutting edge of an information revolution—or is that Wesch's message?

---

7   The correct quotation reads as follows: "The inventor or introducer of the blackboard system deserves to be ranked among the best contributors to learning and science, if not among the greatest benefactors of mankind" (Bumstead 1841).

THE MILLENNIALS AND THE FORMAL EDUCATION SYSTEM

While the above profiles of the Millennials are instructive, they remain descriptive, somewhat superficial, and not at all analytical. To move deeper into an analysis of the Millennials as students, one needs to locate them within the education system that has nurtured them and within which many have excelled; one needs to focus on some of the social circumstances and pressures that have shaped the development of the current generation of students, and one has to come to terms with why so many teachers and university instructors view these students as so disengaged from the mainstream demands of the education system.

Indeed, one of the most disconcerting impressions given by "A Vision of Students Today" is the extent to which the Millennials appear disengaged from the university system. In their study, *Ivory Tower Blues: A University System in Crisis,* James Côté and Anton Allahar (2007:108–14) have also identified students' lack of engagement as one of the most significant characteristics of the Millennials and the key problem facing instructors, university administrators, parents, and even students themselves. Why are these students, who are surrounded by so much information and opportunity, not engaged? The problem is widespread and growing.

Citing *The American Freshman,* an annual publication of the Cooperative Institutional Research Program that provides data on the characteristics of students attending US colleges and universities, Côté and Allahar (2007:16) emphasize that, in 2001, for example, only a third (34.9 per cent) of the students entering university indicated that they had spent six or more hours a week on school work—the lowest figure since the question was first asked in 1987. Despite spending less than an hour a day on homework, high-school grades "continue to soar," and "44.1 percent of freshmen report earning 'A' averages in high school, compared with 42.9 percent last year [2000], and a low of 17.6 percent in 1968" (quoted in Côté and Allahar 2007:16).

Data on Canadian university students collected by the American National Survey of Student Engagement parallel the data collected by the same agency on college and university students in the United States. The survey shows that students, both American and Canadian, fall into one of three groups: those who are fully engaged and meet the work expectations of their professors (about 10 per cent of the students), the partially engaged who do less than expected but "enough to get by" (about 40 per cent), and the disengaged who do the minimum or nothing at all (almost half the students).[8] This low level of engagement is reflected in student preparation for classes and seminars.

Only two per cent of instructors, according to Côté and Allahar (2007:81), think that 80 per cent or more of their students come to class fully prepared. Less than 15 per cent of the professors they sampled think that 60 per cent or more of their students come to class fully prepared while 65 per cent of the professors believe that less than 40 per cent—only two students out of every five—come to lectures and seminars fully prepared. In plain language, almost two-thirds of university instructors feel that they teach in lecture halls and seminar rooms where well over half the class is disinterested and underprepared.

Part of the reason that so many students in postsecondary education are not fully engaged is that many students today are "funnelled into higher education as a result of policies based on the belief that a university education is superior to all other forms of job preparation"—even for occupations that do not have a university degree as a requirement (Côté and Allahar 2007:96). Many Millennials are "pushed into a situation for which they are unprepared academically or emotionally." "The following analogy," Côté and Allahar (2007) write, "can help us understand how these students might experience university":

> Imagine if circumstances were different and we had developed an occupational system where one had to graduate from an art school instead of a liberal arts university to qualify for white-collar jobs. Instead of intellectual criteria, we would all be judged on our artistic abilities. Imagine how you would feel if you were pushed into art school and had no interest in art and little or no artistic ability. Beyond this, imagine your reaction if your future depended on your ability to satisfy the demands of high-level artists and pass their tests. Would you be resentful, lost, wanting to cut corners, or looking for some other way to play the system and get a credential that is likely irrelevant to what you want to do with your life? Welcome to the world of the reluctant intellectual—the disengaged student. (P. 96)

---

8 Côté and Allahar (2007:9) reference data collected by the American-based National Survey of Student Engagement, but these data are consistent with data collected in other research conducted by Côté and Allahar. In a survey of professors, Côté and Allahar (2007:77) found that about 40 per cent of faculty members felt that only 10 per cent of their students (zero to 10 per cent actually) were fully engaged. Forty-five per cent of instructors felt that 21 to 40 per cent of their students were minimally engaged, and another quarter (26 per cent) felt that between 40 and 60 per cent of their students were minimally engaged. Most discouraging, only a quarter of instructors thought that 10 per cent or less of their students were disengaged, 40 per cent felt that 11 to 20 per cent of their students were disengaged, and another quarter (26 per cent) felt that 21 to 40 per cent of their students were disengaged.

Based on his clinical work at the University of North Carolina Medical School's Center for the Study of Development and Learning, Melvin Levine (2005:7) argues in his book *Ready or Not, Here Life Comes* that students entering university "are not equipped with a durable work temperament, having been submerged in a culture that stresses instant rewards instead of patient, tenacious, sustained mental effort and the ability to delay gratification for the sake of eventual self-fulfillment." In other words, they "have grown up in an era that infiltrates them with unfettered pleasure, heavy layers of overprotection, and heaps of questionably justified feedback" (quoted in Côté and Allahar 2007:99). The result is that the Millennials have difficulty in charting their own paths in life and in determining their own real ambitions, genuine strengths, and realistic appraisals of their personal worth, ability, and values. The university environment then confounds these students as professors pose questions about complex issues, questions that require time and prolonged effort to yield provisional answers. Often for the first time, students are faced with a situation in which, even though there is not one correct answer, there are certainly answers that are wrong. To make matters worse, professors assess the answer and not the time, struggle, and effort that it took for the student to arrive at his or her provisional endpoint. The best university instructors assign work that requires students to manage their time independently, prioritize the information they have collected, and integrate it into a cohesive, coherent whole—that is not a familiar experience for many students within the current high-school system (Côté and Allahar 2007:136–7). It is challenging and for some so formidable that they simply disengage.

E-Culture versus Print Culture: "Hot," "Cool," and "Molten Ice" Media

First year students' lives have unrelentingly revolved around chip-based, digital technology—laptops, iPods, and cell phones. They have grown up totally immersed within what one might call "e-culture." Despite all the adjustments and changes that postsecondary instructors and institutions have made to the growth of information technology and to how so much information is transmitted, filtered, stored, and utilized, university education still remains intimately tied to what one might term "print culture." This structurally based tension has significant outcomes.

On the one hand, students now have direct contact with more scholarly information than ever before, and they can reach almost all of it from the comfort of their own rooms. Gaining access to scholarly texts has never been easier or required less time. Project Gutenberg (n.d.), for example, has converted more than 15,000 books to a digital format and made them freely available as e-books. Based almost exclusively on volunteer labour, the project is "the first producer of free electronic books," and it once had the largest single collection of e-books available.

Google has taken a slightly different direction. It has invested millions of dollars to sustain the Google Print Library Project. According to Google (n.d.), the project's aim "is simple." It seeks to make it easier for people "to find books they wouldn't find any other way such as those that are out of print—while carefully respecting authors' and publishers' copyrights." The goal is to "create a comprehensive, searchable, virtual card catalog of all books in all languages that helps users discover new books and publishers discover new readers." To date Google has scanned and digitized more than a million books. Periodical scholarly publications, newspapers, and magazines from around the world are also increasingly available online at no direct cost through university libraries or on a pay-per-access basis.

Along with having unprecedented direct access to so much information, students can produce research papers using sophisticated software packages that check spelling and grammar, offer hundreds of font types and sizes, and allow students to customize their formatting and layout. Desktop publishing is easier than baking a cake. Statistics packages give students discriminatory and analytical powers that continually grow in sophistication and ease of use with each passing semester.

Nevertheless, despite these tremendous gains in access to information and in the means for processing it, there is an enormous gap between the e-cultural experiences, skills, and expectations of students and the print culture perspective of their professors. The lived experiences, background, wants, and desires of students who are coming to prevail in colleges and universities differ significantly from those of the instructors who currently prevail in postsecondary education.

Wesch's introduction of McLuhan in "A Vision of Students Today" is insightful. McLuhan's understanding of the relationship between the medium and message allows one to focus on the key tensions and contradictions that exist between e-culture and print culture.

In *Understanding Media,* McLuhan (1964) argues that different media encourage and permit distinctive types of participation on the part of the consumer. A movie, McLuhan maintains, stimulates one sense overall—vision. Film, as a medium, is highly active in constructing the message it projects. Television is similar, but it requires more effort on the part of the viewer, and a comic book demands even more as the reader must interpret the visual images and actively—though subconsciously—construct the message the cartoonist intended or the reader perceives as intended. McLuhan identified active media, such as film, as "hot media" in contrast to the "cool media" of comic books and written texts, which, paradoxically, require a more active audience in the creation of meaning.

Wesch's videos, like so much of the media information that the Millennials absorb, are definitely "hot" in McLuhan's terms, although the viewer is not completely passive. And even though pause, rewind, fast forward, and play allow the viewer to go back over parts of a YouTube video, a DVD, or a music video, those media "encourage" the viewer to be a passive recipient of the message rather than an interactive one.

Media such as YouTube or music videos make it difficult for the viewer to control the stream of information—to slow it down when it becomes complex or immediately go back to a particular point and see information there juxtaposed with information further ahead. It is also more difficult to outline the whole of the information, its flow and its context. One wonders how many viewers noticed that Wesch put up two different statements about technology three-quarters of the way through the video—"Some have suggested that technology can save us" appears at 3 minutes and 32 seconds and lasts 4 seconds before the background fades and the words are replaced by "Some have suggested that technology alone can save us," which remains visible for 5 seconds.

In a written text, such as this, one can instantly glance back over those two sentences to note the additional word in the second—a small but extremely significant addition. One can read the sentence or sentences slowly and simultaneously reflect on what they mean without worrying about the stream of information getting ahead of one's thoughts—the reader controls the pace completely. One can read through what is familiar quite quickly and easily, skip over the unimportant, and then slow down for new or complex material.

For the Millennials, the practice of slowing down the flow of information, stopping and going back over a point, does not come naturally. Part of the reason is the structural nature of the hot media they rely upon so heavily for their information. The information sources in the Millennials' lives compel them to keep up—the medium sets the pace and it is passively consumed. As in much of their lives, control is external, and the Millennials simply comply and adjust or fall behind, tune it out, and move on to other media and messages.

Another part of the reason for the disjunction between today's students and their professors is the abundance of information these students have been trained to consume and multi-task through at any given point in time. As a consequence, each input receives a quick scan, but few, if any, are accorded undivided attention for any length of time. Through a lifetime of multiple, almost simultaneous information scanning strategies, the Millennials have developed particular learning expectations and techniques appropriate to their e-culture needs, but these are not necessarily conducive to success in the print-culture world of the postsecondary education system.

It is instructive to hone in on the type of information itself that today's students encounter and use most often in their daily lives. In two other YouTube videos, "Information R/evolution" and "The Machine is Us/ing Us (Final Version)," Wesch's (2007b, 2007c) main argument concerns the fluidity, instability, ubiquity, and almost infinite recombinant capacities of information in the cyber world. The information in the cyber world is neither hot nor cool in McLuhan's terms; it is almost "molten-ice," if one were to build on the imagery. The term is internally contradictory but also appropriate to cyber media.

McLuhan identified a medium as hot when it played the most significant role in creating the message—the medium is the message applies directly to hot media. Media were cool when the consumer played a more active role in creating the message—the medium was still the message, but these media and messages required, upon reception, much more creative, human deciphering and construction (constructive, creative capacity was one aspect of the message).

The information Wesch is focused upon is "molten hot" insofar as web-based information is highly packaged, tightly scripted, and ready for instantaneous and largely passive consumption. Millennials grew up with *Sesame Street* (1969–70, 1970–present); they watched information that entertains and is absorbed through constant repetition rather than focused concentration. They have learned to absorb information in small, repetitive, animated doses coming from different angles and perspectives. Their multi-tasking—chatting online, texting another friend, monitoring a video download, Googling for information, and watching a YouTube video while listening to iTunes on their computer—has significantly shaped how they process information. They control the range of information coming in, but they can only process parts of it at one time and thus do so far more passively than actively.

While molten hot, on the one hand, cyber media are also "ice cold" because digital information is "immaterial." It has almost no material constraints; digital information can be changed instantly, manipulated endlessly by anyone who receives it. Electronic information gives enormous potential to the receiver to be highly interpretive, constructive, even interactive in grasping its "content" and meanings. The ice-cold aspects of digital media have positive and negative implications.

On the positive side, the recipient can create and recreate meaning; the information allows for tremendous creative potential and active interaction with—even participation within—the digital information. On the negative side, the boundless possibilities present in hypertexts and digital information can leave a consumer feeling helplessly unable to control or even begin to grasp the infinite scope of such information let alone its full potential. "We no longer find information" Wesch (2007b) indicates, "it can find us." He changes the sentence: "We can make it find us." And then he edits it further: "Together, we can make it find us." The flexibilities of digital information "are not just cool tricks," Wesch (2007b) argues, "they change the rules of order."

The volume of information the Millennials have become accustomed to consuming, its apparently infinite recombinant potential, and the speed with which it passes its "best before date" can be anxiety inducing—especially for students who are not accustomed to setting their own priorities and controlling their lives fully. In the fast-paced, competitive world of the Millennials, infinitely recombinant information discourages consumers from slowing down, pondering, reflecting, and making broader connections. Most important, although an experienced scholar like Wesch can see unlimited potential in the changing rules of order, for students with personal biographies still in flux and limited resources and experiences to draw upon, seeing the overall forest for all the virtual, ever-changing digital trees is difficult to say the least.

Scholarship: Time, Labour, and Detail

What separates universities from other institutions in society is their ongoing commitment to scholarship and, to a great but not exclusive extent, print culture. Both of these commitments conflict with the media and information that the Millennials have used most of their lives, have always relied upon, and with which they are comfortable. To succeed fully in higher education— to genuinely benefit from all postsecondary education has to offer—students entering higher education will have to adjust to the demands and expectations of print culture. And for those who are willing to engage with that culture, the rewards are significant because it will provide the foundation and stability that will enable those students to take full advantage of e-culture and the changing rules of order with respect to information.

The print culture of university professors rests on the labour-intensive, time-consuming study of texts and data. The true scholar builds her or his knowledge over decades of long hours devoted to studying things, concepts, events, and ideas. She or he labours to make precise connections, to apprehend and grasp complex wholes. A scholar's work demands an ongoing, close, careful, and critical commitment to detail because, often, a tiny difference is of monumental significance. A small example from Wesch's (2007a) video can illustrate the point.

Wesch (2007a) misquoted Bumstead: Wesch wrote "The inventor of the system" instead of "The inventor or introducer of the blackboard system." That might seem a trivial error, but, upon close examination, it proves otherwise.

Bumstead had *one very specific system* in mind—the erasable chalkboard as a new means or system of communication within education. Wesch's error—"the system"—moves the mind instantly to notions of a far larger and perhaps even oppressive system, such as "the education system" or, worse, the dystopian sounding invention of "*the* system" that one finds in George Orwell's (1949) *Nineteen Eighty-Four* or Eugene Zamiatan's ([1924] 1952) *We*. Perhaps that is how Wesch actually feels—at least about "the education system," but it is not what Bumstead had in mind (Wesch 2008a).

Many might respond that few, if any, would notice Wesch's error, and it would probably turn out to be irrelevant to anyone watching the video. But, although the first point might be right, the second one certainly is not.

Wesch's videos are all about digital information and the social and political responsibilities that go along with it. He is painstaking in putting them together—they are original productions of images, music, sound, and text. Wesch's error was almost Freudian because, if people do not understand "*the* system"—the system of digitally based information and hypertexts—then everyone is in danger of being dominated by it because people would no longer control their own creations.

Wesch is a scholar; his work is precise; his videos pay close attention to detail in the lives of his students and in the information world that surrounds him and that he studies with care. Drawing the Millennials into the molten ice world of information in the twenty-first century as careful, critical scholars focused on detail while keeping the "bigger picture" in front of them is clearly his goal. It is also the task he sets for students in postsecondary education today. Without identifying it as such, Wesch is pinpointing an important element in the intersection "of man and society, of biography and society, of self and world" for the Millennials, for their instructors, and for everyone living in Canada, the United States, and other technologically enhanced societies today (Mills 1959:5).

Old School—New School: Re-Schooling Both
E-culture and print culture exist together. Each has its advocates and detractors, but institutions of postsecondary education have to adjust to both. To draw upon the strengths of each means that students and professors must adapt to the structural realities of education in the twenty-first century.

Thus, although "old school" professors may lament what students lose by ignoring the print culture that Johannes Gutenberg helped introduce in the mid-fifteenth century with the development of movable type, they have to recognize the extent to which digital media have made it easier and faster for increasingly larger numbers around the globe to access the written word. Digital technology makes print culture more widely available.

Contemporary postsecondary instructors must also recognize that today's students live in a world of continuously changing texts and images, which they download and upload from the Internet at a mouse click. The videos on YouTube, a video sharing website that only began in 2005, might be authentic or cleverly constructed fictions and hoaxes; in either case, they are short audiovisual entertainment-information packages that are a standard part of students' everyday stock of knowledge, conversation, and insight into the world in which they live.

The "new technologies" are also new systems of communication that have to be evaluated in much the same way that Bumstead assessed the erasable chalkboard. The chalkboard allowed an instructor to provide visual illustrations to different points and ideas and, "in real time" (to use the current terminology), alter those images. Digital technology allows an instructor to tap into students' senses in ways that can create a powerfully emotional atmosphere to underline certain material appropriately. Learning can be enhanced significantly as clear, cold logical reasoning is supplemented by dynamic images and emotionally stirring audiovisual essays. Indeed, as a frequently quoted McLuhan (n.d.) aphorism notes, "Anyone who tries to make a distinction between education and entertainment doesn't know the first thing about either."

Instructors and professors must recognize that the Millennials' life experiences, including those within the formal education system, have led them, for the most part, to treat the printed text—the most stable source of knowledge for thousands of years—as simply one ancillary form of information, and one that competes with the symbolically rich, active, Technicolor, audiovisual vignettes, stories, and statements that they can find, produce, quickly edit, save, play, pause, replay, and relay across the globe in seconds or store on their cell phones or iPods for future reference. Cyberspace is a reality that old-school professors must understand and use more extensively.

If old-school instructors need educating, "new-school" students need some schooling too. The students of the twenty-first century have to recognize that there are approaches to information and knowledge that offer deeper, more enriching forms of learning than those with which they are so familiar. Although today's students have not had the same relationship that their Boomer parents had with texts and textual material in "hard copy," they must learn that there is much to be gained by devoting time to an enduring, static printed page.

Slowing down to reread a paragraph and decide if it really is worth labouring over is not easy for students whose educational past has continually emphasized moving forward almost relentlessly. Giving time—devoting large blocks of undisturbed, active, concentrated time and attention to an unchanging, discipline-demanding medium such as a printed text is a difficult task for the current generation of students to embrace—but it is vital to their education.

The cooler the medium, the greater the onus is on the consumer to construct the message. If the medium is the message, the most critically important meaning in a cool medium is the active engagement it demands and enables. Slowing down, stopping, retracing a path—a few pages, a single page, a paragraph, sentence, or specific word—are skills that many first year students need to develop and refine (and some must learn these skills for the first time). Attending to detail and engaging in critical reflection are truly liberating experiences—and both are essential to higher education—but this is a freedom one must struggle to achieve.

Thus, the Millennials need to discover the awe and inspiration of running a finger over the volumes—old and new—on the library shelves. Browsing the stacks is an invitation into a world of contemplative pleasure and mystery that connects generations and eras of knowledge. Most important, it is a vital step towards changing the world as an informed citizen drawing upon a set of developing, fully self-conscious values and commitments.

The work world into which today's first year students will graduate is fully global; trade barriers have fallen, and the competition for work is no longer national, provincial, or local. Governments strive to attract businesses that will bring jobs, and their success is tied to the global capitalism of the late twentieth century (Ferguson 2001; Frieden 2006; Harvey 2005; Hobsbawm 1994). When one country or one region of a country can offer low-cost labour, other countries or regions, if they are to remain competitive, must do the same. There are inescapable global pressures on every aspect of the labour market to provide either low-cost labour or absolutely unique, highly sought after skilled workers. Although the first year sociology student might be thinking of a secure, high-paying job upon graduation, the labour market is currently creating more short-term, poorly paid, low-skill jobs than long-term, highly paid managerial ones.

No student should read these comments with despair; she or he should, however, read them with an acute sense of the intersection of self and world. More important, each student should see the present situation as an invitation to learn more so as to be better able to assess where her or his future lies.

There is no better place to begin such an analysis than in university—although the task and promise of undergraduate study has changed over the last few decades and the overall objectives of a university education are open to question and debate at the present moment in history.

HIGHER EDUCATION: THE PURSUIT OF SWEETNESS AND LIGHT

Allan Bloom's (1987) best-seller *The Closing of the American Mind: How Higher Education Has Failed Democracy and Impoverished the Souls of Today's Students* is a scathing and highly controversial critique of higher education as it stands today. More recently, Peter Emberley and Waller Newell (1994), in *Bankrupt Education: The Decline of Liberal Education in Canada,* and Côté and Allahar (2007), in *Ivory Tower Blues,* have expressed concerns that are similar to Bloom's (see also D'Souza 1992).

Bloom (1987) notes that his book is "a meditation on the state of our souls, particularly those of the young, and their education." It was written from a teacher's perspective, which, despite its "grave limitations" and "dangerous temptations" is "a privileged one." "The teacher," Bloom writes,

> particularly the teacher dedicated to liberal education, must constantly
> try to look toward the goal of human completeness and back at the
> natures of his students here and now, ever seeking to understand the for-
> mer and to assess the capacities of the latter to approach it. Attention to
> the young, knowing what their hungers are and what they can digest, is
> the essence of the craft. (P. 19)

Emberley and Newell (1994) express a similar sentiment. "At the core of liberal education" they write, is "the duty of the teacher to impart and cultivate those talents and excellences which would prepare a student to bear the obligations of citizenship and to begin the exploration of the intellectual and spiritual life." "Liberal education," they continue, speaks to "human equality and freedom" (p. 3).

Bloom's concern for students and his appreciation of the significance of liberal education are deeply heartfelt. "What each generation is" he indicates, "can be best discovered in its relation to the permanent concerns of mankind. This in turn can best be discovered in each generation's tastes, amusements, and especially angers" (Bloom 1987:19).

It is through a fascination with one's students, Bloom (1987) emphasizes, that one becomes aware "of the various kinds of soul and their various capacities for truth and error as well as learning" (pp. 20–1). Knowing this about your students, he maintains, is critical if an instructor is to help them ask *the question* in education and life: What is humankind? "A liberal education," Bloom (1987) continues,

> means precisely helping students to pose this question to themselves, to
> become aware that the answer is neither obvious nor simply unavailable,

and that there is no serious life in which this question is not a continuous concern. Despite all the efforts to pervert it ... the question that every young person asks, "Who am I?," the powerful urge to follow the Delphic command, "Know thyself," which is born in each of us, means in the first place "What is man?" And in our chronic lack of certainty, this comes down to knowing the alternative answers and thinking about them. ... The liberally educated person is one who is able to resist the easy and preferred answers, not because he is obstinate but because he knows others worthy of consideration. (P. 21)

Bloom's central concerns are threefold—higher education's failure to defend and maintain a liberal education; long term and immediate social pressures that deflect students away from engaging with the questions that are central to a liberal education; and the inner structure of universities, including their curricula, that have marginalized the fundamental tenets of a liberal education. Bloom (1987) brings the first two concerns together in a paragraph worth citing at length:

What image does a first-rank college or university present today to a teenager leaving home for the first time, off to the adventure of a liberal education? He has four years of freedom to discover himself—a space between the intellectual wasteland he has left behind and the inevitable dreary professional training that awaits·him after the baccalaureate. In this short time he must learn that there is a great world beyond the little one he knows, experience the exhilaration of it and digest enough of it to sustain himself in the intellectual deserts he is destined to traverse. He must do this, that is, if he is to have any hope of a higher life. These are charmed years when he can, if he so chooses, become anything he wishes and when he has the opportunity to survey his alternatives, not merely those current in his time or provided by careers, but those available to him as a human being. The importance of these years for an American [or Canadian] cannot be overestimated. They are civilization's only chance to get him. (P. 336)

Many disagree with different aspects of Bloom's argument about why universities allegedly fail to provide a genuine liberal education, but even Bloom's sharpest critics agree that the four years a student spends in university are a golden opportunity that is too often wasted. Bloom's notion that those years represent a critical "space between the intellectual wasteland" the student has just left and "the inevitable dreary professional training that awaits" may overstate the "before" and "after," but his phrasing certainly captures the unique opportunity that higher education offers—or should offer—all those who are privileged enough to partake in it.

Bloom's perspective is far from unique; he is just one in a long line of educators emphasizing the importance of grappling with life's fundamental questions. Matthew Arnold ([1868] 1932), the son of Thomas Arnold (who had a profound and lasting effect on the British private school), wrote *Culture and Anarchy: An Essay in Political and Social Criticism* in 1868 to address virtually the same concerns Bloom would tackle over a century later.[9] Arnold wrote the book when English institutions were adjusting to the changes in economic and social life occasioned by Britain becoming a rapidly expanding industrial society, when the beginnings of modernity were becoming evident. He sought to address two fundamental questions: what kind of life should people in a market-driven, industrial society live, and how can the education system best ensure that the quality of people's lives is not impoverished?

"The whole scope of this essay," Arnold ([1868] 1932) advises, "is to recommend culture as the great help out of our present difficulties." Culture, he notes, is the pursuit "of our total perfection by means of getting to know, on all the matters which most concern us, the best which has been thought and said in the world" (p. 6). Through this knowledge, Arnold continues, one could turn "a stream of fresh and free thought upon our stock notions and habits, which we now follow staunchly but mechanically," and liberate people from their current prejudices as well as the petty distractions of everyday life. One could inspire people to seek greatness in themselves and a better world in which they would live.

Although Arnold is often accused of being an elitist, he was very much a progressive reformer. The "stock notions and habits" that he identifies as being "staunchly"—steadfastly, unwaveringly—and "mechanically" followed were those of the British aristocracy as much as those of the emerging middle class, whose members were fixated on financial gain and appearances. Arnold was as critical of the elitist prejudices of the British upper class as he was of the narrow, material, business-driven interests of the middle class. Arnold wanted all Britons to strive for "harmonious perfection." As he writes,

---

9 Appointed Rugby's headmaster in 1828, Thomas Arnold fundamentally reshaped the school. He introduced modern history, modern languages (in addition to Greek and Latin), mathematics, and the prefect system in which students maintained order themselves. Arnold also emphasized the role of athletics in developing character and moral fibre. Along with Canon Kingsley, Arnold is seen as one of the founders of "muscular Christianity"—a movement that influenced everything from religion and education to Baron Pierre de Coubertin's image of the Olympic Games (Beamish and Ritchie 2006:11–30; Fitch 1898; Hall 1994). The Rugby experience is captured in detail in Thomas Hughes's (1857) classic *Tom Brown's Schooldays*.

Culture, which is the study of perfection, leads us ... to conceive of true human perfection as a harmonious perfection, developing all sides of our humanity; and as a general perfection, developing all parts of our society. For if one member suffers, the other members must suffer with it; and the fewer there are that follow the true way of salvation, the harder that way is to find. (Arnold ([1868] 1932:11)

Arnold ([1868] 1932) revisits these themes of human welfare, human perfectibility, and culture from a slightly different perspective:

[B]ecause men are all members of one great whole, and the sympathy which is in human nature will not allow one member to be indifferent to the rest or to have a perfect welfare independent of the rest, the expansion of our humanity, to suit the idea of perfection which culture forms, must be a general expansion. Perfection, as culture conceives it, is not possible while the individual remains isolated. The individual is required, under pain of being stunted and enfeebled in his own development if he disobeys, to carry others along with him in his march towards perfection, to be continually doing all he can to enlarge and increase the volume of the human stream sweeping thitherward. (P. 48)

Because Arnold was a deeply religious person, some have also dismissed his position as conservative, nostalgic, and driven by the theology of the Church of England. But Arnold viewed religion as only one aspect of the quest for human perfection and the highest quality of life. Culture was more encompassing than religion, and Arnold's criticisms of various religious denominations were precisely that they accentuated only one aspect of human potential and thus deflected people away from the real quest for perfection (Arnold [1868] 1932:10–38). "[B]eing in contact with the main stream of human life is of more moment for a man's total spiritual growth ... than any speculative [or religious] opinion which he may hold or think he holds" (Arnold [1868] 1932:30).

Concerning religion, Arnold ([1868] 1932) quotes Martin Luther's commentary on the Book of Daniel: "A God is simply that whereon the human heart rests with trust, faith, hope, and love. If the resting is right, then the God too is right; if the resting is wrong, then the God too is illusory" (p. 30). According to Arnold ([1868] 1932), what one thinks about God and the objects of religion "depends on what man is; and what the man is, depends upon his having more or less reached the measure of a perfect and total man" (p. 30). In other words, what a person is depends upon the extent to which she or he has become cultured in the sense that Arnold understood the term.

Arnold ([1868] 1932) emphasizes this point later in the essay:

> But, finally, perfection—as culture, from a thorough disinterested study
> of human nature and human experience learns to conceive it—is a har-
> monious expansion of all the powers which make the beauty and worth
> of human nature, and is not consistent with the over-development of any
> one power at the expense of the rest. Here culture goes beyond religion,
> as religion is generally conceived by us. (P. 48)

Arnold has a broad, empowering notion of culture and of what it offers
or should offer. He recognizes that it is "at variance with the mechanical
and material civilisation in esteem with us [then and now]" (Arnold [1868]
1932:49). He knows that culture, as the perfection of humanity, contradicts
the strong sense of individualism found in modern societies. He also understands that, in a materially oriented world, there are numerous forces that
seek to trivialize culture as he conceives it.

"The disparagers of culture," Arnold ([1868] 1932) notes—and this applies
today as much as it did in 1868—"make its motive curiosity; sometimes,
indeed, they make its motive mere exclusiveness and vanity." They dispar-
age it as simply "a smattering of Greek and Latin," something that is valued
"out of sheer vanity." Or they call it "an engine of social and class distinction,
separating its holder, like a badge or title, from other people who have not
got it." "No serious man," he states emphatically, "would call this culture, or
attach any value to it, as culture, at all" (Arnold [1868] 1932:43).

What culture was for Arnold ([1868] 1932) is so simple yet so daunting;
it was "the study of perfection" (p. 50). It involves the formation of a spirit
and character that is finely tempered—"a harmonious perfection" in which
"the characters of beauty and intelligence are both present" and unite "the
two noblest of things, sweetness and light" (Arnold [1868] 1932:53–4).

The pursuit of sweetness and light, Arnold ([1868] 1932) maintains, will
make reason prevail: "Culture looks beyond machinery, culture hates hatred;
culture has one great passion, the passion for sweetness and light" (p. 69).
But it has an even greater passion—"the passion for making them prevail":

> It is not satisfied till we all come to a perfect man; it knows that the sweet-
> ness and light of the few must be imperfect until the raw and unkin-
> dled masses of humanity are touched with sweetness and light. If I have
> not shrunk from saying that we must work for sweetness and light, so
> neither have I shrunk from saying that we must have a broad basis, must
> have sweetness and light for as many as possible. Again and again I have
> insisted how those are the happy moments of humanity, how those are

the marking epochs of a people's life, how those are the flowering times
for literature and art and all the creative powers of genius, when there is
a national glow of life and thought, when the whole of society is in the
fullest measure permeated by thought, sensible to beauty, intelligent and
alive. Only it must be real thought and real beauty; real sweetness and real
light. Plenty of people will try to give the masses, as they call them, an
intellectual food prepared and adapted in the way they think proper for
the actual condition of the masses. . . . [B]ut culture works differently. . . .
It seeks to do away with classes; to make the best that has been thought
and known in the world current everywhere; to make all men live in an
atmosphere of sweetness and light, where they may use ideas, as it uses
them itself, freely—nourished and not bound by them. (Arnold [1868]
1932:69–70)

Arnold's work is inspiring. Bring forth sweetness and light: it is hard to
think of a loftier goal in human life. His ideas were also inspired—inspired
by a faith few feel today, even though his faith could have been quite secular.
To believe that humanity can aspire to sweetness and light represents a commitment to humankind, progress, and change. In this respect, Arnold's challenge is daunting—his goal is that the greatest qualities of humanity would
come to prevail for all. Arnold's goals were ultimately social; he wanted to
see the best ideas spread throughout the social whole so that everyone, not
just a cultured elite, would consider them critically and implement them.

In presenting his challenge, Arnold identifies a troubled world and tries
to inspire people to discover the qualities needed to change and improve it.
For Arnold, the solution rests in culture, and he places tremendous faith in
human reason to find the way forward.

As inspiring as Arnold's ideas are, he does not provide much that directly
helps us to understand our world critically and to discern what is needed
to create genuine social change. Fortunately, from its first emergence as a
discipline, sociology has made the question of change central to its focus.
It has sought to discover conceptual frameworks that help us better understand the social world so that we can successfully change it. The next chapter introduces students to these dimensions of sociology through the work
of Mills and what he termed "the sociological imagination."

2 THE SOCIOLOGICAL IMAGINATION: BEYOND "EVERYDAY STOCKS OF KNOWLEDGE"

Even though everyone is born into and has grown up within a vast network of social relationships, few people automatically think "sociologically"—at least not in a manner sociologists would accept. Consciously using a sociological approach to understand, analyse, and inform their everyday conduct is something that some students begin to learn in high school, but most become familiar with this approach only at a community college or university, even though they are already sophisticated social agents in all their daily activities. This should not be surprising—although it often is.

Young children speak, count, and marvel at tadpoles, salamanders, goldfish, puppies, and kittens without being able to recite the rules of spelling, grammar, language usage, mathematics, or biology. They are taught those subjects in school; there, they learn to label, understand, and apply the system of rules for correct speech, proper spelling, pronunciation, and enunciation. In fact, some children wonder why they have to even go to school to learn how to read and spell when they can already speak, listen, and communicate effectively—isn't that enough they wonder.

But there is an important difference between what sociologists refer to as one's "everyday stocks of knowledge" and the knowledge that educational, academic, scientific, and political decision makers have formalized into specific subjects and disciplines, into codified and structured knowledge that is passed on to future generations in mostly formal educational settings. It is within the school system that children learn to reflect consciously upon how they speak or write, what they can do with numbers in a base-ten number system, and how to begin to approach important questions about different life forms. Beyond what people learn from their everyday lives about language, mathematics, or biology, there is an elaborate, extensive, complex body of formal knowledge about each of these aspects of people's lives.

Social life is no different. The subject areas of history, geography, civics, business practice, and sociology are introduced in high school, but they are developed much further as history, geography, political studies, economics, philosophy, anthropology, global development studies, and sociology within community colleges and universities. So even though first year students are sophisticated social agents, the postsecondary education system offers them a body of formal knowledge so that they can build upon their already existing everyday stocks of knowledge.

As a formal discipline, sociology offers something far more important than simply a systematic body of knowledge—as important as that is. Studying sociology as a discipline allows people to approach the world in a totally new and powerful way. Unfortunately, because the sociological perspective is so different from the way people tend to think about the world around them, it is a difficult perspective to learn—although the rewards for mastering it are profoundly empowering.

Thinking sociologically is hard at first because people already possess deeply entrenched ways of understanding the social world around them. People routinely employ a very individualist, personal, almost "psychologistic" or self-centred perspective as they negotiate their way through every aspect of their daily lives. Thinking about the world from "my perspective," from the vantage point of the "I," is very natural because that is how individuals directly encounter the social world. Consider that point for a minute because its basis and implications are significant.

People encounter the world through their senses. For sighted persons, vision is a key sensory input, and they rely on sight heavily for the vast majority of their daily activities. Not surprisingly, then, people tend naturally to understand the world around them as sighted individuals, and this perspective has profound implications.

As an individual looks out on the world through his or her eyes, what and how does that person see? First, eyes allow a sighted person to see straight ahead, with a certain amount of peripheral vision. With two eyes, that person can perceive depth—someone with only one eye has great difficulty accurately determining how near or far an object is from his or her body. Visually, the world appears to lie in front of a person; she or he can easily distinguish objects that are near from those at a bit of a distance or those on the horizon, as far away as the eye can see.

Although each person has some breadth of vision, which is extended slightly by peripheral vision, the individual almost always turns to the left or right to see things not directly in his or her line of sight. Frequently, a person will turn not just the head but the entire body to face things, so objects are directly in front, centred in the person's field of vision to enable that individual to see more, focus better, and engage with the world.

So eyes do more than simply let an individual locate himself or herself spatially within the world; eyes tend to determine the perspective from within which a person thinks about the surrounding world. You feel, on the basis of visual sensory input, like an *individual* who is located in *a world that exists around you.*

Apprehending the world through vision, a person distinguishes himself or herself from other people and the surrounding environment. Because each of us appears, on the basis of vision, to be an individual, we all conduct ourselves as individuals moving within a world in which there are other things and other people—"welcome to my world" can be more than a sarcastic comment!

On the basis of what sociologist Alfred Schutz (1973) termed "the natural attitude," people "naturally"—that is naturally on the basis of their biological sense organs and by naturally not thinking much about it—see themselves, from their own personal perspectives, as individuals. This may be a useful way to think about oneself in some situations, and it is certainly appropriate for some disciplines such as biology and psychology. But it is not the correct perspective for sociology. In fact, even though the longstanding, entrenched nature of the natural attitude makes it very difficult to shift to a sociological perspective, that adjustment is necessary for more than simply gaining sociological insight into one's life.

Making the switch from the personal to a broader sociological framework is critical to genuinely understanding our relationships to others; it is central to understanding the relationships we have to the natural environment; and it is essential to understanding how our lives are pressured, shaped, and directed by the social environments within which we inescapably live.

It is not an overstatement to note that, without a sociological perspective, people are severely limited in their ability to understand themselves and the world in which they live, and they are seriously constrained in their ability to control their lives and to make changes in the social worlds in which they are inevitably and fully engaged. A very simple example will begin to bring this point into focus.

The Web of Social Relations

Almost all of the students in a first year sociology class, drawing upon their understanding of the world through the use of the natural attitude and their everyday stocks of knowledge, tend to think of themselves as individuals who control their own actions, choices, plans, aspirations, and destiny. But, as they sit in their first sociology lecture, if they reflect for a minute—and often the social context will cause them to pause and reflect—they will each recognize that they really are not individuals at all.

A good part of the tension that students feel in their first lecture stems from the fact that every student knows that many of the students swelling the lecture hall are not there simply to obtain a degree; those students want to obtain their degrees with the highest standing possible, so they can continue on to law school, to study medicine or dentistry, to an MBA program or other graduate studies, or simply to stand at the top of the class so they have the most options for work upon graduation. Students who feel that tension and reflect upon it might not choose to be like the others—outstanding grades are not a high priority for everyone—but they know that those "keeners" will have an impact on the grade structure in the course. At the same time, those who are striving for the highest grades possible will initially feel that they are inside a crucible of almost overwhelming competitive pressure.

The professor, knowing that significant numbers of students are motivated, for very calculated reasons, to achieve high grades, can structure the forms of assessment used in the course to take those over-achievers into account. Testing and evaluation can be stringent because a lot of students will be aiming high and working hard. Thus, the tension each student feels is well founded; not only is the first lecture a journey into largely unknown territory but what is known suggests that the overall conduct of the course is out of the individual first year student's control.

The first course in sociology is out of each individual student's control in many other ways too. The professor decides what books the students should buy, the course content, the way material is presented, the speed at which material will be covered, and the ways that students' mastery of course content will be assessed.

But the professor cannot determine those things all alone; the professor is also constrained by university regulations, the course's calendar description, and the expectations of colleagues within the sociology department and within the professor's faculty. So, if each single student's experience is influenced by his or her professor, it is also affected by people at least once removed from that professor. The first lecture in sociology is shaped by a vast network of informal social relationships and pressures, as well as by highly formalized regulations and restrictions.

At the same time, the students in the class have their own networks of relationships and pressures. Think of their parents, siblings, friends, and former teachers. Each of them has certain expectations about how individual students in the course will perform. The students in the class may think that they can ignore these expectations, but, even as they decide to ignore them, they are responding to perceived expectations that emanate from other people in those students' lives.

As the first year student reflects upon attending that first lecture, he or she might begin to feel caught within a gigantic spider web—and that analogy is not a bad one.

Each individual student might want to visualize being linked by a fine thread of a particular colour to each of the people he or she knows directly, all of whom have expectations for that student's performance in sociology or in university. The student can think of a different coloured thread that ties him or her to the introductory sociology course instructor and to all of the associated university personnel (for example, the admissions officer that admitted and registered the student, the dean of the student's faculty, and the professors in each of the departments in which the student is taking courses). All of these people are just once removed from the students' instructors, but they still have an important impact upon each student.

There might be a third coloured thread that links each student to all the others in the lecture hall because the dynamic of the class will also affect all the students in the course and at each lecture. Over time, that thread might bind several students in a friendship that will last throughout the year and could extend far into the future. Of course, a thread that begins as friendship might deepen in colour as two or more students find themselves in a significant, intimate relationship at different—perhaps lasting, perhaps not—points in time during the year or over the course of their undergraduate studies.

By visualizing the various threads that link a student to other people who constitute the student's "first year sociology experience," the individual student quickly recognizes how much he or she and his or her experiences in introductory sociology are integrated into a complex web of social relationships. Although invisible, the threads that constitute the web of social relations and that extend well beyond an individual's immediate life-world tie each and every person on the planet into one network or another. Everyone is inescapably tied to, and acts within, various webs of social connection (Simmel 1955:125–95). At the same time, each person creates or modifies those relationships as he or she acts.

If each of us is irrevocably linked to an increasingly complex and ever-distant network of social relations, then how can we best understand that

complex reality? What is needed to move beyond the natural attitude of people's everyday stocks of knowledge and grasp the complexity of life more
fully? What is required to comprehend the world *sociologically*?

The web of social relations is one way to begin thinking sociologically,
but there is another image that is also helpful—it is captured in the opening, framing scene of Alfred Hitchcock's (1960) *Psycho*.

FROM THE INDIVIDUAL TO THE SOCIAL

On a clear, sunny day from an elevated perspective—perhaps a rooftop, perhaps from the window of a tall building—the camera begins a long, slow,
continuous pan from left to right across the buildings of a downtown in 1950s
America. The camera's gaze lasts a full minute as the scene carefully unfolds.

It might be any city centre, but the viewer learns that it is "Phoenix,
Arizona" on "Friday, December the eleventh" at "two forty-three p.m." The
city's buildings extend as far as the camera can see—the only activity is the
traffic moving slowly away from the camera along a one-way street. As the
camera continues its deliberate sweep, the focus begins to tighten onto a single building, and then it pinpoints one specific window on the fifth floor,
entering the half-opened window under the slightly raised blind.

Adjusting to the darker interior, as one's eyes would when moving from
sunlight into a room with the blind drawn, the camera continues searching
from left to right, panning around a nondescript, rent-by-the-hour hotel
room. The camera comes to rest at the bed.

A man stands almost against the bed wearing his dress pants and gently
towelling what shows of his naked torso. "You never did eat your lunch did
you?" he says in a deep, rich tone to a woman, lying on her back. Her eyes are
fixed on him. In a bra and half-slip, the woman exudes a Marilyn Munro–like
sensuality that is captivating. The two, it turns out, are lovers getting ready
to part after another "extended lunch hour" rendezvous.

In the midst of downtown Phoenix, in one hotel room, two people with
complicated personal circumstances feel dissatisfied and trapped in lives
they do not want. This woman and man seem unable or unwilling to make
the changes that would allow them to achieve the lives they desire—or perhaps they simply do not know how to start making these changes.

Filmed in 1959, *Psycho* overlaps with Columbia University sociologist C.
Wright Mills's (1959) extremely influential book *The Sociological Imagination*
in a number of ways—each can illuminate the other. Together, *Psycho* and
The Sociological Imagination provide an excellent introduction to what it

means and feels like to think sociologically. Before making the links, however, it is important to know a bit about Mills's book.

Mills's Five Main Objectives

The opening chapter of *The Sociological Imagination*—"The Promise"—is widely used in introductory sociology courses. Mills wrote the chapter to give his readers some key concepts and questions that readily orient new students to the way sociologists study the social world around them. At the same time, in sketching out the promise of sociology, Mills makes a strong case for the importance of the discipline.

In particular, though, Mills has five main objectives in mind, all of which relate, in some way, to enabling people to understand and change the social world in which they exist. "Nowadays," Mills (1959) begins, "men often feel that their private lives are a series of traps. They sense that within their everyday worlds, they cannot overcome their troubles, and in this feeling, they are often quite correct" (p. 3).[10]

First and foremost, then, Mills wants to empower people; he wants to give them the tools needed to change the world in which they live and their own lives through that action. Mills believes that the key to such change lies in one particular way of understanding the world—the one used by sociologists working within the classical tradition. As a result, Mills wants to empower people by achieving his second objective, establishing the clas- sical tradition as the dominant orientation to sociology in North America.

This second objective put Mills in conflict with the then-existing establishment in American sociology. As a result, Mills's (1959) third objective was to demonstrate the weaknesses of the "structural-functional perspective" that prevailed in North American sociology from the 1950s into the 1970s and to re-establish the classical tradition as the dominant approach in North American sociology (pp. 25–49).

Fourth, Mills critiques the over-reliance on quantitative, survey-based research in sociology and the accompanying piecemeal approach to social change, which, he argues, characterize the discipline in the postwar period. Mills (1959) describes both characteristics pejoratively—negatively—as "abstracted empiricism" and "the liberal practicality," contrasting their limitations to the classical tradition's bold ambitions for significant social change (pp. 50–75, 76–99).

---

10 Writing in 1959, Mills used the noun "man" and masculine pronouns such as "his" to refer to both men and women, as was customary at that time. To retain the historical accuracy of the document and because introducing more inclusive language in square brackets can be very distracting, quotations from Mills have not been altered to reflect the current, more gender-inclusive practices. The same holds for other early texts. When a new translation is supplied, gender-inclusive language is employed.

Sociology's classical tradition, Mills argues, critically addressed fundamental social issues, and classical sociologists were not afraid to propose sweeping changes to the societies in which they lived. This tradition, according to Mills, had given way to social reformism and then to mere "administrative tinkering" as sociological studies were increasingly narrowed to survey research that focused on very specific, rather isolated aspects of social life. It is Mills's final objective, however, that is of greatest significance at this juncture.

Mills argues that all people—not just sociologists—should and could become more sociologically aware, so they could genuinely understand the social world in which they lived, assess it critically, strive for change, and know how to bring it about. The world continues to be far from perfect, but people can foster genuine improvement if they only develop the particular "quality of mind" that Mills identifies as "the sociological imagination." Understanding, embracing, and using the sociological imagination are the first, crucial steps needed to create change and improve social and political life in North America and the rest of the world. So Mills's final objective is to instil the sociological imagination into the consciousness of all thinking North Americans—an objective that remains as vital today as it was in 1959.

Mills begins his argument by noting that most people—"ordinary men" as he calls them—see the world from their own particular, limited perspective. The average person does not usually connect his or her problems with larger social issues or within a broader social context. Problems are seen from the perspective of the personal, the private. "What ordinary men are directly aware of," Mills (1959) writes, and "what they try to do are bounded by the private orbits in which they live; their visions and their powers are limited to the close-up scenes of job, family, neighbourhood" (p. 3). Similarly, what goes well for people is viewed from the perspective of the personal. "The well-being they enjoy," Mills (1959) continues, is not usually "imput[ed] to the big ups and downs of the societies in which they live" (p. 3).

Seldom aware of the intricate connection between the patterns of their own lives and the course of world history, ordinary men do not usually know what this connection means for the kinds of men they are becoming and for the kinds of history making in which they might take part (Mills 1959:3–4).

Mills's point is that most people view the world around them in very limited, personal terms. He goes further, however—Mills argues that this perspective is restricting and even misleading because people's lives are shaped, to an overwhelming extent, by the broader social context within which they live. To understand their specific situation genuinely—their particular predicament if there are problems in their lives—people require a larger, more encompassing perspective. People will be empowered by learning to use the sociological imagination.

Psycho *and the Sociological Imagination*

Marion Crane is the woman lying on the bed in *Psycho's* opening scene. Moving from the broad context of the city of Phoenix, the viewer is brought directly into a close, personal exchange between Marion and her lover Sam Loomis. They are both feeling, in Mills's words, "that their private lives are a series of traps." Marion's work, her relationship to Sam, and her feelings about how and where they are meeting cause conflict within Marion. She tells Sam, "This is the last time."

Sam also feels trapped: he has debts inherited from his late father, and he is burdened by alimony payments to his ex-wife. Sam wants to keep their relationship alive, but Marion wants more—she wants "respectability." As Sam bemoans his own circumstances, Marion wistfully laments, "I haven't even been married once yet."

"Yeah but when you do," Sam replies, anticipating what she would be like as a partner and perhaps their lives together, "you'll swing."

"Oh Sam," Marion responds with an emotional cocktail of frustration, love, desire, trepidation, and foolish wishful thinking, "let's get married." Marion, it is now fully apparent, wants the "happily-ever-after" life that 1950s America promised.[11]

By moving from the panorama of 1950s Phoenix to the intimacy of the hotel room, the camera is suggesting that one will understand the stories of Marion and Sam by zeroing in on the private and personal level. But Mills would disagree; one must also take into account that Marion and Sam are located in a particular society during a specific period—they live where and when a number of social forces shape their lives and everyone else's. Who are they in the broader social context?

Marion is a secretary working in America for a small real estate company and dreaming of and wishing for all that "the American dream" and postwar prosperity promised (see, for example, Cohen 2003). She is single, longing for love, personal security, and financial stability. Marion desperately, it turns out, wants to escape her identity as a poorly paid white-collar employee who must continually ignore the banal juvenile humour and the weak double entendres of aging male clients, who openly lust over her as they pass through the office. Marion wants what she thinks Sam can offer— what *they* could have together.

Sam is young, handsome, strong, and virile—a stark contrast to the men Marion has to deal with at work day in and day out. But Sam is also trapped

---

11 The contrast between the dream and the reality of marriage in 1950s America is brought out in the next scene when Marion returns to work and asks her fellow secretary what had happened while she was away. The ensuing dialogue about her co-worker's humdrum, tranquilizer-enhanced world is an instructive and realistic contrast to the romantic illusion Marion is embracing.

by a life and work that will never let him realize his 1950s male vision of the American dream. He sees his life blocked by his inherited debts and by the alimony he pays to an ex-wife "who is living on the other side of the world somewhere." The most Sam can offer Marion is living "in a storeroom behind a hardware store in Fairvale [California]."

"Yeah, we'll have a lot of laughs," Sam tells Marion, with defeat in his voice. "[A]nd when I send my wife her alimony, you can lick the stamps," he continues, mocking his predicament.

"I'll lick the stamps," Marion assures him, as her eyes implore Sam to offer a sign of commitment that would match hers.

Through most of *Psycho*, the audience is also trapped by the close-up perspective of the camera, but, in the same way that everyday men and women can escape their own particular, limited points of view, the sociological imagination can reveal within this movie a rich, sophisticated, and critical commentary on American life rather than leaving it as a taut psychological thriller.

Although the panning camera has already revealed the broader macro context within which the micro drama in the hotel room takes place, like the natural attitude of everyday life, the "private orbit" is the movie's primary consideration. The camera zeros in on the lives of Marion and Sam, and it will stay there throughout the movie. To understand *Psycho* sociologically, one must break out of the natural attitude; one must move the camera back to make the "intricate connection between the patterns of [the lovers'] lives and the course of [American and] world history" (Mills 1959:3–4). This is Mills's major point in *The Sociological Imagination*. Sociology and the sociological perspective require the quality of mind that integrates macro and micro, the social and the individual.

To understand the world fully and change it, one needs to grasp "*the interplay of man and society, of biography and society, of self and world*" (Mills 1959:5, emphasis added). One needs to acquire and employ *the sociological imagination.*

Before exploring Mills's major point, his use of the term "imagination" merits some attention. The term and what it signifies can be easily misunderstood—although the word choice is brilliant.

People often associate imagination with making things up; it is something that applies to children's games, fairy tales, science fiction stories, or horror films—all imaginary and unreal. That is not the type of imagination Mills has in mind.

Mills chooses the word imagination to convey several specific ideas that are crucial to his conception of sociological understanding. First, imagination—to imagine or to image—involves creative mental processes and the active role of the mind, both of which are central to the sociological imagination. But it is not a fabricating, make-believe activity; it is an apprehending process—a way of creating a complex mental image of the world by developing an increasingly more comprehensive mental view of the relationship between an individual and his or her social location.

The sociological imagination is a quality of mind that requires one to grasp the social context intellectually, to come to grips with it, draw it together, or apprehend the world critically in a manner that is much more complex than passively relying on one's normal, taken-for-granted stocks of everyday knowledge. It requires attention to the broader social context, panning slowly and attentively across it while paying attention to historical detail before focusing on the individual and personal—and then pulling back again so that the interplay of self and world, biography and society, and the individual and the social can be drawn together and examined as a dynamic whole.

The understanding that is created through the sociological imagination is not at all artificial or constructed out of thin air—it is a mental understanding of the world *as it actually is* through an approach that allows people to understand more than they would by using normal, everyday stocks of knowledge. Mills proposes that to grasp and comprehend the world genuinely—the real world in which people live and act—one must develop this particular, active quality of mind.

Mills (1959) also argues that the sociological imagination enables individuals to understand themselves and their experiences:

> The first fruit of this imagination—and the first lesson of the social science that embodies it—is the idea that the individual can understand his own experience and gauge his own fate only by locating himself within his period, that he can know his own chances in life only by becoming aware of those individuals in his circumstances. (P. 5)

This pivotal conception is central to thinking sociologically.

To understand a particular situation sociologically—your own life chances, for example—you have to think beyond personal experiences. A person must locate himself or herself within the broader social framework of the period and within the context of others who are in a comparable situation, who share similar life chances. As soon as a person makes those identifications, he or she has moved beyond the individual and the psychological to the social and the sociological. However, adjusting the focal point from the self to a group of people who share similar circumstances and comparable fates is a radical shift.

The key to this shift in focus involves locating the individual in the period in which he or she lives and within the context of others who are in similar circumstances—one must "grasp history and biography and the relations between the two within society." This is the sociological imagination's "task and its promise" (Mills 1959:6).

"The sociological imagination enables us to grasp history and biography and the relations between the two within society": this sentence is pivotal to Mills's conception. Any sociological study that fails to examine "problems of biography, of history, and of their intersections within society," Mills (1959:6) maintains, has not completed its intellectual journey.

Stated in another way, to complete its intellectual journey, every study must locate a person's personal biography within a larger set of social relationships or within a social framework.[12] It must also consider the historical location of that larger set of social relations. Finally, it must look at how those two conceptualizations—personal experiences understood as part of a larger set of social relationships and the impact of history on a larger set of social relations—intersect and influence one another. In essence, the sociological imagination involves an understanding of how people (the agents who make or constitute extended sets of social relationships) and historically located sets of extended social relationships (the "products" of human agents) mutually interact with and condition one another.

Psycho and "the Interplay of Man and Society"

One can begin to appreciate the sort of insight the sociological imagination allows by considering the production of *Psycho* from the perspective of the intersection of biography (the film's biography, the audience's collective biography) and social structure.

Hitchcock's movie was a relatively low-budget film—black and white, with a limited set, just five central characters, and a small supporting cast. He did not employ any special effects. Essentially, he used the same techniques he had been perfecting—to great viewer ratings—on his television show *Alfred Hitchcock Presents*, employing them now on the big screen.

---

12 The phrase "larger set of social relationships" is clumsy but more precise than the word "society" for two reasons. First, society usually refers to a large entity that is easily denoted by common sense, such as Canadian society, American society, or contemporary society, and, although locating the individual in a larger context might involve one of those macro entities (or something similar), most sociologists choose to focus on a more restricted set of social relationships, such as undergraduate students or first year undergraduate students. Second, although people use the word "society" almost all of the time in their daily lives, it tends to suggest a particular entity—almost a thing. But people do not really live within a thing—they live within social relationships that tend to have an enduring existence. To avoid the reification of social relationships—to avoid turning fluid, changing social relationships into an apparently static thing—this text frequently uses the term "social relationships" rather than the more common shorthand term "society."

Television was the new medium in the 1950s. It was almost killing Hollywood. So Hitchcock adapted the television close-up, which so fascinated audiences, for the large, full-screen movie theatres of the postwar period. In an irony that was befitting a Hitchcock production, television actually made *Psycho* the success it became. Television, the laboratory where Hitchcock experimented, now served as the unconscious reference point for his feature-length movie—the techniques of television on the silver screen appeared cutting edge.

Psycho also tapped into the sexual repression of the 1950s, capitalizing on a growing desire within urban America to break free of its traditional, puritanical constraints.[13] The shots of Janet Leigh (Marion Crane) in her lingerie—first white and then black—pushed the limits of propriety and tested respectability among the new mass consumption viewers.

The famous shower scene contrasts starkly with the climaxes of today's horror films but was inescapably shaped by 1950s America. The scene's sexual overtones are suggestive but discrete; the violence is muted and restrained, but its impact is sudden, forceful, and chillingly unsettling.

Leading up to the scene, the viewer has followed the conversation between Marion and the young motel owner Norman Bates, watched him peer into her room through a hole hidden behind a picture mounted on the wall, and trailed after him as he retreats back to the house he shares with his mother.

The viewer sees Marion sit at a desk in her robe, calculating what she owes and contemplating her situation. Tearing up the page on which she has made her calculations, Marion steps into the bathroom and flushes the bits of paper down the toilet. Next, we watch as Marion closes the bathroom door, lets the full-length robe fall from her shoulders to the floor, steps inside the shower, and draws the semi-transparent shower curtain, obscuring the view.

The building voyeuristic urge heightens as the translucent shower curtain reveals enough to seduce the viewer into wanting more—and the camera accommodates.

The next shot is from inside the shower, directly at Marion's head and shoulders. She is resolved to return to Phoenix. So perhaps she is simply washing away the stain of her evil deed—stealing from her boss—and the shower is a baptism of renewed faith in honesty and the truth. But the warm water gushing from the showerhead suggests other possibilities.

Marion throws her head back, opening her mouth in response to the pleasure of the water enveloping her body. The viewer (voyeur) watches Marion's

---

13 See Marcuse (1955, 1964), Bell (1960a, 1976), and Harrington (1965) for three similar assessments of sexual repression within the dominant postwar American culture.

hands moving over her shoulders, arms, and neck and sees her eyes close while the warm stream continues to wash down her naked body. A tension builds, but it is sexual—not one that anticipates an impending horror.

From inside the shower and through the curtain, the camera reveals another partially obscure image: the bathroom door opens, and someone slowly approaches. As the shower curtain is ripped open, Marion turns and screams while *Psycho*'s signature music shatters the mood.

The raised knife is thrust downwards; Marion struggles to resist, and the camera's clear focus is lost as a staccato of images: her head and shoulders, an arm, a hand trying to defend, a wound, her midriff, her side, drops of blood in the water. We see traces of blood in the water and hear the knife piercing her flesh, but it is Marion turning towards the wall, the fingernails of her hand scratching the tiles as she begins to slide downwards, that reveals her fate. Turning again, her expression in palpable contrast to the one on her face just moments before, Marion takes her last shallow breaths and, glassy-eyed, slowly reaches forward. The camera focuses directly on her hand, giving the voyeur one last hazy glimpse of her breasts just before she tumbles face first onto the cold, hard tile of the bathroom floor.

The water, still streaming from the showerhead, is once again the only sound. The last image is a faint trace of diluted blood flowing past Marion's ankles and feet into the drain.

Today, the scene appears stark and contrived—perhaps naïve or simplistic. It is almost archaic, but Hitchcock knew his audience and laboured over the carefully sequenced images until they achieved the effect that met his demanding standards (Rebello 1990:100–18). The full shower scene—a minute and forty seconds long—was not a two-take affair. Hitchcock filmed it over seven days using more than 70 different camera angles. The collage of images was painstakingly planned, shot, and edited. It was written and filmed so that the viewer—like any voyeur—would have to fill in the gaps to create the full impact. At one level, the scene is immediately individual in terms of the event it portrays and how the event is witnessed and experienced. But, by drawing back and locating personal biography within the history of social structure, one can see the sociological dimensions of Hitchcock's artistry.

The audiences of the late 1950s and early 1960s were accustomed to using the imagination to create or fill in images. Oral history and books still dominated the culture. Radio was only just being replaced as the main technology for home entertainment, and movies were still relative newcomers on the scene. In fact, the "talkies" were not widespread until 1930.[14] A significant part

---

14 The first feature-length movie to include dialogue was *The Jazz Singer*, which was released in October 1927. Although cinema still developed throughout World War II (1939–45), the auditory and

of the appeal of Hitchcock's low-budget approach was the skill with which he let viewers create their own scenes—stimulate their own horror—by combining an austere set of images using vivid, active imaginations.

Early 1960s North American viewers had not yet experienced the explicit images of violence, destruction, oozing wounds, and tragic, painful death that the nightly news coverage of the Vietnam War would bring directly into their living rooms from 1964 onwards. Hitchcock's audience had not been desensitized by the graphic, made-for-television carnage that prime-time television programs would begin to use increasingly in the late 1960s, as fiction competed with reality for market share. Realistic special effects and the extent to which they could carry the suspense in contemporary movies such as *Friday the 13th, Halloween, Scream,* or *A Nightmare on Elm Street* still lay in the future. *Psycho* and *Scream* each succeeded as box-office attractions because of the way they intersected with the larger social context in which they were produced.

THREE KEY QUESTIONS

The discussion of Mills's conception of the sociological imagination often stops at his key phrase and point of emphasis—grasping "history and biography and the relations between the two within society." But Mills provides his reader with more. Mills presents three sets of questions to help his readers begin to think in broader, sociological terms. Those who use the sociological imagination fruitfully, Mills (1959:6–7) argues, ask three types of questions, each of which is aimed at a very specific aspect of the classical tradition in sociology.

Mills's first set of questions concerns what is often termed the structure of society, and, even though the term "structure" has certain problems, it conveys the notion that social relationships tend to have an enduring, almost structural or thing-like reality to them. The analogy of the web mentioned at the outset of this chapter conveys a conception of the reality, connection, and semi-permanence that Mills intends with the term "structure."

"What is the structure of this particular society as a whole?" Mills (1959:6) tells us to ask. How is it "webbed" or woven together? "What are its essential components, and how are they related to one another? How does it differ from other varieties of social order?" We also need to inquire about "the

imaginative skills audiences brought to movie theatres in the early postwar period remained those of a low-tech culture.

meaning of any particular feature for its continuance and for its change" (p. 6).

His second set of questions moves the sociologist and sociological analysis away from the potential reification of social relationships: in other words, away from an image of a fixed, solid, permanent social structure or static web and towards a critical awareness of the historical and changing dynamic of social relations and relationships.

At the most general level, a sociologist must ask these questions:

> Where does this society stand in human history? What are the mechanics by which it is changing? What is its place within and its meaning for the development of humanity as a whole? (Mills 1959:7)

Using this second set of questions, sociologists should also look closely at the social relationships of particular societies:

> How does any particular feature we are examining affect, and how is it affected by, the historical period in which it moves? And this period— what are its essential features? How does it differ from other periods? (Mills 1959:7)

Finally, sociologists must integrate human agency into their analyses. A third set of questions facilitates this integration: "What varieties of men and women now prevail in this society and in this period? And what varieties are coming to prevail?" Mills (1959) argues that sociologists must consider how social agents are "formed, liberated and repressed, made sensitive and blunted" within their particular social relations and relationships:

> What kinds of "human nature" are revealed in the conduct and character we observe in this society in this period? And what is the meaning for "human nature" of each and every feature of the society we are examining? (Mills 1959:7)

These three sets of questions bring together social structure, history, and human agents and agency (personal biography and action) into an ensemble in which the sociologist must simultaneously consider all three and how they interact with each other.

At the centre of the classical tradition in sociology and of Mills's sociological imagination is a dynamic conception of society, one that requires every sociologist to also consider issues of stability, power, human agency, and social change. No matter what one's interest might be—life in a particular family, prison life, the dynamics of work in Canada, protest movements of various types, even how a sociology course is conducted—these are the kinds of questions the best social analysts ask. They are the intellectual roots of the classic studies in sociology. The importance of these questions in the work of Marx, Durkheim, Weber, and others who work within sociology's classical tradition will become apparent in later chapters in this book.

But we can begin to appreciate the analytical power of the classical tradition's key questions by returning to *Psycho* as a sociological analysis of 1950s America.

Completing "the Intellectual Journey"

The great success *Psycho* enjoyed stemmed directly from its ability to capitalize on the tensions, fears, and frustrations of postwar America—the same emotions that made *The Twilight Zone, The Outer Limits,* and *Alfred Hitchcock Presents* so successful.[15] On the one hand, the 1950s promised a life of order, routine, and progress. Corporations were growing in size, and the white-collar labour force was expanding dramatically. The structure of American society seemed firm and solid. Postwar America offered unlimited satisfaction and freedom, as a bounty of affordable consumer goods was continuously presented to a carefully orchestrated mass market (Cohen 2003).

At the same time, however, the growing white-collar middle class experienced a sense of constraint, insecurity, and subjugation in postwar America. William Whyte's (1956) bestselling work *The Organization Man,* Mills's (1951) *White Collar,* and Sloan Wilson's (1955) semi-autobiographical novel *The Man in the Gray Flannel Suit* captured the mood and life experiences of a growing segment of the population in Canada, the United States, and, to a certain extent, western Europe as its recovery progressed in the latter half of the 1950s. This mood, their works indicate, was closely associated with the emerging social structure of the period.

"The white-collar people," Mills (1951) writes, "slipped quietly into modern society."[16]

Whatever history they have had is a history without events; whatever common interests they have do not lead to unity; whatever future they

---

15 Rod Serling's *The Twilight Zone* ran for five seasons (1959 to 1964) on CBS television (Presnell and McGee 1998; Zicree 1982). *The Outer Limits* ran two seasons (1963–64 and 1964–65) on ABC while *Alfred Hitchcock Presents* ran from 1955 to 1964 on CBS and another year on NBC (McCarty and Kelleher 1985).

16 Mills is an "intellectual craftsman" (see Mills 1959:195–226; 2000:136–9, 150–1, 230, 276–81). His use of "white-collar people" is deliberate and conveys one of the central theses in the book. These people were not a class; they were not just white-collar workers; they constituted a growing, divided, other-directed constituency in postwar capitalist societies. People who, by their numbers and their drift, would have a significant impact on all aspects of social life.

have will not be of their own making. If they aspire at all it is to a middle course, at a time when no middle course is available, and hence to an illusory course in an imaginary society. Internally, they are split, fragmented; externally, they are dependent on larger forces. (P. ix)

Largely taken for granted, the white-collar world, Mills argues, "is characteristic of twentieth-century existence." White-collar people have "transformed the tang and feel of the American experience," he maintains. "They carry, in a most revealing way, many of those psychological themes that characterize our epoch" (Mills 1951:ix).

Whyte's work corroborates Mills's analysis. A growing segment of the "middle class," Whyte (1956) argues, "had left home, spiritually as well as physically, to take the vows of organization life, and it is they who are the mind and soul of our great self-perpetuating institutions" (p. 3). Whyte (1956) continues,

Listen to them talk to each other over the front lawns of their suburbia and you cannot help but be struck by how well they grasp the common denominators which bind them. Whatever the differences in their organization ties, it is the common problems of collective work that dominate their attentions, and when the Du Pont man talks to the research chemist or the chemist to the army man, it is these problems that are uppermost. The word *collective* most of them can't bring themselves to use—except to describe foreign countries or organizations they don't work for— but they are keenly aware of how much more deeply beholden they are to organization than were their elders. They are wry about it, to be sure; they talk of the "treadmill," the "rat race," of the inability to control one's direction. But they have no great sense of plight; between themselves and organization they believe they see an ultimate harmony and, more than most elders recognize, they are building an ideology that will vouchsafe this trust. (P. 4)

The "Protestant work ethic," Whyte (1956) maintains, had been replaced by an "organization ethic" or a "bureaucratic ethic," which converted "what would seem in other times a bill of no rights into a restatement of individualism"—one in which the individual was totally subordinated to the rigid structure of the organization and "Corporate America" (p. 6).

"Where Does This Society Stand in Human History?"
Whyte and Mills both address the second set of questions that are central to classical analyses—where is this society located in history? One gains

from their work a strong sense of where postwar America lay in the history of industrial societies and what some of the implications were as the United States, in particular, and industrial societies, more generally, began to change in the 1950s and 1960s.

Mills also provides details of the corporate world that developed in the wake of World War II, of the daily grind that subserviates individuals to the organization and teaches them their place in the hierarchy, as well as the fact that they can be readily replaced:

> In the enormous file of the office, in all the calculating rooms, accountants and purchasing agents replace the man who did his own figuring. And in the lower reaches of the white-collar world, office operatives grind along, loading and emptying the filing system; there are private secretaries and typists, entry clerks, billing clerks, corresponding clerks—a thousand kinds of clerks; the operators of light machinery, comptometers, Dictaphones, addressographs; and the receptionists to let you in or keep you out. (Mills 1951:x)

According to Mills (1951), the working situation of these accountants and clerks paralleled their economic and social worlds to teach them acceptance or, perhaps, a frustrated and resigned helplessness when they were confronted by the impersonal forces acting upon them:

> In a world crowded with big ugly forces, the white-collar man is readily assumed to possess all the supposed virtues of the small creature. He may be at the bottom of the social world, but he is, at the same time, gratifyingly middle class. It is easy as well as safe to sympathize with his troubles; he can do little or nothing about them. Other social actors threaten to become big and aggressive, to act out of selfish interests and deal in politics. The big business man continues his big-business-as-usual through the normal rhythm of slump and war and boom; the big labor man, lifting his shaggy eyebrows, holds up the nation until his demands are met; the big farmer cultivates the Senate to see that big farmers get theirs. But not the white-collar man. He is more often pitiful than tragic, as he is seen collectively, fighting impersonal inflation, living out in slow misery his yearning for the quick American climb. He is pushed by forces beyond his control, pulled into movements he does not understand; he gets into situations in which his is the most helpless position. The white-collar man is the hero as victim, the small creature who is acted upon but does not act, who works along unnoticed in somebody's office or store, never talking loud, never talking back, never taking a stand. (P. xii)

This was the audience Hitchcock reached—one that he could exploit so perfectly in the broader symbolism of *Psycho*.

White-collar people, to use Mills's term, wanted to escape the "slow misery" of striving to inch one's way up the organizational hierarchy that crushed them in all its bureaucratic impersonality and countless layers. But they also sought reassurance, and, viewed sociologically, one sees how *Psycho* delivers this comfort.

Key aspects of Hitchcock's characters appeal to the audience while their failings evoke a cathartic *Schadenfreude* (pleasure in another's misery). Marion Crane is a family-centred, proper, careful, white-collar worker who wants love and interpersonal fulfilment. Her needs are simple and basic: she is competent, and she shows initiative appropriate for a 1950s woman (Beamish 2009:109–16; Friedan 1963; Millett 1970).

As long as Marion tolerates the tedium of her job, she can have her limited part of the American dream. But succumbing to sexual temptation (Sam) and taking a financial shortcut to escape the slow misery that was filling her life brings serious consequences. Marion Crane pays the ultimate price for jumping onto the open highway to Los Angeles, pursuing the glamour, excitement, and excesses that Hollywood held out for everyone but gave to very few.

Sam represents some of the fundamental traits of the pre-war American male—the strong, confident individual small businessman. But he also embodies the painful future of that dying breed.

Sam has inherited his father's debts; he has lost his wife to divorce (symbolically losing the security of family), and she has moved to "a different world" far removed from quaint Fairvale, California. Sam is now caught between, on the one hand, his small-business roots that had been nourished by his Norman Rockwell–like, small-town existence and, on the other, the growing vibrancy of modern, urban, corporate America, to which he makes frequent flights. Sam has already succumbed to the temptations of the metropolis, and he has experienced its frustrations (the objects he desires slipping through his grasp). He too will pay a price—this time for staying trapped in small town America.

In an exchange that sets the key elements for the sociological subplot of *Psycho,* Marion tells Sam she has to break off their relationship. "What do we do instead," Sam responds, "write each other lurid love letters?" Ignoring her decision to break it off, Sam tries to tempt her back: "I can come down next week."

"No," Marion replies with firmness.

"Not even just to see you? Have lunch—in public?"

"Oh we can see each other," Marion responds with control. "We can even have dinner, but respectably. In my house with my mother's picture on the mantle and my sister helping you broil a big steak for three."

"And after the steak, do we send Sister to the movies, turn Momma's picture to the wall?"

"Sam!" Marion retorts with some exasperation.

"All right," Sam answers, drawing the words out as he spreads his arms, palms up, in a sign of semi-surrender. "Marion, whatever's possible, I want to see you. And under any circumstances—even respectability."

"You make respectability sound disrespectful," Marion laments, pausing over the word "disrespectful."

"Oh no, I'm all for it," Sam responds. "It requires patience, temperance, a lot of sweaty hours; otherwise, though, it's just hard work." Holding Marion in his arms, her back to his chest as he caresses her neck, Sam continues: "But if I can see you and touch you as simply as this, I won't mind."

Releasing her and pacing to the other side of the room, his tone changing to one of helpless frustration, Sam continues: "I'm tired of sweating for people who aren't there. I sweat to pay off my father's debts, and he's in his grave. I sweat to pay my ex-wife alimony, and she's living on the other side of the world somewhere."

"I pay too," Marion replies. "They also pay who meet in hotel rooms."

If we drag the camera's focus back from the tight, close-up of the personal lives of Sam and Marion to the larger context of Phoenix, Bakersfield, Fairvale, and Los Angeles—to the lives of all who watched *Psycho*—we see that this scene constructs the four dominant, interrelated macro themes that resonated so strongly with the audience and made the film such a success.

The first subtext focuses on respectability and desire; it is embodied most fully in Marion. The second centres on sexual repression versus sexual liberation; this theme is embodied by Bates, Marion, Sam, and the state trooper. The third contrasts work and consumption and is most fully represented in Sam sweating to pay off his father's debts and his ex-wife's alimony, which denies him what he most wants—to be able to afford the respectability that Marion desires. Finally, the fourth subtext centres on gender, gender roles, and gender appropriate behaviour. Marion is torn between respectability and desire—a tension appropriate for a woman. Sam is divided between his public role as a provider—"it requires patience, temperance, a lot of sweaty hours ... it's just hard work"—and his personal needs—"but if I can touch you as simply as this, I won't mind." Bates struggles with maturation and the expectations of masculinity and independence in a much different manner than Sam does—one that ends in social pathology. *Psycho*, then, was animated and driven by the dominant social tensions of 1950s North American societies—not psychological ones.

"And What Varieties of Men and Women Are Coming to Prevail?"
Hitchcock's film also explores Mills's third set of key questions—what men and women prevail in the society and what men and women are coming to prevail? The answers to those questions are what really make the film so unsettling—and yet reassuring—to its 1960 audience.

Norman Bates, his mother, and the Bates Motel embody the psychotic aspects of 1950s America. Bates is "very kind;" he is boyishly handsome and earnest, and he seems to be disarmingly, almost painfully, honest and simple. Tied too intimately to his past, his family, and a dying—long dead perhaps—way of life, Bates is less advanced than Sam in making the transition to the realities of postwar America.

The Bates Motel is on the old highway, so it is now passed by and has become moribund. Bates and the motel are trapped in a past that progress will leave further and further behind. The new highway takes people directly into the urban sprawl of a booming Los Angeles, where the future and all its dreams promise to unfold. Yet, like Bates, adults contemplating their lives unfolding in the 1960s hesitated—they felt attraction to what was once forbidden and fear of what it might bring. There was comfort in the familiar past but no going back. Bates represents this tension. He knows that the past is gone and can never be resurrected, yet it continues to haunt him. The passivity that Bates sees in his mounted birds has become deadly, but to assert his own ambition and forge something new in the present is out of the question. This tension tears at Bates, as it did at others marooned in the world of the late 1950s.

The state trooper who finds Marion sleeping in her car at the side of the road embodies another set of tensions. He follows her in his car for a distance before turning off and then reappearing across the road from the used car lot. When watching this sequence, one cannot help but question his motives: What is in the eyes hidden by the trooper's police-issue shades? Is he objectifying Marion as he questions her, or is he genuinely protective? Is he concerned for her welfare or his own interests? Does the trooper represent Marion's conscience, causing her conflict and distress for making poor decisions, or a larger social force that is trying to control her, seeking to halt her struggle for independence? The trooper could embody the security that law and order provide and that had once given Marion comfort back in respectable Phoenix. But the highway patrolman also represents the long, unsolicited reach of arbitrary power. The trooper, like the complex concept of patriarchy that the second wave of the women's movement would begin to deconstruct in the 1960s and 1970s, can be seen to signify all those things depending on time, place, and angle of perception. The trooper represents those who were prevailing in the late fifties and those who, from their positions of power, were holding back others who were struggling to prevail.

Social tensions are deeply woven into *Psycho*'s script, and they were very unsettling for the movie's audience. However, despite the internal turmoil and creeping fears these tensions stirred, Hitchcock reassured those who watched the film in the sixties that they were making the right decisions— or that they could see the correct decisions to make.

Bates, who remains tied to rural life, becomes a schizophrenic, serial killer; Marion dies for "stepping into the private trap" of wanting everything immediately and moving outside her prescribed role. Sam continues to remain frustrated and unfulfilled as long as he stays in Fairvale, and the trooper's watchful eye follows Sam everywhere—though that surveillance is never fully shown in the film.

And the audience?

The white-collar people who flocked to *Psycho* could feel redemption for accepting their fates as "organization men" and honest wives who embraced progress, while simultaneously being excited, entertained, and enlivened by Hitchcock's larger-than-life psycho thriller. The American dream did not have to be a nightmare—one only had to fit in and fill one's prescribed role. One only had to accept the strictures of respectability.

PERSONAL TROUBLES OF MILIEU, PUBLIC ISSUES OF SOCIAL STRUCTURE

People's social lives are constituted through the complex interaction of what Mills (1959) calls "personal troubles of milieu" and "public issues of social structure" (p. 8). Almost everyone is familiar with personal troubles of milieu. Personal troubles, Mills writes, "occur within the character of the individual and within the range of his immediate relations with others; they have to do with his self and with those limited areas of social life of which he is directly and personally aware." "Accordingly," Mills (1959) continues, "the statement and the resolution of troubles properly lie within the individual as a biographical entity and within the scope of his immediate milieu—the social setting that is directly open to his personal experience and to some extent his wilful activity" (p. 8).

Psycho, adopting the natural attitude that focuses on the close-up and the private, dwells on the personal troubles of milieu experienced by Marion and Sam. Marion wants respectability; she wants a life with Sam, but he has debts and burdening financial obligations. Marion is a mere secretary, Sam a small businessman struggling to make ends meet. Their financial troubles undermine their personal happiness and their personal wishes and goals. They both face personal troubles of milieu and seek their own solutions to these problems—Marion opts for a quick but risky solution and steals the money entrusted to her. Like most people, then, Sam and Marion are unable to see their problems as anything other than personal.

"Ordinary" people, Mills (1959) argues, tend to see all of their problems as personal troubles because they view the world from the perspective of an individual. This does not mean that the problems are not real, but it simply underlines the point that most people see *all* of their troubles as personal, individually created problems.

It is important to emphasize, and Mills would have concurred, that the problems people perceive as personal are, indeed, troubles and problems for them as individuals. Sam and Marion do not make up the problem that money poses to their relationship or the conflicted feelings they experience. Personal troubles exist; one cannot simply wish or conjure them away.

At the same time, personal problems are most often linked to what Mills (1959) calls "public issues of social structure" (p. 8). Public issues of social structure are concerned with matters that extend beyond the local environments of the individual and his or her inner life:

> Public issues have to do with the organization of many [personal] milieu into the institutions of an historical society as a whole, with the ways in which various milieu overlap and interpenetrate to form the larger structure of social and historical life. An issue is a public matter: some value cherished by publics is felt to be threatened. Often there is a debate about what that value really is and about what it is that really threatens it. (Mills 1959:8)

One person, such as Marion who is trapped between a wish for respectability and a longing for sexual fulfilment, does not represent a public issue of social structure. But, when a growing number of women feel trapped by the contradiction that exists between respectability and sexual fulfilment, this experience is more than a personal trouble of milieu—it becomes a broader, *public issue* that has been created by *a variety of personal milieu overlapping and interpenetrating each other producing a structure* that constrains these women.

Family, work, friendship, and the law all intersected to create the situation that Marion and many other Marions who watched *Psycho* were experiencing in America and Canada during the late fifties and early sixties. For them, as for us, an analysis of the intersection of social structure and personal biography can achieve the level of understanding needed to inform action that will solve personal troubles and public issues.

The relationship between personal troubles and public issues of social structure is more complex than most usually recognize because there are really three terms at issue—personal troubles of milieu, public issues, and social structure. Mills presents the three concepts within an interrelated pair—personal troubles of milieu and public issues of social structure—but, by separating the terms, one can gain the full insight inherent in Mills's conception.

The significance of Mills's terms is best brought out in four specific points. The first was just discussed but merits underscoring. Although most people experience their problems as personal troubles of milieu, these difficulties are almost always associated with public issues of social structure. The link between personal troubles and public issues of social structure is Mills's basic point, but it can be refined further by attending to the relationship between personal troubles and public issues, on the one hand, and personal troubles and issues of social structure, on the other. This is the second point.

A personal trouble is seen as a *public issue* when the social circumstances are ripe for it to be a public concern—otherwise, the issue remains a personal trouble, festers as a repressed problem, or exists as a general malaise—something people cannot yet recognize and formulate but persistent nonetheless. Not all personal troubles are simultaneously public issues; timing and historical location matter.

The setting of *Psycho*, when and where it takes place, makes Marion's situation more than a personal trouble of milieu. Postwar America "promised" freedom, progress, and a cornucopia of things to buy and own. The economic capacity to produce an abundance of consumer goods and the cultural promotion of the new "consumers' republic" and of the growing Disneyland world, where one's dreams came true, created the social conditions that caused Marion and many other women in the 1950s to feel anxiety generating troubles. As more people felt them, what had been experienced initially as *personal troubles* became *public issues.* They were public issues of *social structure* because the particular overlapping of personal milieu and institutions created a social structure that promised a good deal to many women but delivered to only a few—leaving a large and growing number of women troubled and dissatisfied. So these women began to turn their personal troubles into structurally induced public issues.

If Hitchcock had set the film at the turn of the twentieth century in Canada, the United States, Britain, or Europe, Marion would not have experienced the same personal troubles, and the women during that period would not have expressed those troubles as public issues. In the early decades of the twentieth century, religion played a dominant, constraining role in North America, belief in progress was tempered, and the largely rural economy promised only moderate surplus production but not consumer abundance. Traditional roles, traditional expectations, and traditionally governed life-chances shaped, tempered, and limited people's aspirations and dreams significantly. The intersection of the personal milieu with these different cir-cumstances and institutions did not foster the conditions in which Marion's situation could become widespread. A few women may have felt personal troubles similar to Marion's, but those feelings remained personal troubles of milieu and did not become broader, public issues.

The importance of separating public issues from social structure is most apparent in point three. A small number of women feeling fatigued and numbed by their daily lives could reflect on the constraints and limitations of their roles in the domestic household, for example. But these women might never articulate their troubles and turn them into a public issue because of the power and inertia of "the institutions of an historical society as a whole" and "the ways in which various milieu overlap and interpenetrate to form the larger structure of social and historical life." In fact, these social forces could prevent most women from even feeling and expressing their circum-stances as a simple, personal trouble.

The intersection of personal biography and the history of social struc-ture may lead the majority of people to view all of their problems in per-sonal terms, and their social circumstances might also lead them to develop a naïve or blind understanding of their lives. In this case, people's social cir-cumstances have prevented them from perceiving a particular injustice (per-petrated against them or in which they are complicit) even though someone in a different situation or using a more critically informed perspective would easily see the injustice and repression. This naïve or distorted perception of their actual lives and of the forces that shape them is often termed "false consciousness" by sociologists. False consciousness is a controversial term because it implies that a true consciousness exists, or could exist. But how does one determine what is true and what is false? Similarly, how can some-thing exist that is not thought? If no one is feeling a particular personal trou-ble, then how can someone say that it should exist as truth? These are good questions to ask, but they do not rule out the notion of false consciousness because one of the most important roles that scientists and sociologists fill is the systematic analysis of the natural and social worlds to discover knowl-edge or features that were previously unknown, unrecognized, and, thus, never articulated before.

By combining the overall panorama of Phoenix, the location of the Bates Motel, Fairvale, and 1950s America with the close-up scenes of the lives of

Marion and Sam, a sociological observer can identify and explain many facets of the intersection of the personal and social. In other words, from a detached, systematic, sophisticated, theoretically informed perspective, a sociologist can explain *what* some of Marion and Sam's specific personal troubles are, indicate *how* they are linked to broader issues of social structure, and suggest *why* these troubles have not yet—but will eventually—become public issues. The sociologist can correctly note that Marion and Sam live in a state of false consciousness—a truer consciousness arises through the use of the sociological imagination.

The fourth and final point of emphasis concerns personal troubles of milieu and their resolution. Mills (1959) argues that personal troubles "have to do with self and with those limited areas of social life of which ... [an individual] is directly and personally aware" (p. 8). As a result, their resolution lies within the scope of the individual and his or her wilful activity.

Mills understands that people feel trapped and unsettled in their lives; he wants to give them the tools to alter their circumstances while recognizing that change is up to them—within the scope of their will. One of the key resources Mills offers is a perspective that takes people beyond the close-up and the personal. Mills wants his readers to develop the sociological imagination as a critical, powerful tool for creating significant, meaningful change.

To solve a personal trouble, an individual must rely on his or her wilful activity—in *Psycho*, Marion chooses to steal the money handed to her, but she could have chosen other solutions. If Marion had been able to use the sociological imagination, if she had grasped her personal trouble as part of a larger issue of social structure, she would have seen how her own biography intersected with the history of the 1950s American social structure. This would have provided a completely different perspective and indicated other ways to solve her problems. Marion would have understood her plight much differently; she could have reduced her anxiety and begun to assess her circumstances more objectively—with greater personal distance.

If she had identified the social pressures she was confronting, Marion would have had several courses of action open to her. She could have, for example, begun to connect with other women feeling the same or similar unease and lack of fulfilment—Marion and her officemate probably shared more in common than either realized. Marion could have resolved to interrogate her sense of respectability critically. Where had it come from? Why was it so constraining? Which did she value more—her sense of respectability or her desire to be with Sam (or her own freedom to make her own choices, irrespective of social pressures)?

Marion might have begun to recognize all of the different social forces—each of the personal milieus—that intersected with larger social institutions to create what seemed like a "personal problem." Then, she would have found herself in a far better position to develop a meaningful and effective course of action to create change—change in her personal life as well as change that might have had a wider rippling effect.

If other women were experiencing the same troubles as Marion—and they were—then, as each sought out social solutions to her personal problems, those personal troubles of milieu would begin to coalesce into a public issue of social structure. One of the key, sociological subtexts of *Psycho*, it is now apparent, resonated with the nascent women's movement of the 1960s and 1970s.

To summarize, Mills wants people to understand their society critically and fully; he wants them to gain that understanding to change and improve it. There are some personal troubles that are deeply rooted in an individual's personal milieu and biography and have very little broader impact or significance—but those are actually the exception rather than the rule. The majority of people's personal troubles are linked to broader social relationships—they are public issues of social structure, and they require more than an individual's solitary, wilful activity to solve them. By promoting the use of the sociological imagination, Mills helps people to recognize the social bases of the problems they encounter and the social relationships that can and need to be changed to improve the lives of everyone. Personal troubles might start a person to think about her or his particular circumstances; but, by seeing these circumstances within the context of public issues of social structure, the individual can begin to initiate change that will affect everyone. The subtext of Hitchcock's *Psycho* complements that dimension of Mills's *Sociological Imagination*.

C. WRIGHT MILLS AND INTELLECTUAL CRAFTSMANSHIP

Mills's conception of the sociological imagination and his respect for the classical tradition in sociology stemmed largely from his intimate knowledge of the work of Marx, Durkheim, and Weber—three thinkers who are frequently referred to as the "founding fathers of sociology." Before learning about these three thinkers in the next few chapters and appreciating why the classical tradition influenced Mills's sociology so much and retains its relevance today, one should consider some key questions that students often ask about Mills. What was he like? What happened—how did he die so young? Most important, what did sociology and the sociological imagination really mean to him?

While watching a production of *Medea* at Oberlin College on 20 March 1962, Mills's eldest daughter, Pamela, was called to the phone and learned that her father had died, at the age of 45, from a second myocardial infarction—a heart attack—at his home in West Nyack near New York City. "In the decades since then," she writes, "the ghost of my father has made many appearances, often provoked by gratifying references to his work" (P. Mills 2000:xxi). "Large and vibrant," she notes, the images have ranged from canoeing in Lake Temagami, where Mills built, from the ground up, a summer home, to the cadence of his voice as he read *David Copperfield* to her aloud or to sitting behind her father, feeling the throbbing power of the BMW motorcycle that Mills loved to race along an open road. But among all the memories, the image "that most impressed me," Pamela Mills (2000) indicates, "is that of a muscular figure of energy and determination, overflowing with ambitious plans for the future, envisioning books that would cut through official distortions to produce uncompromising versions of truth as his logical mind perceived it" (p. xxiii).

Mills's second daughter, Kathryn—"the only child in ... nursery school whose father delivered her there on his motorcycle and also let her honk the horn"—remembers being afraid of the dark and the way her father attempted to cure the fear (K. Mills 2000:xvii). "He took me on a daytime tour of our house," she writes, "armed with a flashlight, which he used to light up the far corners of every single closet, every single dark storage place—showing me that there was nothing frightening hiding in the darkness" (K. Mills 2000:xviii).

She continues,

> In my mind's eye, I can still see my father standing by the closet door shining his flashlight into the darkness. Yes, it was possible to light up the far corners. No, we should not be afraid to confront what we find there. I believe that my father's lesson for me was also his message to the world. His was the light of reason, humane purpose, and moral passion, and he struggled to dispel the darkness of apathy, confusion, and irresponsibility. (K. Mills 2000:xx)

Born in Waco, Texas on 28 August 1916, Mills was a robust, strongly independent iconoclast who thought of himself as largely self-made:

> There is a certain type of man who spends his life finding and refining what is within him, and I suppose I am of that type. ... [T]here is nothing I need that can be given to me by others. In the end, a man must go to bat alone. (Mills 2000:40)

Elsewhere, Mills notes that he did well at bat in spite of the circumstances into which he was born, that he did not owe much to his cultural or economic background. In an unfinished manuscript—"Contacting the Enemy: Tovarich, Written to an Imaginary Soviet Colleague"[17]—Mills (2000) writes that his upbringing "contained no intellectual or cultural benefits." He informs his fictitious Soviet friend that he grew up in "houses that had no books and no music in them." Mills heard his first piece of classical music in his second year of university. "Thus intellectually and culturally I am as 'self-made' as it is possible to be" (pp. 28–9). The decision to pursue a postgraduate degree in sociology meant "a further cutting off of self from my family background and the social setting at large as well." Even as he first entered university, Mills (2000) felt set apart: "I think no one I had previously known, including family members, really counted for me as a point of reference. I was cut off and alone, and I felt it at the time" (p. 29).

Nevertheless, as independent and critical of his background as he was, Mills (2000) recognized that he owed a great debt to his parents. He credits his mother with nurturing his sensibilities and his sensitivity to the world around him, enabling Mills to tap into the "tang and feel" of any social situation (p. 41). From his father, a white-collar representative for an insurance company, Mills (2000) "absorbed the gospel and character of work, determination with both eyes always ahead":[18]

> That is part of the America he knows, and it is part of him too. There was a time when I thought he did not possess a feeling for craftsmanship. But I was wrong. It is merely that his line of effort is one I did not understand. Looking back, I see he always did a good job, that he never quit until it was finished. (P. 41)

Mills (2000) ends this letter to his parents, which he wrote in 1939, with these words: "So from both of you I have gotten a living craftsmanship" (p. 41). And it is this concept of craftsmanship and what it entails that rests at the centre of Mills's conception of the sociological imagination.

One of Mills's most important essays is directed explicitly at beginning students in sociology; it deals at length with what he calls "Intellectual

17 The Russian word товарищ (usually tovarishch, tovarish, or tovarisch when written in the Roman or Latin alphabet) means "comrade" and denotes a particularly close friendship rather than a casual one. "Tovarich" was not an error in the collection Mills's daughters published; to maintain the authenticity of his thought and work, they consciously chose to use Mills's own transliteration—Tovarich—in their edited collection of Mills's letters and autobiographical writings (Mills 2000:xiii).

18 Another of Pamela's recollections reflects this same spirit in Mills: "I am no older than seven, and I see his hazel eyes behind horned-rimmed glasses intently focused on my face, teaching me to always look people straight in the eye when I talk to them. He wants me to be like he is—self-confident, straightforward, no-nonsense" (P. Mills, 2000:xxii).

Craftsmanship" (Mills 1959:195–226).[19] Although Mills (1959:224–6) presents the full argument in eight major points, there are five aspects of intellectual craftsmanship that are more critical than the others.[20] An overview of those points allows one to appreciate Mills's commitment to sociology as a craft and may also serve to inspire first year students wondering what might be required to reach the self-made heights that Mills attained despite his modest beginnings.

"To the individual social scientist who feels himself a part of the classic tradition," Mills (1959) writes, "social science is the practice of a craft" (p. 195). Intellectual craftsmanship begins with a full commitment to the integration of work and life. The best scholars, Mills informs the beginning student, "do not split their work from their lives." They take both too seriously and strive to use each to enrich the other.

> Scholarship is a choice of how to live as well as a choice of career; whether he knows it or not, the intellectual workman forms his own self as he works toward the perfection of his craft; to realize his own potentialities, and any opportunities that come his way, he constructs a character which has as its core the qualities of the good workman. (Mills 1959:196)

In other words, the integration of life and work allows the scholar to use individual life experiences to reflect critically upon intellectual work.

Mills (1959) also stresses a second dimension of integration—the integration of biography and social structure, the constant shifting from one perspective to the other that, in the process, develops "an adequate view of a total society and of its components" (p. 211). It is this nimbleness of mind—imagination—that separates the craft worker from the mere technician. Mills emphasizes that it is playfulness of mind, backed by a fierce drive to make sense of the world, that is central to intellectual craftsmanship. Moreover, the mental dexterity of scholarship is not an innate quality—it is a skill that one can develop and perfect through constant practice over time. One is not born a scholar; one becomes one through work, imaginative creativity, and commitment.

If the ability to integrate is the first element in intellectual craftsmanship—one that enables the craft worker to develop his or her character and skills through hours too numerous to count of concentrated, exhausting, yet

---

19 See also the "What Does It Mean to be an Intellectual?" section of Mills's open letter to Tovarich (Mills 2000:276–81).

20 The five aspects discussed here do not directly parallel Mills's eight-point survey. They do, however, directly reflect the key points Mills made in his essay, and they outline the foundation of the intellectual's craft.

also playful, creative mental labour—the second is an active, ongoing commitment to learning. Mills's long-time friend, Ralph Miliband (1968), emphasizes that every working day—"and every day was a working day"—Mills was engaged in silent debate with authors across the political and intellectual spectrum as he read books, journal articles, essays, and newspapers. "I have never seen anyone read as creatively as Mills did," Miliband (1968) writes. "He couldn't even read a detective story without pencil in hand" (p. 6).

The third building block in intellectual craftsmanship is the concerted, difficult balancing act of applying critical reason to an empirically informed analysis. Gaining enlightenment from a world where insight is obscured by ideology, prejudice, and misrepresentation is a fundamental craft of sociological analysis, according to Mills. "All social scientists," Mills reminds us, "are involved in the struggle between enlightenment and obscurantism" (quoted in Miliband 1968:6).

Gathering empirical information is also critical to good sociology, as Mills maintains and demonstrates in his own work, but the main purpose of empirical inquiry "is to settle disagreements and doubts about facts, and thus to make arguments more fruitful by basing all sides more substantively" (Mills 1959:205). But, Mills continues, although "facts discipline reason," "reason is the advance guard in any field of learning." A critical mind—one committed to intellectual craftsmanship and all that it entails—employing the sociological imagination is the fundamental requirement of good sociology.

The fourth component to intellectual craftsmanship is the dissemination of one's research, which entails a commitment to public scrutiny and criticism. For Mills, however, it was more than just making an argument publically available; the craftsman presented the best-honed argument possible. Mills laboured over the act of writing—it never came easily to him, and he was rarely satisfied with the final result. No project was ever the masterpiece he wanted it to be. In 1949, labouring over the manuscript of the book many regard as his best, Mills (2000) wrote candidly to his close friend William Miller. The reflection merits quotation at length:

> I am disillusioned about *White Collar* again. I can't write it right. I can't get what I want to say about America in it. What I want to say is what you say to intimate friends when you are discouraged about how it all is. All of it at once: to create a little spotlight focus where the alienation, and apathy and dry rot and immensity and razzle dazzle and bullshit and wonderfulness and how lonesome it is, really, how terribly lonesome and rich and vulgar and god I don't know. Maybe that mood, which I take now to be reality for me, is merely confusion which of course might be so and still worthwhile if one could only articulate it properly.

I can write an ordered statement of this and that; I can go lyric for a paragraph or two, I can moan well and feel sad sometimes without showing sentiment too cornily; but I cannot get them all into each sentence or even each chapter. I think, I really do, that my medium is not studies of *White Collar* people etc. but that I ought to launch out in some new medium that is not so restricting, but I don't have the guts to do that because my skill, my tested talent, is in handling the facts and contour according to my own brand of "social science." It is all too god damn much to try to do. The problem is the old problem of creation. How many minutes in a lifetime do we ever get that are creative in any sense? (P. 136)

Even an intellectual giant like Mills, struggling to organize and present his thoughts on paper, feels the same crushing doubts that every first year student will experience a number of times over while working on various writing assignments in the course of his or her undergraduate studies.

Creating an argument—presenting it so it is clear and compelling—is an intimidating task each and every time one must prepare something for public consumption and scrutiny. However, as daunting as the task may be, it is an unavoidable requirement of an intellectual's craft. Successful novelist and accomplished American essayist Harvey Swados deeply admired Mills for his "unending and humble desire to learn how to commit to paper with precision and fluency all that he believed" (quoted in Wakefield 2000:8). Writing with skill, precision, and fluency is a central component of intellectual craftsmanship. This accurate and creative presentation of information and ideas is also one of the final steps that will turn the sociological imagination from mere potential into an actual, active force in the world.

The final aspect of intellectual craftsmanship that Mills (1959:198–204) emphasizes is keeping files and a journal. In a pre-digital age, Mills kept paper files comprised of newspaper clippings, notes he had jotted down, outlines for projects, and endless lists. Mills's files are the physical embodiment of how his life and work coalesced—a comment overheard or an apparently random flyer often went into his files along with extensive notes taken from the work of other scholars. Keeping files, Mills maintains, helps develop one's self-reflective habits and keeps one's "inner world awake."

According to Mills (1959), taking notes is critical to the intellectual craft. The mere taking of a note, he instructs, "is often a prod to reflection" (p. 199). Mills kept two sorts of notes. The first type captured the structure of an author's argument and noted important details. One could refer back to these notes for substantive information or to confirm the form and content of an argument. The second type—one that becomes more predominant as Mills gains experience—does not reflect the original author's argument but takes his or her ideas and recasts them within Mills's own developing position.

The files begin as almost random collections, but over time they coalesce into identifiable interests and projects. But the files are more than repositories of information. Simply keeping a file and updating it involves an active engagement with ideas—it is intellectual production. At the same time, a scholar's files can stimulate his or her sociological imagination and provide new questions or angles of inquiry. By simply resorting and rearranging a file, Mills notes, one may stumble upon different connections not seen previously or discover a hole in the information assembled, thus stimulating a new avenue of inquiry.

Perhaps the most profound comment Mills made on his files is one that brings together the physical dimensions of scholarly activity—the collecting and sorting of information—with the demanding, creative task of assimilating and presenting that information in a clear, cohesive, precise argument. "Books," Mills (1959) writes, "are simply organized releases from the continuous work that goes into them" (200–1). For the true crafts worker, no project is ever perfect, so publications are all steps along the road to that unattainable goal, which she or he never ceases striving to reach.

In his tribute to Mills, Miliband (1968) writes what may stand as a fitting conclusion to this chapter.

> C. Wright Mills cannot be neatly labelled and catalogued. He never belonged to any party or faction; he did not think of himself as a "Marxist"; he had the most profound contempt for orthodox Social Democrats and for closed minds in the Communist world. He detested smug liberals and the kind of radical whose response to urgent and uncomfortable choices is hand wringing. He was a man on his own, with both the strength and also the weakness which go with that solitude. He was on the Left, but not of the Left, a deliberately lone guerrilla, not a regular soldier. He was highly organized, but unwilling to *be* organized, with self-discipline the only discipline he could tolerate. ... In a trapped and inhumane world, he taught what it means to be a free and humane intellect. "Get on with it," he used to say. "Work." So, in his spirit, let us. (P. 11)

PART TWO

THE CLASSICAL
TRADITION

3

MARX AND THE DIALECTIC OF DYNAMIC, UNSTABLE SOCIAL FORMATIONS

Sociology is a child of the Enlightenment although key elements of its lineage extend back to Francis Bacon's *The Advancement of Learning* of 1604 and *Novum organum scientiarum* (New Instrument of Science) of 1620, René Descartes' 1637 *Discours de la méthode pour bien conduire sa raison, et chercher la verité dans les sciences* (*Discourse on the Method of Rightly Conducting the Reason and Seeking for Truth in the Sciences*) and his 1641 *Meditationes de prima philosophia, in qua Dei existentia et animæ immortalitas demonstratur* (*Meditations on First Philosophy in which the Existence of God and the Immortality of the Soul are Demonstrated*) as well as Isaac Newton's 1687, three-volume *Philosophiæ naturalis principia mathematica* (*The Mathematical Principles of Natural Philosophy*).[21] But it is the Enlightenment—usually dated from the rise of the eighteenth-century French *philosophes'* works through to the French Revolution of 1789—that was critical in shaping sociological thought and its overall ethos.

The spirit of the Enlightenment, especially as it influenced the emergence of sociology, can be captured in three words—freedom, mastery, and progress. Enlightenment thinkers sought to escape the darkness of ignorance; the cruel, unknown vicissitudes of nature; the arbitrary constraints of religious dogma and mysticism; and the shackles of tradition. Knowledge

---

21 See Bacon (1864), Descartes (1911, 1963), and Newton (1953) for modern translations or reprints of these texts.

obtained through the powers of human reason—enlightenment—would allow humankind to understand, control, and master the natural and social worlds and enable "the people" to create the conditions in which they controlled events and decisions rather than being the passive, powerless subjects of nature, the monarch, and the pope in Rome. Progress would be measured by the extent to which knowledge advanced, people controlled their lives, and freedom spread to more and more members of society. The three terms intertwined to form a revolutionary force in western Europe during the eighteenth century.

Some of the key works of this period, which capture the spirit of freedom, mastery, and progress, include David Hume's *Treatise of Human Nature* (published anonymously in 1739) and his 1748 *Enquiry Concerning Human Understanding,* which laid the foundation for British empiricism (Hume [1739–40] 1941, [1748] 1966). By focusing on "the nature of things themselves," Charles-Louis de Secondat, baron de La Brède et de Montesquieu— almost always referred to simply as Montesquieu—wrote, in 1748, what is regarded by many as one of the first real studies in sociology, *De l'ésprit des lois* (*The Spirit of the Laws;* see Montesquieu [1748] 1989). In 1762, Jean-Jacques Rousseau ([1762] 1963) published *Du contrat social, ou Principes du droit politique* (*The Social Contract, or Principles of Political Right*) to address questions of freedom, order, and governance in a manner that would fundamentally challenge Hobbes's ([1651] 1968) *Leviathan* of 1651. Finally, Adam Ferguson's ([1767] 1971) *An Essay on the History of Civil Society* and Adam Smith's ([1776] 1976) *An Inquiry into the Nature and Causes of the Wealth of Nations* also addressed fundamental questions of freedom, social organization, and social progress.

Despite a common spirit, there were at least three different intellectual traditions that emerged from the Enlightenment and shaped sociology from its birth as a discipline. A largely Gallic tradition—the dominant one in North America up to the late 1950s—extends from Descartes and Montesquieu through Rousseau to Claude Henri de Rouvroy, comte de Saint-Simon and Auguste Comte and, ultimately, to Émile Durkheim (see Chapters 6 and 7). This tradition, which tends to be quantitative and somewhat ahistorical, is opposed by (or complemented by, depending on one's willingness to draw together opposites) a largely German tradition that emphasizes the importance of interpretive meaning in understanding social life.

The interpretive tradition is closely associated with the work of Wilhelm Dilthey, Heinrich Rickert, Georg Simmel, and Max Weber (see Chapters 8 and 9). Interpretive sociology also tends to be more historical than the more natural science-like positivist tradition of Saint-Simon, Comte, and Durkheim (Aron 1964, 1965, 1967).

Finally, even though the ideas of Karl Marx and, later, of Marxists circulated outside of sociology and, in many ways, opposed it as a "bourgeois science," a number of debates, which were primarily carried out in the 1960s, over the methodology, purpose, and objectives of sociology led to a serious reinvestigation of the sociological aspects of Marx's work (Giddens 1971; Gouldner 1970; Marcuse 1954; Zeitlin 1968). Since then, Marx's ideas have exerted a profound effect on the discipline, and his thought constitutes a third tradition extending from the Enlightenment into contemporary sociology. This chapter and the next focus on Marx's work in some detail.

For many students, Marx's name is only meaningful because of the way it has been associated with the former Soviet Union. As a result, Marx is a controversial figure, at best, and often a demonized one, given Soviet history. To others, however, Marx was just one of the old, classical political economists whose work is long, pedantic, and dry.

Socialist scholar Isaac Deutscher (1971) once recounted his early attitude to reading Marx:

> His exposition seemed to me too slow and leisurely for someone like myself, who was impatient to understand the world and to change it quickly. I was relieved to hear that Ignacy Daszynski, our famous member of parliament, a pioneer of socialism, ... admitted that he too found *Das Kapital* too hard a nut. "I have not read it," he almost boasted, "but Karl Kautsky has read it and has written a popular summary of it.[22] I have not read Kautsky either; but Kelles-Krauz, our party theorist, has read him and he summarized Kautsky's book. I have not read Kelles-Krauz either, but ... Herman Diamand, our financial expert, has read Kelles-Krauz, and has told me all about it." (P. 257)

There are many people who have not read Marx or any of the summaries of his work and have relied, instead, on others' opinions to come to firm conclusions about how good or evil, intelligent or foolish Marx and Marxism were or are. That is unfortunate because Marx was a gifted thinker, writing at a vital point in time, when a wide array of ideas and perspectives competed for attention and adherents.

Most of Marx's work is complex and sophisticated; his analyses are multilayered, and the reader needs to take time to understand them, although

---

22 Ignacy Daszynski was the founder of the Polish Socialist Party and played a significant role in founding the briefly lived "Polish People's Republic" (1918–39). Kazimierz Kelles-Krauz was a member of the Polish Socialist Party who corresponded with Kautsky and entered into a number of Marxist debates on the nature of "historical materialism," the Hegelian basis of Marx's work, and the impact of nationalist interests on the prospects for socialism (Kautsky 1898–1903; Snyder 1997). For the summaries of Marx discussed in this quotation, see Kautsky (1886, 1925).

some of his writing is clear and didactic. Easy to understand or not, Marx is, nevertheless, a key figure in the development of contemporary sociology, and no student today should skip over his work too quickly.

To present Marx's ideas, this chapter will review some background material to contextualize Marx fully and then examine, in some detail, the preface to Marx's 1859 *Towards the Critique of Political Economy* (Marx [1859] 1980:99–103; Marx [1859] 2005). The preface was chosen for specific reasons.

The "1859 preface," as it is often called, represents one apparently clear, didactic introduction to the "guiding thread" of Marx's analyses of the political economy of different social formations. But the preface is more complex than first meets the eye; it is a multilayered analysis, and the discussion of the preface allows one to see the complexity and sophistication of Marx's ideas in a very short, seemingly straightforward text (see also Ryazanov 1930).

Before discussing the 1859 preface, the chapter will focus on the intersection of Marx's biography with the structure of social thought during his lifetime to show what aspects of his ideas prevailed and what aspects came to prevail in later readings and interpretations of his work. Marx may have thought of himself as a social revolutionary, but the Marx who came to prevail was very much a critical sociologist whose work shaped scholars' understandings of the world in a fundamental manner.

FROM POETRY AND GERMAN IDEALISM TO POLITICAL ECONOMY AND THE PROLETARIAT

Marx was born in 1818 in Germany's oldest city, Trier, which is located in the Rhineland not far from the French border. Closer to Paris than Berlin, Trier was, during Marx's youth, a liberalized, progressive city that was saturated with the spirit of the Enlightenment and the French Revolution and with republican political views.

Marx was the eldest son in a comfortable middle-class family of nine children (four of whom lived to adulthood). Marx's father Heinrich was a lawyer, and his mother Henrietta a stay-at-home mom. A bright fellow who was home schooled to the age of 12, Marx underachieved in high school, but his parents still hoped he would, like his father, become a lawyer.

In 1835, his first year of study at the University of Bonn, Marx was actively involved in student life. He spent a night in jail with friends for "disturbing the peace of the night with drunken noise" and was wounded in a duel (McLellan 1973:17). Marx spent much of the time during his first year at university writing romantic poetry for his sweetheart Jenny von Westphalen back home, reading Hegel, and debating political issues with a group of like-minded, liberally oriented students (Adoratsky 1934:2–4). Concerned that his son was too focused on romance and frivolity, Heinrich had Marx transfer to the University of Berlin, but Marx found new diversions that kept him from his studies—left-leaning political philosophy and debate stimulated by the work of Hegel.

Hegel, by the end of his teaching career in Berlin, had developed a large following of radically oriented students who filled his lectures. Following Hegel's death, Schelling was appointed as Hegel's successor. Schelling opposed Hegel's system and represented a position that was far more favourable to the conservative Prussian monarchy. His lectures, however, prompted the growth of a group known as the "Left Hegelians," who advocated the radical elements in Hegel's thought in opposition to Schelling and conservative interpreters of Hegel's works.

Marx found the debate swirling around Hegel and the Left Hegelians quite intoxicating, so he joined the Doctors' Club, as it was popularly known—a group of academically oriented, Left-Hegelian students and faculty members—attended lectures by liberal, left-leaning Hegelian professors, and wrote extensively on philosophy and the philosophy of law. From his experiences in the Doctors' Club, Marx began to consider a career as a professor, and, in 1841 at the University of Jena, he completed a doctoral dissertation entitled "The Difference between the Democritean and Epicurean Philosophy of Nature" (Marx 1968c). Marx might well have become a professor except that Bruno Bauer, a close friend in the Doctors' Club and a potential sponsor of Marx's academic aspirations, lost his position at the University of Bonn for publishing a piece portraying Hegel as an atheist and Antichrist.[23]

With an academic career blocked, Marx ([1859] 2005:60–1) began working as a journalist for the liberal-oriented *Rheinische Zeitung* (Rhineland Gazette). Away from the academic world of ideas and philosophical disputes, Marx was forced to examine the real issues and problems that affected people's lives. As a result, Marx found himself covering debates on the peasantry's right to fallen wood in the forests—a longstanding right the nobility was in the process of rescinding—and the ensuing deteriorating living conditions of the Mosel peasantry. Throughout this period, Marx argued from a progressive, liberal, industry-oriented perspective that opposed the Prussian monarchy and favoured a republican governing structure.

While serving as the editor of the *Rheinische Zeitung*, Marx became increasingly disenchanted with his former Left-Hegelian friends and their

---

23 It is not certain whether Marx collaborated with Bauer on the piece, but it was widely speculated that the two had co-authored *The Trump of the Last Judgement on Hegel the Atheist and Anti-Christ* (McLellan 1973:42).

continuous proposals that communist society could be established if the real, potential ideas in Hegel's thought were brought into being. Determined to address the "communist musings" of the Left Hegelians, Marx began to immerse himself in the writings of the French socialists—Charles Fourier, Étienne Cabet, Louis Auguste Blanqui, Pierre-Joseph Proudhon, Armand Barbès, and others.

The pro-industry and pro-republican articles published in the *Rheinische Zeitung* and Marx's critical editorials became an excuse for the Prussian monarchy to shut the paper down in 1843. Forced out of work, Marx moved to Paris and became fully engaged in the French socialists' and communists' animated debates. He experienced, at first hand, the living and working conditions of the German immigrant workers in Paris, and he was deeply impressed by the spirit of solidarity that characterized their associations and meetings.

In addition to his familiarity with Moses Hess's contributions to the *Rheinische Zeitung*, which would ultimately take the shape of his essay "The Essence of Money," Marx was also strongly influenced by Engels's ([1844] 1975) *Outlines of a Critique of Political Economy*. Both pieces reinforced Marx's belief that, to bring about social change, one had to focus upon workers' real social experiences and the material-economic questions that he had first confronted at the *Rheinische Zeitung*.

In the process of breaking with Hegel and the Left Hegelians, Marx (Marx [1843] 1927, [1844] 1975) became convinced that the proletariat was the key to significant social transformation. During a lengthy critique of Hegel's analysis of constitutional monarchies, Marx discussed the fundamental exploitation of people under nineteenth century capitalism in Germany and asked this question:

> Where then is the *positive* possibility of German emancipation?
> *Answer:* In the formation of a class with *radical chains*, a class of bourgeois society which is no class of bourgeois society, an estate which is the dissolution of all estates, a sphere which possesses a universal character by its universal suffering and claims no *particular* right because no *particular wrong* but *wrong generally* is perpetrated against it; which can no longer invoke an *historical* but only a *human* title; which does not stand in any one-sided opposition to the consequences but in an all-round opposition to the premises of the essence of the German state; a sphere, finally, which cannot emancipate itself without emancipating itself from all other spheres of society thereby emancipating all the other spheres of society, which, in a word, is the *total sacrifice* of mankind, thus which can gain for

itself only through the *full recovery of mankind.* This dissolution of society as a particular estate is the *proletariat.* (Marx [1843] 1927:619–20)

From that point on, Marx immersed himself in the study of political economy—developing his ideas concerning the nature of class-divided societies, investigating the central importance of the economy in shaping society, and discovering the conflict and the dynamic that would create social change.

Political Economy and German Idealism

Classical political economy did more than shape Marx's work; it was one of the traditions of social analysis that influenced sociology as it was coming into existence. The roots of political economy lie in the work of Hume and extend into Adam Ferguson, Adam Smith, and Dugald Stewart (1968)— members of the "Scottish Enlightenment." Each of these thinkers emphasizes the social context within which people live to explain behaviour.

Hume's *Treatise on Human Nature* suggests that there is a common and consistent "nature" to humanity; Ferguson ([1767] 1971) accepts that assumption although his conception of human nature differs from Hume's. Ferguson strongly opposes Hobbes and Rousseau's notion that a "state of nature" preceded the existence of civil society. For Ferguson, civil society is an "historical-natural constant ... beyond which there is nothing to be found" (Foucault 2008:298). Ferguson's ([1767] 1971) baseline premises in *An Essay on the History of Civil Society* involve the following:

> Man, in the perfection of his natural faculties, is quick and delicate in his sensibility; extensive and various in his imaginations and reflections; attentive, penetrating, and subtile, in what relates to his fellow creatures; firm and ardent in his purposes; devoted to friendship or to enmity; jealous of his independence and his honour, which he will not relinquish for safety or for profit: under all his corruptions or improvements, he retains his natural sensibility, if not his force; and his commerce is a blessing or a curse, according to the direction his mind has received. (P. 171)

There is a lot packed into that description. In the perfection of "natural faculties," humankind is quick and delicate in sensibility, imaginative, attentive to others, and firm and ardent in purpose. Humankind would not give up independence or honour for safety or profit, and this natural sensibility remains under all social conditions. All of these elements, Ferguson ([1767] 1971:23–9) establishes in his essay, favour the spontaneous synthesis of individuals. One does not need an explicit social contract, a renunciation of rights, or the delegation of natural rights to a sovereign to create an integrated civil society. However, the natural social bonds of civil society can be jeopardized by the economic foundation of a particular social formation—"commerce is a blessing or a curse, according to the direction his mind has received." This is Ferguson's chief concern in the essay, so he focuses on the social impact resulting from the increasing dominance of industrial production, the growth of the division of labour, and the continual simplification of work tasks in the manufacturing industries.

Ferguson ([1767] 1971) fears that the increasing division of labour will have significant deleterious consequences for people in capitalist societies:

> Many mechanical arts ... require no [mental] capacity; they succeed best under a total suppression of sentiment and reason; and ignorance is the mother of industry as well as of superstition. Reflection and fancy are subject to err; but a habit of moving the hand, or the foot, is independent of either. Manufacturers, accordingly, prosper most where the mind is least consulted, and where the workshop may, without any great effort of imagination, be considered as an engine, the parts of which are men. (P. 280)

Modern industry, according to Ferguson, will affect the development of workers' intellectual capacities and their "natural faculties." Ferguson sees a tension—a contradiction—between civil society's natural, integrative features that promote humanity's natural faculties and the suppression of those faculties within an increasingly divisive and competitive market economy.

"From the tendency of these reflections," Ferguson ([1767] 1971) explains at the end of his essay, "it should appear, that a national spirit is frequently transient, not on account of any incurable distemper in the nature of mankind, but on account of their voluntary neglects and corruptions" (p. 343). As Ferguson's history indicates, humankind, through its political leaders, could promote and stimulate the national spirit, but it could also let that spirit decline, and the nation would then decay and come to ruin. The key contradiction for Ferguson lay in the tension between capitalist commerce and humankind's natural faculties, which were being distorted by the growing dominance of a market-based economy.

Smith and Stewart were not particularly concerned with a nation's spirit, but they did find Ferguson's attention to the fundamental bases of social organization quite significant. Smith and Stewart examine the impact of the economy and its political consequences on the social whole (hence the term "political economy" and why it would rival the term "sociology").[24] Smith

---

24 The term political economy first appeared in 1615 in *Traicité de l'economie politique* (Treatise on Political Economy) by Antoine de Montchréstien ([1615] 1889). The term was first used in English in Sir James Stewart's ([1770] 1776) *An Inquiry into the Principles of Political Economy*. James Mill ([1821]

([1776] 1976), for example, notes three particular points related to human nature, the economy, and society at the outset of his much celebrated *An Enquiry into the Nature and Causes of the Wealth of Nations*. First, he notes that humanity had a "natural propensity to truck, barter, and exchange one thing for another" (Smith [1776] 1976:25). Bringing goods to the market, haggling over their value, and trading them, all these economic activities were simply part of human nature.

Second, Smith ([1776] 1976:26–30) argues that, by nature, each person pursues his or her own self interest, but this does not lead to a war of all against all, as Hobbes ([1651] 1968) had argued; it actually integrates people. In view of the first propensity of humans to barter and trade, the pursuit of individual interest furthers the collective interests of all because what one person enjoys doing—and others might not—is shared through barter and exchange in the market. Each person pursuing his or her own self interest, then, yields a number of different products that can be exchanged to meet all of the community's various needs and wants.

Finally, Smith ([1776] 1976) uses his famous pin-making example to show that the key to the wealth of a nation is the division of labour. "The greatest improvements in the productive powers of labour," he writes, "and the greater part of the skill, dexterity, and judgement with which it is any where directed, or applied, seem to have been the effects of the division of labour" (p. 13). Smith argues that a group of workers in which each worker performs just one task in succession—straightening the wire, cutting it, sharpening the point, or putting on the head—is far more productive than one in which each worker builds the entire pin individually.

On the basis of his socio-economic analysis, then, Smith maintains that the wealth of nations depends on the propensity to truck, barter, and exchange; on the pursuit of individual interest; and on the added productive capacity arising from the systematic division of labour in production. Smith shows, in effect, that a free and open market is the most conducive social arrangement for meeting everyone's needs. But Smith also recognizes that the growing division of labour in market-based societies has limitations that citizens and governments cannot ignore.

1844) noted that "Political Economy is to the State, what domestic economy is to the family. The family consumes; and, in order to consume, it must supply. Domestic economy has, therefore, two grand objects; the consumption and supply of the family. The consumption being a quantity always indefinite, for there is no end to the desire of enjoyment, the grand concern is, to increase the supply ... The same is the case with Political Economy. It also has two grand objects, the Consumption of the Community, and that Supply upon which the consumption depends." These are the central issues of political economy from Ferguson, Smith, Simonde de Sismondi ([1815] 1966), and David Ricardo ([1817] 1891) right through to the work of Marx.

In the little-read section on education in Chapter 1 of Book 5 of *The Wealth of Nations,* Smith ([1776] 1976:758–87) recognizes that market forces will not support the appropriate development of the institutions needed to ensure the education of everyone in a free-market or laissez-faire society. Smith agrees with Ferguson that a completely unrestricted division of labour will diminish the intellectual capacities of workers and that this outcome is not in the common interest.

There are two choices: restrict the extent to which industries refine the division of labour and simplify work tasks—a solution Smith does not favour because it is contrary to the natural propensities that most stimulate the wealth of nations—or ensure that workers are able to develop themselves outside of the workplace. This is the solution Smith favours.

As a result, Smith, the champion of laissez-faire capitalism, demonstrates the need for some state involvement in the society as a whole. Through tax revenue, the state is best placed to provide formal educational opportunities for workers who would otherwise be completely dulled by the division of labour.

The key point to note is that Ferguson, Smith, and Stewart, followed by other British political economists such as Thomas Malthus (1827), David Ricardo ([1817] 1891), James Mill ([1821] 1844), Robert Owen ([1814] 1927), and John Stuart Mill (1848), would also develop their analyses of society on the basis of the economy.

A second rival to sociology as the science of society began with Immanuel Kant, whom Hume "interrupted from his dogmatic slumber," giving his "investigations in the field of speculative philosophy a completely new direction" (Kant [1783] 1968:118). Kant's influence and concerns extend to Johann Gottlieb Fichte, Friedrich Wilhelm Joseph von Schelling, and Georg Wilhelm Friedrich Hegel—the central figures in German idealism.

Unlike Plato and Descartes, Hume had mounted the argument that the only true and certain knowledge humankind has is supplied by the senses. In response to Hume's ([1748] 1966) arguments, Kant proceeded to explore the limits and possibilities of human reason. Kant's *The Critique of Pure Reason* sets out the relationship that exists between the external world and humankind's possible knowledge of that world. The external world, Kant ultimately argues, is never directly known—humanity wrestles with perceptions of that world, perceptions that are shaped by the categories of the mind. Because the categories filter or shape how the external world is perceived, it is impossible, according to Kant, to actually know the external world "in and of itself." In other words, absolute certain knowledge of the external world cannot be attained by human reason.

Fichte, Schelling, and Hegel each explore the same problem. Was Kant correct or could the human mind overcome the apparent gap between the world and humanity's ideas of that world? The goal of scholarship, they argue, is to refine these mental images or ideas so that they reflect, as fully as possible, the objective world they represent and use that knowledge to guide social and political decisions and conduct. The role of the human mind and the development of human consciousness, then, are the central concerns of idealist philosophy.

This tradition emphasizes the active side of humanity in the creation and interpretation of the social world. Kant, Fichte, Schelling, and Hegel did not philosophize for the intrinsic joy of developing their own minds; they wanted to provide humans with the best knowledge and the best tools to shape and improve the societies in which they lived. The German idealists were socially engaged and, in that sense, shared the same ultimate objectives as any other social thinker who sought to understand the world in order to change it. In this sense, German idealism was very much a motive force for and a product of the Enlightenment. Hegel, in particular, emphasizes human freedom, which, he argues, can be attained through the progressive development of philosophical knowledge until it allows human beings to comprehend fully —or master—the world in which they live. The advance of philosophy, the mastery of "Absolute Reason," and the increased freedom this provides to human action equate with positive development, and, indeed, Hegel sees history as the march of human progress.

Constituting Marx's Intellectual Legacy

Marx's particular approach to social analysis began with German idealism; it was soon influenced by British and French political economy, and he later incorporated insights from French revolutionary thought and some elements of German romanticism. At no point in his life, however, did Marx ever think of himself as a sociologist. In fact, Marx, his close friend and collaborator Friedrich Engels, as well as many of the early Marxists, such as Wilhelm Liebknecht, August Bebel, Franz Mehring, Eduard Bernstein, Karl Kautsky, Laura Marx Lafargue (one of Marx's daughters), Paul Lafargue (Laura's husband), and Eleanor Marx (Marx's other daughter), would most likely have been offended that sociologists would one day claim Marx as one of their own.

The way Marx was drawn into the pantheon of sociology's founding fathers is an interesting sociological study in itself. During the last quarter of the nineteenth century, Marx, Engels, and other collaborators unwittingly completed some of the groundwork as they began to present Marx's ideas as a systematic whole.

By the time the first International Workingmen's Association—founded in 1864—began to break up in 1876, Marx was established as a key leader of the socialist movement in Europe. As a result, there was an emerging "Marxist movement" and a growing number of socialists who considered themselves Marxists. There were, however, two major problems.

First, Marx never developed a clear statement of his principles or a thematic account around which Marxists could rally. In fact, aside from his writings as a journalist in 1842–3; *The Poverty of Philosophy* ([1847] 1950); the *Manifesto* of 1848; his 1849 serial publication of *Wage-Labour and Capital* ([1849] 1933); his historical essays *The Class Struggles in France* (1935), also published serially in 1850; *The Eighteenth Brumaire of Louis Napoleon* ([1852] 1937); *Towards the Critique of Political Economy* ([1859] 1980); and three editions of volume one of *Capital* ([1867] 1983, [1872] 1987, [1875] 1989), Marx had not really put very much in print from the vast corpus of his lifetime's work.[25]

Second, because Marx drew from at least three, not necessarily compatible, intellectual traditions—German idealism, political economy, and French revolutionary thought—his ideas are complex, and they were always in a state of flux, making it impossible to form a definitive statement about *What Marx Really Meant* (to borrow G.D.H. Cole's 1934 book title). One can make claims about a theory of society on the basis of Marx's writings and call it "Marxist," but doing this is something different than presenting "Marx's position"—an extremely important but almost always neglected distinction.[26]

To establish the Marxist position, Engels, Kautsky, Bernstein, Bebel, Mehring, the Lafargues, Eleanor Marx, and others consciously set out to develop a concise "Marxist theory" that would produce the critical insights needed to assist revolutionaries in the overthrow of bourgeois society. The core of their endeavour is the *Manifest der Kommunistischen Partei* (*Manifesto of the Communist Party*), Marx's 1859 preface, and the 1886 pamphlet by Engels ([1886] 1935) entitled *Socialisme utopique et socialisme scientifique* (*Socialism: Utopian and Scientific*).

---

25 To get some perspective on what Marx left unpublished, one could note that the German texts for volumes two and three of *Capital* (Marx and Engels 1963b, 1964b) are 518 and 919 pages in length, the *Theories of Surplus Value* (Marx and Engels 1965a, 1967a, 1968) total 1,514 pages, the *Grundrisse* (Marx 1953) is 1,102 pages, the *German Ideology* (Marx and Engels 1969) is 520 pages of text, the Paris manuscripts of 1844 a mere 121 pages (Marx 1968a), and Marx's 1843 critique of Hegel is 148 pages (Marx 1968b)—that totals over 4,700 pages of text.

26 Whether Marx would have wanted his ideas to be consolidated into a perspective named after him is questionable according to reputable scholars of Marx's work (Haupt 1982; Jones 1982; Rubel 1957, 1974, 1981b; Rubel and Manale 1975:vii–xii). In a letter to Conrad Schmidt on 5 August 1890, Engels shows that he and Marx are aware of some of the pitfalls of establishing a school of thought: "The materialist conception of history has a bunch [of dangerous friends] nowadays for whom it serves as a pretext to *not* study history," Engels writes. "Just as Marx said of the French 'Marxists' in the late [18]70s, 'One thing I do know for sure is that I am not a Marxist'" (Marx and Engels 1967b:436).

The development of a Marxist theory did more than serve as a guide to revolutionary change; it also functioned as an important framework for social analysis. Because the Marxists focused on the most problematic and contradictory aspects of capitalist society, Marxism became a potential framework for sociologists who wanted a radical understanding of society. As a result, the early formulation of Marxism was one of the reference points that sociologists had in mind when they began to include Marx among the founders of sociology.

In addition to formulating a concise statement of Marxism, Engels, Kautsky, Bernstein, and Bebel began to transcribe, edit, and publish Marx's voluminous manuscripts.[27] These publications added new material for understanding Marx's analysis of capitalist society—and other social formations—making his work that much more interesting for sociologists.

Following the Russian Revolution in 1917, the Communist Party of the Soviet Union also began systematically to collect and publish portions of Marx's literary estate (Külow and Jaroslawski 1993:16–28; Ryazanov 1925). These posthumous publications were influential in reshaping how Marx's intellectual legacy and his impact upon sociology were interpreted. Two texts were particularly decisive—three draft notebooks from 1844 published under the title *Ökonomisch-philosophische Manuskripte aus dem Jahre 1844* (*Economic and Philosophical Manuscripts of 1844*) and Marx's 1857–8 preliminary draft of his entire critique of political economy published as the *Grundrisse der Kritik der politischen Ökonomie (Rohentwurf)* (*Foundations for the Critique of Political Economy* [*Rough Draft*]).

In 1844, Marx drafted the three fragmentary manuscripts in Paris in preparation for a book he promised, but never delivered, to the publisher Carl Leske. The Paris manuscripts were independently transcribed and simultaneously published in 1932 by the Soviets and Kröner Verlag in Germany (Marx 1932a, 1932b, 1975). The dramatic rethinking of Marx's ideas that the manuscripts triggered was quickly interrupted by the outbreak of World War II in 1939. Following the war, the discussion began again in earnest, growing in intensity during the 1960s once these manuscripts were translated into French and English and absorbed by a broader scholarly community (Marx 1959, 1962, 1963).[28]

27 The plans for Part IV of the new Marx-Engels *Gesamtausgabe* (*Complete Works*) gives one sense of what Marx left unpublished. Part IV will contain Marx's study notebooks and various draft manuscripts—*over and above the unpublished material noted earlier in this chapter!* To date, 10 of the projected 32 volumes of Part IV have been published, 8 volumes comprising about 6,900 pages (Marx and Engels 1976–91) and 4 more of about 4,400 pages (Marx and Engels 1992–2005).

28 Selected portions of the 1844 Paris manuscripts were available in English in 1956 (Bottomore and Rubel 1956). The most significant portions of the manuscripts were made widely available in German with the 1950 publication of an inexpensive edition that drew from the 1932 Soviet and Kröner Verlag editions (Marx 1950). Upon their first publication, Marcuse (1932) immediately recognized the

The timing of a limited run publication of the *Grundrisse* in two volumes during World War II—the first in 1939 and the second in 1941—meant that the work was not really discussed until it was reissued in a single volume in 1953 (Marx 1939, 1941, 1953; see also Musto 2008 and Rosdolsky 1977:xi–xiv). The *Grundrisse* led to additional rethinking of Marx's work and confirmed how much his conceptual framework and mode of analysis was influenced by Hegel. At the same time, the *Grundrisse* demonstrated the extent to which Marx's work compared favourably to that of many critical sociologists writing in the postwar period.

Marx's Work: A Dynamic, Unstable, Dialectical Whole

On the basis of all the material that scholars may now easily access—a good portion of Marx's handwritten manuscripts still lie in the former Institute for Marxism-Leninism in Moscow and in the Institute for Social History in Amsterdam—there is no doubt that Marx was an extremely gifted, synthetic thinker who drew together a number of different perspectives (Rojahn 1998). However, rather than producing a single, clear system—as some contend—Marx's work might be described as an unfinished, dynamic, unstable whole. One can view these qualities in a positive light because they mean that Marx's works are extremely suggestive and stimulate considerable thought and debate. But one can see them negatively as well because they make it impossible to know what Marx really meant, what is most important, or even where to start.

Because of the complex nature of Marx's ideas, there are more books claiming to state or clarify his position than there are for any other social theorist.[29] Each author feels she or he is presenting the "real Marx" even though each "Marx" is quite different and one is often the complete opposite of another.[30] Although a few authors distort or misrepresent Marx's ideas for

---

importance of the Paris manuscripts. Pappenheim (1959), Fromm (1961), Popitz (1967), Mészáros (1970), Schacht (1970), Maguire (1971), and Ollman (1971) all made important contributions to the systematic study of the Paris notebooks. Aptheker (1965) and Fromm (1965) published symposia indicating the growing interest in this aspect of Marx's thought. On the history of the manuscripts, see Rojahn (1983, 1985).

29 Attempts to clarify Marx have taken many forms, including two comic books in the Pantheon Documentary Comic Book series: *Marx for Beginners* (Rius 1976) and *Marx's Kapital for Beginners* (Smith and Evans 1982). One may also purchase the Coles Notes (Lichtman 1979), SparkNotes (SparkNotes Editors 2007), or Cliff Notes on Marx. Limited as these are, they are far superior to the overwhelming majority of Soviet-produced summaries of Marx.

30 There are numerous examples one could use to demonstrate this point, and some are discussed later in this chapter. For example, there is the "revolutionary Marx" of the Social Democratic Party presented by Karl Kautsky (1927a, 1927b) versus the "revisionist Marx" of evolutionary socialism presented by Eduard Bernstein (1969, 1909; see also Haupt 1982; Jones 1982; Labriola 1904). There is the "young Marx" versus the "old Marx" (Althusser 1977a, 1977b, 1977c; Bell 1960b; Schmidt 1972) and the "Marx of continuity" (Festcher 1985; Mészáros 1975:217–26) bridging the young and old. One can point to Kautsky's revolutionary Marx versus Lenin's (1943) assessment of it in "The Proletarian Revolution and the Renegade Kautsky." One could note that the view of Marx and Marxism in Lenin's

political reasons, most of them simply try to present Marx's ideas as a clear, meaningful (and often consistent) whole. To accomplish this task, the author often places her or his emphasis on specific aspects of Marx's work and brings the other parts, which are not necessarily fully consistent with the aspects selected as central, into line. The result is a more consistent whole but one that masks the tensions, revisions, and reconceptions that lie within Marx's unfinished project and, in the end, misrepresents Marx's *oeuvre*.

Part of the difficulty of grasping Marx's ideas fully is due simply to the complexity and dynamic nature of the social formation he wanted to comprehend and change—industrial capitalism. There were times over the course of his adult life when Marx felt that he had discovered the key (or keys) to understanding and explaining capitalist society, but most of the time he knew he was struggling with that very task.[31] Although Marx wrestled with how best to examine, explain, and criticize capitalism, he was, nonetheless, very certain about how *not* to proceed with these projects, and he never shied away from making scathing criticisms of those who had different perspectives.[32] Two points result.

First, reading some of Marx's criticisms of others often provides critical insight into what Marx rejected as well as aspects of what Marx would propose instead.

Second, when one reads something by Marx or cites from his work, it is always critical to identify the work, when it was written, and where it might have stood within the whole corpus of his project. Marx's ideas shifted over time, and it is possible to cite statements that appear to completely contradict each other, but, once these ideas are seen in their full context, the contradiction usually disappears, although a tension between the two statements will remain. *When* Marx said something and *the context* in which it was said are as important as *what he said*. This is true of many sociologists, but it is

---

(1972) *Philosophical Notebooks*, which emphasizes the significance of Hegel's dialectic in Marx's thought, differs from that in Lenin's (1927) *Materialism and Empirio-Criticism*, which subordinates the evolution of society to the laws of nature as conceived by Darwin and rejects idealist elements completely (Lichtheim 1965:244–58, 325–51). Finally—in this note, which is not comprehensive— one should mention *The Postmodern Marx* of Carver (1998), Derrida's (1994) *Specters of Marx*, and Bensaïd's (2002) *Marx for Our Times*.

31 When drafting the *Grundrisse* in 1857–8, Marx sketched out five different plans for the project. He discussed several more with Engels and others in his correspondence (Beamish 1992:161–8, 181; Rubel 1981a, 1981c).

32 One might note Marx's *The Holy Family, or Critique of Critical Criticism: Against Bruno Bauer and Consorts* (Marx and Engels [1845] 1975), which was a rejection of his former Left-Hegelian comrades who were writing for the Berlin-based newspaper the *Allgemeine Literatur-Zeitung* (General Literature Gazette); his critique of Ludwig Feuerbach, Bauer, Max Stirner, and others in 1845 (Marx and Engels 1932, 1939, 1976); his 1847 polemic against Joseph-Pierre Proudhon (Marx [1847] 1950), *Herr Vogt* in 1860 (Marx [1860]1982); and Marx's ([1881] 1962, [1881] 1975) critique of Adolf Wagner's *Allgemeine oder theoretische Volkswirtschaftslehre* (*General or Theoretical Political Economy*).

especially true of Marx, who left his life's work—the critique of political economy—unfinished when he died.

There is, however, another reason that Marx's work is so complex. Marx's perspective—the very approach he uses to grasp the whole of capitalism—relies very heavily on Hegel's (1841) dialectical logic (Marcuse 1954). As a result, although Marx's work may be described as unfinished, dynamic, and unstable, it is really more accurate to say that Marx's work is *best* described as "a dynamic, unstable, 'dialectical whole.'" All dialectical wholes are unstable and thus dynamic, but Marx's position is more so than others.

Marx's analyses are less stable than Hegel's *Phenomenology of Mind* (1807, 1977), the *Lectures on the History of Philosophy* (1840, 1844, 1892–6), or the *Encyclopaedia of Philosophical Knowledge* ([1830] 1983), for example, because Marx tries to grasp the totality of an actual social formation and not simply construct a conceptual map of the history of social thought. This point merits some elaboration.

In *Capital*, Marx (1914:xlviii; [1890] 1976:103) notes that Hegel was the first to present the dialectical aspects of history in their "general forms of motion in a comprehensive and conscious manner," but, with Hegel, the dialectic "is standing on its head." Hegel's dialectic deals simply with the development of ideas. The dialectic, Marx continues, "must be inverted, in order to discover the rational kernel within the mystical shell." The dialectic must be used to grasp the material world in which real people walk, labour, and act. So Marx attempts to accomplish that task—to develop a comprehensive analysis of capitalism as a real social formation that took into account its dialectical dynamic. This sounds extremely complex, but it is not as mystifying as it might first appear—the key is to remember what "dialectic" means and where it comes from.

Hegel's conception of the dialectic is indebted to classical Greek philosophy and the work of Socrates. In the Socratic method, through the dialectical back and forth of dialogue, one continually probes knowledge to find its limitations. As continuous questioning uncovers limitations or errors in thought and understanding, one revises ideas to develop more complete (or comprehensive) knowledge than before. Hegel maintains, then, that, by incorporating new insights with corrected, previously existing knowledge, basic human understanding (*Verstand*) develops into something more powerful and complete; it becomes reason (*Vernunft*). This development occurs through two processes.

The first process is one of negation—through the critique of existing, imperfect knowledge (the very point of Socratic questioning). The second is a process of transcendence; new knowledge is incorporated into what was previously known creating a new, more nuanced, and complete form of knowledge. Hegel argues that the processes of negation and transcendence, through the dialectic (or through the mind's own disciplined, inner searching and dialogue), allows humanity to advance its knowledge from simple forms of understanding to an ultimate, all encompassing form of absolute reason. Absolute reason would fully grasp all of reality's complexity. Hegel also maintains that this advancement to absolute reason is naturally inherent in the way humans develop their conscious awareness of the world. Over the course of history, humanity elevates its knowledge from naïve understanding to comprehensive, absolute reason through the natural, dialectical dynamic of thought and mind (Hegel 1840, 1844, 1892–6, 1983).

Marx, however, did not believe that conceptual awareness was the real basis for the advancement of human societies. For Marx, the real processes of negation and transcendence—the real dialectic of change—occurs within social relationships themselves rather than in the realm of ideas. To distinguish his position from that of Hegel and other idealists, Marx calls it "materialist."

The term materialist also draws attention to the ultimate focus of Marx's analyses—the real, practical, everyday lives of those exploited by capitalism. At the same time, the term emphasizes Marx's primary goal—to create change in those real, palpable conditions of life. Significant change, Marx maintains, only occurs when social relationships in the real, material world of existence take place.

Marx uses the term materialist to distinguish his work from that of the idealists, to show where his work concentrates, and to emphasize what must be transformed in order to achieve real social change. This was all he meant by the term. He did not, as later Soviet Marxists would contend, believe that there was a dialectic of history that was located in the "material dialectic of Nature," which unfolded on the basis of natural laws. Marx was never a materialist in that sense; for Marx, the dialectic of change involves human agents instigating and carrying through social change (Fetscher 1985; Schmidt 1971).

Marx argues that pre-communist social formations are characterized by their own dialectic of social relations of production, their own internal tensions and contradictions, which are irresolvable within those formations. Through a process of negation and transcendence, human history moves through a series of newer, more advanced social formations. Marx maintains that the processes driving change are internal to each of the pre-communist social formations in their entirety.

One can now begin to appreciate why Marx's work might seem so complicated and be so multifaceted. One of his greatest challenges—once he thought he had sorted out the convolutions of capitalist society—was to determine how he could present his ideas so that people would grasp them.

That proved to be very problematic and led to a number of attempts on his part and then by Engels, followed by later Marxists trying to find the best way to convey Marx's ideas to a popular audience without compromising them too much. The search for a way to present Marx's ideas has some significant political and intellectual consequences, including when and how Marx entered the pantheon of sociology.

THE CRITIQUE OF POLITICAL ECONOMY

In the graveside eulogy for his closest comrade, Engels ([1883] 1958:167; [1883] 1962:335) portrayed Marx's work, and thus the essence of Marxism, in the following way:

> Just as Darwin discovered the law of development of organic nature, so Marx discovered the law of development of human history: the simple fact, hitherto concealed by an overgrowth of ideology, that mankind must first of all eat, drink, have shelter and clothing, before it can pursue politics, science, art, religion, etc.; that therefore the production of the immediate material means of subsistence and consequently the degree of economic development attained by a given people or during a given epoch form the foundation upon which the state institutions, the legal conceptions, art, and even the ideas on religion, of the people concerned have been evolved, and in the light of which they must, therefore, be explained, instead of vice versa, as had hitherto been the case.
>
> But that is not all. Marx also discovered the special law of motion governing the present-day capitalist mode of production and the bourgeois society that this mode of production has created. The discovery of surplus value suddenly threw light on the problem, which all previous investigations of both bourgeois economists and socialist critics, had been groping in the dark looking for the solution.[33]

---

33 The concept of surplus value (*Mehrwert* or "more value" in German) is actually rather simple. To produce a commodity, a capitalist must purchase raw material and machinery and hire workers to produce a good that will be sold in the market. The capitalist must calculate the cost of the raw material, machinery, and labour that is present in each commodity. The capitalist calculates the portion of value that is transferred from the machinery, the raw material used, and the wage costs of the workers. The production process is designed so that it will generate more than just cost recovery; it must also generate a profit or "more value" than the value that went into the production of the commodity. Surplus value (*Mehrwert*) is the source of profit for the capitalist, and Marx's contribution is his analysis showing that *the worker* is the real source of this extra value that the capitalist could collect for his or her own—not the division of labour, as Smith argued, or differential rent, as Ricardo maintained, or the abundance of nature, as the French Physiocrats claimed (Marx 1933).

Engels drew all of these ideas directly from the most concise statement Marx had published about his overall approach to the systematic study of capitalist society—his preface to *Towards the Critique of Political Economy.*[34]

The 1859 preface became the specific reference point within Marx's own writings that Engels and the early orthodox Marxists would use in their consolidation and popularization of a doctrine of Marxism.[35] The revolutionary movement Marx had spent much of his life trying to build and lead would, it turned out, find its predominant textual inspiration in just over 500 words in the preface to one of Marx's least read, most obscure books. Marxism, at the end of the nineteenth and turn of the twentieth century, would be constituted as a self-contained system of thought that offered a Darwinist-like scientific understanding of social history.[36] It was presented in opposition to a number of other socialist and anarchist positions, as well as to bourgeois social and political theory, including the emerging discipline of sociology.

Marx's pursuit of a comprehensive critique of capitalist society draws together ideas from fields as disparate as classical Greek philosophy, German idealism, European history, political economy, and a host of different and divergent socialist thinkers. The scope of Marx's research also ranges from classical and contemporary European literature to the ethnological analyses of different early social formations. He combines this material with his own personal experiences within an emerging and active communist movement.

---

34 The link Engels makes between Charles Darwin and Marx is interesting for three reasons. First, by coincidence, Marx's *Critique* and Darwin's *Origin of the Species* both appeared in 1859. Second, Engels wants to capitalize on that coincidence by connecting the two names in an attempt to lend greater scientific credibility to Marx's work and Marxism in view of the parallels that appeared to exist between some aspects of Marx's preface and Darwin's notion of evolution, development, and the survival of different species. Finally, consistent with the spirit of the time and, in many ways, sharing the same ambitions as Comte and other social scientists, Engels also wants to create a theory of dialectical change that applies to both the natural and social worlds. Engels hopes to one day establish a new science of historical materialism that will replace its non-dialectical bourgeois rivals (Engels 1935, 1940). This objective had numerous negative consequences and significantly impeded a real understanding of Marx's theory of social change (see Korsch 1970, 1971).

35 The term "orthodox Marxism" emerged from a struggle over the political platform of the German Social Democratic Party at the turn of the twentieth century. In *Evolutionary Socialism*, Bernstein ([1899] 1909, [1899] 1969) argued that the party should forsake its longstanding commitment to revolution and pursue social reform through parliamentary legislation. Those opposed, who wanted to maintain the party's commitment to revolution, proudly referred to themselves as orthodox Marxists, calling Bernstein's supporters "revisionists." But the revisionists saw things differently. Exploiting the religious connotation of the term "orthodox"—orthodox believers usually follow a very narrow, strict reading of religious texts—the revisionists suggested that "orthodox Marxist" revolutionaries in the party were slaves to certain Marxist texts and to Marxist orthodoxy; the revisionists, who were willing to revise their understanding of capitalism based on an analysis of social change, were Marx's true heirs, they claimed.

36 It was long believed that Marx had asked Darwin if he could dedicate *Capital* to him. It turns out that the letter upon which the claim was made was actually from Eleanor Marx's partner, Eduard Aveling—a great fan of Darwin's—to Darwin about a book Aveling was writing (Avineri 1967; Fay 1978).

So, Marx's insights into capitalist society stem from an impressive breadth and depth of knowledge.[37]

Throughout 40 years of active intellectual and political engagement, Marx continually struggled with how he could bring the prodigious volume of work into a single, coherent, persuasive argument. He felt the enormity of his task in 1843–4, and it only grew larger as his work progressed. Working frantically to publish his critique "before the deluge" during the economic crisis of 1857–8, Marx (1953) appears to settle on the following order for his argument:[38]

(1) the general, abstract determinants which are found, more or less, in all forms of society ... (2) The categories which make up the inner structure of bourgeois society and on which the fundamental classes rest. Capital, wage-labour, landed property. Their relationship to one another. Town and country. The 3 great social classes. Exchange between them. Circulation. Credit system (private). (3) Concentration of bourgeois society in the form of the state. Viewed in relation to itself. The "unproductive" classes. Taxes. State debt. Public credit. The population. The colonies. Emigration. (4) The international relation of production. International division of labour. International exchange. Export and import. Rate of exchange. (5) The world market and crises. (P. 28–9)

Between this outline and the publication of the *Critique* in 1859, Marx drafted at least 10 more plans and outlines for his project (Beamish 1992:54–9; Rubel 1968:lxxvi–cxxi). By April 1858, for example, Marx had decided to write separate books focused on capital, landed property, wage-labour, the state, international trade, and the world market.[39]

The book on capital, Marx informed Engels in an April 1858 letter, would include sections on capital in general, competition ("the action of many capitals on each other"), credit, and share capital (Marx and Engels 1978:312).

---

37 One more indication of the breadth of Marx's scholarship is the size, scope, and content of his personal library; see Kaiser (1967) and Marx and Engels (1999). Kaiser (1967:89) notes that Marx read with feverish zeal, making numerous marginal notations in his books, often denouncing authors for their errors.

38 Marx ([1859] 2005) mentions this same "general introduction" in the second paragraph of the 1859 preface, saying it had been "dashed off" but left unpublished "because on closer consideration it appears confusing to anticipate results that are still to be demonstrated" (p. 60).

39 Marx ([1859] 2005:60) presents the same outline with some additional commentary in the opening paragraph of the 1859 preface. One more indicator of how Marx's project expanded is the realization that the book on capital became six books: volume 1 of *Capital* entitled "The Process of Capitalist Production," first published in 1890 (Marx and Engels 1962b); volume 2 entitled "The Process of Circulation of Capital," first published in 1893 (Marx and Engels 1963b); volume 3 entitled "The Process of Capitalist Production as a Whole," first published in 1894 (Marx and Engels 1964b); and the so-called volume 4 of *Capital*, which covers, in three books, the history of theories of surplus value (Marx and Engels 1965a, 1967a, 1968).

By May 1858, Marx had decided that capital in general would require two volumes, and, when he finally delivered the manuscript for the *Critique* to the publisher in January 1859, it consisted of one chapter on the commodity and another on money and simple circulation. Despite its opening subtitle "Section One: Capital in General," the 1859 *Critique* did not contain any of the copious material Marx had amassed on capital!

The points to note from this story are the following. First, Marx changed his plans numerous times over the course of his adult life, and each change was precipitated by Marx's desire for a deeper and more detailed examination of particular aspects of political economy.

Second, as he progressed towards the final drafting and revising of volume one of *Capital*, Marx continued to refine and expand his theoretical and empirical insights into the economic infrastructure of the capitalist relations of production (Beamish 1992).

Third, in the evolution of his expanding critique of political economy, Marx's intellectual energies became increasingly focused upon the essential relations of capital. Capital would serve as the departure point for his critique of capitalist society, but the detailed presentation of that departure point had become a life's work (and more).

Fourth, Marx never published his entire critique of political economy. The project had outgrown the powers of one single individual. Marx had amassed more material than he could ever manage to bring together in his lifetime.

Finally, and most important, it was on the basis of this prodigious volume of work that Marx wrote his 1859 preface to *Towards the Critique of Political Economy*. Short, concise, didactic, and written at a strategic moment in the publication of Marx's critique of political economy, the preface became, for Engels and later Marxists, a central statement of Marx's approach to the study of industrial capitalist societies. The preface can easily appear as Marx's final word; but it is not.

In true dialectical fashion, the preface is an accurate consolidation of Marx's main approach to the critique of political economy. But it is also internally unstable and incomplete. The preface needs to be negated and transcended—expanded and developed further—and the forces of negation are in the preface itself. Reading the preface carefully also allows one to grasp the internal dialectic of Marx's conceptual framework.

The Economic Infrastructure, the Ideological Superstructure

In the 1859 preface, Marx ([1859] 2005:60–1) provides an overview of his intellectual labours between 1843 and 1859 and of the ideas he had developed over that decade and a half. He notes that the "guiding thread" that emerged for his analysis of society and social change was quite straightforward (Marx [1859] 2005:61).

In the social production of their lives, humankind, independently of its will, enters determinate, necessary relations, relations of production (*Produktionsverhältnisse*) that are appropriate to a determinate stage of development of their material forces of production (*materiellen Produktivkräfte*).

Marx argues that people, whether they like it or not, are born into or enter into a particular set of social relations that pre-dates them. In making this statement, Marx actually claims two things. First, as Marx and Engels (1932:10, 1939:6–7) indicate in an unpublished work, *The German Ideology*: "The premises from which we begin are not arbitrary ones, not dogmas, but real premises ... real individuals, their activity and the material conditions under which they live" (Marx and Engels 1939:6–7). One can distinguish humankind from animals "by consciousness, by religion, by whatever else one wants," they argue. But "humans distinguish themselves from animals as soon as they begin to *produce* their means of subsistence. ... Insofar as humans produce their means of subsistence, they indirectly produce their material life itself" (Marx and Engels 1932:10).

Production, Marx and Engels maintain, is fundamental to social life; it is an ontological condition of humankind. But, they also note that the form of production changes with time. Although social relations of production, in general, are one of the universal conditions of humankind, the actual social relations of production will vary with time and place. Marx ([1859] 2005) makes the same point in the 1859 preface.

In the social production of their lives, Marx ([1859] 2005) argues, people will enter into "determinate, necessary relations, relations of production that are appropriate to a determinate [or specific] stage of the development of their material forces of production" (p. 61). This means, as he makes clear a few sentences later, that history and change are also fundamental (or ontological) to the human condition.

Having established that humankind enters into certain, historically created, social relations of production, Marx makes his next important claim. He argues that the "totality of these relations of production shape the economic structure of society" (Marx [1859] 2005:61). More important, the economic structure of society is "the real basis upon which a legal and political superstructure rises and to which determinate social forms of consciousness are appropriate" (p. 61).

These statements present the famous "base and superstructure" or "infrastructure and superstructure" conception that characterizes orthodox Marxism. There is an economic base (or infrastructure) that determines or shapes the superstructure: "The mode of production of material life conditions the social, political, and intellectual processes of life overall" (Marx [1859] 2005:61).

Although it might seem unnecessary to provide a diagrammatic representation of the "base and superstructure" model at this time, because the model becomes more complex, a basic diagram is helpful. Figure 1 shows the components of the superstructure and the economic base, as well as the direction of determination or conditioning that Marx identified.

The *mode of production*, one reads, is comprised of two basic elements: the *social relations of production* and the *material forces of production*. The social relations of production—"or property relations"—encompass the ownership and control of the forces of production (see Figure 2).

In slave societies, for example, the patrician class owns and controls the forces of production, and slaves are used to produce the basic goods and services needed for the society to exist. In feudal societies, the king or queen and feudal lords own and control the forces of production. Serfs are given access to the land as well as certain rights and privileges in exchange for an allocation of their production. In capitalist societies, industrial capitalists own the factories, purchase and own machinery and raw material, and, by paying wages, hire workers who make the products (or commodities) the owner will sell in the market. Master and slave, lord and serf, owner and employee characterize three different "relations of production" or "property relations."

The "material forces of production" encompass the material elements that are involved in production. In slave societies, the material elements are slaves using their labour to convert raw materials into goods for consumption. In capitalist societies, the material forces of production include the factories, the machinery, the raw material, and the physical workers, which all combine to produce commodities for sale in the market.

Up to this point in the 1859 preface, Marx's premises and propositions lead to two provisional conclusions. First, the mode of production is the key to understanding all social relations, including the "social, political, and intellectual processes of life overall" that constitute the superstructure. The second conclusion is a corollary of the first. It is not consciousness or ideas

SUPERSTRUCTURE
legal and political superstructure;
determinate forms of consciousness

BASE
Economic Structure of Society:
totality of the relations of production

FIGURE 1: *The Basic "Base and Superstructure" Model*

SUPERSTRUCTURE
legal and political superstructure;
determinate forms of consciousness

BASE
Economic Structure of Society:
totality of the relations of production

The Mode of Production:
the social relations of production;
the material forces of production

FIGURE 2: *Conceptualizing the Mode of Production*

| SUPERSTRUCTURE |
| social, political, and intellectual |
| processes of life overall |

↑

| BASE |
| *Mode of Production:* |
| social relations of production; |
| material forces of production |

FIGURE 3: *The Social, Political, and Intellectual Processes Overall*

that determine or shape social life; on the contrary, social life (living within a society) determines consciousness.

Figure 3 presents the essential relations that Marx seems to have had in mind while writing the preface. Although Marx begins with conceptions of the state as the superstructure ("the legal and political superstructure"), he also includes "determinate social forms of consciousness," ones appropriate to the relations of production in the base. He then suggests the more inclusive idea that "the mode of production of material life conditions the social, political, and intellectual process of life overall." This general conception is the most inclusive of all his formulations.

Contradiction and Revolutionary Change

If the relations of production as a whole constitute the basic infrastructure of society, they are also central to the social dynamism and change that characterize society and social history. On the basis of his studies, Marx ([1859] 2005) argues that, at "a certain stage of their development, the material productive forces of society come into contradiction with the existing relations of production. ... From forms of development of the productive forces, these relations [of production] transform into their fetters. It gives rise to an era of social revolution" (pp. 61–2). With change in the economic foundation, "the whole immense superstructure sooner or later revolutionizes itself" (Marx [1859] 2005:62).

Before examining the specific dynamic that Marx sees in social history, it is important to re-emphasize the sources of his conceptions.

The idea that there is an internal dynamic to social change was inspired by Marx's reading of Hegel. Hegel argues that historical change results from the development of ideas. Marx, however, rejects the notion that new theories, bodies of ideas, or changes in the legal and political superstructure are the driving forces of history and result in significant revolutionary change.

From the mid-1840s onward, Marx develops the position that the genuine, far-reaching transformation of society can only result from change within its material infrastructure. Moreover, his analyses convince him that it is the dynamic, contradictory nature of the economic infrastructure—the internal dynamic of the mode of production—that generates the social contradictions that lead to revolutionary social change.

Three important conclusions arise from this overview of Hegel and Marx's assertion of the primacy of the economic infrastructure. First, on the basis of his own life experiences, his study of political economy, and the changes he saw in the world around him, Marx, along with political economists such as Malthus, Ricardo, Jean-Baptiste Say (1817), and Smith, firmly believed that social analysis had to begin with the economic infrastructure of society. Marx, then, asserts a theme that was common to the contemporary literature on the political economy.

Second, Marx wanted to create social change. He was opposed to capitalism (a social system that he felt squandered the full potential of humankind). To create revolutionary social change, he wanted revolutionaries to focus upon the most important features of society that had to be transformed. The dominant tradition of the humanities in Germany led most reformers, including socialists such as Bruno Bauer, his brother Edgar, and Hess and Wilhelm Weitling, to focus upon the realm of ideas rather than the real material relations of society.[40] So, in breaking from Hegel and proposing his critique of capitalist society through political economy, Marx advocates a form of social analysis that would create genuine, meaningful—indeed, revolutionary—social change.

Third, and most important, in asserting his own particular position, Marx, it seems, rules out the notion that ideas or changes in the superstructure could be sources for fundamental social change. Is this because Marx thought that the superstructure was of little consequence, or is it that he wanted to make his position most emphatically? For the generation of orthodox Marxists, the answer is clear: the superstructure is simply a reflection of the infrastructure. Revolutionary change can come only from the contradictions in the economic infrastructure. The superstructure is determined by the infrastructure. As a result, the superstructure, as a mirror reflection of the infrastructure, is not of much importance.

Even though this became a widely accepted interpretation of Marx's 1859 preface, it arose from a rather simplified, narrow understanding of Marx's specific terms and of his argument as a whole. Marx fully recognized the unstable, dialectical unity of the social whole, and he wanted to convey the full interrelated texture of social life, but one cannot present such complexity all at once. As a result, Marx began with the infrastructure, enumerated its key elements, and then proceeded, in his more complete works such as the *Grundrisse,* to show the full, interrelated complexity of social life. This intricacy is one of the primary reasons that Marx's project kept expanding in size and why he continually revised his plans for presenting his entire critique of

---

40 Marx had addressed this tendency in German socialism critically in his sardonic critique of some of his former associates, for example, the Bauers, in *The Holy Family* (Marx and Engels 1957:3–224, [1845] 1975) and in the last section of the *Manifesto* under the heading "German or 'True' Socialism" (Marx and Engels 1848:18–20, [1848] 1934:31–4).

political economy. The simple "base determines superstructure" model was only one step in a presentation that was more complex and sophisticated than many orthodox Marxists recognized.

Still, the 1859 preface does present the idea that the motor of historical change is the tendency of the material productive forces to grow and come into conflict with the social relations of production, ushering in an age of social revolution. What was the basis of this dynamic? Why did Marx think that the forces of production would continually develop and come into conflict with the social relations of production? The dynamic of production is easy enough to understand: one need only think of a factory and its long assembly lines to conceptualize the dynamic of production. But how does the everyday dynamic of production create contradictory forces that lead to the existing relations of production serving as a fetter on their further development, and how does that lead to revolutionary change?

Technological Determinism

The dynamic tension that Marx sees within capitalist society and presents in his brief 1859 preface is more complex and layered than first meets the eye. One can progress through three different levels of analysis within Marx's preface statement. By beginning with the most basic reading and proceeding to more nuanced readings, one gains helpful insight into how, as noted earlier, Marx's conception of capitalist society is best described as a dynamic, unstable, dialectical whole; one may see the way Marx layers the elements of dynamic tension that he perceived within capitalist economies.

The first reading of the dynamic tension between the forces of production and the social relations of production is quite straightforward. The social relations of production in capitalist society facilitate, encourage, and, in fact, require production for profit. A capitalist factory owner employs workers to turn raw material, through the use of various machines, into commodities that the capitalist will sell for a profit in the marketplace. To increase profits, the factory owner is always looking for ways to improve and speed the production processes. The key focus in this reading of the conditions that create revolutionary change is the role of machinery.

"At a certain stage of their development, *the material productive forces of society* come into contradiction with the existing relations of production [my emphasis]" (Marx [1859] 2005: 61–2). Machinery is obviously the key, the material productive force that permits capitalists to increase productivity and thereby increase profits. As a result, it seems apparent and logical that Marx had machinery and technology in mind when he noted the conditions that would create revolutionary change.

The idea that machinery is the key to social change is found in many writers' works, and it is often termed "technological determinism." Technology, in this type of argument, determines the course of social change and development. And a number of statements throughout Marx's work, when taken out of context, appear to be quite technologically deterministic. The statement most often used to claim that Marx is a technological determinist is found in *The Poverty of Philosophy,* Marx's critique of Proudhon's *The Philosophy of Poverty*: "the hand-mill gives you society with the feudal lord; the steam-mill, society with the industrial capitalist" (Marx [1847] 1950:127). The statement reads like a causal relationship—a lower form of technology ("the hand-mill") allows for a feudal society to exist while a more developed form of technology ("the steam-mill") creates the more complex society of industrial capitalism.

Certainly, one of the major forces of change in nineteenth-century capitalism was technological development. And such development took place extremely rapidly and on a massive scale. So people reading Marx's preface in 1859 had good historical reasons for thinking that Marx had machinery in mind. Such a reading equates "the motor of history," appropriately enough, with technological development. As technology advances, society progresses.

As familiar as Marx was with technologically deterministic arguments, it is unlikely that his conception of change is that narrow, although he would certainly have seen technology as one of the major sources of change. By reading the preface very narrowly, however, generations of orthodox Marxists, critics of orthodox Marxism, and commentators on Marx's texts have argued that Marx is a technological determinist, and the proof, they all maintain, is in this section of the 1859 preface. As one element in Marx's understanding of the dialectical tensions within the material relations of production, technology is important—but it is not the only element.

Economic Determinism

A technologically determinist reading of the 1859 preface places the emphasis upon how the development of "the material productive forces of society" creates the contradictions that lead to revolutionary social change. However, if one shifts the emphasis to the latter half of the sentence concerning how change will occur, one may develop a different aspect of the dynamic of change that Marx outlines in this work. "At a certain stage of their development, the material productive forces of society come into contradiction with *the existing relations of production* or, what is only a legal expression for it, *with the property relations within which they have operated to that point in time* [my emphasis]" (Marx [1859] 2005:6–62). This reading will produce an "economically deterministic" argument, and this argument, too, was taken up and explored by orthodox Marxists, their critics, and commentators on Marx.

In an economically deterministic argument it is not machinery or technology that drives history and social change but the economy as a whole. The economy determines or shapes the types of contradictions that will emerge and create, animate, or drive revolutionary change. This reading is also sometimes referred to as "economic reductionism" because the course of history—the source of the major tensions that create social change—is "reduced to" the economy. As in the case of technological determinism, sound historical reasons exist for thinking that Marx subscribes to economic reductionism, but those interpretations ignore the dialectical aspects of Marx's presentation and insights.

In the course of his own lifetime, Marx lived through several economic crises. In the *Manifesto,* his essay *Wage-Labour and Capital,* and at some length in the draft manuscript for the third volume of *Capital,* Marx outlines a theory of what he calls "overproduction." Marx argues that, in the regular dynamic of the capitalist economy, the drive for profit puts pressure on capitalists to continually increase their productive advantage over others. That drive leads to technological innovation and more efficient production, but better technology and increased productive efficiency often lead to the replacement of workers by more efficient machines. The surplus workers are then relegated to what Marx terms "the reserve army of the unemployed," which creates a dilemma for capitalists pursuing profit. The reserve army of the unemployed is too poor to purchase goods in the market, so, as more and more workers are replaced by machines, the number of potential consumers for this growing surplus of commodities falls. That is one problem, but the situation gets worse.

 The unemployed workers compete with the employed for jobs and are willing to work for less money just to secure employment, which puts a dampening effect on workers' wages, often causing them to fall. Thus, a second major problem arises. Through capitalist competition for increased profits, even the workers with jobs find themselves in economically insecure positions or economically worsening situations. This employment instability also leads to decreased consumer demand and falling sales. Consequently, in the pursuit of profits, capitalists inevitably run the risk of unleashing one of the many periodic crises of overproduction that characterized late nineteenth- and early twentieth-century capitalist societies. The system itself, then, seems to generate its own contradictions and potential downfall.

Before writing the 1859 preface, Marx had already described this situation graphically in the *Manifesto of the Communist Party:*

Modern bourgeois society with its relations of production, of exchange and of property, a society that has conjured up such gigantic means of production and of exchange, is like the sorcerer who is no longer able to control the powers of the nether world whom he has called up by his ✓ spells. (Marx and Engels [1848] 1934:14–5)

In the *Manifesto*, Marx notes the numerous economic crises during which "modern productive forces" revolted "against modern conditions of production," with each crisis more threatening than the last.

In these crises, there breaks out an epidemic that, in all earlier epochs, would have seemed an absurdity—the epidemic of over-production. Society suddenly finds itself put back into a state of momentary barbarism; it appears as if a famine, a universal war of devastation, had cut off the supply of every means of subsistence; industry and commerce seem to be destroyed. (Marx and Engels [1848] 1934:15)

Marx ominously argues that history was showing through these crises that the "productive forces at the disposal of society no longer tend to further the development of the conditions of bourgeois property; on the contrary, they have become too powerful for these conditions, by which they are fettered, and as soon as they overcome these fetters, they bring disorder into the whole of bourgeois society, endangering the existence of bourgeois property" (Marx and Engels [1848] 1934:15).

The tendency for the rate of profit to fall is a different dimension of the same problem that the pursuit of profit creates. Marx argues that workers, through the sale of their ability to do work—or their labour-power—are the sole source of value and surplus value, which are actualized into profit. Although details of the theory of value and surplus value are not important here, the argument that Marx makes in *Wage-Labour and Capital* (Marx [1849] 1933) and presents in greater detail in the draft manuscript for volume two of *Capital* (Marx and Engels 1963a:101–52) shows that the tendency for the increased mechanization of production sets in motion a tendency for the rate of profit to fall. Each worker a capitalist employs generates a continually shrinking rate of profit, as more technology is introduced into production. The only way to offset the loss in profits inherent in this tendency is to find a technological advantage that will increase the rate of profit over less technologically advanced competitors, to increase the speed with which products are produced and sold, or to find new markets.

The first solution is only a stopgap measure and part of the vicious cycle inherent in the tendency for the rate of profit to fall. Every advance in technology might bring brief respite, but it exacerbates the situation in the long run because more workers will have been replaced by the new technology. More machinery means fewer workers and a decreased rate of profit.

Speeding the rate of commodity turnover requires technological innovation, so it too contributes to the same vicious cycle that pushes the rate of profit downwards.

The last solution is only effective as long as new markets can be found. It buys time, perhaps, but, inevitably, the crisis will emerge as all the markets become saturated. Worse yet, as Marx notes in the *Manifesto*, "the conquest of new markets" and "the more thorough exploitation of the old ones" simply "pav[es] the way for more extensive and more destructive crises" and diminishes "the means whereby crises are prevented" (Marx and Engels [1848] 1934:15).[41]

The final dimension of the economically determinist reading of the 1859 preface concerns the contradiction that exists between the planned efficiency that characterizes capitalist production and the free-flowing competition of the capitalist market. Marx was not the only person who recognized that the private ownership of the means of production—one of the centrally defining features of capitalist society—would create problems over the supply of commodities that were produced and put onto the market. Before Marx, Ferguson ([1767] 1971), Smith ([1776] 1976), Sismondi ([1815] 1966), and James Mill ([1821] 1844), for example, all noted the potential problems associated with overproduction.[42] Perhaps this was what Marx had in mind as he wrote that "the material productive forces of society come into contradiction with the existing ... property relations."

All of the economic crises Marx identifies ultimately stem from the drive to increase or maintain levels of profit through increased efficiency in production. But the outcome is overproduction, a tendency for the rate of profit to fall, and the creation of an impoverished reserve army of the unemployed. One solution—a solution that a number of socialists put forward with different emphases—is to coordinate the economy as a whole—to introduce the same rational planning to the total economy that each capitalist uses in his or her particular enterprise. Centralized planning, of course, conflicts

---

41 There was a lively debate between Marxists and mainstream economists over the various "breakdown theses" that exist in Marx's work. See, in particular, Grossman (1929), who started the debate by demonstrating the tendencies were correctly predicted, Böhm-Bawerk (1949), who responded, Hilferding's (1949) response to Böhm-Bawerk, and Luxemburg's (1951) argument that capitalism would only expand so far until it would break down under its own contradictions.

42 Modern economists also recognize the problems associated with the regulation of supply and demand. The most significant struggle in economic thought and public policy is between those who argue that the economy needs regulation versus those who want it completely unregulated. This debate pits the work of John Maynard Keynes (1936) and the Cambridge school against that of Friedrich von Hayek (1931, 1934), Ludwig von Mises (1934), and the Austrian school.

with the tenets of a free market. It conflicts, in other words, with the exist-ing property relations.

All of these "economically deterministic" readings of the 1859 preface were supported by the history of capitalist society in the late nineteenth and early twentieth century. As a result, they would all have assisted Marx in seeing the internally generated, dialectical dynamism of capitalist society as it stemmed from within its economic infrastructure. Marx's preface, then, reflects each of these different layers of the contradictory nature of capitalist production.

Labour-Power, Consciousness, Political Action

There is a third level of argument within the preface. This one includes the first two but is more comprehensive and thus goes beyond them. Although it includes the first two levels of analysis, the third one brings into play the significance of class consciousness within the proletariat.

In the *Manifesto,* Marx focuses upon the central role of class struggle in history. According to some, his description of the means by which tech-nology, crises of overproduction, and the falling rate of profit create crises seems to imply that social transformation is a more or less automatic, almost mechanistic, process—that one need only wait for the conditions of revolu-tion to emerge and then erupt, leading to the revolutionary transformation of capitalist society. Many orthodox Marxists insisted that this was, indeed, Marx's position. But, as one reads the preface more closely, it is also appar-ent that Marx has made room for the "revolutionary subject"—the prole-tariat—to become conscious of its situation and begin to push for change.

Drawing upon his background in analytical philosophy and Marxism, Gerald Cohen (1978) intensively dissected the key concepts in the 1859 pref-ace. He argues that the means of production within the mode of production are more complex than most commentators have noted. What are the mate-rial forces of production in Marx's work, Cohen asks. What are they in any capitalist enterprise? The material forces of production break down into three basic elements: the means of production, which are comprised of the raw material and machinery that are used to produce commodities; the spaces where production takes place (factories in the case of industrial production); and the human labour-power that is required to carry out productive work.

The technological explanations for social change are encompassed in the dimensions that are relevant to the means of production narrowly under-stood. Economic determinist explanations still all apply because the same contradictions between the property relations and the relations of produc-tion will continue to be in effect. The new elements are the acknowledged presence of labour-power and its congregation in factories.

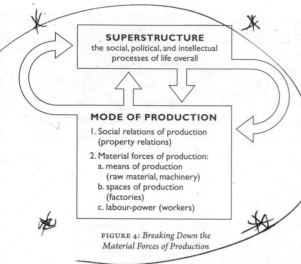

SUPERSTRUCTURE
the social, political, and intellectual
processes of life overall

MODE OF PRODUCTION

1. Social relations of production
   (property relations)

2. Material forces of production:
   a. means of production
      (raw material, machinery)
   b. spaces of production
      (factories)
   c. labour-power (workers)

FIGURE 4: *Breaking Down the Material Forces of Production*

On the one hand, it is surprising that the central importance of labour-power in Marx's 1859 preface could have been overlooked for so many years. Workers and their labour-power are a key element in Marx's analysis of capitalist production. Labour-power, according to Marx, is the sole source of surplus value. The proletariat is the revolutionary force that Marx thinks will change the world. And the conditions under which workers live and work are central to all of Engels and Marx's major analyses of capitalist society. Figure 4 presents this expanded model of the key elements in Marx's 1859 preface.

As was the case earlier, this layer of analysis in the preface incorporates technological determinism and economic determinism. The key differences within this deeper, more comprehensive understanding of the dynamic that Marx points to are the identification of labour-power as a factor in social change, the role that ideas will play, and the unique environment within which they will germinate and grow.

The social relations of production under capitalism centre on the generation of profit. Value and surplus value, the bases for profit, are created in the production process when workers animate machinery to turn raw material into finished products that are sold on the market. Over the course of the nineteenth century and into the twentieth, employers consolidated production into larger and larger mechanized factories to gain the efficiencies of a growth in productive scale, improved mechanization, and increased control over the workers (Smith [1776] 1976). Marx notes this trend in the *Manifesto* (Marx and Engels [1848] 1934:16–7). In the technologically determinist and economically determinist levels of analysis in the preface, workers are seen as mere factors of production. They are much like other raw materials and treated as an expense. But labour-power is more than simply a factor in production. Labour-power is irrevocably tied to a human being.

Why is that important? It is important for four very specific reasons. First, humans are conceptual beings. Humans reflexively monitor their actions; they conceptualize the tasks they are asked to perform; they consciously engage with the world around them. As a result, one key factor within the material forces of production that constitute part of the mode of production (which constitutes the economic infrastructure), is the group consisting of *conscious human workers.*

Ideas and consciousness are not located solely in the superstructure. The very presence of labour-power, of humans, among the material forces of production indicates that one of the processes Marx explicitly locates in the superstructure—"intellectual processes of life"—is also present in the infrastructure. Marx's model must be thought of as much more integrated than the distinct, two-tiered conception that most people derive from the 1859 preface. Marx's conceptual understanding of capitalist society is heavily indebted to Hegel, and all of Hegel's analyses—his work on the phenomenology of mind, the history of philosophy, the encyclopaedia of knowledge, or the philosophy of law, for example—are synthetic wholes. Marx may argue that Hegel looked in the wrong place in his efforts to understand the dynamic of history, but Marx is never critical of Hegel's overall conceptual framework.[43] Marx, too, sought to grasp and present capitalist society as a dialectically unstable, synthetic whole; he did not want it understood as a hierarchical, stratified layer cake.

Second, while workers are conscious producers and use their minds as much as necessary to fulfil their work tasks, their consciousness expands beyond the specific tasks they must carry out in the production process. Reflexively monitoring their work experiences will encompass more than recognizing when they need to carry out a specific production task.

As a result, workers take in and assess the conditions under which they work. They inevitably develop a political consciousness of their role in the production process and of their place in the factory, as well as perceptions concerning their treatment by employers. Workers develop political consciousness in the work process. This fact, too, brings another explicitly defined aspect of the superstructure into the infrastructure—political consciousness.

Third, because workers' reflexively monitor their conditions of work and because industrial production brings together an increasing mass of workers, a growing political force is created. This force was becoming evident in industrial Britain during the second half of the nineteenth century. Even though capitalist owners controlled the majority of resources and could establish most of the rules that would structure the workplace, the power that those rules and resources generated was not all in the hands of the employer. The emergence of trade unions and the impact that workers in

---

43 Marx ([1890] 1976) argues that "For Hegel, the process of thinking, which he even transforms into an independent subject, under the name of 'the Idea,' is the creator of the real world, and the real world is only the external appearance of the idea. With me the reverse is true: the ideal is nothing but the material world reflected in the mind of man, and translated into forms of thought" (p. 102).

Britain had on parliamentary legislation to curb the length of the working day and introduce some basic worker protections demonstrated that the workers were politically conscious and active. The workers of the late nineteenth and early twentieth century were becoming an increasingly powerful political force. Marx also emphasizes this trend in the *Manifesto* (Marx and Engels [1848] 1934:17–8).

Finally, when Marx reviews his early intellectual labours in the preface, he notes that his critique of Hegel had "led to the conclusion that legal relations and forms of state cannot be comprehended by themselves or on the basis of the so-called general development of the human mind or spirit" (Marx [1859] 2005:61). Instead, he maintains, "they are rooted in the material relations of life whose totality Hegel, following the lead of the English and French in the eighteenth century, brought together under the name 'civil society.'" And, he continues, "the anatomy of civil society is to be sought in political economy" (p. 61).

To clearly distinguish himself from Hegel and many other socialists and to emphasize what he believed was his most important contribution to the understanding of societies and their dynamics, Marx used the term "materialist" to identify his position. However, there was a tendency among orthodox Marxists to inflate the notion of materialism in Marx's work and to regard ideas as purely side effects or by-products of the "material relations of society." But Marx was never a crude materialist. The statements cited previously demonstrate what he meant, and the preface provides a more elaborate explanation of his position. The interpretation of the preface to follow begins with Marx's comments on Hegel and then moves to the importance of labour-power to bring out the full meaning of Marx's position in 1859.

The vast majority of social analysts, from Socrates, Plato, and Aristotle in antiquity through to classical political theorists such as Hobbes, John Locke, Montesquieu, Rousseau, Saint-Simon, Comte, and John Stuart Mill, are concerned with issues of power. They tend to see power solely in terms of the state—hence Hobbes's ([1651] 1968) *Leviathan*, Locke's ([1694] 1967) *Two Treatises on Government*, Rousseau's ([1762] 1963) *Social Contract*, Montesquieu's ([1748] 1989) *Spirit of the Laws*, Saint-Simon's (1975) *The Industrial System* (published in 1821), and Comte's (1974) *Plan of Scientific Studies Necessary for the Reorganization of Society* (published in 1822).

Marx argues that this view of power is wrong. While the state holds tremendous power, that power can only be understood by examining "the material relations of life," which Hegel and Rousseau discuss under the label "civil society." Marx goes a step further: the "anatomy of civil society"— the anatomy of the material relations of civil society—"is to be sought in political economy."

For Marx, materialism represents the realities of everyday life in civil society, and, to begin to analyse civil society, one should begin with its anatomy—political economy. None of this excludes the importance of ideas, per se, in either civil society or in political economy; they are just not the place where one should begin the study of power and social dynamics.

There is a fifth point related to this more inclusive, nuanced understanding of Marx's preface, and it relates to Mills's notion of the intersection of personal biography and the history of the social structure. One of the reasons Mills emphasizes this intersection is his appreciation of Marx's work. By recognizing the role that conscious human labour-power plays in the production process and the awareness that develops, one can see that intersection very clearly and, most important for Marx, within a strategic area of social life. One can also see how that dynamic—working under the demanding and exploitative conditions of unregulated, nineteenth-century capitalism—would lead to particular forms of conscious resistance to the system and to a new type of worker beginning to prevail. The intersection of workers' biographies (their personal histories of keeping pace with automated production running at full speed) and the structural demands of profit production within capitalist social relations of production shaped worker consciousness and resistance in very specific ways during Marx's era and beyond (see Hobsbawm 1964, 1999; Thompson 1970). One is now in a position to grasp the full dialectical whole that Marx sketches in his 1859 preface.

In setting out an apparently two-tiered conception of base and superstructure, Marx uses terms that set the economic base opposite the "legal and political superstructure." He then establishes the key elements within "the totality of the relations of production"—the social relations of production and the forces of production. He then sets these opposite a broader conception of the superstructure, which he identifies as the "social, political, and intellectual process of life overall." When one breaks down the material forces of production into their key elements—material means of production, spaces for production, and labourpower—it becomes clear that what was originally presented as a two-tiered conception is actually fully integrated (see Figure 5). Social, political, and intellectual processes may be found within labour-power in Marx's

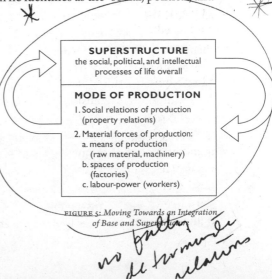

SUPERSTRUCTURE
the social, political, and intellectual
processes of life overall

MODE OF PRODUCTION

1. Social relations of production
(property relations)

2. Material forces of production:
a. means of production
(raw material, machinery)
b. spaces of production
(factories)
c. labour-power (workers)

FIGURE 5: *Moving Towards an Integration of Base and Superstructure*

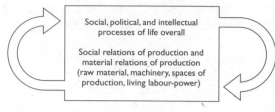

FIGURE 6: *Marx's Model as a Conceptual Totality*

analytical point of departure—the base—as well as within the larger social institutions such as the family, education, the church, and the state, which constitute "the social, political, and intellectual processes of life overall."

The social whole has a number of tensions and contradictions. To begin to enumerate those contradictions, Marx maintains, one has to begin with the base and work from there, keeping in mind that, intellectually, one is grasping an unstable, dynamic, contradictory whole. This is the conceptual framework Marx sought to sketch out in his 1859 preface.

When one then breaks down the material forces of production into the means, spaces, and animate components of the production process, labour-power must serve the double function of being part of the production process and part of the "social, political, and intellectual processes of life overall." Figure 6 captures this more integrated model.

The arrows are important; Marx argues that to understand the social whole, one must start with the anatomy of civil society (which is to be sought in the economic infrastructure). After critically grasping the social and material relations of production and their relationship, as the arrow on the left indicates, one may proceed to considering the elements of the superstructure. Based on one's knowledge of the economic infrastructure, one can now more fully grasp how the material practices in the economic infrastructure shape (or determine) the elements contained in the superstructure. Once one has grasped how the social, political, and intellectual processes of life are shaped by the infrastructure, one can then, as the arrow on the right indicates, return to the social and material relations of production and consider them more fully in light of one's knowledge of the superstructure. Analysis now becomes a recurring cycle in which one gains a deeper, more complex and synthetic understanding of the social whole.

Marx's 1859 Preface, the Enlightenment Legacy, and Sociology

If the Enlightenment's legacy to sociology can be captured in the words "freedom," "mastery," and "progress," it is clear that Marx's contribution to sociology draws upon these same themes as they are developed within his 1859 preface to *Towards the Critique of Political Economy*. Marx's fundamental concerns in this preface are freedom from exploitation, greater equality in the sharing of social resources, and the full expression of human potential. Each of these, in Marx's view, requires some fundamental change in the structure of society, and the key to understanding what will bring about that change lies in the anatomy of civil society—in its political economy.

Marx believed that the intellectual critique of political economy—his analysis of the mode of production—followed by the requisite changes to the social relations and material forces of production would allow humanity to master its material conditions of existence. That knowledge and the practices it set in motion would bring to fruition the Enlightenment's dream of greater human freedom and progress towards a more advanced social formation.

Conflict, power, tension, struggle, and revolutionary transformation are also all part of Marx's analysis of capitalist society. One of the main reasons his work was drawn into sociology is the attention his perspective brings to questions of power and to the political processes that occur within the texture of everyday life. In Marx's analysis, civil society may be characterized by exploitation and inequality, but that is due to a specific set of property relations. Those relations, in turn, are constituted and reconstituted in the everyday activities of workers in their workplaces. In that process of constitution and reconstitution, however, the rules and resources that structure the production process and the sale of goods in the marketplace are continually in flux. Through the flow and reflexive monitoring of everyday activities, workers and citizens gain new levels of awareness and political insight and seek change.

Marx ends the preface with an ominous challenge. Quoting from Dante's *Divine Comedy,* he notes that "the same challenge must be made at the entrance to science as at the entrance to hell: 'Here must all distrust be left; All Cowardice must here be dead'" (Marx [1859] 2005:64). Marx's sociology challenges sociologists to examine the world around them critically, irrespective of what they will find. One must trust one's findings, no matter how painful, if they have been obtained through a careful, unbiased analysis of the social world. These dimensions of Marx's work, along with the questions he posed and the framework he employed, drew Marx into the pantheon of early sociologists.

Although Marx wrote in the late nineteenth century, his work remains alive today because the intersection of his personal and intellectual biography with the history of the social structure placed him at a particularly propitious vantage point. From this perspective, he could capture the dynamics of modern society as it was being consolidated and anticipate the impact of industrial capitalism as it expanded across Europe. The next chapter focuses upon the *Manifesto of the Communist Party* not because it is the *communist* manifesto but because it is also a manifesto of *modernity* (Berman 1988). The *Manifesto* presents, in vivid imagery, the dynamic vitality of the modern world as it was unfolding in the 1840s and as it continued to develop, with greater speed and deeper impact, over the next century and a half. Reading the *Manifesto* in this light brings Marx directly into the most pressing debates in sociology today.

4 MARX, THE *COMMUNIST MANIFESTO*, AND MODERNITY

The anonymous 23-page *Manifest der Kommunistischen Partei* that rolled off the presses located in the office of the Bildungs-Gesellschaft für Arbeiter (Educational Society for Workers), 46 Liverpool Street, London, in February 1848 had little impact upon the revolutionary insurrections that took place in Berlin, Cologne, Königsberg, and other parts of Prussia that March.[44] Part of the reason was due to the Prussian government's diligence in intercepting and confiscating large numbers of the pamphlet, but its late arrival and the Communist League's low profile among revolutionaries also undermined its impact. Nevertheless, the *Manifesto* was circulated among and read by many bourgeois and working class revolutionaries in 1848.

Despite its rather undistinguished beginning, the *Communist Manifesto* (as its title became after the 1872 Leipzig edition) gained a much higher profile following the Paris Commune of 1871. Under changed social and political circumstances and after almost 20 years of underground discussion, the *Manifesto* had attained a growing reputation for its cogency, power, and

---

44 The anonymous, first edition of the *Manifesto* went through four printings, with the first printing appearing in serial instalments in the *Deutsche Londoner Zeitung* (German London Gazette) from March 3 to July 28, 1848. The second edition, a 30-page anonymous pamphlet, was most likely published in April or May 1848 and, along with an 1866 edition, served as the basis for all future editions of the *Manifesto*. Although the preamble to the *Manifesto* states that it would appear in English, French, German, Italian, Flemish, and Danish, with the exception of a Swedish translation in 1849, only the German text appeared in 1848–9 (Andréas 1963:15). The *Manifesto* now appears in more than 35 languages; 544 editions were printed between 1848 and the beginning of the Russian Revolution in 1917.

insight, and it became, in the second half of the nineteenth century, the principle statement of how and why the revolutionary workers' movement in western Europe would succeed in transforming society into a more egalitarian social formation. In addition, Marx, the pamphlet's principal author, enjoyed a significantly higher political profile in 1871 than he had held as an exiled German émigré living and writing in Brussels in 1848.

By 1871, Marx had been living in London, the centre of British political radicalism and the home of other socialist and communist refugees, for 22 years. By then, Marx had published *Towards a Critique of Political Economy*, which presented the preliminary arguments for his critique of bourgeois political economy and a powerful summary, in the preface, regarding how societies changed and the apparent inevitability of a communist society in the future. Also, Marx had assumed a leading role in the International Working Men's Association, founded in 1864, and he had published the first volume of his magnum opus *Das Kapital* ([1867] 1983).[45]

From 1871 onwards, the *Communist Manifesto* has been recognized as one of the most important social documents of the modern era. Correctly or not, the *Manifesto* has been used by disadvantaged, repressed, exploited groups in widely differing parts of the world as an inspiration, and sometimes as a blueprint, for social change. It has been used by different communist states to justify various policies and decisions as well as a particular interpretation of history. Finally, the *Manifesto* has been used by critics of social democracy, socialism, or communism as an example of all that is wrong and evil in those movements.

Written during a key period in European history, the *Manifesto* captures the dynamics of market societies as they were becoming dominant across western Europe. England, by this time, had undergone almost a century of industrial development, France was becoming increasingly industrialized, and Germany was then undergoing industrialization as a weak middle class began to struggle for power against well-established landed and military interests. Although similar documents were written at that time, the *Manifesto* has endured because of its vivid imagery and the way it expresses the essential dynamic of modern industrial capitalist society as its prodigious potential was just beginning to become fully apparent.

---

45 The first International Working Men's Association (the "First International") was founded in 1864 in St. Martin's Hall, London. It held its first congress in Geneva in 1866 and held together until 1876. Marx was a member of the General Council throughout the First International's existence although he was in constant conflict with the leaders of the various strands of socialism that the organization brought together. Marx fought with the German workers who followed Ferdinand Lassalle, the Italians supporting Giuseppe Mazzini's republican nationalist leanings, the French mutualists who backed Proudhon's particular anarchist program, the Owenites who promoted Owen's socialist ideas, and the workers who followed Mikhail Bakunin's anti-state anarchism (Cole 1954:88–133).

The *Manifesto* was also a significant accomplishment in Marx's quest for recognition as a scholar, social critic, and revolutionary leader. It represents one of the high-water marks in Marx's life for three particular reasons.

First, by 1848, Marx had arrived at fundamental solutions to the major theoretical and philosophical issues with which he had been struggling since he switched to the University of Berlin in 1836. In 1848, Marx believed he had identified the key factors that would provide genuine insight into societies and their dynamics—aspects of the material world, which he felt revolutionaries could use to create the social change they all thought was necessary to improve the human condition.

Second, the *Manifesto* represents the victory of Marx's intellectual vision in the political arena. Following two different international conferences organized by the League of the Just and held in London, Marx was entrusted with preparing the document that would present the league's new position on socialism and on the transition to a communist society. Drafting the *Manifesto* moved Marx from the obscurity of his writing desk at his home in Brussels to the public stage of the European socialist movement. At the same time, it allowed Marx to draw together all the work he had been slaving over to arrive at his particular sociological understanding of capitalist society (as barebones as that analysis might have been at the time).

Finally, in writing the *Manifesto*, Marx is able to demonstrate his skill and craft as a revolutionary writer—the rhetoric and imagery he uses emphasizes the importance he places upon the development of a revolutionary consciousness within the working class. Class struggle requires a clear, unambiguous class consciousness, and the *Manifesto* sought to provide workers with a moving and motivating understanding of their reality and their role in history and to inspire them to take action. This dimension of the *Manifesto* has proven to be one of its most enduring qualities for today—if one wants to capture the imagery of modernity, the anonymous 1848 pamphlet does it extremely well.

Even though Marx is the pamphlet's author and the work represents the League of the Just's acceptance of his particular analysis of capitalist society, it was not then, and is not now, a set of uncontested, scriptural truths. The *Communist Manifesto* emerged as the result of a complex process in which personal biographies (those of Marx, Engels, Hess, Karl Schapper, and Joseph Moll, in particular); the history of social structure (of Britain, France, and Germany, mostly); and the types of men, women, and political associations (such as the League of the Just, which became the Communist League) prevailing at that time all played important roles.

Rather than representing a single, monolithic position—one that puts forward the uncontested, universal views of the Communist League—the

Manifesto is the product of debate, struggle, negotiation, some compromise, and Marx's own particular style of presentation and argument. The *Manifesto* is an extremely interesting compromise of the intensely competing views that gave the Communist League unity and a vision, but this was a historically located and temporally bound unity and perspective—one that would, and needed to be, adjusted, debated, and contested as the social world around the socialist movement changed (Beamish 1998). It was also a tremendously compelling and historically important vision of bourgeois society and of the future of the industrial world.

THE *MANIFESTO* AND MODERNITY'S DYNAMISM

Marx begins the *Manifesto* powerfully and ominously: *"Ein Gespenst geht um in Europa—das Gespenst des Kommunismus* [A spectre moves about Europe—the spectre of communism]" (Marx and Engels 1848:3).[46] He continues,

> All the powers of old Europe have entered into a holy alliance to exor-
> cise this spectre: Pope and Tsar, Metternich and Guizot, French Radicals
> and German police-spies.[47] Where is the party in opposition that has
> not been decried as communistic by its opponents in power? (Marx and
> Engels [1848] 1934:9)

Two points arise from these facts—first it is clear that all European powers acknowledge communism to be a powerful force. Second—and here Marx negates or inverts the ominous opening—it is high time that "Communists should ... meet this nursery tale of the spectre of Communism with a manifesto of the party itself." The opening section, then, takes one from a frighten-

---

46 The first English translation of the *Manifesto*—produced by Helen Macfarlane and serialized in Julian Harney's *The Red Republican* throughout November 1850—lost some of Marx's dramatic imagery: "A frightful hobgoblin stalks throughout Europe. We are haunted by a ghost, the ghost of Communism" (Beamish 1998:239, note 63).

47 Marx is taking some literary licence here by collapsing two events into one. The 1815 Congress of Vienna, which proclaimed a loose alliance of European powers called the "Holy Alliance," was spearheaded by Klemens von Metternich, an Austrian prince who was a staunch reactionary opposed to any ideas of liberalism. In this 1815 alliance of Russia, Austria, Prussia, and England, Metternich sought the return of conservative, absolute monarchies. A smaller "holy alliance" was forged by Metternich between the Russian Tsar Alexander I and Prussia's Frederick Wilhelm III. The pope, though sympathetic to the forces of reaction, was never part of either alliance, and Guizot, who expelled Marx from Paris, was never important enough to represent France in any of these alliances. Finally, both alliances were conservative insofar as their main targets were liberal reformers—not the communist or workers' movements (which they would most certainly have also opposed).

ing spectre to a down-to-earth dismissal of such fictions and the presentation of the international communist movement.

Part I of the *Manifesto* returns to vivid imagery to present its dominant
theme:

> The history of all hitherto existing societies is the history of class
> struggles.
>
> Free man and slave, patrician and plebeian, lord and serf, guild-master
> and journeyman, in a word, oppressor and oppressed, stood in constant
> opposition to one another, carried on an uninterrupted, now hidden,
> now open fight, a fight that each time ended, either in a revolutionary
> reconstitution of society at large, or in the common ruin of the contend-
> ing classes. (Marx and Engels [1848] 1934:10)

Through the use of a carefully crafted history, Marx proceeds to sketch
out the two great titans that would soon confront each other—the bourgeoisie and the proletariat.[48] As Marx argues, "Our epoch, the epoch of the
bourgeoisie ... has simplified class antagonisms," so modern society "is more
and more splitting up into two great hostile camps, into two great classes
directly facing each other—bourgeoisie and proletariat" (Marx and Engels
[1848] 1934:10).

In broad, powerful strokes, Marx sketches out the rise of the bourgeoisie
as a class and the implications this has for life in the emerging modern world:

> [T]he modern bourgeoisie is itself the product of a long course of devel-
> opment, of a series of revolutions in the modes of production and of
> exchange.
>
> Each step in the development of the bourgeoisie was accompanied
> by a corresponding political advance in that class. An oppressed class
> under the sway of the feudal nobility, an armed and self-governing asso-
> ciation in the medieval commune: here independent urban republic (as
> in Italy and Germany); there taxable "third estate" of the monarchy (as in
> France); afterward, in the period of manufacturing proper, serving either
> the semi-feudal or the absolute monarchy as a counterpoise against the
> nobility, and, in fact, cornerstone of the great monarchies in general—the
> bourgeoisie has at last, since the establishment of Modern Industry and
> of the world market, conquered for itself, in the modern representative

---

48 The noun "proletariat" is derived from the Latin noun *"proles"* meaning "offspring." The *proles* were an
impoverished, subordinate class in ancient Rome. Each member of that class was a proletarian, and,
collectively, they were the proletariat. The only economic assets proletarians had were their sons—
their offspring (hence the *proles* had nothing to offer other than their offspring).

state, exclusive political sway. The executive of the modern state is but a committee for managing the common affairs of the whole bourgeoisie. (Marx and Engels [1848] 1934:11–2)

The bourgeoisie, Marx argues, was a revolutionary class that radically transformed society as it rose to dominance from within the feudal order. Some of those changes centred on the social relations among people; for example, market society fundamentally changed the basis of human interaction, the nature of work, and the reality of every occupation:

> The bourgeoisie, wherever it has got the upper hand, has put an end to all feudal, patriarchal, idyllic relations. It has pitilessly torn asunder the motley feudal ties that bound man to his "natural superiors," and has left no other nexus between man and man than naked self-interest, than callous "cash payment". ... It has resolved personal worth into exchange value, and in place of the numberless indefeasible chartered freedoms, has set up that single, unconscionable freedom—Free Trade. In one word, for exploitation, veiled by religious and political illusions, it has substituted naked, shameless, direct, brutal exploitation.
>
> The bourgeoisie has stripped of its halo every occupation hitherto honoured and looked up to with reverent awe. It has converted the physician, the lawyer, the priest, the poet, the man of science, into its paid wage labourers. (Marx and Engels [1848] 1934:12)

As a consequence, Marx continues, the modern era is unlike any before it—tradition, the mystification of magic or religion, and "natural rights" no longer structure social relationships. The cash nexus and the ethos of unrestricted trade dominate production, interpersonal relations, and the social structure as a whole.

While replacing a veiled form of exploitation with a naked, direct form that leaves factory workers toiling long hours for meagre wages, the bourgeoisie demonstrates the power of industrial, market-based production. The accomplishments of the bourgeoisie are breathtaking; it has produced "wonders far surpassing Egyptian pyramids, Roman aqueducts, and Gothic cathedrals" (Marx and Engels [1848] 1934:12).

According to Marx, the most important revolutionary change that the bourgeoisie accomplished in the transformation of feudal society into a market-based one was the constant revolutionary change of the "instruments of production, and thereby the relations of production, and with them the whole relations of society":

Conservation of the old modes of production in unaltered form, was …
the first condition of existence for all earlier industrial classes. Constant
revolutionizing of production, uninterrupted disturbance of all social
conditions, everlasting uncertainty and agitation distinguish the bourgeois epoch from all earlier ones. All fixed, fast-frozen relations, with their
train of ancient and venerable prejudices and opinions, are swept away,
all new-formed ones become antiquated before they can ossify. All that
is solid melts into air, all that is holy is profaned, and man is at last com-
pelled to face with sober senses his real condition of life and his relations
with his kind. (Marx and Engels [1848] 1934:12–3)

Marx's imagery is powerful, and it remains fresh when one thinks of the
contemporary world in which the drive to shorten time and shrink distances
now dominates people's lives. In the globalized world, the sun never sets and
information circles the globe constantly and almost instantaneously, so "all
that is solid" really does melt "into air," and people recognize that they have
few choices outside of meeting the demands of tighter schedules, as time
and space shrink within an increasingly ruthless and fiercely competitive
global marketplace.

Over the next six paragraphs, Marx illustrates graphically the tremendous change that modernity had already brought to the face of the globe
by the middle of the nineteenth century, as markets expanded, production improved, and modernity revolutionized the world in its own image.
Concentration, centralization, and increasingly rationalized production characterized this modern era. The bourgeoisie, Marx's argument confirms, was
rapidly becoming a new Promethean force in the history of humanity:

The bourgeoisie, during its rule of scarce one hundred years, has created
more massive and more colossal productive forces than have all preced-
ing generations together. Subjection of nature's forces to man, machinery,
application of chemistry to industry and agriculture, steam navigation,
railways, electric telegraphs, clearing of whole continents for cultivation,
canalization of rivers, whole populations conjured out of the ground—
what earlier century had even a presentiment that such productive forces
slumbered in the lap of social labour? (Marx and Engels [1848] 1934:14)

To this point in the text, the bourgeoisie seems all powerful—omnipotent. But, Marx continues, there are two forces that will undermine the power
of the bourgeoisie and take modernity in a different direction.

The first force is rooted in the economic relations of market-based society itself—contradictions within the mode of production. The bourgeoisie

initially arose within feudal society as the means of production and exchange began to change and feudal production was replaced by capitalist production. As the bourgeois order began to establish itself, feudal production, Marx argues, was "no longer compatible with the already developed productive forces" (Marx and Engels [1848] 1934:14). Feudal production became restrictive—an anachronism, "so many fetters":

> They had to be burst asunder; they were burst asunder.
>   Into their place stepped free competition, accompanied by a social and political constitution adapted in it, and the economic and political sway of the bourgeois class. (Marx and Engels [1848] 1934:14)

The essential features of feudal production were kings, lords, and aristocrats holding title to large tracts of land and the landless serfs or peasants who were tied to the land, working it in return for traditional protections and rights. The church guided and restricted behaviour, emphasizing the acceptance of toil in this life for the everlasting rewards in an afterlife. Wealth was accumulated in goods through plunder and war; the manor's production met immediate needs alone. The key features of feudal production were its heavy reliance on tradition and its enduring stability.

Capitalist production was completely different—it centred on "wage-labour," and its goal was the pursuit of unlimited financial wealth. The pursuit of (potentially) unrestricted wealth introduced a totally new dynamic—one that would require continual improvements in the speed of production and the sale of goods, with capital augmenting itself through turnover during every cycle.

Peasants who had left the manor and found refuge in the emerging cities were freed from their feudal obligations, but, to survive, they had to sell the one good they had to exchange on the market—their ability to do work (their labour power). Capitalists with sufficient resources to own implements of production (tools and, eventually, machines) and to purchase raw materials could also hire wage workers to produce goods for the market. So an entirely new mode of production—a new economic foundation to society—emerged, and it revolved around the sale and purchase of free wage labour and the pursuit of profit. Wealth was created by the profit—or surplus value—workers produced as they laboured in factories, and the accumulation of money became the central motive force within the economy (Dobb 1947; Marx [1890] 1976:270–80, 873–95). Although this new mode of production created wonders—it too, according to Marx's analysis, had its own dynamic and set of contradictions:

Modern bourgeois society, with its relations of production, of exchange
and of property, a society that has conjured up such gigantic means of
production and of exchange, is like the sorcerer who is no longer able
to control the powers of the nether world whom he has called up by his
spells. For many a decade past, the history of industry and commerce is
but the history of the revolt of modern productive forces against modern
conditions of production, against the property relations that are the conditions for the existence of the bourgeoisie and of its rule. It is enough to
mention the commercial crises that, by their periodical return, put the
existence of the entire bourgeois society on trial, each time more threat-
eningly. In these crises, a great part not only of the existing products, but
also of the previously created productive forces, is periodically destroyed.
In these crises, there breaks out an epidemic that, in all earlier epochs,
would have seemed an absurdity—the epidemic of over-production.
Society suddenly finds itself put back into a state of momentary barbarism; it appears as if a famine, a universal war of devastation, had cut off
the supply of every means of subsistence; industry and commerce seem
to be destroyed. And why? Because there is too much civilisation, too
much means of subsistence, too much industry, too much commerce. The
productive forces at the disposal of society no longer tend to further the
development of the conditions of bourgeois property; on the contrary,
they have become too powerful for these conditions, by which they are
fettered, and so soon as they overcome these fetters, they bring disorder
into the whole of bourgeois society, endanger the existence of bourgeois
property. The conditions of bourgeois society are too narrow to comprise
the wealth created by them. And how does the bourgeoisie get over these
crises? On the one hand, by enforced destruction of a mass of productive
forces; on the other, by the conquest of new markets, and by the more
thorough exploitation of the old ones. That is to say, by paving the way
for more extensive and more destructive crises, and by diminishing the
means whereby crises are prevented.

The weapons with which the bourgeoisie felled feudalism to the
ground are now turned against the bourgeoisie itself. (Marx and Engels
[1848] 1934:14–5)

There are few more accurate, graphic descriptions of the dynamic, ever-
expanding nature of modernity: growing production that results in overproduction, increasing productive power that escapes from the sorcerer
and pulls everything helplessly along into its swirling orbit, the conquest of
new markets creating a brief respite before giving way to even greater crises.

In the *Manifesto* of 1848, Marx argues that, already, the dynamic of modernity has created more than its own, internally generated crises—it has also "forged the weapons that bring death to itself; it has also called into existence the men who are to wield those weapons—the modern working class—the proletarians" (p. 15).

Over the next five paragraphs, Marx sketches the dynamic of modernity and indicates how it produced the force that will oppose the bourgeoisie. Wage workers must find work, and, as modern industry develops, they are brought together in increasingly larger factories where they are reduced to mere appendages of the machines that run endlessly; "as the use of machinery and division of labour increases, in the same proportion the burden of toil also increases" through longer working hours and the increased speed of the machinery. By building the factory system, modern industry "has converted the little workshop of the patriarchal master into the great factory of the industrial capitalist," Marx writes:

> Masses of labourers, crowded into the factory, are organised like soldiers. As privates of the industrial army, they are placed under the command of a perfect hierarchy of officers and sergeants. Not only are they slaves of the bourgeois class, and of the bourgeois state; they are daily and hourly enslaved by the machine, by the over-looker, and, above all, by the individual bourgeois manufacturer himself. The more openly this despotism proclaims gain to be its end and aim, the more petty, the more hateful and the more embittering it is. (Marx and Engels [1848] 1934:16)

Marx uses the next section of the *Manifesto* (10 paragraphs) to indicate the dynamics within the capitalist mode of production that turned the workers, who initially struggled against capital as individuals, into a unified, powerful class that grew in size and in political power as its grievances mounted (Marx and Engels [1848] 1934:16–7). With the development of industry, Marx argues,

> the proletariat not only increases in number; it becomes concentrated in greater masses, its strength grows, and it feels that strength more. The various interests and conditions of life within the ranks of the proletariat are more and more equalised, in proportion as machinery obliterates all distinctions of labour, and nearly everywhere reduces wages to the same low level. The growing competition among the bourgeois, and the resulting commercial crises, make the wages of the workers ever more fluctuating. The increasing improvement of machinery, ever more rapidly developing, makes their livelihood more and more precarious; the collisions between

individual workmen and individual bourgeois take more and more the character of collisions between two classes. Thereupon, the workers begin to form combinations (trade unions) against the bourgeois; they club together in order to keep up the rate of wages; they found permanent associations in order to make provision beforehand for these occasional revolts. Here and there, the contest breaks out into riots. (Marx and Engels [1848] 1934:17)

Marx has now set the stage for the two titans of the modern world to face one another, and, although dynamics can obscure this conflict, he suggests that the overall relationship between capital and wage labour is one of growing antagonism and polarization and that time will see the increasing consolidation of power within the working class. At this point, Marx argues, not only will the proletariat grow in strength, but the forces of right and justice will grow along with it:

All previous historical movements were movements of minorities, or in the interest of minorities. The proletarian movement is the self-conscious, independent movement of the immense majority, in the interest of the immense majority. The proletariat, the lowest stratum of our present society, cannot stir, cannot raise itself up, without the whole superincumbent strata of official society being sprung into the air. (Marx and Engels [1848] 1934:19)

Even though its mandate is the universal emancipation of humankind from class rule, the revolutionary struggles of the working class, according to Marx, will begin in national struggles—"The proletariat of each country must, of course, first of all settle matters with its own bourgeoisie" (Marx and Engels [1848] 1934:20). Ironically, in the pursuit of its own narrow economic interests, in following the imperatives of market-based society, the bourgeoisie had produced the class that would, on the basis of those same dynamics, grow to not only oppose it but ultimately overthrow it.

The essential conditions for the existence and for the sway of the bourgeois class is the formation and augmentation of capital; the condition for capital is wage-labour. Wage-labour rests exclusively on competition between the labourers. The advance of industry, whose involuntary promoter is the bourgeoisie, replaces the isolation of the labourers, due to competition, by the revolutionary combination, due to association. The development of Modern Industry, therefore, cuts from under its feet the very foundation on which the bourgeoisie produces and appropriates products. What the bourgeoisie therefore produces, above all, are its own grave-diggers. Its fall and the victory of the proletariat are equally inevitable. (Marx and Engels [1848] 1934:20)

The Manifesto and Sociology

As a sociological analysis, the *Manifesto* is a groundbreaking text for four reasons. First, the *Manifesto* presents a version of one of Marx's most important contributions to sociology—the argument that social formations and social history can be best understood by carefully examining their real, material social relations. Focusing upon, gathering information about, and studying social processes is now so central to sociology that it is hard to believe that this approach once had to be asserted—but in the mid-nineteenth century, there were still a number of competing and very different approaches to the study of various social formations.

The power of speculative philosophy had to be challenged, and social theorists such as Marx did so, arguing that ideas did not create social formations nor were societies the actualization of ideas as they came into being. Instead, every social formation was the product of real human activity. Societies were the larger product of the interaction patterns of individuals that constituted and reconstituted social relationships of a relatively enduring nature.

Second, Marx goes further in the *Manifesto* than simply saying that one must focus on the material conditions of a social formation to study it properly. He presents an argument that he will later outline in his 1859 preface to *Towards a Critique of Political Economy*—it is the economic infrastructure of society upon which one should most carefully focus. The significant emphasis Marx places upon the determining role of the economic infrastructure has led to extensive debate in the social sciences. Irrespective of where sociologists finally fall in this debate—whether they think Marx overly emphasizes the centrality of the economy in shaping the power relationships that tend to constitute social relationships and social formations more generally—it was within the Communist League's congresses and in writing the *Manifesto* that Marx first successfully established this position in a public forum.

Third, consistent with his focus upon the economic infrastructure, Marx identifies class struggle as one of the major motive forces of history. Marx was not the first to emphasize the class nature of bourgeois society, nor was he the only one to see class struggle as an inherent dynamic in social relationships, social formations, and social history. But the idea that major social change occurs through class struggle is firmly associated with his name, his theoretical position, and his approach to social analysis. The main reason for that association is the *Communist Manifesto*. When questioned in March 1852 about his major contributions to the working class movement, Marx replied,

[N]o credit is due to me for discovering the existence of classes in society or the struggle between them. Long before me bourgeois historians had described the historical development of this class struggle and bourgeois economists, the economic nature of the classes. What I did that was new was to prove:

(1) that the *existence of classes* is only bound up with *particular historical phases in the development of production,*

(2) that the class struggle necessarily leads to the dictatorship of the proletariat,

(3) that this dictatorship itself only constitutes the transition to the *abolition of all classes* and to a *classless society.*[49] (Marx and Engels 1955:69)

The final contribution that Marx makes to sociology in the *Manifesto* is a somewhat contradictory yet vitally important one. Marx identifies two forces that will overturn bourgeois society—the internal contradictions of the economic infrastructure (Marx and Engels [1848] 1934:14–5) and the "men who are to wield those weapons [that will bring about the death of the bourgeoisie]—the modern working class—the proletarians" (p. 15). Many commentators on Marx have focused on the economic contradictions of bourgeois society as the major source of social change, but, in the *Manifesto* and elsewhere, Marx also emphasizes the "subjective" side of social change—the development of class consciousness and the desire on the part of classes to make change.

For Marx, the capitalist mode of production had its contradictions and internal dynamic, but change would not occur without real men and women acting and creating change. Yes, capitalist production brought workers together in unprecedented numbers within single factories, often located in large cities; it created working conditions that led to numerous grievances; it provided the opportunity for workers to develop their own understandings

---

49 In that same letter, Marx writes the following: "Finally, if I were you, I should tell the democratic gents *en général* that they would do better to acquaint themselves with bourgeois literature before they venture to yap at its opponents. For instance they should study the historical works of [Augustin] Thierry, [François] Guizot, John Wade and so forth, in order to enlighten themselves as to the past 'history of the classes.' They should acquaint themselves with the fundamentals of political economy before attempting to criticise the critique of political economy. For example, one need only open Ricardo's *magnum opus* to find, on the first page, the words with which he begins his preface: 'The produce of the earth—all that is derived from its surface by the united application of labour, machinery, and capital, is divided among *three classes* of the community; namely the proprietor of the land, the owner of the stock or capital necessary for its cultivation, and the labourers by whose industry it is cultivated'" (Marx and Engels 1955:68).

and interpretations of the world; and it provided the opportunity for them to press for social change. Still, although it is often overlooked, the interpretive role of human agents, who collectively pursue the goals they see as important within the context of their particular historical and social location, is central to Marx's sociological perspective.

Marx fully expected a revolutionary transformation of European society in the 1840s—he believed it would happen because the material conditions of existence for workers were such that they would want to rebel; they would want to change society in radical ways to their benefit. Marx also believed, based on his own lived experiences, that workers would develop a revolutionary consciousness, and this consciousness, coupled with a desire for change created from within their everyday lives, would lead them to action. The role of human understanding—how people grasp the world around them—*is* part of Marx's sociological insight, although he does not spend much time developing this aspect of his sociological understanding of industrial capitalist society.

Thus, the *Manifesto* also reflects the core ethos of the Enlightenment, as Marx carries it forward in his work—the themes of freedom, mastery, and progress reverberate throughout the document. History, as Marx presents it, is a continuous dialectic of progress, until freedom from exploitation and class division is gained through the ongoing struggle. As soon as the bourgeoisie established its mastery over the remnants of the feudal aristocracy, it began to create the conditions from which it would be challenged by a class that represents the universal interests of humanity rather than partial, class interests. The material conditions of capitalism, Marx argues, create the circumstances under which the proletariat will gain the political will and material means to transform society and move it forward to a higher level of universal development. In the *Manifesto*, then, Marx brings freedom, mastery, and progress together with the French Revolution's themes of liberty, equality, and fraternity to form a striking and inspiring synthesis.

On the basis of this discussion of Marx's work, it is clear how much Mills's conception of the sociological imagination draws from Marx, although there are important differences in emphasis. To begin with, Mills (1959) argues that the sociological imagination involves the intersection of biography with the history of the social structure. Marx's position is very similar, although it would be more accurate to state that, for Marx, the intersection of the history of the social structure with the biography of social classes is the critical aspect. In both cases, however, the objective dimensions of society (the social relationships that are constituted and reconstituted), the subjective dimensions of society (the human agents who constitute social relationships and seek to maintain or change them), and their intersection within a specific socio-historical context must all be taken into account for a sociological study to meet its task and promise. Both Marx and Mills can be described as holistic thinkers who were extremely aware of the dynamic tensions and contradictions that existed in the social formations they studied and criticized.

Second, both Marx and Mills wrote from the vantage point of the societies in which they lived and concentrated on the social formations they wanted to examine. Consequently, Marx focused on the early industrializing period of capitalist society in western Europe. His work emphasizes the dramatic changes that occurred in the nature of the political economy in England, France, and Germany as industrial capitalism swept aside the remnants of feudal power, privilege, tradition, and governance. Marx wrote when a variety of social critics—socialists, anarchists, and liberal reformers, for example, as well as reactionary, conservative traditionalists and Christian reformers—were intensely engaged in exposing the problems inherent in market-based society and proposing a variety of solutions that would alter civil society fundamentally. Chief among those proposals was the redistribution of property or an alternative form of ownership and control of the productive forces in society and the results of social production.

The point in time and, as a result, the nature of the social formation about which Mills wrote were different in key ways, even though some of the fundamental aspects of capitalist society still prevailed in North America and western Europe during the mid-twentieth century. The social product of 1950s Canada, the United States, and western Europe was far greater than it had been in 1848. The absolute standard of living of wage workers and the conditions under which they laboured were far better in the world Mills inhabited in 1955 than the one Engels ([1845] 1975) described in 1845. Most important, the composition of the labour force had changed by the mid-twentieth century, the perceived routes that workers had for ameliorating their working conditions and life chances were different, and their commitment to political change had altered as the strata of white-collar workers grew absolutely and proportionately in North America and western Europe. Three of Mills's most important studies—*New Men of Power: America's Labor Leaders* (1948), *White Collar* (1951), and *The Power Elite* (1956)—all addressed these changes (see also Mills 1963).

The most significant difference between Marx's socio-political world and the one Mills addressed, however, was the threat of thermonuclear war, the "immediate causes" of which lay "in the fearful symmetry of the cold warriors on either side: an act of one aggravates the other; the other reacts, in turn aggravating the one" (Mills 1958:9). Behind those apparent immediate causes were intermediate causes although the "ultimate causes" were, according to Mills, "part of the very shaping of world history in the 20th century." But despite this enormous change in the global power structure—indeed partly because of it—Mills championed the classical tradition and its particular sociological imagination as the way to understand events in order to change them. Furthermore, as Mills (1962) maintains in *The Marxists*, the sociological imagination is heavily indebted to Marx—his empirical work and his conceptual grasp of capitalist society.

Consequently, Marx cannot be ignored if one wants to deepen one's grasp of the sociological imagination and of the classical tradition in sociology, Mills (1962) argues: "Many of those who reject (or more accurately, ignore) Marxist ways of thinking about human affairs are actually rejecting the classic traditions of their own disciplines" (p. 10). At the same time, Mills (1962) maintains that there is no longer any "'marxist social science' of any intellectual consequence" either:

There is just—social science: without the work of Marx and other marxists, it would not be what it is today; with their work alone, it would not be nearly as good as it happens to be. No one who does not come to grips with the ideas of marxism can be an adequate social scientist; no one who believes that marxism contains the last word can be one either. Is there any doubt about this after Max Weber, Thorstein Veblen, Karl Mannheim—to mention only three? We do now have ways—better than Marx's alone—of studying and understanding man, society, and history, but the work of these three is quite unimaginable without his work. (P. 11)

In addition to Weber, Veblen, and Mannheim, Mills could have mentioned Émile Durkheim although Mills was highly critical of the path that many sociologists had taken on the basis of the positivist dimensions of Durkheim's work. Durkheim's contributions will be the focus of the next chapter, but, before turning to Durkheim, let us reflect on one of Mills's suggestions in the *Images of Man: The Classic Tradition in Sociological Thinking*—the sociological frame of reference can begin with "the acquisition of a vocabulary that is adequate for clear social reflection," a vocabulary that involves only 20 or so pivotal terms (Mills 1960:17). With regard to Marx, what might be his most pivotal contribution to that vocabulary?

MARX AND A VOCABULARY FOR CLEAR SOCIAL REFLECTION

On the basis of the material presented in this chapter, we can identify several pivotal terms from Marx that enable "clear social reflection"—"economic infrastructure," "proletariat," "revolution," or "materialism" are all excellent candidates. As we read more of Marx's work, the terms "alienation," "the labour process," "the labour theory of value," and "the fetishism of the commodity" present themselves as possible contenders. But, if we have to choose only one concept at this moment, the best one might be *Klassenkampf* (class struggle), and several reasons recommend it as a key Marxian contribution to sociological vocabulary.   *CLASS STRUGGLE*

First, the term *Klassenkampf* (class struggle) is widely associated with Marx and with his most celebrated revolutionary pamphlet—the *Communist Manifesto*. "The history of all hitherto existing societies is the history of class struggles," Marx provocatively writes in the first section of his rallying cry to the proletariat (Marx and Engels [1848] 1934:10).

As a term that is popularly associated with Marx, "class struggle" serves to remind us that the popular, often superficial familiarity with Marx's work is frequently very uninformed and misleading. Therefore, it is not just the term but also the term and its full meaning that should be kept in mind. To do this, we must think of class struggle within the full context of Marx's work (after all, Marx took no credit "for discovering the existence of classes in society or the struggle between them" [Marx and Engels 1955:69]). Properly understood, class struggle suggests at least seven aspects to Marx's work that are both critical to his sociology and important contributions to the classical tradition.

First, the notion of class clearly indicates that social change centres on the actions of many people—not individuals. Second, the notion of class struggle also emphasizes that groups pushing for social change are located in particular, objective locations within the social whole. The working class exists as a class of wage workers that will struggle for change due to the particular way in which the means of social production are distributed and controlled. Third, class struggle simultaneously reminds us that there is a subjective element to social change—a particular class consciousness within human agents must develop before they will push for change (revolutionary change or reform). Fourth, the notion of struggle and class struggle bring to the fore Marx's belief that social formations are dynamic, unstable, contradictory, dialectical wholes. At the same time, that realization reminds us that Marx's work, although powerful and insightful, was never completed to his satisfaction; Marx did not finish his project, and, as Mills (1962:11) emphasizes, Marx's work is neither the definitive word in sociological analysis nor the definitive contribution to the classical tradition.

The term itself—especially in its German original, *Klassenkampf*—appears, initially at least, as precise and provocative, but it is really suggestive of several forms of conflict. *Kampf* is clearly "struggle," but the notion of struggle (particularly in German) carries a range of meaning that stretches from combat to strife and even to a simple encounter. This potential ambiguity is important within the overall context of Marx's work as a sociologist because it reminds us that he was fully aware of the different forms that class struggle could take at varying points in time under changing social conditions with differing objective outcomes in view. That is the fifth point: *Klassenkampf* is provocative but also nuanced, which is how Marx's work should be understood.

Sixth, class struggle, as an objectively based aspect of social change, takes the sociologist directly into the economic infrastructure of society, which is, according to Marx, the correct departure point for a critique of political economy and the basis for a truly critical social analysis. The economic infrastructure is more than simply the relationship between the physical means of production and the social relations of production (the property relations or class relations); the economic infrastructure involves real and living working men and women as one component of the means of production, the conditions under which they work, and their growing consciousness of those conditions in association with the social relations of production. It is the subtle ways in which class consciousness develops and is directed within the context of specific relations of property ownership that is fundamental to Marx's overall analysis of capitalist society and to his conception of class struggle.

Finally—although this list could be extended much further—*Klassenkampf* reminds us of the impact that the Enlightenment had upon Marx's work. According to Marx, freedom—freedom from exploitation—increases as the working class recognizes and masters the circumstances in which it is located and then engages in the political struggle to overcome them. Progress towards greater freedom, equality, and human fulfilment were Marx's major objectives, and *Klassenkampf* encapsulates the Enlightenment aspect of Marx's project very well.

Although other terms from Marx contribute to our understanding of social relations and processes, "class struggle" is an important one to incorporate into a vocabulary "adequate for clear social reflection"; it enhances intellectual craftsmanship and helps stimulate the sociological imagination.

Use last 2 pages as outline

5 FROM DESCARTES TO DURKHEIM: TOWARDS A SCIENCE OF SOCIETY

The second key figure within the classical tradition is Émile Durkheim. Although Comte named the discipline "sociology," Durkheim is justifiably considered the principal founder of sociology as an empirical discipline. Durkheim secured sociology's first foothold in higher education when he established the Department of Sociology at the University of Bordeaux in 1895 and began, a year later, the publication of the first sociology journal— *L'Année sociologique*—and he also dedicated his career to demonstrating the unique nature and strengths of the empirically based, systematic study of society. *Les régles de la methode sociologique* (*The Rules of Sociological Method*), which Durkheim published in 1895, charted a new, formal path for the study of the social world—not one without controversy, to be sure, but Durkheim's work was clearly central to the future directions of sociology as a discipline.

Born in Épinal, France in 1858, Durkheim had a life and academic career that were far more tumultuous, contested, and controversial than most commentators have indicated. For example, some speak or write dismissively of the "dead, white, European males" (the DWEMs) who founded sociology (the usual reference is to Marx, Weber, and Durkheim, but it could include others). They write as though the DWEMs all lived similar lives, as if they were all privileged patriarchs, securely established in the dominant class, maintaining and reproducing the system that gave them their advantages. Durkheim would have had great difficulty reconciling his personal or academic life with that characterization (Peyre 1960).

Far from being a member of the ruling elite, Durkheim was marginalized as a member of the Jewish minority within a country and educational system that the Roman Catholic Church dominated. Durkheim experienced anti-Semitism in a number of overt and subtle ways, and his social standing was frequently fragile and uncertain.

Durkheim experienced one particularly painful period in his life. His son André, once a student under Durkheim at the Sorbonne and on his way to becoming his father's intellectual collaborator, was conscripted into the army and killed in action on the Bulgarian front during World War I in the spring of 1915 (Lukes 1973:555). A very short while later, due to Durkheim's religious affiliation, his residency in France was challenged and the ensuing senate debate was covered in the daily newspapers. In January 1916, *Libre parole* called him "a Boche with a false nose"—a phrase combining an offensive slang term for a German with blatant anti-Semitism—and accused him of being a Jewish collaborator with the German war effort (Lukes 1973:557).

But Durkheim was resilient, and, as Lukes's (1973:99–102) extensive biography indicates, Durkheim pursued his intellectual labours within a caring, supportive extended family environment. Durkheim was not an exclusionary, dominating patriarch. Along with his wife Louise (née Dreyfus), his son André, his daughter Marie, various nephews (the most famous of whom was Marcel Mauss), and other friends and colleagues, Durkheim worked collaboratively on the advancement of sociology as they edited, proofed, and kept *L'Année sociologique* going in its early years. The deaths in World War I of several friends and supporters who had worked in the Durkheim household were deep personal losses and had a devastating impact upon French sociology because the household's work had become such a shared undertaking.[50]

Jeffrey Alexander (1986) emphasizes that Durkheim came into maturity "in the crucible of the formation of the Third Republic in France" (p. 94). That experience helped Durkheim crystallize some particular concerns and issues that he explored throughout his career as a sociologist. Durkheim recognized that French society had to change if it were to become more stable; he believed that stability would only come with greater social justice (particularly in the distribution of economic product). He also thought that the state needed to be restructured to ensure greater justice but that this restructuring should not occur at the expense of individual freedom. "Durkheim," Alexander (1986) notes, "described these goals as socialism, but he insisted, to use contemporary terms, that this be socialism with a voluntaristic or human face" (p. 94).

---

50 The impact of war on French sociology extended into World War II when the Nazis invaded Paris, forcing Marie to flee and leave behind all of Durkheim's books and manuscripts, which the occupying forces destroyed (Meštrović 1988).

Similarly, Durkheim's intellectual struggles have been largely overlooked in most of the standard accounts of his work as a sociologist. Part of the reason is the extremely influential presentation and interpretation of Durkheim's work in the magnum opus of Talcott Parsons (1949)—*The Structure of Social Action*. In critiquing utilitarian theory and individualist accounts of social action—one of the main objectives of *The Structure of Social Action* and a perspective Parsons actually shares with Durkheim—Parsons (1949:352–5) emphasizes the holistic, functionalist, organic, and positivist dimensions of Durkheim's work at the expense of the more historically and empirically based accounts of the dynamic tensions in social life, accounts that Durkheim addressed from his first review essays in 1885 through to *Les formes élémentaire de la vie religieuse* (*The Elementary Forms of the Religious Life*) of 1912.[51]

Parsons's interpretation was so dominant partly because of the stature Parsons and his work held in the post–World War II period and also because of the limited range of Durkheim's work available in English translation. Additionally, although Durkheim's key studies—*De la division du travail social* (*The Division of Labour in Society*; [1893] 1902), *Les régles de la methode sociologique* (*The Rules of Sociological Method*; [1895] 1912, [1895] 1938), *Le suicide* (*Suicide*; [1897] 1951, [1897] 1983), and *Les formes élémentaire de la vie religieuse* (*The Elementary Forms of the Religious Life*; 1912, [1912] 1915)— were all published during his lifetime, a number of additional works were published posthumously, which further constrained sociologists' exposure to his ideas. *Sociologie et philosophie* (*Sociology and Philosophy*; [1924] 1953, [1924] 1969), *L'éducation morale* (*Moral Education*; 1925), *Le socialisme; sa definition, ses debuts, la doctrine saint-simonienne* (*Socialism: Its Definition, Goals and the Doctrine of Saint-Simon*; [1928] 1958, [1928] 1971), *L'évolution pédagogique en France* (*The Evolution of Educational Thought in France*; [1938] 1969, [1938] 1977), *Leçons de sociologie: physique des moeurs et du droit* (Sociology Lessons: The Physics of Morals and the Law; 1950), *Pragmatisme et sociologie* (*Pragmatism and Sociology*; 1955, [1955] 1983), and *Durkheim's Philosophy Lectures* (2004) were not available until much later in the twentieth century, and none of them was translated until after Parsons's book had already become one of the most influential studies in North American sociology.

These additions to Durkheim's published work are critical because they allow scholars to appreciate the development of Durkheim's ideas more fully and to understand some of the important struggles—as well as the reasons for them—that he went through in sharpening his conception of sociology. Far from following a simple, internally driven developmental progression,

---

51 For more on the nature and impact of early North American interpretations of Durkheim, see Alexander (1986:91–3) and Giddens (1972:38–48). Compare with Parsons (1949:301–450, 1968).

Durkheim's work evolved through its author's active engagement with the social and intellectual environment.

Although French thought from Descartes through Montesquieu and Rousseau to Saint-Simon and Comte was the primary influence in Durkheim's work, he also drew critically from other traditions and perspectives. One such focal point is the individualist theory of the English utilitarians and their instrumental, rationalist explanations for the emergence of collective order. The social and the individual, Durkheim (1960:137) maintained throughout his career, are dissimilar, and sociology must focus on the way and extent to which the social creates a socialized individual rather than beginning with fictitious, isolated individuals and explaining society as the outcome of their individual, rational calculation. Opposition to the utilitarians' individualist explanations of social interaction and of the emergence of social relations, then, helped shape Durkheim's commitment to the notion of society as a pre-existing, *sui generis* entity into which individuals are born, an entity that socializes the individual.

In a similar manner, Durkheim criticized the materialist reductionism of the orthodox Marxists. The social whole cannot, Durkheim maintained in opposition to the growing influence of various Marxist positions in France, be reduced to the instrumental rationality of economic man. Nor is the superstructure simply a direct, automatic reflection of the economic infrastructure. Durkheim placed far more emphasis on the role of ideas and of the collective consciousness than did the orthodox Marxists of his day.

Finally, as explanations of how societies are held together, Durkheim rejected the ahistorical and metaphysically based arguments of the idealist holists, such as Hegel, or of those proposing a universal moral imperative, such as Kant. Rather than following the philosophers' attempts to discover a single, absolute criterion of morality—Hegel's absolute reason or Kant's categorical imperative, for example—and using it as a measuring rod for different societies in history, Durkheim argues that one must start with the complex moral rules that actually exist within a society and determine how these arose from particular social arrangements. Morality, cohesiveness, and solidarity are all, in Durkheim's view, created within a social whole.

In view of his debates with various intellectual traditions, the central thread running through Durkheim's work is his struggle to reconcile the valid point that "society always embodies collective ideals which surpass the experience and activities of the individual" with the equally valid point that "in the course of social development, traditional values seem to become increasingly dissolved," creating an increased individuation of the members within contemporary society that allows each individual greater and greater freedom (Giddens 1972:2).

Before focusing directly on Durkheim, this chapter will highlight some of the key elements within French social thought that influenced Durkheim's particular approach to sociology. What becomes most apparent in such an overview is the extent to which Durkheim accepted some aspects of earlier French social thinkers while also sharply rejecting others—forcing him to clarify exactly what an empirical social science would involve.

DESCARTES AND MONTESQUIEU

Descartes is a pivotal thinker in the early development of the empirical, observationally based social science that Durkheim advocated. Descartes wrote his *Discours de la méthode pour bien conduire sa raison et chercher la vérité dans les sciences* (*Discourse on the Method of Rightly Conducting the Reason and Seeking Truth in the Sciences*) in 1637 to establish firmly the basis for certain knowledge. His system of methodological scepticism begins by doubting anything that is not clearly true (Descartes 1911:92, [1637] 1966:47). In order for problems to be resolved properly and adequately, Descartes then argues, they should be divided into as many parts as necessary, and the analysis must begin with those elements that are the simplest and easiest to understand. Progressing to the more complex, the analysis must ensure that no possible explanations are overlooked or left out of consideration.

This *Discourse* was groundbreaking in the seventeenth century for four reasons. First, in opposition to the classical tradition in philosophy (the scholastic theology and church doctrine that had dominated the intellectual world since medieval times), Descartes shifts the focal point for the pursuit of true knowledge from metaphysical contemplation or religious doctrine to a method involving rigorous observation of the world. The foundation for certainty starts with rigorous deductive practices, according to Descartes, but those deductions then have to be tested through observation and the careful consideration of those observations. This standard for empirically based knowledge became central to Durkheim's aspirations for sociology as a scientific undertaking.

Second, Descartes' conception of method and his radical doubt cast all previous knowledge into question; unless knowledge is derived from rigorous deduction and observation, it cannot make any claim to certainty or truth. So all previously accepted truths about the natural or social world can no longer be accepted automatically simply because they existed or were supported by tradition or traditional beliefs. Descartes' method, then, undercuts tradition as the justification for existing ways of doing things and existing social and political relationships.

Third, Descartes' method firmly supported the then-emerging inductive methodologies of the natural sciences and maintained that the scientific method should apply to all forms of human knowledge in order for that knowledge to be reliable, unbiased, and certain.

Finally, Descartes' method positions critique as central to the scientific method—all claims must be open to scrutiny, criticism, and confirmation before they can be accepted as true.

Although other philosophers would refine Descartes' rules of method over the next two centuries, his philosophy was central in fundamentally changing the way scientists—natural and social—approached the gathering, synthesizing, and testing of knowledge from the mid-seventeenth century onwards. Descartes' method was also the thin edge of the wedge that ultimately divided philosophical thought from scientific thought. Because of Descartes' method, some social scientists came to believe that philosophy produces largely speculative knowledge that might serve as a source for hypotheses while science empirically tests hypotheses to develop positive knowledge that is highly, if not completely, certain. This distinction would lead some sociologists to argue that sociology could only develop further if it broke away from philosophy completely and pursued the systematic collection of "social facts" or empirical information.

Montesquieu is often identified as the first, genuine precursor of sociology—and for good reason. Although Montesquieu, like Hobbes before him and Rousseau who followed, was mainly concerned with forms of government, his approach to understanding the state and the social order is highly sociological—more sociological, in fact, than that of almost any other scholar of his day who attempted a systematic analysis of political or social issues. In fact, Durkheim (1960) argues that, although it is a mistake to link the birth of a science to a particular thinker—"since every science is the product of an unbroken chain of contributions and it is hard to say exactly when it came into existence"—it is Montesquieu "who first laid down the fundamental principles of social science" (p. 61).

Montesquieu came from a privileged background and was genuinely interested in the realm of ideas, the world of letters, and the various salons of eighteenth-century France. Montesquieu read widely, kept detailed notes from his readings, and genuinely sought to advance knowledge. Finally, he travelled extensively and used those opportunities to meet other men and women of letters as well as scientists and other scholars (Cohler 1989:xii–xviii).

Montesquieu's works include the *Lettres persanes* (*Persian Letters*; [1721] 1975) and *Considérations sur les causes de la grandeur des Romains, et de leur décadence* (*Considerations on the Causes of the Greatness of the Romans and their Decline*; [1734] 1968), but it is *De l'esprit des loix* (*The Spirit of the Laws*;

[1748] 1989) that represents the culmination of his life's work (Montesquieu [1748] 1989:xliii).[52] *The Spirit of the Laws* draws upon over 300 sources and contains 3,000 references and 2,000 notes. Although rich in insight, the text is poorly organized, lacks a coherent argument, and ranges over almost every domain of human behaviour and into questions of philosophical judgement, even though it claims to be a treatise on law. Despite those weaknesses, it was ground-breaking in several important respects.

First, *The Spirit of the Laws* was one of the most empirical works in social thought produced in the mid-eighteenth century. On the basis of his own observations or those found in the historical record, Montesquieu develops in the text several basic principles about how societies are governed. From these simple principles, he argues, one can virtually predict the histories of the nations under study. Laying this groundwork for an empirical approach to the study of social and political life, then, was Montesquieu's major contribution to sociology (Durkheim 1960:3–24).

In *The Spirit of the Laws*, Montesquieu classifies societies on the basis of how they are governed, and he identifies three types—despotic governments, monarchies, and republics (which can take an aristocratic or a democratic form). Each form of government is characterized by a "nature" and a "principle." "He derives these three types not from any a priori principle [as Aristotle did]," Durkheim (1960) notes, "but from a comparison of the societies known to him from his study of history, from travellers' accounts, and from his own travels" (p. 25).

The "nature" of government refers to who (or what group) holds sovereign power—a despot, a king, or a legislative body—while the "principle" refers to the passion or spirit that animates those who govern. Fear is the principle of despotism; honour the principle of monarchy; and virtue the principle of a republic. Good governments, Montesquieu concludes after more than two decades of research, have a nature and principle that are consistent with the dominant spirit of the people who make up the society as a whole.

Although many of his arguments are difficult to accept today, Montesquieu's work has sociological import because it breaks down the social whole into its component parts and then examines how they work together to produce a whole that is greater than the simple sum of its parts. To comprehend the laws of a society fully, he maintains, one has to see them as part of a larger system within which they serve a particular purpose. In

---

52 In a letter written in the same year that *The Spirit of the Laws* was published, Montesquieu notes, "I can say that I have worked on it my whole life: I was given some law books when I left my *collège*; I sought their spirit, I worked, but I did nothing worthwhile. I discovered my principles twenty years ago: they are quite simple; anyone else working as hard as I did would have done better. But I swear this book nearly killed me; I am going to rest now; I shall work no more" (quoted by Cohler 1989:xi; see also Montesquieu [1748] 1989: xlv). *The Spirit of the Laws* was his last book.

order to do that, one has to understand the different parts of a social system as they and the system itself develop over time. This, in turn, means that one has to examine the system's underling causes—both physical and moral.

According to Montesquieu's *The Spirit of the Laws,* physical causes—for example, the climate, terrain, and population density—play a role in a social system's development, but moral causes are of much greater importance because they shape a society's spirit. Building his argument on the basis of historical material drawn from Roman, Chinese, and European history, Montesquieu argues that this spirit grows out of a society's dominant religion, its laws, maxims, mores, customs, styles of thought, and the atmosphere in a nation's capital or court (Montesquieu [1748] 1989:308–33, especially p. 310). Law, in Montesquieu's analysis, is only one way of controlling people's conduct—which makes Montesquieu among the first to focus upon mechanisms of social control other than the power of a centralized state or government.

Four aspects of Montesquieu's approach set him apart from Hobbes and Rousseau and were influential in Durkheim's conception of sociology. First, Montesquieu places a heavy emphasis on the importance of empirical observation in the study of societies. Although contemporary sociologists might think that his claim to have developed his principles from "the nature of things themselves" is overstated, there is a far greater empirical basis to his work than one finds in that of other social and political thinkers of this period. In conjunction with the work of Saint-Simon and Comte, this would become a central feature of Durkheim's sociology.

Second, Montesquieu bases his holistic approach to the study of forms of government and the laws regulating human action on a unique analysis of more basic social processes—customs, mores, and styles of thought. Durkheim also adopts a holistic approach to understanding social phenomena, drawing in a similar manner upon customs, mores, and styles of thought to serve as the key indicators of a social formation.

Third, Montesquieu's notion of the spirit of a society resonates strongly with Durkheim's concept of the *conscience collective* (collective conscience and consciousness). Both Montesquieu and Durkheim see this spirit or consciousness developing within the social whole and also changing as the social formation and the relationships among individuals change.

Finally, in *The Division of Labor in Society,* Durkheim ([1893] 1933) focuses upon two different types of law—repressive and restitutive—to serve as indicators of which form of social solidarity, mechanical or organic, dominates within a social formation. Montesquieu created the basis for that undertaking by linking the nature of laws within a society to the spirit of the society as a whole. Durkheim did not fully agree with Montesquieu's analysis, but he certainly profited from Montesquieu's approach.

SAINT-SIMON AND *THE INDUSTRIAL SYSTEM*

Claude Henri de Rouvroy, comte de Saint-Simon is one of the more interesting and tragic figures in sociology.[53] Saint-Simon lived through the French Revolution and its turbulent aftermath. As a result, he experienced and felt, at first hand, the powerful optimism of the French *philosophes'* Enlightenment rationalism, he believed in progress, and he shared the hope that the French monarchy's demise and the fall of French feudalism would usher in a new era of human freedom. But the Reign of Terror (September 1793 to July 1794) left Saint-Simon deeply concerned with the problem of social order in the post-feudal era.[54]

Saint-Simon's works parallel, to a large extent, his personal and intellectual fortunes and misfortunes. These works include *Lettres d'un habitant de Genève* (*Letters from an Inhabitant of Geneva*), first published in 1802; *Mémoire sur la science de l'homme* (*Memoir on the Science of Humankind*) and *Travail sur la gravitation universelle* (*A Work on Universal Gravitation*), two manuscripts from 1813; *Réorganisation de la société Européene* (*The Reorganization of European Society*), a booklet written with Augustin Thierry in 1814; his contributions to the periodicals *L'industrie* between 1816 and 1818, *L'Organisateur* between 1819 and 1820, *Du système industriel* (*The Industrial System*) between 1821 and 1822), and *Catéchisme des industriels* (*The Catechism of Industry*) between 1823 and 1824; and, finally, his book *De l'organisation sociale* (*On Social Organization*; [1825] 1964) and his unfinished *Nouveau Christianisme* (*The New Christianity*). Saint-Simon's writings are extremely broad in scope, and, although he left no genuinely enduring work, his legacy is one of intriguing insights that led later thinkers in many directions. Saint-Simon is best regarded as a catalyst for those who came afterwards.

From 1800 to 1813, Saint-Simon was primarily concerned with the unity of knowledge based on Newton's law of gravitation—the clearest example of scientific thought in Saint-Simon's estimation. In 1814, Saint-Simon turned to issues of social organization, and his work *The Reorganization of European*

---

53 The material on Saint-Simon's biography presented here is based on Markham (1964) and Taylor (1975), but see also Durkheim ([1928] 1958:82–9).

54 *La Terreur* (The Reign of Terror) was a period of brutal repression that followed the Jacobins' seizure of power in June 1793. (The Jacobins constituted a powerful political force in the French Revolution.) The Jacobin-controlled Convention passed "the Law of Suspects," which permitted arrest for any "crime against liberty." The Jacobins terrorized their domestic enemies using the guillotine to display publicly the revolutionary government's power.

Society drew considerable, positive attention. From 1816 to 1825, Saint-Simon considered the coming of industrial society, what its structure would be like and the implications it had for the future of humanity. This period culminated in *On Social Organization*. Finally, Saint-Simon's unfinished *New Christianity* aimed to establish a new sense of religiosity, one appropriate to an industrial society and able to constitute the cohesive force that religions had provided throughout human history.

Saint-Simon's contributions to the development of sociology are numerous, and they were important for Durkheim. First and foremost, Saint-Simon championed the development of an empirically based science of society (Durkheim [1928] 1958:90–109). Following Montesquieu, Saint-Simon's work, and that of his successors, reinforced the break from metaphysical and speculative social thought and affirmed the use of an empirical, scientifically inspired approach to the study of society. Although he never developed the idea systematically, Saint-Simon sought to establish a "social physics" that would eventually lay out the laws of social development. These laws would be complemented by his "social physiology," which would focus on the scientific study of human interaction. Both of these concepts were catalysts in the development of what would emerge as a sociology that sought to employ the same methodology as the natural sciences.

Second, Saint-Simon's emerging sociology was heavily influenced by conservative thinkers such as the Marquis de Condorcet and Louis de Bonald. In his *Letters from an Inhabitant of Geneva*, Saint-Simon uses the structure of medieval society as his enduring reference point. According to Saint-Simon, medieval society was comprised of different orders, which were arranged in an important, functional hierarchy that eliminated all class conflict. At the base, there were the producers (the feudal serfs) who were coordinated by a ruling, or temporal, elite (the nobility), and the entire society was integrated by the spiritual elite—the Roman Catholic Church.

These three orders—the spiritual elite, the governing elite (or temporal elite), and the productive classes—became the template for Saint-Simon's conception of both social structure and the evolutionary development of societies through history (Saint-Simon 1975:70–7). This conception of society as an integrated, functional, evolving entity is the third point of importance in his work.

Although Saint-Simon viewed society in holistic and functional terms, he also saw it as an evolutionary, developmental entity. According to Saint-Simon—although Comte would later articulate this point more clearly as "the law of three stages"—human history moves through an identifiable progression of stable, organic civilizations. Western history began with classical Greece and Rome, societies that had a polytheistic ideology, a slave economy, and a monolithic state. By the eighth century, this polytheistic and slave-based social formation had given way to medieval society, which was characterized by Roman Catholic theology, a feudal economy, and a ruling nobility. The benefits of medieval society were a more humane means of production (indentured versus slave labour), a more systematic theology, and the separation of temporal and spiritual power within the state.

In the fifteenth century, Saint-Simon argues, as craftwork grew and independent workshops became increasingly important in social production, one sees the beginning of the emerging industrial society within medieval Europe. Craft, guild, and eventually industrial production meant that more and more serfs and peasants found work in the cities as wage earners freed from the life-long obligations of serfdom. Enlightenment rationality and science became the new spiritual system (or theology), and the state, in Saint-Simon's view, would be increasingly controlled by industrialists and scientists to ensure the maximum technological and industrial development. In *The Industrial System*, Saint-Simon praises the virtues of this emerging industrial society.

Industrial societies, Saint-Simon maintains, will eliminate war and poverty through the tremendous productivity that large-scale, scientifically planned industrial production can deliver. There will be work for all, assigned on the basis of ability and merit, and all will have the opportunity for advancement in an open, classless, knowledge-based society. Continuous development will be ensured by the central role of science in the spiritual realm, and the state will change from one of government characterized by class power and national rivalries to one of social welfare or administration that is scientifically managed by skilled technocrats. In this emerging industrialized society, Saint-Simon sees the scientists, artists, and men of letters as constituting the spiritual elite, the industrialists the temporal elite, and the workers the highly valued, direct economic producers.

Later sociologists, particularly those working in the French tradition, take all three of these ideas—a science of society; a holistic, organic conception of society as a complex entity comprised of functionally interdependent orders (or institutions); and the stage theory of history—and develop them further. Although these three items mark Saint-Simon's main contributions to sociological thought, his empirical study of the industrialization process in France influenced sociology in another profound, though less direct, manner.

Saint-Simon's understanding of industrial production and the process of industrialization was influenced by Sismondi's 1819 publication, *Nouveaux principes d'économie politique* (*New Principles of Political Economy*; Durkheim [1928] 1958:70–3; Sismondi [1815] 1966). Through his use of Sismondi, Saint-Simon draws upon the ideas of Smith, Ferguson, and other British political economists as they were filtered by Sismondi. Two more personal influences, however, also converge in this dimension of Saint-Simon's thought.

First, Saint-Simon's own analyses of industrialization (a term he introduced to sociology) led him to agree with various political economists that the economy, in general, and the specific productive processes stemming from it, shape society. Second, Saint-Simon's own personal experiences in France furthered his belief in the central importance of the economy in shaping a social formation.

Unlike Smith, Ferguson, and other political economists, Saint-Simon lived through a number of changes in governmental regimes—some of them highly revolutionary—but his experiences suggested that changes in governments or ruling elites do not alter society fundamentally. Genuine social change, Saint-Simon's experiences indicated, is directly related to the way the economy is structured, organized, controlled, and operated; they do not come from the form of the state or from changes in government, as the leaders of the French Revolution had maintained. Instead, it was modern industrialization—a fundamental change in the productive organization of society—that was uprooting traditional governments and traditional social formations in Saint-Simon's day.

This aspect of Saint-Simon's work did not influence the development of French sociology directly, although it would be picked up in other strands of French social thought. Saint-Simon's studies of industrial society, the importance they place on the productive processes in society and on the significance of the industrialists as the new temporal elite, influenced thinkers as different and divergent as mutualists such as Pierre-Joseph Proudhon, who wanted to organize society on the basis of a central bank and mutually cooperating enterprises, and socialists such as Marx who focused on the central importance of the mode of production and the exploitation of the immediate producers (the working class).

Saint-Simon's insights into industrialization also influenced twentieth century sociologists such as Raymond Aron, Daniel Bell, and Ralf Dahrendorf, who argued that capitalist society, which was characterized by classes and class conflict, gave way to an industrial society in which classes had disappeared or were no longer the divisive forces they had been (Aron 1961, 1962; Bell 1960a, 1973; Dahrendorf 1959, 1967).[55] Class conflict, they came to believe, had been transformed into the open and fair processes of collective bargaining between the interests of labour and those of management.

---

55 It is interesting to note that, even though Aron, Bell, and Dahrendorf come from three different countries—France, the United States, and the Federal Republic of Germany respectively—and from somewhat different sociological traditions, they all subscribe to the industrial society thesis.

Industrial society had become a fully integrated, smoothly functioning society based on industrialized mass production.

Saint-Simon synthesized many different influences into his various writings, and his work was an inspirational source for a variety of very different intellectual and political projects. Read by many and recorded at an important time in French and European history, Saint-Simon's insights are significant, but the systematization of his thought is flawed. The task of systematizing and developing Saint-Simon's scattered ideas fell to his former secretary, Auguste Comte, who sought to establish the new science of society.

COMTE AND SOCIOLOGY AS A POSITIVE SCIENCE

From 1817 to 1824, Comte served as Saint-Simon's recording secretary, and it is clear from Comte's subsequent work that the elder Saint-Simon had a tremendous impact on his thought. At the same time, Comte was a strong, independent thinker in his own right who ultimately broke from Saint-Simon and set out his own—some would argue grandiose—goals. In 1822, Comte published his *Plan de travaux scientifiques nécessaires pour réorganiser la société* (*Plan of Scientific Studies Necessary for the Reorganization of Society*)—the blueprint for his ambitious plan to change the moral, intellectual, and social landscape of Europe.

Viewed in total, Comte's work involves five key elements. First is the idea that human societies and human knowledge had progressed through three stages. As Comte boldly notes at the outset of his six-volume *Cours de philosophie positive: Discours sur l'esprit positif* (*Course in Positive Philosophy: A Discourse on the Positivist Spirit*),

> Studying the total development of the human intelligence in its various spheres of activity, from its first trial flights up to our own day, I believe I have discovered a fundamental law to which it is subjected from an invariable necessity ... This law is that each of our principal conceptions, each branch of our knowledge, passes successively through three different theoretical states: the theological or fictitious, the metaphysical or abstract, and the scientific or positive ... Hence there are three mutually exclusive kinds of philosophy, or conception systems regarding the totality of phenomena: the first is the necessary starting point of human intelligence; the third its fixed and final state; the second is only a means of transition.
> (Comte 1974:19–20, n.d.:5–6)

Comte also notes that, due to the varying complexity of the different sciences, the least complex develops first and the most complex at the end. As a result, the scientific or positive stage first developed in astronomy and physics and then in chemistry and physiology before finally shaping social physics (or sociology).[56] Comte's first goal, as outlined in his *Plan of Scientific Studies Necessary for the Reorganization of Society*, is to establish the positivist form in all branches of knowledge, including the study of societies.

The second key element of Comte's thought is his notion of positivism. He views positivism as a system of knowledge based exclusively on the methodology of the natural sciences. "Positivism," Comte (1974) argues, "is first of all characterised by that necessary and permanent subordination of imagination to observation which constitutes the scientific spirit, as opposed to the theological or metaphysical spirit" (p. 139). Comte's goal was to treat social phenomena in exactly the same way that natural phenomena were treated in the natural sciences. The main emphasis in social thought, according to him, should be centred fully and squarely on the collection and examination of empirical, observationally based knowledge.

Comte's real concern, however, is understanding social stability and social change—the third element of importance in his work. "Order and progress," Comte (1974) notes, "which antiquity regarded as irreconcilable, constitute, from the nature of modern civilization, two equally necessary conditions whose combination is at once the principal difficulty and the principal strength of every political system" (pp. 126–7). "No order," he continues, "can now be established, and above all can now endure, if it is not fully compatible with progress; and no great progress can be effected, unless it tends to consolidate order" (Comte 1974:127).

Picking up this theme, Comte contrasts the existing situation in France with his notions of order and progress. He depicts the period following the French Revolution and continuing up to the writing of his *Course in Positive Philosophy* as one of revolution, an ensuing reaction, and a return to an ongoing revolutionary struggle—a period, in other words, of tremendous social instability. The former defenders of Louis XVI's *ancien régime* reacted to

---

56 Comte first designated the positivist study of society as "social physics" but abandoned the term in 1838 in favour of his newly minted term "sociology." He derived the word from the Latin word *socius* ("companion," "associate") and the Greek term *lógos* (which has various meanings including "word," "speech," "logic," and "thought"). Thus sociology would deal with thought regarding association or the logic of association. The first book with sociology in its title was Herbert Spencer's 1873 *The Study of Sociology*. Part of the reason Comte abandoned social physics was the publication of Belgian statistician Adolphe Quetelet's book *Physique sociale* in 1835, but the deeper reason was a shift in Comte's own thought. Up to 1838, Comte had regarded mathematics as the methodological basis of all the sciences, including his social physics. However, as he progressed further and further into the *Course of Positive Philosophy*, he began to give greater emphasis to the importance of history. His use of the Latin and Greek terms suggests that Comte came to view sociology as being focused on the logic of, or thought about, human association.

the revolutionary changes of 1789 by trying to re-establish the monarchy and the feudal order. Comte understands this as an attempt by the aristocracy and clergy to turn back the clock—to return to the lower theological stage of development.

Those who sought to resist the gains of the revolution, in Comte's view, were motivated by irrational desires and lacked a coherent plan. "In the half century during which the revolutionary crisis of modern societies has been developing," he writes, "one cannot disguise the fact that all the great efforts in favour of order have been guided by a retrograde spirit, and the principal efforts for progress by radically anarchical doctrines" (Comte 1974:127).

Comte (1974) maintains, then, that "the development and the propagation of science, industry, and even the fine arts" result from the rise of the positivist spirit as society moves into its highest stage of development. "It is the ascendancy of the scientific spirit which preserves us today" (p. 131). Because of this belief, he sought fervently to establish positivism in general and sociology—the positivist study of societies—in particular.

Comte also presents the principles of social physics at great length in the *Course in Positive Philosophy*—in far too much detail to discuss here. There are, however, three key aspects worth noting, and these demonstrate his conception of a scientific sociology—it is Comte's conception of sociology as a science that represents the fourth key element of his thought.

Positive philosophy, according to Comte, would ensure that observation, "which constitutes the scientific spirit," would replace "imagination" as the basis for knowledge. Referring to his elaboration of the fundamental sciences, which he presents in three earlier volumes, Comte (1974) notes that positive philosophy

> restricts its activity to discovering or perfecting either the exact coordination of the facts as they stand, or the means of undertaking new investigations. It is this habitual tendency to subordinate scientific conceptions to the facts—it being the sole function of these conceptions to demonstrate the interconnection of the facts—that must be introduced into social studies, where vague and ill-defined observation still offers no sufficient foundation for truly scientific reasoning, and is continually being modified by imagination under the stimulus of very lively passions. (P. 139)

What Hobbes, Montesquieu, and Saint-Simon suggested is fully and formally asserted by Comte—observable facts are the groundwork of science, both natural and social.

Second, positive philosophy rejects the notion of absolute truths—all of its findings and observations are relative—that is related to a particular situation. If we consider "the actual scientific conceptions in positive phi-losophy," Comte (1974) writes, "we see that in contradistinction to theo-logico-metaphysical philosophy it has a constant tendency to make all those notions relative which had been considered absolute" (p. 140). "From the purely scientific point of view," he continues, "it seems to me we may regard the contrast between the relative and the absolute as expressing the antipa-thy between modern and ancient philosophy":

> Every study of the inner nature of beings, of their primary and final
> causes, etc. must obviously be absolute, while every investigation of the
> laws of phenomena is eminently relative, since it presupposes that the
> progress of thought is dependent on the gradual improvement of obser-
> vation, exact reality being never, in any subject, perfectly disclosed: so
> that the relative nature of scientific conceptions is inseparable from the
> true notion of natural laws, just as the chimerical attachment to absolute
> knowledge accompanies the use of theological fictions or metaphysical
> entities. (Comte 1974:140)

In other words, because of the absolute spirit inherent in political studies under the theological and metaphysical forms of thought, the only means by which people could propose solutions to social and political problems was through the search for conclusive and unqualified truth. And these solu-tions were inevitably cast in all or nothing terms: some men are born free while some are born slaves in Plato's *Republic*, only the Leviathan could pre-vent the war of all against all in Hobbes, humankind needed to return to its former state of nature to escape the problems of the current social contract, according to Rousseau. Gradual reform can find no genuine place in these absolutist metaphysical systems; however, gradualism, progressively better understandings, and reform are all consistent with the new scientific world-view of positivism.

Finally, Comte (1974) argues that positive sociology allows for one other important advantage for social reform—the capacity for rational prediction. "The very idea therefore of rational prediction presupposes that the human mind has definitely quitted the region of metaphysical idealities in politics, in order to take its stand on the firm ground of observed realities through a sys-tematic and constant subordination of imagination to observation" (p. 145).

This dimension of positive sociology has tremendous political implica-tions—social systems and social problems can be observed carefully and systematically, leading to relative insight appropriate to that time and the given knowledge of a society. This analysis would suggest reforms, which, once in place, would allow for further careful observation and a prediction of outcomes if nothing more were done or if other changes were made. This leads to the fifth and final key idea in Comte's thought—positive sociology as a science of social statics and social dynamics (Comte 1974:147–50).

Positive sociology focuses on societies as they are at given moments in time—the science of social statics. On the basis of that science, reforms can be implemented that lead to an evolutionary development of the society—Comte's social dynamics. Comte draws upon biology for an analogy to make his point clear—social statics deals with the anatomy of a society and social dynamics with its physiology. With this example, Comte brings the metaphoric similarity of societies and biological organisms into the centre of his positive sociology, and that organic analogy will be adopted by ensuing sociologists to their great profit and loss. For Comte, the notions of social statics and social dynamics link to his conceptions of order and progress. Comte considers social change to be the evolutionary development of science and all social formations.

To summarize, Comte's key contributions to the emergence of sociology are the following. It was Comte who, for better or for worse, named the positive study of societies "sociology." Comte insisted that knowledge passes through three stages—the theological, the metaphysical, and the positive. The positive stage, according to him, emphasizes the central importance of observation and rejects the theological and metaphysical conceptions of absolutes. On the basis of positivist knowledge, scientifically based knowledge can inform social reform and thereby remove the threat of reaction or revolution, so there will be a stable relationship between order and progress. Reform also allows for progressive change—scientifically planned and monitored progress.

Comte associates his conceptions of order and progress with his conceptions of social statics and social dynamics, and all these concepts lend support to his use of an organic analogy for the study of societies—the anatomy and physiology of society. Finally, the law of the three stages and the triumph of positive science as well as the conceptions of order and progress, social statics and dynamics, and social anatomy and physiology are all consistent with Comte's idea that all realms of knowledge can be known on the basis of the same rational, observationally based, positive science. Comte was one of the most passionate advocates for what is often called the unity of the sciences—the belief that there is one true scientific method and that it can be applied to both natural and social phenomena.

FORMS OF SOCIAL SOLIDARITY AND *LA CONSCIENCE COLLECTIVE*

Durkheim's major contributions to the development of sociology really stem from his 1893 study *The Division of Labor in Society*. His other key contributions to sociology—*The Rules of Sociological Method* ([1895] 1938), *Suicide* ([1897] 1951), and *The Elementary Forms of the Religious Life* ([1912] 1915)—consider in greater detail specific aspects of some of the central issues Durkheim addresses in *The Division of Labor*. Despite the apparent focused specificity of *The Division of Labor,* it constitutes the departure point for almost all that followed in Durkheim's career—including his work on methodology, his debate with French Marxists, and his conception of socialism. In *The Division of Labor*, Durkheim introduces the most important concept in his sociology—*la conscience collective*—and expresses his commitment to a particular conception of "positive sociology" (Durkheim [1893] 1933:79, 32).[57]

In view of the strategic importance of *The Division of Labor* in Durkheim's work, it is worth noting how it provided the impetus behind the encompassing sense of sociology that emerges from his research and writing. The quick overview to follow will highlight the relationship between Durkheim's first systematic, sociological study and the key dimensions of his sociology.

Faced with the emerging tensions of modernity that Durkheim experienced firsthand in the Third Republic, the growth of class conflict that culminated in the massive Decazeville strike of 1886—overlapping with the period in which Durkheim toiled over *The Division of Labor*—and the cleavages that led to and were fostered by the growing challenge of European socialism, French intellectuals at the end of the nineteenth century felt an immediate and urgent need to know whether an industrializing society could ever become stable. Durkheim was no exception. In the preface of the first edition of *The Division of Labor*, he acknowledges that this work "had its origins in the question of the relations of the individual to social solidarity" (Durkheim [1893] 1933:37; Gouldner 1958:xxiv–xxv).[58] The changing nature of social cohesiveness—social solidarity—remained a central element in all of Durkheim's sociology. But, it should be emphasized, it was the *changing nature of social solidarity within specific social contexts* that Durkheim made

---

57 The French noun *conscience* contains two meanings—consciousness as well as conscience. Both are important because, according to Durkheim, the dominant social consciousness also serves as a guide to behaviour—as a conscience of what is appropriate and what is not. Parsons (1949) argues that, because the way the term is translated may result in "an interpretive bias, ... [i]t seems best here [in *The Division of Labor*] to leave it untranslated" (p. 309, note 3; see also the translator's comments in Durkheim [1893] 1933:ix).

58 The subtitle of the first edition of *The Division of Labor* was *étude sur l'organisation des sociétés supérieures*, which translates to "a study of the organization of the advanced societies."

the focus of his work—he was not engaged in the pursuit of some abstract question of social order or some universal explanation for social order or social solidarity.

Because the demise of traditional societies across western Europe was associated with so much social strife, dislocation, and conflict, the transition from traditional to modern society became the focal point of a growing body of academic analysis. The theme is addressed to some extent in Montesquieu's and Rousseau's works, and it is certainly central to the work of Saint-Simon and Comte who, according to Durkheim ([1928] 1958), viewed it very differently (Gouldner 1958:x–xv). The theme also resonates with work in Germany undertaken by sociologists such as Ferdinand Tönnies (1887, [1887] 1957), Albert Schäffle (1896), and Paul von Lilienfeld (1873).

Although *The Division of Labor* concentrates almost exclusively on the substantive problem of social solidarity, Durkheim also uses it to introduce another of his major contributions to sociology: the question of methodology in sociology.

In *The Division of Labor*, Durkheim first presents his case—elaborated more fully in *The Rules of Sociological Method* and in *Suicide* and also central to his discussion of *Socialism and Saint-Simon*—for sociology as a positive science (Durkheim 1972:117–20, 121–2). "This book," the opening sentence of the preface of *The Division of Labor* reads, "is pre-eminently an attempt to treat the facts of the moral life according to the method of the positive sciences" (Durkheim [1893] 1933:32). In making this decision, Durkheim criticizes the approach others used to explain social solidarity while presenting the key elements of his own, empirically inspired approach to the methodology of the social sciences (Durkheim [1893] 1933:44–6).

The question of stability in the modern world concerns the relationship between the individual and the social whole. In many respects, Durkheim's entire sociology stems from how he presents this relationship within both *The Division of Labor* and some of his subsequent studies. As a result, Durkheim's key concepts—society as a *sui generis* phenomenon that pre-exists individuals and the internalization of an externally existing *conscience collective*—developed out of his analysis of the changing form of solidarity within what he calls "the advanced societies."[59]

In *The Division of Labor*, Durkheim ([1893] 1933) poses two specific questions:

---

59 Perhaps the most controversial aspect of Durkheim's sociology is his use of language and his apparent reification of (or giving reality to) entities that do not have a real, palpable existence. But Durkheim is very careful to emphasize that these references are analogies—ways to help conceptualize social phenomena—and not reifications. Thus, for example, when he writes in *The Rules* that "social facts" can be treated "like things," he is constructing a simile and not a statement of identity. This issue is addressed at greater length later in this chapter.

Why does the individual, while becoming more autonomous, depend
more upon society? How can he be at once more individual and more
solidary? Certainly, these two movements contradictory as they appear,
develop in parallel fashion. This is the problem we are raising. (P. 37)

His answer involves the social effects of the division of labour. "It appeared
to us," he writes at the end of his first preface, "that what resolves this apparent antinomy is a transformation of social solidarity due to the steadily growing development of the division of labor. That is how we have been led to
make this the object of our study" (Durkheim [1893] 1933:37–8).

Consequently, it is the general question of social cohesion and stability,
examined within the context—an increasingly controversial context—of
advanced societies that leads Durkheim to focus on the division of labour.
This specific focus would lead him to more general insights and to claims
that he would pursue in detail within the context of other specific, empirical social situations, such as rates of suicide or forms of religion. As a result,
from a very specific social issue—the relationship of individuals within a
social whole—Durkheim begins a study that ultimately leads to his particular approach to understanding the intersection of personal biography with
the history of social structure.

The Division of Labour in Society

The central argument in *The Division of Labor* distinguishes Durkheim
from almost all other commentators on and analysts of either the division of labour—for example Smith, Say, and Sismondi—or the differing
natures of traditional and modern societies—for example, Saint-Simon,
Comte, Tönnies, Schäffle, and Lilienfeld. The work also draws together
those two seemingly disparate topics into one integrated analysis that features Durkheim's key contributions to sociology. It is a fascinating study
and presentation.

At the outset, Durkheim ([1893] 1933:49–56) demonstrates that the division of labour is much more than an economic phenomenon and that to view
it solely in economic terms misses its most important social function. The
key aspect of the division of labour, for Durkheim, rests in its fundamental
role as the basis for social cohesion.

Acknowledging that "everybody knows that we like those who resemble
us, those who think and feel as we do," Durkheim ([1893] 1933) notes that
"the opposite is no less true":

It very often happens that we feel kindly towards those who do not
resemble us, precisely because of this lack of resemblance. These facts are

apparently so contradictory that moralists have always vacillated concerning the true nature of friendship and have derived it sometimes from the
former, sometimes from the latter. (P. 54)

Quoting Aristotle and Heraclitus, Durkheim shows that both positions
extend back to classical philosophy and to ancient Greek conceptions of
morality. "These opposing doctrines," Durkheim ([1893] 1933) maintains,
"prove that both types are necessary to natural friendship. Difference, as
likeness, can be a cause of mutual attraction" (p. 55). But not all differences
can serve as the basis of friendship—only those differences that "instead of
opposing and excluding, complement each other" constitute the basis for
friendship:

> As richly endowed as we may be, we always lack something, and the best
> of us realize our own insufficiency. That is why we seek in our friends
> the qualities we lack, since in joining with them, we participate in some
> measure in their nature and thus feel less incomplete. So it is that small
> friendly associations are formed wherein each one plays a role conform-
> able to his character, where there is a true exchange of services. One
> urges, another consoles; this one advises, that one follows advice, and it is
> this apportionment of functions, or to use the usual expression, this divi-
> sion of labor, which determines the relations of friendship. (Durkheim
> [1893] 1933:55–6)

Durkheim then moves from the personal to the social in his investigation of the division of labour. This shift is the first step in Durkheim's study
of the relationship between the division of labour in a society and that society's form of social solidarity:

> We are thus led to consider the division of labor in a new light. In this
> instance, the economic services that it can render are picayune compared
> to the moral effect that it produces, and its true function is to create in
> two or more persons a feeling of solidarity. In whatever manner the result
> is obtained, its aim is to cause coherence among friends and to stamp
> them with its seal. (Durkheim [1893] 1933:56)

To open the way for his argument that the division of labour serves as the
basis for "the integration of the social body to assure unity," Durkheim uses
Comte's notion that the division of labour is "the most essential condition
of social life, provided that one conceives it 'in all its rational extent; that
is to say, that one applies it to the totality of all our diverse operations of

whatever kind, instead of attributing it, as is ordinarily done, to simple material usages'" (Durkheim [1893] 1933:62–3).

The empirical study of social solidarity presents one fundamental problem: social solidarity "is a completely moral phenomenon which, taken by itself, does not lend itself to exact observation nor indeed measurement" (Durkheim, [1893] 1933:64). One needs an observable indicator of social solidarity that one can empirically study and measure—the indicator that Durkheim ([1893] 1933:64–8) selected was the law.

This decision is critical for two reasons in particular. First, it moves the analysis of social solidarity—the basis for a moral order—away from abstract philosophy directly into the concerns of sociology. Sociology, it turns out, can develop an empirically based understanding of the moral order within a society. Also, Durkheim suggests, to inform social policy, social solidarity can and should be studied through an empirically based sociology rather than through the well-worn paths of abstract philosophical argument.

Second, the examination of law as an indicator of social solidarity requires (and allows) Durkheim to introduce his central conception—*la conscience collective*—which is the social substratum of the legal system. Different types of law are indicative of different types of social conscience or consciousness and different types of social solidarity.[60]

Before focusing on the two types of law that Durkheim discusses, let us examine his notion of the *conscience collective*. Because the term is so critical to his sociology and also to the way he links law to forms of solidarity, it is worth citing Durkheim's presentation at length.

> The totality of beliefs and sentiments common to average citizens of the same society forms a determinate system which has its own life; one may call it the *collective* or *common conscience*. No doubt, it has not a specific organ as a substratum; it is, by definition, diffuse in every reach of society. Nevertheless, it has specific characteristics which make it a distinct reality. It is, in effect, independent of the particular conditions in which individuals are placed; they pass on and it remains. It is the same in the North and in the South, in great cities and in small, in different professions. Moreover, it does not change with each generation, but, on the contrary, it connects successive generations with one another. It is, thus, an entirely different thing from particular consciences, although it can be realized

---

60 The study of law in *The Division of Labor* also provides insight into another relationship that Durkheim presents in some of his later work—the connection between different levels of social integration and the extent to which an individual follows or deviates from the expected course (or norms) of behaviour, a relationship that represents or allows for changes in the existing collective conscience/consciousness. According to Durkheim, deviance plays an important function in determining the limits of what is accepted by the overall collective conscience in society.

only through them. It is the psychical type of society, a type which has its properties, its conditions of existence, its mode of development, just as individual types, although in a different way. Thus understood, it has the right to be denoted by a special word. The one which we have just employed [*conscience*] is not, it is true, without ambiguity. ... [and even though it might be preferable] to create a [new] technical expression especially to designate the totality of social similitudes ... the use of a new word, when not absolutely necessary, is not without inconvenience. ... [Therefore] we shall employ the well-worn expression, collective or common conscience, but we shall always mean the strict sense in which we have taken it. (Durkheim [1893] 1933:79–80)

Durkheim has packed so much into that lengthy paragraph.

The *conscience collective* is not a palpable thing—it cannot be seen directly, touched, smelled, or tasted—and yet it exists. This entity exists separately from the conscience or consciousness of each individual, yet it comes into existence through all individuals thinking, judging, and acting. Because it is the product of those individuals and has an existence that is separate from them—virtually external to them—it is there before they are born into a society, and it will endure after they are gone. But it is not set in stone—the collective conscience or consciousness may change over time, even though it demonstrates a relatively enduring content. Finally, the collective conscience/consciousness is enormously encompassing, even though few people can enumerate all of its aspects with any precision. It is captured quite well in the very simple, yet deeply profound phrase, "it's just done that way," which suggests operational instructions about how to do things as well as a moral assessment of what one ought to do.

The term *conscience collective* is ambiguous in some ways—but it can be examined and elaborated upon. Most important, it can and must be examined and elaborated upon through a discussion of different indicators drawn from real social life. It is through the *conscience collective* that the individual and society are actually brought together in social action.

With this pivotal term in place, the remainder of Durkheim's argument in *The Division of Labor* centres on the extent to which one of the two basic types of law—repressive or restitutive—serves as an indicator for a particular form of social solidarity and the implications that this has for life in the modern world.

Durkheim ([1893] 1933:102–5) argues that repressive law is a highly intense response on the part of the individuals in a society in which this form of law dominates to anyone who has transgressed the ideals embodied in the *conscience collective*. It is, Giddens (1972) explains, "an expression of anger on the part of the community, the avenging of an outrage to morality" (p. 6; see also Foucault 1995:3–32). Repressive law, Durkheim ([1893] 1933:70–110) details at length, is consistent with traditional, face-to-face societies—societies characterized by what he terms "mechanical solidarity" (pp. 105–9).

Durkheim ([1893] 1933:129) uses the term mechanical solidarity to emphasize that the individual is bound almost directly to the society through a *conscience collective* that provides a single, powerful, total belief system. The term also conveys an analogy that links this form of organization with that of a simple organism, one having a mechanical unity insofar as each cell is wholly compatible with every other and necessary for the survival of the whole—if any part of the organism splits off, the organism as a unity would die.

On the other hand, restitutive law corresponds to a social solidarity "of a totally different kind" (Durkheim [1893] 1933:111). Restitutive law does not involve the suffering of the individual but simply "*the return of things as they were,* in the reestablishment of troubled relations to their normal state" (Durkheim [1893] 1933:69).[61] Restitutive law, Durkheim ([1893] 1933:111–29) documents, is only possible in societies in which individuals are increasingly dependent upon other individuals carrying out specialized social functions—in other words, in societies with an advanced division of labour.

This second type of solidarity—organic solidarity—represents a solidarity in which each individual "depends on society, because he depends upon the parts of which it is composed": it is "a system of different, special functions which definite relations unite" (Durkheim [1893] 1933:129).

According to Durkheim, mechanical solidarity dominates "only if the ideas and tendencies common to all members of the society are greater in number and intensity than those which pertain personally to each member." He continues, "Solidarity which comes from likenesses is at its maximum when the collective conscience completely envelops our whole conscience and coincides in all points with it" (Durkheim [1893] 1933:129–30).

Organic solidarity, on the other hand, presumes people are different. Under the conditions of mechanical solidarity, "the individual personality is absorbed under the collective personality"; whereas organic solidarity is "only possible if each one has a sphere of action which is peculiar to him":

> It is necessary that the collective conscience leave open a part of the individual conscience in order that special functions may be established

---

61 "What distinguishes [restitutive] sanction," Durkheim ([1893] 1933) writes, "is that it is not expiatory, but consists of a simple *return in state.* Sufferance proportionate to the misdeed is not inflicted on the one who has violated the law or who disregards it; he is simply sentenced to comply with it. If certain things were done, the judge reinstates them as they would have been. He speaks of law; he says nothing of punishment. Damage-interests have no penal character; they are only a means of reviewing the past in order to reinstate it, as far as possible, to its normal form" (p. 111).

there, functions it cannot regulate. The more this region is extended, the stronger is the cohesion which results from this [organic] solidarity. In effect, on the one hand, each one depends as much more strictly on society as labor is more divided; and, on the other, the activity of each is as much more personal as it is more specialized. .... Here, then, the individuality of all grows at the same time as that of its parts. Society becomes more capable of collective movement, at the same time that each of its elements has more freedom of movement. This solidarity resembles that which we observe among the higher animals. Each organ, in effect, has its special physiognomy, its autonomy. And, moreover, the unity of the organism is as great as the individuation of the parts is more marked. Because of this analogy, we propose to call the solidarity which is due to the division of labor, organic. (Durkheim [1893] 1933:131)

Durkheim uses the remainder of *The Division of Labor* to examine the dynamic that leads from mechanical to organic solidarity.

In the latter part of his study, Durkheim, explicitly and implicitly, addresses a number of established positions in the literature examining the transition from traditional to modern societies, and he puts forward his own assessment of the importance of his particular analysis of the division of labour, social solidarity, and the presence of a *conscience collective*.

Ferdinand Tönnies's *Gemeinschaft und Gesellschaft* (*Community and Civil Society*), which Durkheim (1972:146–7) reviewed while working on *The Division of Labor*, had quickly become the authoritative study on the transition from traditional to modern society. In a review that appeared before he published *The Division of Labor*, Durkheim notes that he agrees "with the general lines of analysis and the description of *Gemeinschaft* which he has given us" but that he does not accept Tönnies's analysis of *Gesellschaft* (modern, civil society). To begin with, Durkheim rejects Tönnies's method:

> Tönnies devotes more time to the systematic analysis of concepts than to the observation of facts. He proceeds by conceptual argument; we find in his writing the distinctions and symmetrical classifications which are so beloved of German logicians. The only way to avoid this would have been to proceed inductively, that is, to study *Gesellschaft* through the law and the mores which correspond to it, and which reveal its structure. (Durkheim 1972:146)

Equally as important, Durkheim (1972) notes, "If I have properly understood his thought, *Gesellschaft* is supposed to be characterized by a progressive development of individualism, the dispersive effects of which can only be prevented for a time, and by artificial means, by the action of the state" (p. 146). This, Durkheim continues, is the view of the utilitarians—there is no true collective life. "I believe," Durkheim counters, "that the life of large social agglomerations is just as natural as that of small groupings. It is no less organic and no less internal." There is a natural, collective solidarity within modern civil societies. "In order to prove this," Durkheim (1972) writes, "it would need a book" (p. 147). That book is *The Division of Labor.*

Thus, Durkheim's analysis of the nature of organic solidarity is directed against Tönnies's presentation of *Gesellschaft,* and it is the latter part of the study that is particularly important to Durkheim's critique and position.[62] Durkheim wants to establish that modern civil societies are not an aberration—that the "natural" form of social association is not solely a property of traditional societies. Second, and equally important, he wants to demonstrate that there is a natural social solidarity within modern civil societies— order does not have to be imposed by a powerful, central state.

These concerns also put Durkheim in opposition to another sociologist whose work had gained tremendous prominence—British sociologist Herbert Spencer (1876, 1893, 1896). Spencer was one of the strongest advocates of viewing societies as if they were natural organisms—what was true of biological phenomena was equally true of social phenomena. As a result, according to Spencer, the same principles of evolution that applied to the natural world applied to the social world. Thus, just as the later forms of organic life displayed greater differentiation and multiplicity in both structure and function so did the social world progress through an evolutionary development from the simple to the complex.

Durkheim's critique of Spencer shows the extent to which he willingly accepts biological analogies but clearly sees social phenomena as distinct from those of the natural world. The forms of social solidarity that Spencer attributes to advanced societies, Durkheim ([1893] 1933:200) argues, are completely spontaneous and natural—the outgrowth of the evolutionary process of increased differentiation and thus the growth of the division of labour. In this view of the social world, Durkheim notes,

> Society does not have to intervene to assure the harmony which is self-
> established. The typical social relation [in Spencer's conception] would
> be the economic, stripped of all regulation and resulting from the entirely

---

62 This portion of *The Division of Labor* also provides a clue to why Durkheim calls the solidarity of modern civil society "organic." It is a term one expects to find associated with face-to-face, traditional societies, but Durkheim's use of the term suggests that the solidarity found in advanced societies is equally as natural—equally as organic to those societies—as the seemingly spontaneous solidarity discussed in all the literature on traditional societies.

free initiative of the parties. In short, society would be solely the stage where individuals exchanged the products of their labor, without any action properly coming to regulate this exchange. (Durkheim [1893] 1933:203)

Durkheim, however, proceeds to demonstrate not only that contractual relations, guided by restitutive law, grow within advanced civil societies but also that non-contractual social relationships grow. All of this demonstrates the fundamental importance of the socially created *conscience collective*. Increasing differentiation and multiplicity within societies are, Durkheim argues, distinctively different from those processes in the natural world.

In summarizing the main arguments of his book, Durkheim ([1893] 1933) maintains that, even though advanced society has become increasingly dependent upon an advancing division of labour, "it does not become a jumble of juxtaposed atoms." Instead, its "members are united by ties which extend deeper and far beyond the short moments during which exchange is made" (p. 227).

Men cannot live together without acknowledging, and consequently, making mutual sacrifices, without tying themselves to one another with strong, durable bonds. Every society is a moral society. In certain respects, this character is even more pronounced in organized societies. Because the individual is not sufficient unto himself, it is from society that he receives everything necessary to him, as it is for society that he works. Thus is formed a very strong sentiment of the state of dependence in which he finds himself. He becomes accustomed to estimating it at its just value, that is to say, in regarding himself as part of a whole, the organ of an organism. Such sentiments naturally inspire not only mundane sacrifices which assure the regular development of daily social life, but even, on occasion, acts of complete self-renunciation and wholesale abnegation. On its side, society learns to regard its members no longer as things over which it has rights, but as co-operators whom it cannot neglect and towards whom it owes duties. Thus, it is wrong to oppose a society which comes from a community of beliefs to one which has a co-operative basis, according only to the first a moral character, and seeing in the latter only an economic grouping. In reality, co-operation also has its intrinsic morality. There is, however, reason to believe, as we shall see later, that in contemporary societies this morality has not yet reached the high development which would now seem necessary to it. (Durkheim [1893] 1933:228)

In this summary, Durkheim presents the empirical insights that he had gained from his study of the growing division of labour in advanced societies and the changing form of social solidarity upon which it was based. At the same time, however, he imparts his own optimistic, normative view of what the future should hold—a future in which the *conscience collective* will accord greater justice for all members of society and in which everyone shares a moral position that safeguards the social whole and the individuated individual at the same time. On the basis of this summary statement at the end of *The Division of Labor,* one gains a glimmer of insight into Durkheim's notion of what lay ahead in the future and into his conception of what a truly socialist society would be like.

6

DURKHEIM AND THE SYSTEMATIC STUDY OF SOCIAL FACTS

Although the central concern in *The Division of Labor* is the question of social order or social solidarity, this study also triggered Durkheim's concerns about establishing sociology as an independent, scientific discipline. As a result, in the preface to the first edition of *The Division of Labor,* drawing upon Descartes, Durkheim ([1893] 1933) argues that science "presupposed a complete freedom of mind" and that "we must rigorously submit ourselves to the discipline of methodical doubt" (p. 36). The arguments he presents in the study, Durkheim argues, rest on authentic proofs given with "the greatest possible exactness." "To subject an order of facts to science," Durkheim ([1893] 1933) continues, "it is not sufficient to observe them carefully, to describe and classify them, but what is a great deal more difficult, we must also find, in the words of Descartes, *the way in which they are scientific,* that is to say, to discover in them some objective element that allows an exact determination, and if possible, measurement" (p. 36–7). The latter part of this sentence is the challenge Durkheim takes up in his next major publication, *The Rules of Sociological Method*—a text that fundamentally shaped the methodology sociologists would employ in their study of the social world as well as how they would conceptualize the world they sought to systematically study.

In the preface to *The Rules,* Durkheim ([1895] 1938) writes that he wants to extend "scientific rationalism" to the study of human behaviour. "It can be shown that behaviour in the past, when analyzed, can be reduced to relationships of cause and effect" (pp. xxix–xl). To do this, however, Durkheim has to answer the question he posed in *The Division of Labor*; he has to discover some "objective element" that sociologists can focus upon, one that allows for "an exact determination, and if possible, measurement." The first chapter of *The Rules* addresses that question: Is there such an objective element in sociology, can it be determined exactly, and can it be measured? In other words, "what is a social fact?"

"Social Facts" and the Systematic Study of Societies

The opening chapter of *The Rules* begins with this statement: "Before inquiring into the method suited to the study of social facts, it is important to know which facts are commonly called 'social'" (Durkheim [1895] 1938:1). Before discussing method, Durkheim wants to establish the real subject matter of sociology. There are many facts one might gather and learn about people, but, Durkheim continues, if "all these facts are counted as 'social' facts, sociology would have no subject matter exclusively its own, and its domain would be confused with that of biology and psychology" (p. 1).

For Durkheim, the subject matter of sociology is distinct from biology because it deals with shared ideas and patterns of conscious action as well as with social institutions and structures. Although those social structures and processes might be analogous to biological structures and their functions, they are distinct enough to separate easily the subject matter of sociology from that of biology.

With respect to psychology, Durkheim argues that it is concerned with the thought processes internal to the individual. To distinguish itself from psychology, sociology would instead be concerned with processes that are *external to the individual*. This simple but decisive distinction indicates that *social facts* are phenomena in every society and differentiates them from the facts considered in all other realms of science: I can recognize social facts because they "are defined externally to myself and my acts, in law and custom." A social fact is something that exists "outside the individual consciousness" and is "endowed with coercive power" by virtue of which it imposes itself upon social actors independently of their will (Durkheim [1895] 1938:2–3).

There is "a category of facts with very distinctive characteristics: it consists of ways of acting, thinking, and feeling, external to the individual, and endowed with a power of coercion, by reason of which they control him." Durkheim ([1895] 1938) continues:

> These ways of thinking could not be confused with biological phenomena, since they consist of representations and of actions; nor with psychological phenomena, which exist only in the individual consciousness

and through it. They constitute, thus, a new variety of phenomena; and it
is to them exclusively that the term "social" ought to be applied. (P. 3)

Three important aspects of sociology, as Durkheim conceives it, are
present in this definition of social facts. First, as Peter Berger (1963) notes,
Durkheim believes that the subject matter of sociology is society, which is
an identifiable entity that "confronts us as an objective facticity":

It is *there*, something that cannot be denied and that must be reckoned
with. Society is external to us. It surrounds us, encompasses our life on
all sides. We are *in* society, located in specific sectors of the social system.
(P. 91)

So the search for social facts—the facts of importance to sociology—is
the search for aspects of human existence that are external to people ("outside the individual consciousness") and "endowed with a coercive power."
Social facts shape and control human behaviour.

Second, this attempt to define social facts is completely consistent with
the positivist image of sociology that Comte promoted. Durkheim's rules of
sociological method are far more sophisticated and certainly far less polemical than those outlined in Comte's *Course of Positive Philosophy*, but they
are firmly located in the tradition that links sociology to other forms of scientific study.

Finally, Durkheim's sociology is based on an important, unarticulated,
premise despite appearances to the contrary, people are not really free.
People may have the freedom to act in ways they choose, but the options
from which they select are constrained within and, even more important, the
consequences of their choices are set by a particular social context. A key element to *social* being is constraint. The forces that impinge upon people and
guide or constrain their actions should be the focus of sociology. To demonstrate the point, Durkheim discusses children and how they are brought up.

"All education," he writes, "is a continuous effort to impose on the child
ways of seeing, feeling, and acting which he could not have arrived at sponta-
neously" (Durkheim [1895] 1938:6). In the process of individuation, individuals are separated from one another and identified by personal and potentially
unshared facts—the focus is upon what makes each person unique. But
that is not the area of interest for sociologists; sociologists are interested in
individuals in their *association* with others, in what might be better termed
their socialized state. Through the process of socialization—the opposite
of individuation—individuals are subjected to and influenced by external
social forces, and these create common and shared social behaviours: "The

unremitting pressure to which the child is subjected is the very pressure of the social milieu which tends to fashion him in its own image, and of which parents and teachers are merely the representatives and intermediaries" (Durkheim, [1895] 1938:6).

It is "the collective aspects of the beliefs, tendencies, and practices of a group that characterize truly social phenomena," according to Durkheim ([1895] 1938:7). Social practices may begin as regularized ways of behaving within a group, but, as they endure, they can become group habits or traditions. They can even become strongly held customs with a moral connotation—called mores—or they can be formalized into laws. Widely held "currents of opinion," ways of thinking about the world in general or even ways of varying one's thinking in response to different situations, Durkheim argues, all exist outside individuals and are developed within a society and internalized by individuals through the processes of socialization. People's conduct is contoured and shaped through the internalization of these social forces.

Drawing upon the results obtained in *The Division of Labor*, Durkheim reasons in *The Rules of Sociological Method* that the subject matter of sociology and the social facts sociologists should study are very specific in nature. He notes that his discussion of social facts allows him to "formulate and delimit in a precise way the domain of sociology":

> It compromises only a limited group of phenomena [namely, social facts].
> A social fact is to be recognized by the power of external coercion which
> it exercises or is capable of exercising over individuals, and the presence
> of this power may be recognized in its turn either by the existence of
> some specific sanction or by the resistance offered against every individual effort that tends to violate it. (Durkheim [1895] 1938:10)

In addition, social facts are group habits, generalized patterns of action, traditions, mores, and even legal codes that are communicated to individuals and socialized into them. All of these social forces, which are ultimately internalized by the individual, exist outside the individual and are there before his or her birth or entry into society. For Durkheim, the subject of sociology is this conglomeration of social forces that exist outside the individual—social forces that have an autonomous reality of their own. They are, in Durkheim's words, *sui generis*—self-generated—and represent a reality that is greater than the sum of the individuals who make up a society.

Social Facts, Social Control, and the Conscience Collective

In *Invitation to Sociology,* Berger develops and explores Durkheim's conception of social control—the constraining aspects of the social facts that sociologists focus upon and study (Berger 1963:66–78). Building on Durkheim's comments about children, Berger (1963:66) notes that one of the first things a child is taught before she or he goes out into the social world as an independent person is her or his home address. It is an almost pedestrian point, but it is equally profound—people are born into particular social locations, and all of their earliest experiences are shaped by the very small orbits of those locations. As children are able to leave the home, it still remains as an extremely powerful point of personal and social identification.

As children begin to identify themselves socially, Berger argues, they begin to recognize an increasingly larger array of social attributes—or social facts—pertinent to their specific lives. For example, people can identify themselves by gender, racial or ethnic background, city of birth, city of domicile, school status or occupation, income, and membership in specific organizations or associations. People can identify their friendship groups, political interests and orientations, and the media sources that give them their day-to-day information.

When people locate themselves within society, they will see themselves at the intersection of specific social forces that shape their behaviour. All of this is consistent with Durkheim's notions about society, social facts, and the proper subject matter of sociology. This conception also reflects Mills's notion of how important it is for sociologists to understand the intersection of personal biography with the history of social structure.

As a person identifies himself or herself socially, the numerous social forces or social facts that shape, contour, and control his or her behaviour become evident. Social control, Berger argues, has two very important dimensions to it. On the one hand, social control has a formal dimension—the ways and means by which "a society [brings] its recalcitrant members back into line" (Berger 1963:68). Berger (1963:68–73) demonstrates that these ways and means include physical violence; political, legal, and economic regulation and sanction; or group pressures such as persuasion, ridicule, gossip, and opprobrium (or shunning). Berger (1963:74–8) also indicates that there are several realms of social control. Some forms of social control are very general and overarching, such as the legal system, which applies to everyone, or the dominant morality of a society or group. Other forms are exercised in more specific settings, such as the school, the workplace, the family, or within friendship groups.

This point leads to the second important dimension of social control—the aspect emphasized by Durkheim—which is that all of social life fundamentally entails social control. Human beings are not totally free—at least not to the well-informed sociologist. People's actions are shaped or influenced by their social location, and, even when they resist all social constraints, they are, nonetheless, implicated in the dynamics of social control. This informal dimension of social control is fundamentally important to Durkheim's sociology.

Berger (1963) argues that every one of us is located "at the centre of a number of concentric circles, each one representing a system of social control" (p. 73). This image helps clarify Durkheim's notion that living in society means that one is faced with "many forces that constrain and coerce" one's thoughts and actions. To paraphrase Berger, the individual student who thinks consecutively of all the people she or he has to please—roommates, friends, professors, parents, former teachers, people in the local community who held particular aspirations as the student off to university, future employers or graduate admissions officers, and the police and authorities within the legal and political system—then the student would get "the idea that all of society sits right on top of him [or her]." She or he "had better not dismiss that idea as a momentary neurotic derangement," Berger (1963:78) warns, because the sociologist—no matter what the student's therapist might suggest—will strengthen that conception rather than tell her or him to "snap out of it."

According to Durkheim, then, society predates us; it has an existence independent of the individuals who comprise it, in other words, a *sui generis* or self-generated existence; it shapes and patterns our conduct; and, when the fundamental dimensions of social control fail, there are informal mechanisms of social control as well as formal mechanisms. The forces shaping and controlling human behaviour constitute the social facts that sociologists must gather and analyse. Who people are and what they do and will attempt in the future—these factors relate strongly to where people are located in society (their country, province, and city of birth and domicile; their parents' socio-economic status; the schools they attend; the friendship groups they develop; their affiliations; and their location in the work force, to name just a few of the social facts pertinent to everyone). Indeed, it is because there are so many social forces that shape individual behaviour that even political theorists such as Hobbes and Rousseau actually had to look beyond simply the role of the government or the state in the creation and maintenance of social order. The existence of these social forces is one of the main reasons that sociology is such a vital area of human inquiry.

DURKHEIM AND THE STUDY OF SUICIDE

Establishing sociology as a discipline was one of Durkheim's major objectives. *The Division of Labor in Society* and *The Rules of Sociological Method* were crucial steps towards that objective, but it is in his third major work, his study of suicide, that Durkheim (1951) demonstrates the importance and power of sociological analysis by undertaking what seems to be an impossible challenge—a sociological explanation of suicide. In this landmark study, Durkheim examines what appears to be the most decisive, individual decision a person can make—deliberate self-inflicted death—and demonstrates that a number of social factors predispose some and protect others from making that very critical decision.

Suicide is a sociological classic for three reasons. First, it successfully employed the methodology that Durkheim had outlined in *The Rules*—the collection and analysis of particular social facts. Second, by showing how much sociology could contribute to a problem that seemed so far outside of its area of analysis, *Suicide* demonstrated the power of sociological analysis. Finally, the study had a long-lasting impact upon one of the most interesting areas of sociological study—the sociology of deviant behaviour.

Suicide also led Durkheim to think about the notion of *conscience collective* further. In *Suicide,* he introduces the notion of "collective representations" to complement his earlier concept. There are two interrelated reasons for the change in terminology.

First, in *The Division of Labor*, Durkheim is interested in comparing the forms of social solidarity found in face-to-face societies with those found in societies characterized by increasing complexity. The notion of a common conscience or consciousness, which Durkheim first notes in face-to-face societies—those characterized by mechanical solidarity—serves as the critical focal point in this comparison. Thus, although *conscience collective* is very useful in making the comparison between mechanical and organic solidarity as fully and explicitly as possible, it is not as helpful in understanding complex societies.

This difficulty is the second reason for moving from *conscience collective* to "collective representations": Durkheim needs a term that will allow him to explore the dynamics of social solidarity in increasingly complex societies. As the division of labour proceeds and societies become more complex, he argues, different institutions and belief systems generate, foster, and reinforce a particular *conscience collective*, and the social conscience becomes embedded within a number of different social—or collective—representations. The term "collective representations" allows Durkheim to focus on different sources that present appropriate behaviour to individuals. Formal religious systems are one key source, and they offer differing collective representations—a critical point in Durkheim's study of suicide—but there are other sources of morality within an increasingly complex society, such as the education system. As a result, the overall *conscience collective* within a society, Durkheim begins to think, comes from a variety of collective representations. These collective representations are the embodiment of different cognitive, moral, and religious beliefs and sentiments.

In general, Durkheim identifies three different categories of suicide— egoistic, altruistic, and anomic—and each relates to the way that different individuals see the world around them.

With respect to egoistic suicide, Durkheim's analysis demonstrates that religious representations, even in an industrial society, play an important role in who would and who would not commit suicide. Catholicism and Protestantism, which are based on fundamentally different collective representations of how the individual relates to the scriptures and therefore to God, leave believers differently vulnerable to egoistic suicide. In the Catholic Church, the pope is clearly and decisively God's messenger; the pope and his cardinals hold full authority in the interpretation of the Holy Scriptures. Church liturgy reinforces the pope's authority; the church is thoroughly hierarchical with the roles and responsibilities of pope, cardinals, priests, and parishioners well-defined. The Catholic credo is also highly unified and has a long, consistent history.

The collective representation of the proper relationship between the layperson and God is dramatically different within Protestantism. The dominant difference is the direct link between parishioner and God—although Church authorities aid in the interpretation of the scriptures, it ultimately falls to the parishioner to find his or her own meaning within the holy texts. The very structure of the Protestant Church and the reasons for its emergence form a very different social basis for the collective representations of religious meaning, religious affiliation, and religious obligation. These different collective representations lead Protestants and Catholics to see and understand the world in fundamentally different ways, according to Durkheim.

In the absence of a strong, centrally controlled religious credo, the spiritual bonds giving support and comfort to Protestants are much less encompassing and cohesive than those in the Catholic Church. When Catholics have problems, they can rely on the church establishment for unfailing guidance and on the aid of the parish priest; in short, they find that they are not alone in facing difficult situations.

Protestants, on the other hand, have a less authoritarian religious belief system to rely upon; they have to commune directly with God when in search of solutions to deeply perplexing problems. Protestant parishioners are left much more to their own devices than are Roman Catholics. The greater degree of individualism permitted by the Protestant faith, Durkheim argues, leaves Protestant parishioners more vulnerable to egoistic suicide.

If religion is one source of specific and powerful collective representations that influence people's decisions regarding suicide, there could well be others, and Durkheim's study of the data on suicides shows that this is indeed the case. Durkheim ([1897] 1951:171–216) found that marital status also created different collective representations among men and women. Although marital status had no impact on women's decisions about suicide, married men were less apt to commit suicide than single men. Also, for both married men and women, the larger the family unit, the less likely they were to take their own lives.

In sum, according to Durkheim's research, the more others depend on an individual's social actions within a social situation the less likely it is that the individual will pursue his or her own goals exclusively. Marital status (for men) and family size (for married men and women) create the social conditions in which people see themselves as part of a larger social unit, and this perspective, in turn, tempers feelings of excessive individualism or egoism and directly affects the propensity to commit egoistic suicide.

The notion of collective representation also applies to tightly organized, highly integrated social situations (Durkheim [1897] 1951:217–40). The data that Durkheim studied showed that, in smaller, closed societies, several forms of suicide arose because the collective representations of those groups or societies placed the social whole well above the individual. As a result, individuals in those social situations were much more willing to sacrifice themselves for the greater collective good than to preserve their own individual lives. Durkheim concludes that, when collective representations value the individual less than the social whole, one finds a higher incidence of altruistic suicide.

Durkheim's example of altruistic suicide is also connected to a religious belief system. He notes that, in India at that time, "the Hindu was already inclined to self-destruction under Brahminic influence" (Durkheim [1897] 1951:223–4). According to Durkheim, that tradition stipulates that once a man attains a certain age and has at least one son, he has fulfilled his life on earth and is free to "have nothing more to do with life." Durkheim ([1897] 1951) quotes from *The Laws of the Manu*: "The Brahmin who has freed himself from his body by one of the methods employed by the great saints, freed from grief and fear, is honourably received in the abode of Brahma" (p. 223). However, Durkheim ([1897] 1951) spends considerably more time examining altruistic suicide in the military, arguing that "the profession of a soldier develops a moral constitution powerfully predisposing man to make away with himself" (p. 239).

The third condition conducive to suicide, according to Durkheim, is one in which the normal, dominant collective representations of society are broken or significantly changed, leaving the individual with no guidelines to follow—people feel directionless and insecure (Durkheim [1897] 1951:241–76). Durkheim argues that, as religion loses its influence and as the distribution of goods, services, and wealth falls more and more to the growing capitalist market, individuals feel that there are fewer and fewer certainties in their lives. This loss of normality or "normlessness" leaves people in a state of anomie.[63]

"In one sphere of social life," Durkheim ([1897] 1951) argues, "the sphere of trade and industry, [anomie] is actually in a chronic state":

> For a whole century, economic progress has mainly consisted in freeing industrial relations from all regulation. Until very recently [1893], it was the function of a whole system of moral forces to exert this discipline. First, the influence of religion was felt alike by workers and masters, the poor and the rich. It consoled the former and taught them contentment with their lot by informing them of the providential nature of the social order, that the share of each class was assigned by God himself, and by holding out the hope for just compensation in a world to come in return for the inequalities of this world. It governed the latter, recalling that worldly interests are not man's entire lot, that they must be subordinate to other higher interests, and that they should therefore not be pursued without rule or measure. (Pp. 255–6)

But, Durkheim continues, "religion has lost most of its power. And government, instead of regulating economic life, has become its tool and servant" (p. 256). In the absence of regulation, Durkheim notes, people employed in industrial or commercial occupations are more likely to commit anomic suicide than those who find their livelihoods in more stable environments.

The emerging dominance of the market economy posed a significant challenge to Europe during Durkheim's era because trade and industry were rapidly becoming the central social institutions in people's lives. As a result,

---

63 The term "anomie" has its English equivalent—anomy—in seventeenth century theology where it represents a state of lawlessness or a disregard of divine laws. The *Oxford English Dictionary* (OED) cites its first use in 1591 by William Lambarde in *Archion; or a commentary upon the High Courts of Justice in England*: "That were to set an Anomy, and to bring disorder, doubt, and incertaintie over all." Durkheim's use of the word stems from this meaning and is recognized by the OED as establishing a new definition for the term: "Also commonly in French form anomie. [F. (Durkheim *Suicide*, 1897).] Absence of accepted social standards or values; the state or condition of an individual or society lacking such standards."

Durkheim's study of suicide had far-reaching implications because, in view of the declining moral and guiding force of religion, a new institution was needed to integrate members of industrial capitalist society together to prevent deviant, asocial, or destructive behaviours from becoming more and more widespread and entrenched in people's lives.

At the end of *Suicide,* Durkheim ([1897] 1951:361–78) examines some potential forms of social integration. He argues, tentatively and with several important qualifications, that the *syndicates*—occupational organizations— have the potential to constitute the social groupings that will be able to generate the type of collective representations that can integrate people into an industrializing French society and prevent suicide or a growing sense of social isolation (Durkheim [1897] 1951:386–92).

Durkheim's study of suicide has a number of important implications for sociology. First, it demonstrates the power of sociology as a positive science to explain and predict social behaviour—even behaviour that seems to be completely personal and individually controlled. Second, it establishes a particular methodology for sociology—the use of large-scale studies and data to examine the relationship between an independent variable (for example, a man or a woman's religious affiliation) and a dependent variable (self-inflicted death) on the basis of a number of intervening variables— age, marital status, family size, or economic condition. Third, Durkheim's study of suicide suggests that society is greater than the sum of its parts and has an existence independent of the individuals who comprise it. Finally, it argues that it is through the generation of particular collective representations, which arise from specific social circumstances and change as those circumstances change, that people internalize ways of seeing the world. Those representations then guide and control people's behaviour—including the apparently individual decision to commit suicide.

Durkheim's analysis of suicide indicates its author's perception that people are ultimately controlled by the social worlds in which they live. Following from Durkheim, Berger suggests that people are located at the centre of a set of concentric circles, each one representing a set of particular social facts. The mechanism by which external social facts are internalized is the social generation of particular collective representations of the world. As one lives within a world that is represented in particular ways, one's actions are then contoured by those understandings and images. Those who live in largely religious situations interpret all their actions according to the dominant collective representations of religion; those who live in abject poverty see the world in a very different way, and the collective representations stemming from genuine survival-of-the-fittest life experiences shape how these individuals think about the world and act within it.

DURKHEIM AND SOCIOLOGY AS A SCIENCE

Durkheim is one of the founders of sociology partly because he played a major role in establishing Europe's first department of sociology and then launched and edited sociology's first academic journal—*L'Année sociologique*. As important as those endeavours were, Durkheim's real importance centres on three specific accomplishments.

First, Durkheim is a pivotal figure in the development of an empirical approach to the study of society, an approach that looks towards the natural sciences. The general orientation to an empirically based science began with Francis Bacon (1864), Galileo Galilei (1967), and Descartes, all of whom contributed to the development of the scientific method during the seventeenth century. It was extended to the study of society by Montesquieu, Saint-Simon, and Comte. In the work of Durkheim, an empirically based scientific approach is consolidated and presented in a manner that led to its further development by ensuing generations of sociologists. Less polemical, more measured, and far more methodical than Comte's writings, Durkheim's research and publications systematically build the foundation for an empirically based, positivist orientation to sociology.

Durkheim's *Rules of Sociological Method* proposes a methodology for sociology that later sociologists adopt and develop. *Suicide* sets the early standard for the empirical collection and analysis of social facts. Later sociologists will improve upon Durkheim's treatment of quantitative data, but Durkheim's work establishes the basic principles and methodology. In addition, Durkheim's empirical orientation to sociology is consistent with that of scholars who later maintain that the natural and social sciences are part of a unified, single approach to understanding the world. As one considers Durkheim's methodology, it is apparent why it is so central for sociologists who are committed to the unity of the sciences.

Those who support an empiricist or positivist approach to science argue that true scientific knowledge is built up from a number of axioms or propositions; these begin with basic, simple propositions that are logically coherent and build towards more complex propositions and conclusions. Positivists maintain that one must be able to test at least some, or all, of these statements to see if they might be falsified by empirical observations. Empiricists also argue that scientific knowledge is cumulative. As data are gathered and propositions are tested, new, more complex relationships and propositions can be formulated and tested, leading, ultimately, to a comprehensive theory. Finally, those who support a positivist approach to science believe in the integration of all the sciences—natural and social. Durkheim's work is consistent with this particular perspective and important in both establishing it and spreading its acceptance and influence among other social thinkers.

Durkheim's second major contribution to sociology stems from the most important of the social facts that he identified—the *conscience collective*. Durkheim recognized that people are born into societies—or particular locations in societies. A society physically surrounds people; people are, to draw upon Berger's (1963:91) image, located at the centre of a number of concentric circles. But it is more than that: it is the manner in which a society is internalized that is critical.

People become a part of society through the process of socialization—a process in which a number of social facts or forces that are external to the individual are internalized by him or her. The key concept here is the *conscience collective*. It really is through the collective conscience that the individual and society are brought together and through the full and proper understanding of this concept that one can grasp the central element of Durkheim's sociology.

The collective conscience is the key, *sui generis* social fact in Durkheim's sociology. It is greater than the sum of individual consciences and consciousnesses; it is external to each individual, and it is through the internalization of the *conscience collective* that an individual's behaviour is shaped and controlled.

The question of social order had haunted the classical thinkers from Plato and Aristotle through Hobbes and Montesquieu to Rousseau. Durkheim's work brings the question of social order directly and explicitly into the realm of sociology and connects it with an understanding of how societies function. More important, his ideas about social control are much more far reaching than those of the classical thinkers.

For classical theorists, the solution to the problem of order rests with the state. A strong state or a just state is responsible for maintaining social order. For Durkheim, the problem of order rests with society and his notion of the collective conscience. Durkheim argues that every society, located within its own particular history, develops a specific *conscience collective* that is appropriate to its specific social makeup. Through the socialization process, individuals internalize the dominant, socially accepted behaviours, attitudes, and beliefs. It is through this internalization process that the relationship of the individual and society—personal biography and the history of the social structure—remains dynamic and changing.

In the event that the dominant ways of acting are not internalized, or only partially accepted, social order is still maintained because there are a number of mechanisms of social control that ensure some measure of compliance by all individuals in a society. The mechanisms of control include physical violence; political, legal, and economic regulation and sanction; and group pressures such as persuasion, ridicule, gossip, or shunning. Indeed, these informal mechanisms of control that operate in daily life, such as mockery, are the most important for the ongoing functioning of a society in an orderly fashion.

Finally, although Durkheim is not recognized very often for his political activities, his work did carry forward the ideas and aspirations of Saint-Simon and Comte for the orderly development of social change. Living within the cauldron of the Third Republic, Durkheim knew how important social change would be for the future of France, and, like Saint-Simon, he was sceptical about revolutionary change. Consequently, Durkheim's empirical sociology studies the key forces involved in social change so as to enable the development of social policy that would ensure an orderly progress towards an increasingly cohesive and just society. The *conscience collective* is, on the one hand, one of Durkheim's key analytical concepts—one the other, it also serves in his discussions of socialism as a reference point for future hope.

DURKHEIM AND A VOCABULARY FOR CLEAR SOCIAL REFLECTION

On the basis of the material covered in this chapter, there are two key terms that Durkheim could add to the vocabulary one needs for "clear social reflection"—social facts and *conscience collective*—although social facts alone might be sufficient.

The term "social facts" emphasizes several key aspects of Durkheim's work and delineates his contributions to the classical tradition. First it underscores his efforts to establish sociology as an empirically based science—efforts that grew out of a strongly positivist strand of French thought. For better or for worse, Durkheim wanted to establish sociology as a positive science by drawing heavily upon the work of Saint-Simon and Comte and upon their efforts to use the methodology of the natural sciences for the study of society. Saint-Simon, Comte, and Durkheim, more than any other sociologists in the eighteenth or nineteenth centuries, believed in the unity of the sciences.

Because social facts are external to an individual, the term "social facts" also reminds us that sociology has a distinct subject matter that focuses on the manner in which an individual is incorporated within or socialized into a pre-existing society comprised of other individuals who interact with one another on an ongoing basis. The internalization of social facts—the process of socialization—creates the important social bond that is central to

Durkheim's sociology, and his conception of internalization leads directly to the notion of different forms of social solidarity.

The idea of social solidarity is critical to Durkheim for two reasons. First, the bonds of social solidarity—mechanical or organic—indicate that society predates the individual, is greater than the mere sum of its parts, and will continue to exist long after the individual is gone. Second, the fundamental basis for social solidarity is the *conscience collective*—one of Durkheim's most significant concepts (and, consequently, one that might be noted along with "social facts" as key to sociological vocabulary).

It is through the *conscience collective* that the individual and social are brought together—it is the central concept in Durkheim's conception of society as a whole, the source for tension and dynamism, and the focal point of almost all his work.

The notion of the collective conscience and consciousness has parallels to Marx's concept of the dominant ideology and Weber's concern with the enduring "frames of mind" that are critical to his sociology. As a result, *conscience collective* is a useful focal point for comparing and contrasting the main ideas in Marx, Durkheim, and Weber while also serving as a critical concept in one's "vocabulary for clear social reflection."

7 WEBER AND THE INTERPRETIVE UNDERSTANDING OF SOCIAL ACTION

Max Weber is regarded by most sociologists as the third major figure in the classical tradition of sociology. Born in Erfurt on 21 April 1864, Weber spent most of his childhood in Berlin, where his father, a prominent attorney, served as a member of the national parliament from 1872 to 1884. As a result, the Weber household was the site of numerous political discussions and debates as professors, parliamentarians, and other politically engaged figures came and went on a regular basis. In addition to these influences, Weber's mother, a devout Protestant, played an important role in shaping her son's outlook on the world. As a result, Weber was an extremely disciplined, principled, politically engaged scholar with a highly developed work ethic and a deep commitment to scholarship of the highest standard.

Although Weber was a full-time lecturer in Roman, German, and commercial law at the University of Berlin after 1892, his academic career really began when, in 1894, he became a full professor of economics at the University of Freiburg. In 1896, he moved to the University of Heidelberg, where he assumed the chair in political economy previously held by Karl Knies, one of Weber's former teachers and an economist of significant stature within Germany at the time. Weber's tenure as a professor was short-lived, however; he suffered from a debilitating emotional breakdown in 1897 and was unable to return to teaching, although he did not withdraw from scholarly work completely. In 1903, Weber became the lead editor of the prestigious *Archiv für Sozialwissenschaft und Sozialpolitik* (*Archive for Social Science and*

Social Policy), which placed him at the centre of the most important method-ological and substantive debates in the social sciences and humanities within turn-of-the-century Germany. In fact, it was as the editor for the *Archiv* that Weber first began to advocate for the approach to the social sciences that he pursued for the remainder of his active, academic life. Like Durkheim, Weber had a very specific notion of how social research must be conducted if it were to make a genuine contribution to social and political life.

Wanting to shape the social sciences did not mean that Weber wrote in a popular, accessible manner. On the contrary, Weber's formidable body of scholarly work is characterized by its painstaking research and thorough doc-umentation. Weber is renowned—and sometimes vilified—for his attention to detail and nuance. Weber's work is often difficult to read because of the lengthy, complex sentences he constructs in order to carefully qualify each thought and present his arguments with the greatest possible precision. A reader must labour over Weber's texts to extricate all of his meaning and pro-found insight, but the rewards for taking the time to sift carefully through the density of Weber's arguments are enormous.

The vast corpus of Weber's work can be grouped under four headings— his studies in methodology (Weber 1949b, 1968b, 1968c, 1968d, 1968f), his more or less empirical studies (for example, of the relations of production in the ancient world or of economic history; Weber [1892] 1966, 1927, [1923] 1958, 1976), his studies of religion (Weber 1922, 1923a, 1923b, [1930] 1958, [1930] 1969), and his general treatise on sociology entitled *Economy and Society*, which was left incomplete at his death in 1920 (Weber 1956, 1968a).[64] The discussion of Weber in this chapter will focus upon selected essays on methodology and his discussion of the basic principles and concepts of an interpretive sociology, which constitute the opening chapters of *Economy and Society*. Chapter 8 will examine one of Weber's most celebrated works—*The Protestant Ethic and the Spirit of Capitalism*—which brings together all four areas of Weber's work and can serve as the basis for useful comparisons with the work of Marx and Durkheim; that chapter will also examine Weber as a bridging figure between the modernist approach of classical sociology and the postmodernist perspectives one finds in a good deal of sociology today.

In many ways, Mills's conception of the sociological imagination is most heavily indebted to Weber's legacy. For Weber, sociology involves the devel-opment of a comprehensive understanding of social action. According to

---

64 Because much of Weber's most important work was published either posthumously or reissued in col-lections that brought essays on one theme together in one volume, the publication dates for material cited in this chapter do not bear a close relation to when Weber actually wrote or first published many of his pieces. English translations are much later, and do not follow the original sequence of publica-tion at all.

Weber, social life is the product of meaningful social action, and sociologists must strive to develop an interpretive understanding of the social world from the perspective of the human agents involved in it and then locate that meaningful action within the broader social framework within which it developed. Meaning, interpretive understanding, social action, and social context are key concepts for Weber, as they are for Mills.

How did Weber arrive at this particular conception of social action and the task of sociology? This chapter focuses primarily on the manner in which Weber's involvement in a critical debate on methodology in the social sciences and humanities (*Geisteswissenschaften*) led to his emphasis upon sociology as the systematic, interpretive study of social action. The chapter then examines Weber's commitment to scholarly activity, his understanding of what is entailed in science and scholarship as forms of social action, and the implications this understanding has for the role of science and sociology in determining the fundamental principles upon which a society should be ordered and governed.

THE HISTORICAL SCHOOL, ORTHODOX MARXISM, AND INTERPRETIVE SOCIOLOGY

Writing in Germany at the end of the nineteenth and during the first two decades of the twentieth century, Weber was faced with two competing and mutually exclusive approaches to method within the social sciences and humanities (*Geisteswissenschaften*) in Germany. On the one hand, there was the longstanding, extremely influential approach of the historical school and, on the other, the emergence of historical materialism as the orthodox Marxists were developing it.

The position of the historical school was quite straightforward and very well established. Proponents of the methodology of the historical school maintained that the work of historians, economists, and other social analysts involved the collection of facts pertinent to any and all events in social life. The objective was to produce as complete and exhaustive an account as possible—one that was fully based on the facts and emphasized the unique nature of each social event. The only legitimate approach to the study of human social life, in their view, was an ideographic one in which the scholar concentrated on the unique nature of each event.

Any attempt, the supporters of the historical school maintained, to see regularities in social life or social history was completely misguided. They vehemently opposed any argument claiming that there were nomothetic or law-like tendencies in social life. The suggestion that one might try to establish generalizations from the unique events of everyday life, members of the historical school maintained, was completely inappropriate for any undertaking within the humanities or social sciences.

Eduard Meyer's (1902) *Zur Theorie und Methodik der Geschichte* (*On Theory and Methods in History*) is one of the main statements from the conservative historical school. R.G. Collingwood (1962) captures succinctly the essence of Meyer's position (and that of the historical school):

> Against all this [generalization in history], Meyer contends that the proper object of historical thought is historical fact in its individuality, and that chance and free will are determining causes that cannot be banished from history without destroying its very essence. Not only is the historian as such uninterested in the so-called laws of this pseudo-science, but there are no historical laws. (P. 178; see also Weber 1949b, 1968f)

This unqualified emphasis on the ideographic nature of social life and its attendant focus on the collection of the primary facts of any social situation would remain the dominant orthodoxy among many scholars in the social sciences and was certainly true of the vast majority of historians well into the middle of the twentieth century. Historians only began to abandon their strident emphasis on the empirical and the unique with the rise of social history in the 1960s (see Carr 1961; Thompson 1970).

At the other end of both the political and methodological spectrum, historical materialism, as it was being developed by Engels and the first generation of Marxists, was emerging. Engels, as noted in Chapter 3, initiated the process of presenting all of Marx's varied works in the form of a system. The two most influential pieces that Engels wrote are *Socialism: Utopian and Scientific* ([1886] 1935)—a relatively concise summary of the main principles of and approach to "scientific socialism," which Engels produced in pamphlet form in 1880—and the larger 1878 text, *Anti-Dühring: Herr Eugen Dühring's Revolution in Science* ([1878] 1939) from which the pamphlet was drawn.

Following Engels death in 1895, the further development and elaboration of Marx's historical materialism fell primarily on the shoulders of August Bebel, Eduard Bernstein, and Karl Kautsky. It was Kautsky who played the most central role because of his previously close association with Engels and his energy, commitment, and dedication to the continuing development of the orthodox Marxist position (Kautsky 1935).

Just before Marx's death, Kautsky founded what would become one of Marxism's most influential journals—*Die Neue Zeit* (*New Times*). Under Kautsky's editorship, the journal published portions of Marx's literary estate, but it also engaged in commentary and analysis of current social issues from a Marxist perspective. Through its various critical essays, the journal attracted the attention of mainstream sociologists who engaged in debate with the journal, thereby stimulating interaction between the Marxists and German sociologists.

Then, with his 1887 publication *Karl Marx's Oekonomische Lehren* (*The Economic Doctrines of Karl Marx*), Kautsky established himself as the heir apparent of Engels—as Marxism's main theoretician and the chief architect of the Marxian system (Kautsky 1887, 1925). The book provided readers with a popularized, easy-to-grasp summary of Marx's economic theories and brought the principles of a materialist analysis to a wide readership.

Kautsky's key contribution to orthodox Marxism, however, is *Die materialistische Geschichtsauffassung* (*The Materialist Conception of History*)—a massive 1,801-page, two-volume presentation of the materialist conception of history from Kautsky's particular orthodox Marxist perspective (Kautsky 1927a, 1927b).[65] Despite the scholarly and political energy Kautsky invested in *The Materialist Conception,* his presentation met with considerable criticism. This critique of the orthodox Marxist perspective came from the traditional historians in Germany, from German legal scholars, and from a growing body of German sociologists, as well as from certain revisionist Marxists, Austro-Marxists, and Hegelian Marxists. These different criticisms of the orthodox Marxist approach to historical materialism are important insofar as they situate Weber's writings on methodology.

The most strident attack on historical materialism came from the historical school. Scholarship from this perspective emphasized the specific facts of unique historical events. Consequently, Eduard Meyer, Rudolf Stammler, Wilhelm Roscher, Karl Knies, and others within the school presented a position in diametrical opposition to the orthodox Marxist's claim that there are dialectical laws of social life that explain and lead to a succession of modes of production and that this succession, in turn, leads to communism. In short, the historical school disputed the historical processes that Marx had identified in his 1859 preface to *Towards the Critique of Political Economy* and in the *Communist Manifesto.*

The Hegelian-Marxists' critique, presented by Karl Korsch (1922, 1923, 1929, 1970), Georg Lukács (1923, 1970), and Antonio Labriola (1904),

---

65 Kautsky, it should also be noted, was actively recruited for the preparation and wider dissemination of Marx's major economic works. Engels entrusted Kautsky with the responsibility of transcribing, editing, and publishing the manuscripts for Marx's so-called fourth volume of *Capital—The Theories of Surplus Value* (Marx 1921a, 1921b, 1921c, 1921d). Kautsky also painstakingly checked all Marx's references in the three volumes of *Capital* (Marx was far from meticulous in his referencing), added a complete bibliography, and translated all foreign citations and terms into German to produce a *Volksausgabe* or popular edition of *Capital.* Kautsky produced the first volume on his own; his son Benedikt assisted him with the second and then assumed the primary editorial role with his father assisting on the two parts that constituted volume three (Marx 1914, 1926, 1929a, 1929b).

supports the argument that history can unfold in a particular direction due to the internal contradictions of different modes of production but holds that those contradictions, in and of themselves, are not sufficient to create change or to guide it towards a higher stage of history. Drawing upon the Hegelian heritage in Marx's work, Korsch, Lukács, and Labriola argue that consciousness is a key factor in the historical process—one that orthodox Marxists discount far too much. Maintaining that Marx's historical materialism focuses on the material factors of history, Korsch, Lukács, and Labriola argue that consciousness and ideology are, in fact, one of the material constituents of social history and that one has to examine the ways in which consciousness and ideology facilitate and constrain the material practices of humankind within different social formations. This view of the role of consciousness in social processes became important for Weber and informs his contributions to the debate between the historical school and the proponents of historical materialism.

When this debate was lively, Weber was at the University of Heidelberg. He had attracted a small but active group of like-minded thinkers there, and they constituted an informal Weber circle. Weber and this circle of academics played a dominant role in the development of German sociology. The circle included a number of people who attained significant stature in their respective disciplines. Heinrich Rickert, one of the more influential philosophers in the systematic demarcation and separation of the *Geisteswissenschaften* from the *Naturwissenschaften,* was a close friend of Weber's. Lukács, who was deeply interested in the sociological study of literature and aesthetics, was a student of Weber's (and of Simmel's). Georg Simmel was also Weber's friend and collaborator, and he became an influential figure in the development of German sociology, although with a lower profile than Weber.

This circle of academics weighed in on the issue of historical materialism. Interestingly, the critique from the Weber circle is not directed primarily at Kautsky and the orthodox Marxists. Instead, Weber and his colleagues mainly target the historical school—especially its unyielding emphasis on the idiosyncrasies of social life and its refusal to develop any conception of generalization. In making the critique, Weber and his colleagues accept certain aspects of the historical materialist position, but they are also critical of historical materialism's shortcomings, as they see them. Not surprisingly, Weber argues that consciousness and the formation of human understanding in the social world cannot be reduced solely to the economic base, as the orthodox Marxists maintained.

Weber and the Methodology of the Social Sciences

Weber enters the dispute over the method appropriate to the *Geisteswissen-schaften* with a searing rebuttal of Stammler's ([1894] 1924) *Wirtschaft und Recht nach der materialistischen Geschichtsauffassung: Eine sozialphilosophische Untersuchung* (*Economy and Law According to the Materialist Conception of History: A Socio-Philosophical Investigation*), an attack on historical materialism by one of the historical school's leading thinkers. Weber (1968c, 1977) constructs a four-part response entitled "R. Stammler's 'Refutation' of the Materialist Conception of History." It was one of eight essays on methodological questions and issues that Weber wrote between 1903 and 1918.[66]

Weber's critique of Stammler establishes three main points. First, Weber argues that Stammler completely misrepresents many key aspects of historical materialism and then proceeds to attack a caricature of the orthodox Marxist position. This aspect of Weber's critique takes up most of the essay, but its next two points are most significant for this discussion.

Weber's second main point focuses on how complex questions of method are and on the need to explore them with great care and precision. One must clearly establish one's fundamental premises and demonstrate how the arguments that follow build from those premises.

Finally, Weber claims that "something like a methodological pestilence" was beginning to prevail in the social sciences (quoted in Weber 1977:11). One essay on methodology would lead to a refutation, followed by an answer to the refutation, followed by yet another restatement of the original refutation. The result, according to Weber: a pestilence or plague of inward looking and self-referential essays that contributed little to the real advancement of sociological knowledge. The main problems of methodology, Weber argues, can only be resolved on the basis of the actual analysis of the empirical social world—on the basis of genuine lived experience.

In a critique of Mayer, which establishes the same point regarding Stammler, Weber (1968c) insists that only "through the identification and solution to *substantive* problems are the sciences established and their methods developed. Purely epistemological or methodological reflections have never contributed anything of decisive importance" (p. 217). In other words, based on his extensive knowledge of history as well as his keen insight into contemporary social life, Weber maintains in this passage that sociologists

---

66   Weber published four parts of his Stammler critique, promising a fifth that he did not publish in his lifetime. Weber (1949a, 1968d, 1968f, 1975) wrote equally critical review essays against Roscher, Knies, and Meyer, although his critique of Roscher and Knies and of their approach to the historical study of economics also remained incomplete (Weber 1968d, 1975). Weber's widow, Marianne, republished some essays on this topic along with several draft manuscripts that Weber had left unfinished at his death. The collection was later updated and expanded slightly by Johannes Winckelmann, who succeeded Marianne Weber as the executor of her husband's literary estate (Weber 1968b).

have to refine their methodology through their investigations of people's real lived experiences and not through abstract argument.

Consistent with the emphasis upon meaning and understanding found within the German *Geisteswissenschaften,* Weber's sociology is built upon the role that meaning plays in all forms of social action. He elaborates this foundation in an unfinished draft of his systematic treatise on interpretive sociology:

> Sociology (in the sense in which this highly ambiguous word is used here) is a science [*Wissenschaft*] concerning itself with the interpretive understanding [*deutend verstehen*] of social action [*soziales Handeln*] and thereby with a causal explanation of its course and consequences. "Action" signifies human conduct (whether overtly or covertly, by omission or acquiescence) that is associated with subjective *meaning.* But an action is "social" action ["*soziales*" *Handeln*] when its intended meaning takes account of the behaviour of *others* and is thereby oriented in its unfolding [*Ablauf*]. (Weber 1956:1, 1968a:3)

The importance Weber places on the interpretive understanding of human social action has five implications for his work.

First, it means that Weber approaches sociology as "a comprehensive science of *social action*"—with the emphasis upon social action. Weber wants to understand "social action"—the *specific categories of human action which, throughout the course of the action, took into account the behaviour of others and the meaning they and the initiator of the action attached to it.*

Second, Weber views sociology as "a *comprehensive science* of social action"—with the emphasis upon comprehensive science this time. Sociologists have *to interpret and understand* social actions and produce *comprehensive accounts of social action.* To understand or grasp the meaning of social action, Weber argues, sociologists must assume an interpretive position—a *verstehende Ansatz*—rather than simply collect quantitative data based on a variety of external social facts. An interpretive position involves either trying to understand the meaning the person carrying out the action might be intending or what meaning a person's actions might convey to others—sometimes it involves both. The key is to try to understand interpretively "the intended meaning" associated with an action as it is conducted.

A comprehensive account has to go beyond simply describing an action—it has to place the action into as full a socio-historical context as possible, and it has to explore the meaning different agents ascribe to that action. A comprehensive science explores all of the information that it can find, and, in the humanities and social sciences (the *Geisteswissenschaften*), meaning is of critical importance.

Third, Weber notes that, in all cases, "'understanding' [*Verstehen*] involves the interpretive grasp [*deutende Erfassung*] of the meaning present in one of the following contexts":

> (a) the actually intended meaning for the specific action (as in the historical approach); or (b) the average of, or an approximation to, the actually intended meaning (as in cases of sociological mass observation); or (c) the meaning appropriate to a *pure* type [*reinen Typus*] (an ideal type) of a common phenomenon. (Weber 1956:4, 1968a:9)

Although recognizing the three respective levels of understanding, Weber views only one of those levels of understanding as the ultimate objective for sociology as a form of systematic inquiry—as a comprehensive science of social action:

> Sociology constitutes—as we have frequently assumed as self-evident— *type*-concepts and seeks *general* rules of events. This is in contradistinction to history, which seeks causal analyses and explanation of *individual, culturally* significant actions, structures, and personalities. (Weber 1956:9, 1968a:19)

Sociology, in contrast to history, then, should move away from the specific and unique to establish more generalized knowledge and theories of social action. Sociology involves a process of abstraction—the process of moving from the specific to the more general and, ultimately, to broadly inclusive analyses of social behaviour.

Ideal Types or Pure Types

It is important to explore this point further because it is critical to understanding Weber's work as a sociologist and his aspirations for sociology as a comprehensive science of social action. On the one hand, Weber's quest to produce empirically based, generalized understandings of social action is completely consistent with the objectives of other sciences. In this respect, Weber, Marx, Durkheim, and even Bacon, Galileo, and Hume share a common objective—to develop generalized knowledge that begins with careful, detailed observations of the empirical world and proceeds, through the process of abstraction, to the identification of generalized trends, which might ultimately become universal laws. The key objective of scholarship (science or *Wissenschaft*) is the development of the most widely applicable knowledge possible. (In the natural sciences the goal is often universally applicable knowledge while, in the social sciences, although some may aspire to discover universal laws, most would argue that economists, political scientists, and sociologists can only achieve knowledge that one may generalize to specified locations, circumstances, and periods of time.)

On the other hand, Weber differs from Marx, Durkheim, Bacon, and Galileo in two important respects. First, unlike Bacon and Galileo, Weber was not trying to develop universal laws. Weber did not believe that sociology could ever aspire to uncovering the universal laws of human behaviour, although he did believe, as did Durkheim and Marx, that sociologists could develop different concepts and generalized interpretations of social action, ones that they could use to understand social action under any conditions—past or present or anticipated in the future.[67]

Second, Weber differs from Durkheim, Galileo, and Bacon with respect to the type of knowledge sociology should be pursuing. Knowledge must begin with the direct observation and study of the empirically existing world—all agree on that point. But, rather than simply collecting directly observable facts or social facts in the form of variables that can be related causally to one another, Weber argues, sociologists must offer sociological explanations and generalizations. Sociologists have to develop an *interpretive understanding* of social action. The process of abstraction and the attention to meaning that Weber has in mind when he discusses this interpretive understanding is apparent in one of his major contributions to sociology—Weber's fourfold typology of social action.

On the basis of all the different and varied types of social action that he encountered in his research, Weber hypothesizes that it is possible to categorize all meaningful social action into one of four distinct pure types: goal-rational, value-rational, affective, and traditional action:

Goal-rational action (*zweckrationales Handeln*) is *rational action*—mentally calculated action—*that is aimed at achieving a particular goal.*

Value-rational action (*wertrationales Handeln*) is *rational action guided by a particular value or belief.*

---

67 Weber was very aware that the social world changed, as did sociologists' understanding of it. As a result, the concepts adequate for understanding western European societies in the early twentieth century were not necessarily the ones that would still be in use at the end of the century or those needed to examine life in the twenty-first century. Thus, although Weber believed that sociologists should strive for and could often develop concepts enabling the examination of social life in the past, present, and, potentially, into the future, he also knew that changes in society might require the development of new concepts and the rejection of some that had been used previously.

Affective or emotional action is action *guided by desires or emotions* (fear, anger, hate, vengeance, lust, or love, for example).

Traditional action is action *guided by the dictates of tradition.*[68]

Each of these types of action describes the external nature of the action and the subjective meaning the action holds for the person carrying it out; each also takes into account the behaviour of others and the anticipated meanings they might associate with the action.

For Weber, this conceptualization of action—this process of abstracting from the immediately observable activities one finds in everyday life—leads to the development of concepts or, as Weber prefers, "ideal types" or "pure types." (Weber uses these terms interchangeably.) In other words, the generalizations that sociologists develop from observation establish a general framework, based on generalized concepts, which can then be used as reference points or the basis for comparison with actual events and meaningful actions in the reality of everyday life or in the recorded history of other periods. Weber explains both the advantages and disadvantages of these generalized concepts:

> As is the case of every generalizing science the abstract character of the concepts of sociology is responsible for the fact that, compared with actual historical reality, they are relatively lacking in fullness of concrete content. To compensate for this disadvantage, sociological analysis can offer a greater precision of concepts. This precision is obtained by striving for the highest possible degree of adequacy on the level of meaning. (Weber 1968a:20)

In essence, Weber takes what could be considered a weakness—sociology must abstract from (or move away from) the real world of lived experience and thereby lose the fullness of concrete content—and regards it as a strength. The concepts that sociologists develop can incorporate all aspects of meaning (for example, the impact of mystical, prophetic, and affective or emotional dimensions of action along with the rational and calculated dimensions) to produce an enriched concept that one can then use as a reference point for analyses.

---

68 On the basis of this typology of social action, Weber (1956) also develops his typology of what he calls "the three *pure* types of legitimate domination [*drei reine Typen legitimer Herrschaft*]" that one finds in societies throughout history. Weber argues that there are three pure types of legitimate domination— traditional, charismatic, and rational (or legal-rational). See Weber (1956:122–76, 1968a:941–1374).

As a result, an ideal type (or pure type) is viewed by Weber as a deliberate conceptualization that sociologists produce on the basis of their comprehensive understanding of the social action in people's everyday lives. The sociologist constructs the ideal type so that it sharply and precisely identifies the key characteristics that are pertinent to the action under study (for example, goal-rational action). The ideal type brings to conscious awareness aspects of action that are often only partially conscious or that are subconscious, thereby enriching the analysis the sociologist can undertake.

The tendency to produce ideal types operates, consciously or not, in all systematic discussions of cultural or social behaviour. Whenever people discuss or write about religion, power, crime, or even bureaucracy, they stylize, simplify, and accentuate certain aspects so the analysis can focus on the most important features of the issue at hand.

Economists, for example, develop specific concepts (supply, demand, monopoly, or monopsony) so that they can make the economy intelligible.[69] They do not discuss the economy in all of its concrete detail and daily flux. Economists approach the economy conceptually.

The same is true of sociology—sociologists can discuss capitalism, for example, intelligently when they begin with the main concepts or features that comprise capitalism as a pure case (or pure type or ideal type).[70] On the basis of that pure type, they can then examine Canada as a capitalist society and compare it to the United States, Russia, or the United Arab Emirates, let's say.

In the construction of ideal types that are consciously created as abstractions derived from the complexity of reality, sociologists sacrifice one thing to gain another. They sacrifice the detail and flux of the phantasmagoria of everyday life, but they gain the enriched insight ideal types can generate by accentuating particular, key features while also including aspects of meaning that are missed or lost in the immediate context of the life-world. The pure type approach that Weber advocates for the humanities and social sciences allows him to maintain the central significance of meaning to social action while also contributing to a science of society that produces meaningful generalizations about social action and social life.

---

69 Monopoly and monopsony are distinct concepts differentiating the conditions of the market in precise and important ways. A monopoly is a one-seller market; a monopsony is a one-buyer market. In a monopoly, the seller has the advantage and may drive prices accordingly; in a monopsony, the purchaser has greater influence over the prices in the market. The best situation for a business is a monopoly in the market in which it sells products—so it can keep sale prices and profits high—and a monopsony in the market in which it purchases raw materials and labour—so it can keep costs to a minimum.

70 Werner Sombart (1991), who shares Weber's approach to understanding in the social sciences, argues that the key constituent elements of a capitalist society are (1) the spirit or outlook (characterized by acquisition, competition, and rationality), (2) the form (or institutional order), and (3) technology.

This leads to the final implication that Weber's emphasis upon sociology as a comprehensive science of social action has for his sociology in general and for his work on the methodology of the social sciences in particular. Weber uses his approach to sociology to examine the degree to which sociology, in particular, or science, in general, can serve as the ultimate guide to human action. Can science—especially social science—serve as the ethical guide to human action? Put in different terms—are there limits to scientific knowledge?

SCIENCE AND ETHICS: THE LIMITS OF GOAL-RATIONAL ACTION

Weber lived through the turmoil in Europe that led to World War I; he lived through the war and long enough to experience all of the political tensions and personal anxieties that Germans, in particular, and others in Europe experienced after the war.

Besides the economic and political insecurities that caused and followed World War I, Weber's generation often experienced spiritual and ethical uncertainty, as faith and religion seemed to be giving way to doubt and to various and relative worldviews. As early as 1882, Nietzsche's "The Parable of the Madman" had announced God's demise:

> God is dead. God remains dead. And we have killed Him. ... Led out [of churches] and called to account, ... [the madman] is said always to have replied nothing but: "What after all are these churches now if they are not the tombs and sepulchres of God?" (Nietzsche [1882] 1974:181–2)

Although the philosophy behind the parable is complex, Nietzsche is not using it to mourn the death of God; he advocates humankind taking charge of its own affairs rather than passively accepting the dictates of the church. Whether Nietzsche's contemporaries agreed with him, his parable struck a chord at the turn of the twentieth century because many people then were looking for a moral compass that could guide human behaviour. They wanted a firm basis for ethical conduct. If not in traditional religions, could this basis be found in science?

As a scholar committed to the idea that social science should inform people's lives at every level, from the mundane matters of daily life to the formation of national policies, Weber (1946b; 1968e) wrestles with this question—can science be the ultimate source of ethical conduct? Weber's answer is no. In reaching this conclusion, he makes some important contributions concerning both how one should understand scientific inquiry as meaningful human action and how one must understand ethical decision making as a type of meaningful human action.

Weber's answer to the question of whether science can serve as the moral compass of human social action stems directly from his fourfold typology of social action. Looking at science as meaningful social action—action that has meaning to the agent and takes into account the behaviour of others (Weber 1956:1, 1968a:3)—Weber notes that the goal of science is to produce propositions of fact and statements of causality or, in the case of the social sciences, comprehensive interpretations of social action. The social action that characterizes scientific or scholarly action is goal-rational action. Scientists and scholars *use rational means (the specific techniques of their field of science or scholarship) to pursue a specific goal—universally valid truth.*[71]

As the pursuit of universally valid truth, science might seem capable of serving as the moral compass for the modern world. But, Weber argues, scientific action is not simply or exclusively goal-rational action. The action of scholars and scientists is also value-rational action (*wertrationales Handeln*) because these truth seekers are committed to a specific value. Scientific action, Weber maintains, is fundamentally committed to *the value of truths demonstrated by universally valid facts or arguments.*

Before a scholar can engage in scientific activity as a goal-rational action, she or he must have already made a commitment to the value of truths demonstrated by universally valid facts or arguments. Any scholar who manipulates data; fails to examine alternative hypotheses (no matter how uncomfortable or unpopular); or in any other way fails to subject her or his findings, arguments, and conclusions to rigorous analysis and critique does not place a high enough value upon the pursuit of truth to be a genuine scholar or scientist. Without this unyielding commitment to the value of scientific truths, scientific action can never serve as the means for the discovery of universally valid truths.

Scientific action, it turns out, is goal-rational and value-rational action. It is within the value-rational dimension of scholarship, Weber's work demonstrates, that the real problem lies for anyone's hope that science might serve as the ultimate moral compass for society or as the basis for a system of absolute ethics. The value-rational dimension of scholarly action poses

---

71 The phrase "universally valid truth" can cause some confusion because even though the objectives of natural scientists and social scientists or scholars seem to differ in terms of their interest in universal laws (in the case of the natural sciences) versus empirically based, accurate, generalized understandings or theories (in the case of the social sciences and humanities), they all share the goal of producing knowledge that has *truthful validity that anyone can examine and test.* The goal of modernist scholars is to develop accurate statements (truths) about the natural and/or social worlds that are based on the systematic, theoretically informed scrutiny of the real worlds within which humankind lives.

three limitations to science's potential to act as the definitive moral compass for society or as a determiner of universal ethics.

First, scientific activity is, in and of itself, a value-rational activity. As such, it represents one specific commitment to a particular value—the importance of the pursuit and discovery of universally valid truth. But, as one specific value commitment, it cannot also serve as an unbiased, independent arbiter of various other different, competing values.

On what basis, then, can anyone, even a scientist, argue that the pursuit of the universally valid truths of science is a higher value than the pursuit of truth through the Holy Scriptures, for example, or through Plato's theory of forms? A commitment to a particular value or value system, Weber maintains, is a judgement of value (*Werturteil*, meaning a commitment to value or a value judgement). As such, it cannot be assessed, supported, or undermined by any other judgement of value, including a value commitment to some transcendental position of supreme wisdom.

A judgement of value, a commitment to a value, means precisely this— placing a high value on a key notion or set of notions (*Wert-ur-teil*).

That judgement can be based on reasoned calculation, faith, or emotional attachment, or it might be taken out of fear or because of the charismatic attraction of certain values, but it is not based on any absolute measure and cannot be based on any absolute measure (at least not within the knowledge system to which Weber subscribed). Therefore, Weber argues, science, being a judgement of value, is limited and cannot stand as the definitive moral compass for contemporary society.

The second reason scientific knowledge cannot serve as an absolute reference point, according to Weber, is quite simple. The world (natural and social) is infinitely complex. It can never be fully known.

Science generates abstract theories that give meaning to the world, allow humankind to interact meaningfully with it, and, to a certain extent, control it. But even the most advanced scientific insights remain incomplete. Science makes the world intelligible—but not fully known and comprehended.

Scientists commit themselves to an impossible task—they commit themselves to a fundamental value judgement that is, ultimately, unrealizable (although commitment to that value ensures that their work unerringly *strives* towards the realization of that value). Scientists seek to discover universally accepted truths that can advance scientific knowledge, but the abstract laws they generate will never achieve an absolute form of knowledge because an infinite, changing world can never be fully known.

That the final aim of science will remain unachieved does not mean that scientific activity is useless, however. Scientists have produced countless accomplishments in the process of trying to reach science's ultimate goal,

but attaining *universal truths* for an infinitely complex and continually changing world *is not possible.*

Finally, the ways in which science develops and advances do not and
cannot lead to the development of absolute knowledge. Weber argues that
scholars assess the world in which they live and work, and, in the process,
they discover certain questions, problems, or issues that become important
to them. Through a process of relevance—what Weber terms value-relevant
action (*Wertbeziehung*—a relationship of value)—scholars choose the issues
they will research and study.

Part of the reason a question or issue becomes relevant is internal to a
scholar's discipline at a particular point in time. Thus, for example, members of the historical school in the early 1900s chose to examine historical
materialism critically because it was rivalling scientific theory, which they
thought was seriously flawed.

Another part of the reason was that historical materialism was associated
with a rising socialist movement in Germany, and the politically conservative
members of the historical school wanted to undermine historical materialism as a scientific basis for German socialism. In this instance, the value relevance of historical materialism for scholars in the historical school was due to
factors and events in the broader social environment in which they all lived.

The historical school became relevant to Weber because of his interest
in questions of method and his belief that the school's position was influential but also wrong and needed to be addressed.

Based on his own experiences and his interpretive understanding of how
issues or questions become relevant to other researchers, Weber acknowledges that the questions scholars address are related to issues that hold value
relevance for them. The value relevance that motivates a scholar to pursue a
particular question may be strictly scholarly, but it may also involve broader,
extra-scientific concerns.[72]

This issue can be approached in a manner that is more complex, but the
outcome is the same. If scientific action is a form of value-relevant action,
one might think that scholars would only pursue questions directly related to
the search for universally valid truths. In that case, they would never be interested in a question because of its political importance or personal relevance;
the only relevance a question could have would be exclusively related to the

---

72 Once a scientist or scholar chooses a value-relevant question or issue, she or he, as a scientific scholar,
is then committed to suspending all personal interest in the question and pursuing that question on
the basis of a commitment to the value of scholarship (that is, the value judgement or value commitment to the pursuit of universal truth). Scholars are committed to the pursuit of universally
valid truths because that is both the goal of science and the value that determines acceptable from
unacceptable behaviour and action as a scientist.

pursuit of universally valid truths (and any political or personal relevance would be coincidental).

Although this claim is problematic, assume for a moment that all scientists pursue questions and study issues *solely because of the contribution doing so will make to universally valid truth*. Will this result in the inevitable advancement of science towards its value-relevant goal of universally valid truth? Unfortunately—no.

Prior to the time when humankind finally achieves absolute, universal knowledge, the selection of topics and issues would be tied to value-relevant interests and questions stemming from less than perfect knowledge. Consequently, there would be no guarantee that the scientific community would pursue the absolutely necessary value-relevant questions that would lead to absolute universal truth. Having an imperfect comprehension of the world, scientists might ask and pursue the right questions, but, more likely, it would be only by chance that they would choose the correct issues to lead to absolute knowledge. And in a world of infinite complexity, the odds of posing the correct questions time and again as knowledge advances towards an absolute truth are astronomically stacked against science. As a result, the way in which problems are chosen is a serious obstacle to the scientific community ever finding the path to absolute knowledge—despite the fact that, once a problem is chosen, scientists follow the value-rational commitment to pursue universal truths.

In summary, Weber's position is that scientific action cannot serve as the basis for a system of universal ethics or as the ultimate moral compass for a society for three specific reasons. First, as a form of social action, science is a form of value-rational action. It represents one value-based form of action among many. Even though those who live in an increasingly rationalistic age might highly esteem a value commitment to scientific knowledge, there are no absolute grounds upon which that valuation can be proven as the correct one. In an age dominated by Roman Catholicism, for example, the value commitment to Christianity would be higher and scientific action would hold less value. Similarly, if C.S. Lewis's (2001) arguments about God and Christianity in *Mere Christianity* are accepted, then, even in this highly secular age, science would not be the route to absolute knowledge. In both cases just mentioned, scientific action and religious action represent value-rational forms of action and none of them, despite what might be felt from within each of those value commitments, can serve as a universal value system other than through faith—a value commitment to be sure.

Second, if it were possible for scientific action to produce absolute, universal truth (or truths), then the case that science could serve as the basis for a system of absolute ethics would be strong. However, according to Weber, science can never really attain the goal it steadfastly pursues. It cannot achieve that goal for three reasons.

First, the real world in which humankind lives is infinitely complex and changing. Infinite complexity is the first challenge, and its changing nature makes the problem even worse.

Second, science sacrifices the fullness of concrete reality for the precision of the concepts it develops. The precision of concepts in science means that the conceptual apparatus of science is never static—it must develop as more is learned about the real worlds in which people live.

Third, even if the infinite complexity of the natural world could be encompassed by the conceptual systems of science, the objective behind establishing an absolute ethical system is not the ethical guidance of natural objects—it is to guide human conduct. A system of absolute ethics would guide people's actions in their personal, social, and political lives; as a result, it is the universally valid truths of *social action* that are most central to the issue of an absolute ethical system. But the world of social action and the meanings that are central to it are *always changing* (see also Giddens 1984). Science could not possibly provide the absolute knowledge needed to guide human action (that is, meaningful social action).

Finally, science cannot serve as the basis for a system of universal ethics because of the way scientists and scholars conduct their work. Researchers select their research topics and agendas based on the questions they find relevant. They base their research on value-relevant issues. Value relevance, however, even when the scholar is committed to the pursuit of universally valid truth, cannot serve as an infallible guide to absolute knowledge because even scientific interests are shaped within a world of imperfect knowledge—an infinitely complex world that is imperfectly understood.

On the basis of all these arguments, Weber draws one of his most significant conclusions. The goals or ends that an individual, a group, a society, or even all of humankind chooses to pursue can never be determined by an infallible ethical system based upon science (Weber 1946a, 1958). Scientific knowledge is limited; it is just one form of knowledge among many, and, as a result, it can never be an infallible guide to human action. The goals that individuals, groups, or societies pursue are determined within the realm of political discussion, debate, and decision making. Once these goals are chosen, then science can serve as an important guide to reaching those goals. Science can serve as one of the most effective means of goal-rational action, but it cannot determine any system of absolute ends.

It is here that one can further appreciate Weber's complexity as a sociologist. On the one hand, Weber outlines the highest standards for scholarship—especially scholarship in the social sciences. Scholars should undertake, to the fullest of their ability, the pursuit of absolute truths, even though Weber knows that this quest is impossible to achieve. In this sense, Weber holds science and scholarship in the highest regard possible, yet he is also wary of science—not because scholars might fail to live up to the highest standards of their calling (although this was a concern for Weber) but because of the pedestal upon which people in the modern era had placed science. Weber was acutely aware that, in an increasingly secular world in which the performance imperatives of industrial capitalism dominated, goal-rational action had become a dominant force in all aspects of social life. Goal-rational action was already almost sacrosanct, and it would be increasingly regarded as beyond reproach—above critique—despite the fact that goal-rational action was only one type of social action and not one that could establish an infallible set of ethical principles. According to Weber, the discussions, debates, and decisions about the overall goals of a society and about proper human conduct should take place within the political realm. Therefore, the political system should be open, inclusive, and vibrant. Science could inform the pursuit of particular social goals once these had been decided, but it should not be the dominant, decisive force. But Weber feared that science—the most dominant form of goal-rational action in the modern period—had become overly influential and decisive in his day and that it would increasingly place humanity within an "iron cage of reason."

8 THE SPIRIT OF CAPITALISM, MODERNITY, AND THE POSTMODERN WORLD

The discussion on Weber in Chapter 7 focused mainly on his work in methodology and indicated how that led to his particular emphasis upon sociology as the interpretive study of social action. The chapter then examined Weber's notion of pure (or ideal) types and the four pure types of social action he identified—affective, traditional, goal-rational, and value-rational action. The final section explored the limitations that Weber's understanding of social action places upon science and scholarship as the means for determining a system of ethical conduct and social governance.

Two aspects of Weber's thought were noted but not addressed at length in the last chapter's discussion of science and social action. The first is Weber's position on the infinite complexity of the social world and how it might situate him as a bridging figure between classical modernist sociology and the postmodernist conceptions of sociology found in contemporary approaches to sociological analysis. This theme is taken up at length in the second major section of this chapter.

The second is the idea noted at the end of Chapter 7—Weber's fear that the growing domination of goal-rational action in the modern world could leave humanity trapped in an "iron cage of reason." This prospect Weber discusses in his most widely cited essay "Die protestantische Ethik und der Geist des Kapitalismus" (translated in 1930 and published as the monograph *The Protestant Ethic and the Spirit of Capitalism*). However, this essay—originally published in numbers 20 and 21 of the *Archive for Social Science and*

Social Policy in 1905 and then republished in a revised, expanded form in 1920—does more than express a concern about the future impact of goal-rational action; the work embodies almost all of Weber's major concerns as a sociologist. It deals with the impact of religion on a society and the impact of a dominant "frame of mind" on how people interpret and understand the world around them; it addresses issues of method, and it demonstrates Weber's acumen as a historical sociologist. Because of the work's comprehensive nature, the first part of this chapter will explore *The Protestant Ethic and the Spirit of Capitalism* in detail.

The Protestant Ethic and the Spirit of Capitalism

In his discussion of methodology that critiques Meyer, Weber (1968f) notes, "Purely epistemological or methodological reflections have never contributed anything of decisive importance" to the development of methodology in the social sciences (p. 217). Weber can make this claim because he had studied the social world extensively and could draw upon that substantive background in all of his discussions of methodology in the humanities and social sciences. One area of significant inquiry was the impact of the different religions of the world on the societies in which they existed or dominated, and one finds *The Protestant Ethic and the Spirit of Capitalism* within that body of work.

About *The Protestant Ethic*, Weber notes that he employs "the somewhat pretentious phrase, the *spirit* [*Geist*] of capitalism" in the title. He then asks, "What is to be understood by it?" His answer follows:

> If any object can be found to which this term [the spirit of capitalism] can be applied with any understandable meaning, it can only be ... a complex of elements associated in historical reality which we unite into a conceptual whole from the standpoint of their cultural significance. (Weber [1930] 1958:47)

In plain language, "the spirit of modern capitalism" is a culturally significant entity that is comprised of a number of social factors. The act of drawing together and studying the complex unity of several factors is typical of Weber's approach to sociological analysis; equally important and characteristic of his work is the examination of how these different factors combine to yield a specific social impact.

Weber undertook this study because he felt that, although capitalism had a relatively long history, its modern form was significantly different from its earlier forms. Comparing capitalism in fifteenth or sixteenth century Florence, for example, to capitalism in eighteenth century Pennsylvania confirmed, in Weber's mind, that modern capitalism is animated by a different set of values—a different spirit—than were earlier forms. How did this unique spirit arise? Did it emerge from the internal dynamic of capitalism itself (as orthodox Marxists suggested) or from other sources (as other economic historians asserted)?[73] If there were other sources, what were they exactly?

Weber argues that the type of economic rationalism that had begun to dominate western Europe and North America depended on more than the advanced development of technology. The economic rationalism of modern capitalism rested on people's willingness to organize their lives in a particular, rational manner. This willingness to engage in goal-rational action—to determine the most efficient means to a particular end—represents the spirit of capitalism that Weber sought to investigate.

Weber opens his discussion about the "*Geist des Kapitalismus* [the spirit, mind, culture, and ethos of capitalism]" with a number of maxims drawn from Benjamin Franklin, words that capture the spirit of life under modern capitalist conditions:

> Remember, that *time* is money. He that can earn ten shillings a day by his labour, and goes abroad, or sits idle, one half of that day, though he spends but sixpence during his diversion or idleness ought not to reckon *that* the only expense; he has really spent, or rather thrown away, five shillings besides. (Weber [1930] 1958:48, [1930] 1969:40)

Weber notes the significance of this orientation to money and life. For him, the spirit of capitalism speaks in these words, and they form a particular view of the world, an ethic or philosophy. As he writes,

> Truly what is preached is not simply a means of making one's way in the world, but a peculiar ethic. The infraction of its rules is treated not as foolishness but as forgetfulness of duty. ... It is not mere business astuteness, that sort of thing is common enough; it is an *ethos* [emphasis in German original]. (Weber [1930] 1958:51, [1930] 1969:42)

---

73 Part of Weber's argument in *The Protestant Ethic and the Spirit of Capitalism* is aimed at refuting arguments put forth by other economic historians. Although not important for this discussion, it is worth noting that some economic historians of Weber's day attributed the rise of modern capitalism to the intensification of avarice (the desire to acquire). Others saw modern capitalism as a natural evolutionary development from early capitalism (with an intensified rationality). Still others said it was the result of the practices that particular high-profile, charismatic capitalists employed and that others copied. Finally, some saw modern capitalism developing from the practices of Jewish merchants who turned to industrial production rather than simply mercantilism. This last argument was partly inspired by a sometimes latent and sometimes manifest anti-Semitism in European scholarship and served as the fuel for anti-Semitism in Europe as it began to increase during periods of political and economic crisis in the first third of the twentieth century.

But what was the source of this ethos?

For Weber, the secret to understanding the ethos or spirit of capitalism lay in the religious belief system of the seventeenth-century Puritan churches—the Calvinists, Methodists, Congregationalists, Baptists, Quakers, Independents, and Mennonites—and stemmed from John Calvin's particular teachings.

Previous to the Reformation, Roman Catholicism served as the divine justification for the feudal order in medieval Europe. Catholic doctrines were a major force in the consolidation of the feudal formation, as well as a key locus of resistance to any change threatening feudalism's overall hierarchical structure or central dynamics. But the Roman Catholic Church was not omnipotent, and Catholicism's success in bringing order and stability led to its obsolescence as a guiding doctrine for millions of Europeans as the spiritual, political, and economic landscape changed dramatically in the sixteenth century.

The consolidation of feudalism created the social conditions for expanding trade and travel, and the import of exotic goods from afar served as a stimulus for kings and lords to direct more of the productive activity on their estates to the creation of goods that could be exchanged. This shift had disastrous implications for the feudal peasantry: they were slowly squeezed off the land and lost almost all of their feudal rights. As more and more peasants were forced off the land into a destitute existence—during the fifteenth and sixteenth centuries, the European peasantry became a mass of homeless wanderers eking out their existence wherever and however possible—the teachings of the Catholic Church began to lose meaning for people.

The newly emerging and austere social conditions of the displaced population became fertile soil for a religious belief system that gave dignity to poverty and destitution and turned self-denial and sacrifice into a sacred calling. This was one of the roles that Calvin's ascetic Protestantism would fill.

According to Calvin, religion was a highly individual, personal matter. One could and must communicate as directly as possible with God. More important, Calvin believed in the god of the Old Testament, a highly judgemental creator who sought to test people to determine who were the most worthy of heaven. Calvin believed that God would admit only a tiny fraction of humanity into heaven—everyone else was condemned to eternal damnation.

Although God would not disclose in advance which people would enter heaven (the elect), he had created a life on earth that would test and prepare humanity for his final decision. Life on earth was unjust, demanding, irrational, and burdensome: some in the afterlife would have these burdens removed and rejoice in an eternal life with God in heaven. Others—the vast majority—would not. But suffering was God's way of deciding who merited everlasting life in his kingdom. Earthly hardship and an ascetic lifestyle were God's way of drawing individuals into direct communication with him.

Calvinism, then, presents a bleak worldview—no matter what one does, only a tiny minority is predestined to everlasting life. Calvinism, as a religion, accepts the existing world of impoverishment and urges believers to lead a life committed to stoic survival in the hope that they are among the elect. But, like life itself, all is uncertainty: one can never be sure of one's place among the elect—one must simply believe in God, trust his judgement, faithfully follow the scriptures, and pray for salvation.

The Puritans followed Calvin's teachings but developed them further. Still believing in predestination, the Puritans read the Holy Scriptures to see exactly what God expected from humankind on earth. These texts, they believed, clearly indicated that God wanted people to rise above their natural condition—to tame and control all of their natural desires and conduct their lives in ways that conformed strictly to God's commandments and glorified the Lord in heaven. More important, the Puritans believed that it was the absolute duty of all people to have faith that they were among the chosen and to conduct their lives accordingly. Further, the seventeenth-century Puritans believed that if they could prove themselves capable of mastering their natural desires and of leading righteous, dignified lives, then that would prove to themselves that God had given them the ability to conduct their lives as he wanted, and this meant that they were among God's elect.

The Puritans' religious beliefs represent more than a religious doctrine; they comprise a value system, a frame of mind, a set of meaningful actions that Puritan believers can use to guide their daily actions and determine whether they are among God's elect. The Puritan religion espouses a highly disciplined, restrained, passionless way of life that completely tames the natural inclinations of humankind. This Protestant asceticism, Weber argues, directs all of its force against the spontaneous enjoyment of life.

This doctrine did not arise directly from the economic and social circumstances of sixteenth-century Europe, according to Weber, although it is certainly closely related to them. One important link between the ethos of ascetic Protestantism and economic life is the notion of a "calling."

In separating himself or herself from his or her natural condition, an individual receives from God a particular calling through which he or she can glorify the Lord. The calling gives order and direction to life. A person's calling dispels doubt and anxiety because it is a way of demonstrating commitment to the glorification of God. Also, and most important for Weber's argument, the idea of each person having a calling moves the spirit of ascetic

Protestantism directly into the economic sphere. Weber finds an important "elective affinity" (a mutually reinforcing association) between the spirit of ascetic Protestantism, in general, and the calling, in particular, and the emerging overall ethos of modern capitalism.

Weber establishes this link in two different ways. On the one hand, he does it through an analysis of language. On the other, he examines the actual historical relationship between the notion of the calling and the behaviours of ascetic Protestants.

With respect to language and meaning, Weber engages in a lengthy discussion of the term "calling" and of the meanings associated with the word, which, in German, is *Beruf*. Part of the discussion is directly within the text of the essay (Weber [1930] 1958:79–88, [1930] 1969:66–74), but he also writes a lengthy footnote that explores the history of the word and, most important, that examines how the terms *Beruf* and "calling" are introduced into Protestant theology through the translation of ancient Hebrew, Greek, and Latin texts into German and English (Weber [1930] 1958, note 3:207–11; Weber [1930] 1969, note 55:101–6).

Weber's discussion shows that, when Martin Luther translated the Bible into German, there was already an economic connotation to the term *Beruf*. A *Beruf* is a profession. A *Beruf* is a position to which one is called as a vocation for the non-material rewards it offers through personal fulfilment. A *Beruf* is different in this regard from a *Stelle* (an occupational position) or from *Arbeit* (work). The inherent rewards and fulfilment in a vocation are partly what led Luther to use *Beruf* to convey to the German reader what was entailed in the biblical term he was translating.

The typical German reader would see the word *Beruf* and recognize it as connoting not only a professional station in life but also a vocation that necessitates personal commitment and leads to personal fulfilment. The economic term suggests some of the biblical meaning, which is much more elevated because of its religious affiliation. Placed within the context of the Holy Scriptures and ascetic Protestantism, the word *Beruf* or "calling" is an important linking point between religious belief and economic behaviour based on particular religious principles and meanings. As Weber argues in *The Protestant Ethic and the Spirit of Capitalism*, the notion of pursuing a calling for the glory of God made the acquisition of capital acceptable within Protestantism, even though the enjoyment of wealth or its pursuit for its own sake was not:

> This worldly Protestant asceticism ... acted powerfully against the spontaneous enjoyment of possessions; it restricted consumption, especially

of luxuries. On the other hand, it had the psychological effect of freeing the acquisition of goods from the inhibitions of traditionalistic ethics. ... The campaign against the temptations of the flesh, and the dependence on external things, was. ... not a struggle against rational acquisition, but against the irrational use of wealth. ... [I]n conformity with the Old Testament and in analogy to the ethical valuation of good works, asceticism looked upon the pursuit of wealth as an end in itself as highly reprehensible; but the attainment of it as a fruit of labour in a calling was a sign of God's blessing. And even more important: the religious valuation of restless, continuous, systematic work in a worldly calling, as the highest means to asceticism, and at the same time the surest and most evident proof of rebirth and genuine faith, must have been the most powerful conceivable lever for the expansion of that attitude toward life which we have here called the spirit of capitalism. ... When the limitation of consumption is combined with this release of acquisitive activity, the inevitable practical result is obvious: accumulation of capital through ascetic compulsion to save. (Weber [1930] 1958:170–2, [1930] 1969:179–80)

In sum, Weber argues that, as the influence of the Puritan outlook expanded, "it favoured the development of a rational bourgeois economic life." Moreover, he maintains that this outlook was "the most important, and above all the only consistent influence in the development of that life. It stood at the cradle of the modern economic man" (Weber [1930] 1958:174, [1930] 1969:181).

Having established the dynamic of ascetic Protestantism and its integration into economic activity, Weber turns to the ways in which that ascetic ethos was generalized as well as how it continued to operate in social and economic life even as the importance of religion declined in an increasingly secular Europe.

Weber argues that Franklin's maxims about time and money parallel the ethos of ascetic Protestantism; the idea of work as renunciation and disciplined activity had become widespread by the eighteenth century, when Franklin penned these words of "Advice to a Young Tradesman." As Puritan asceticism began to

dominate worldly morality, it did its part in building the tremendous cosmos of the modern economic order. This order is now bound to the technical and economic conditions of machine production which to-day determine the lives of all the individuals who are born into

this mechanism, not only those directly concerned with economic acquisition, with irresistible force. (Weber [1930] 1958:181)[74]

The Protestant Ethic and the Marx-Weber Relationship

The Protestant Ethic and the Spirit of Capitalism is an empirical examination
of the impact that different denominations of Protestantism had upon the
development of capitalism. At the same time, however, because of its level
of abstraction and generalization, it is an extended, implicit critique of the
methodology supported by Stammler, Meyer, Roscher, Knies, and other
members of the historical school, a methodology emphasizing historical
specificity and the gathering of discrete "facts."

However, the work can also be seen as a challenge to historical materialism. In fact, at the end of the entire essay, Weber acknowledges that some
will see the piece as an attempted refutation of historical materialism (Weber
[1930] 1958:183, [1930] 1969:190). The heavy emphasis on the role of ideas
in Weber's account of the Protestant ethic and the rise of capitalist society
seems to challenge directly the Marxist emphasis on the economy as the
main or even sole driving force in history. To clarify where he stands with
respect to that framework, Weber writes the following in the last paragraph
of *The Protestant Ethic and the Spirit of Capitalism*:

> Here we have only attempted to trace the fact and the direction of its
> [ascetic Protestantism's] influence to their [social agents'] motives in
> one, though a very important point. But it would also further be nec-
> essary to investigate how Protestant Asceticism was in turn influenced
> in its development and its character by the totality of social conditions,
> especially economic. Modern man is in general, even with the best will,
> unable to give religious ideas a significance for culture and national char-
> acter which they deserve. But it is, of course, not my aim to substitute for
> a one-sided materialistic interpretation an equally one-sided spiritualis-
> tic causal interpretation of culture and of history. Each is equally possi-
> ble, but each, if it does not serve as the preparation, but as the conclusion
> of an investigation, accomplishes equally little in the interest of historical
> truth. (Weber [1930] 1958:183, [1930] 1969:189–90)

---

74 Although there is nothing specifically inaccurate in the translation by Parsons, it does not convey
Weber's text fully. Weber was more concerned with the increasing impact of the mechanistic worldview than Parsons suggests. Here is an alternative translation: "This order is now bound to the technical and economic assumptions of mechanistic-machine-driven production which today determines
with an irresistible force the lives of all the individuals who are born into this mechanized existence
[*Triebwerk*]—not just those directly concerned with economic activity—and will perhaps so continue
until the last ton of fossilized coal is burned" (Weber [1930] 1969:188).

There are several points of importance in this paragraph.

First, the statement "modern man is in general, even with the best will, unable to give religious ideas a significance for culture and national character which they deserve" indicates Weber's notion that, in an increasingly secularized and industrialized Europe, religion's influence on people's lives was becoming progressively less obvious. Weber seeks to emphasize that, despite their low profile, religious ideas still have a powerful and important impact, although not necessarily as religious ideas and dogmas. This point shows Weber's belief that ideas and values from the past penetrate deeply into the present and extend into the future even though the way they are understood across time can alter.

Next, Weber's statement that he is not aiming "to substitute for a one-sided materialistic interpretation an equally one-sided spiritualistic causal interpretation of culture and of history" carries three important messages. First, it shows Weber's awareness that his argument will be seen as a critique of historical materialism and his desire to be sure that, although it is indeed such a critique, it will not be misconstrued. He does not want to substitute a "one-sided spiritualistic causal interpretation of culture and history" for a one-sided materialism.

Second, the statement and Weber's essay as a whole certainly comprise an implicit dismissal of historical materialism as the orthodox Marxists had been developing it. The phrase "a one-sided materialistic interpretation [of culture and history]" clarifies Weber's position on historical materialism for his readers.

Finally, the statement underlines Weber's rejection of all one-sided or single-factor explanations of social life. Weber's work always maintains a delicate balance among various features and forces, which, in his view, shape social meaning, social action, and, as a result, larger social formations. Weber is even more explicit about his rejection of single-factor analyses in one of the essay's notes:

> For those to whom no causal explanation is adequate without an economic (or materialistic as it is unfortunately still called) interpretation, it may be remarked that I consider the influence of economic development on the fate of religious ideas to be very important and shall later attempt to show how in our case the process of mutual adaptation of the two took place. On the other hand, those religious ideas themselves simply cannot be deduced from economic circumstances. They are in themselves, that is beyond doubt, the most powerful plastic elements of national character, and contain a law of development and a compelling force entirely their own. Moreover, the most important differences, so far as non-religious

factors play a part, are, as with Lutheranism and Calvinism, the result of political circumstances, not economic. (Weber [1930] 1958, note 84:277–8; Weber [1930] 1969, note 277:269–71)

So where does Weber stand vis-à-vis Marx in explanations of culture, society, and economic history? Are their perspectives the same? Are they compatible? Or are they fundamentally different?

The answer to those questions depends partly on how one interprets Marx's position—and, as the discussion in Chapter 3 shows, there are several levels at which one can read Marx's 1859 preface statement outlining his materialist position. But no matter how much importance contemporary Marxists give to the realm of culture and consciousness, there are certain aspects of Weber's work that they cannot accept as compatible with their materialist position. Similarly, Weberians find parts of Marx's work useful and compatible, but, fundamentally, the theoretical differences between Marx and Weber are significant enough that it would be incorrect to argue that the two men share a common theoretical orientation. Two major points of incompatibility between Marx and Weber centre on the direction or outcome of history and the role of meaning.

According to Marx's studies of history and political economy, history is moving towards a particular outcome. Marx, much more than Weber, was influenced by the grand narrative of progress that was a legacy of Enlightenment thought. Weber, however, sees no universal direction to history; his sociology centres on case studies rather than on sweeping analyses and predictions. Marx thought that his study of history, political economy, and the dynamics of industrial capitalist society had discovered forces that would create long-term, sweeping social change and progress. Weber was more cautious—especially on the question of progress.

Although there is debate over the extent to which Marx's analyses actually support the notion that capitalism will give way to socialism, it is impossible to escape the fact that Marx stated a number of times, in a variety of contexts and in various ways, that the dynamics of capitalist society would lead to periods of revolutionary tension and conflict (and possibly revolutionary change). It is also certain that Marx advocated for the revolutionary transformation of capitalism to socialism.

Weber did not believe there was an apparently inevitable course to history. He did not accept Marx's ([1859] 2005) conclusion in the 1859 preface to *Towards the Critique of Political Economy* that "the forces of production developing themselves within the womb of bourgeois society create ... the material conditions for the solution of this antagonism [between the forces and relations of production]" and that, through their dynamic, "the prehistory of human society closes with this social formation" (p. 62). In addition, Weber did not embrace Marx's claim in the *Manifesto* that "the development of modern industry ... cuts from under its feet the very foundation on which the bourgeoisie produces and appropriates products. What the bourgeoisie therefore produces, above all, are its own grave-diggers. Its fall and the victory of the proletariat are equally inevitable" (Marx and Engels [1848] 1934:20).

Weber was far more cautious about making any claims concerning the long-term direction of history although, as noted earlier in this chapter, he did acknowledge that there were certain historical trends, which, if they were not altered, would continue to unfold. In Weber's view, the social, economic, and political trends in Europe, if they continued, would lead to societies that were increasingly bureaucratic, dominated by goal-rational action, and organized on the basis of a legal-rational order (the rule of law).

Goal-rational action and legal-rational authority were trends that would, according to Weber's research, unfold for some time into the future, but he decisively rejected any notion that "laws of society" existed that were comparable to "laws of nature." A sociologist might discover certain trends, but different social forces could arise at any time and redirect the path of social history. On the basis of his own particular methodological perspective, Weber never thought that social history was following a single trajectory. History was far more open ended for Weber than it was for Marx.

Although Antonio Labriola, Karl Korsch, and Georg Lukács argued that Marx's materialist analysis took into account issues of consciousness, class consciousness, political struggle, and class struggle, the trajectory of Marx's own work suggests that he firmly believed that the deep, underlying dynamics of capitalist production were of fundamental importance for sociologists and political activists to grasp—more important, that they were crucial to social change. The *Grundrisse* makes clear Marx's profound awareness of the complexity of the capitalist mode of production and of the ways in which its apparent contradictions and weaknesses might be resolved or mitigated. This understanding is likely why he spent so much of his life exploring the political economy of capitalism deeper and deeper without preparing his full analysis for publication. But despite all of the tendencies and countertendencies that Marx examines in his voluminous study notebooks and drafts, he never seems to move away from the conviction that to discover the secret of capitalist society, one has to begin with an understanding of the labour process within the specific context of the capitalist political economy.

Weber, too, is aware of the importance of economic relations, but his sociology clearly emphasizes the significance of meaning and meaning construction in social life. Weber's emphasis on interpretive understanding places the dominant accent of his sociology in a different place than on the economic factors that comprise Marx's primary focus. The work of each might complement the other, but, in the final analysis, Marx maintains that the economic relations of society have to be changed to produce a better society whereas, for Weber, social action is complex, multifaceted, and inescapably tied to social meaning. Even a radical change in the economic infrastructure, without an equally radical transformation of the dominant ideology within a society and of the meanings people associate with their social actions, will not, according to Weber, produce a fundamentally different society.

WEBER, MODERNISM, AND POSTMODERNISM

Weber's emphasis upon sociology as a comprehensive science of social action places him at what can now be seen as an interesting intersection between modernism and postmodernism. The quest for a comprehensive science of social action in which scholars make a value commitment—or judgement of value—to the pursuit of universally valid truth, grounds Weber squarely in the tradition of modernism. Even though he refuses to believe there are any universal laws or grand narratives of human history, Weber still commits to the strictures of scientific procedure and the principle of objectivity (that is, the knowledge gained through scholarly or scientific inquiry accurately captures or reflects the reality of the object under study, and the knowledge produced is not distorted or misrepresented by the values, beliefs, or personal biases of those conducting the analysis). Modernist scholars and scientists want to know the fundamental or essential reality of the empirical world in which they live; they strive to move beyond the everyday experiences of knowing the world as the phantasmagoria of the infinitely complex, concrete, life-worlds in which people live. Modernist researchers focus on what earlier scientists and scholars have identified as the most meaningful aspects of the infinitely complex world and build upon that knowledge base. Modernists produce and develop meaningful concepts or ideal types (pure types) that sacrifice the fullness of real events to gain the advantages of an abstract, stylized, simplified, and even distorted or accentuated understanding of the complex social and natural worlds.

Conceptual ideal types (or pure types) refine researchers' understandings of the phenomena they study. Scholars develop them on the basis of an unwavering value commitment to the pursuit of universally valid truth. As a result, these pure types are continually open to critical scrutiny by others who are also seeking to grasp the infinite complexity of reality interpretively. Ideal types serve as the reference point for comparisons with the fullness of concrete events and actions and, as such, allow researchers to penetrate more deeply into a more systematic and analytical understanding of the worlds they are studying. Ideal types provide the opportunity for scholars to refine their concepts further, and, most important, these types serve as the vehicles through which scientists may make statements about generalized patterns or processes.

A commitment to the unyielding pursuit of universally valid truth does not require one to be committed to the discovery of universal laws in science (natural or social), but it does allow a scholar to determine the consequences that will follow from his or her conceptual analysis and to understand how that may extend into the future (even the very distant future). These generalizations are recognized as provisional, yet, at the same time, they stand as the best understanding, from a scientific perspective, of what the past and present hold for the future. Charting the past and present to predict and potentially control the future is central to the modernist perspective, and Weber is committed to these aspects of modernism.

But for all of Weber's desire to rein in the fullness of concrete life and grasp it in the form of pure types, his particular conception of sociology as a comprehensive science of social action opens up the possibility for others to emphasize the limitations related to the construction of ideal types and to consider the ways in which ideal types might fundamentally misrepresent the complex natural and social worlds they are designed to grasp abstractly. Weber's premises and arguments take sociology well down the road to the perspective that many now identify as postmodern. In this sense, read from the vantage point of the twenty-first century, Weber's work provides a bridge that leads from modernism to postmodernism.

As a bridging figure, Weber can be seen as a sociologist who anticipates many of the questions and theoretical problems that postmodernists later identify. His emphasis upon the interpretative perspective and his decision to make social action the focus of sociology can be seen as methodological and theoretical interventions addressing the shortcomings of modernism, shortcomings that, at the time, were just beginning to become apparent.

On the other hand, one can argue that Weber's work in methodology allows sociologists in the contemporary world to hold fast to the tenets of the classical tradition. This argument would show that the legacy of the Enlightenment has always been misunderstood—because people put too much faith in the Enlightenment's promise—and that Weber simply reminds us of the limits to thought that were always part of Enlightenment reason. Instead of giving in to postmodernism, Weber's sociology might be regarded as a framework that can re-establish the dominant concepts of modernism and the classical tradition—the pursuit of universally valid truth on the basis of precise, conceptually based observation of the natural and social worlds that is open to critique and unfailingly committed to the value judgement of scientific objectivity.

In either event, because he wrote during the first two decades of the twentieth century and lived in Germany through World War I and into the early interwar years, Weber had to struggle to understand a social world that was in considerable turmoil and transition. As a result of his social location and the intellectual debates with which he engaged, Weber developed an approach to sociology that helps us understand the emerging social reality while still maintaining the analytical, methodological, and scholarly principles and objectives of modernism. The final section of this chapter explores the terms "modernism" and "postmodernism" and investigates how Weber's work can be viewed as a bridge between those two divergent conceptions of the world.

Modernism

Since the end of World War II, there have been three different encyclopaedias of the social sciences or sociology: the *Encyclopaedia of the Social Sciences* (Seligman and Johnson 1957), the *International Encyclopedia of the Social Sciences* (Sills 1968), and the *Blackwell Encyclopedia of Sociology* (Ritzer 2007). Each of those encyclopaedias was produced under very different social conditions and theoretical understandings of the social and natural worlds. As a result, one finds not only different emphases and foci in the entries that are common to all of them—see, for example, the entries on Durkheim, Marx, and Weber on feudalism, the family, science, and sociology—but entries in one that are not found in the other two. For the student of contemporary sociology, it is interesting to note that neither "modernity" nor "postmodernism" is an entry in the first two encyclopaedias, despite the fact that the widespread use of these terms in sociology today suggests their longstanding history within the discipline.

In place of "modernity," one can examine other terms in the *Encyclopaedia of the Social Sciences* and the *International Encyclopedia of the Social Sciences* to determine why the term "modernity," per se, was not identified as a key term. One can also examine the terms that were used in its place to see what they convey about sociological thought at the time of the two earlier encyclopaedias. Exploring this terminology is useful in understanding how and why the concepts of modernity and postmodernism are so important to contemporary sociologists as well as why neither term was explicitly included in earlier comprehensive compilations of knowledge in the social sciences.

In the *Encyclopaedia of the Social Sciences,* instead of modernity, one finds the term "modernism." Horace Kallan (1957), the author of this encyclopaedia's entry under the term, notes that "modernism may be described as that attitude of mind which tends to subordinate the traditional to the novel and to adjust the established and customary to the exigencies of the recent and innovating" (p. 564). Modernism, he continues, places a high value "upon the new as distinguished from the contemporary or the past" (p. 564).[75] Modernism, in this entry, is almost a generic concept describing a general process that encourages innovative change.

For the contemporary reader, the most striking feature of this 1957 entry is the absence of a strong link between modernism and the rise of the scientific worldview during the Enlightenment. To be sure, Kallan locates the ascendance of the modernist worldview within the context of the French Revolution and the *philosophes'* approach to the underlying rationality of reality, but he spends only two sentences on a relationship that sociologists in the latter part of the twentieth century would see as crucially important. "Never regarded as modernist in itself," Kallan (1957) writes, "science has been the occasion of modernism in everything else—from economics, sex, and politics to religion and art." "Modernism," he continues, "indeed might be described as the endeavour to harmonize the relations between the older institutions of civilization with science" (p. 565).

On the whole, however, Kallan's (1957) conception of modernism is best captured in the following:

> The modernistic attitude, in sum, arises where a fission develops in the social or intellectual order because a new invention or discovery has become powerful enough to impose adjustment to itself upon the resistant environment which it has entered as an interloper. The process of adjustment begins in some individual or small group whose life or work has been dislocated. Automatic at first, it soon gets rationalized into a program which wins adherents from a wider and wider range of personalities and vocations. None who ally themselves with the program are likely in the beginning to have any thought of conflict or rebellion. That comes as their conduct and labours arouse anxieties, the fears, and finally the active antagonism of the masters of the traditional establishment—the princes and nobles of the church, the academicians of the arts, the academics of the schools. Antagonism leads to self-consciousness, formal definition and propaganda. Freely cooperative individuals become a disciplined school. Their program becomes in its turn a dogmatic object of faith and authority now fighting for its life not only against the established order it rejected but also against a fresh innovation which rejects it. (P. 567)

---

75 It is worth noting that the 1957 encyclopaedia does not contain an entry on postmodernism or post-anything, for that matter.

Kallan's presentation of modernism from the perspective of the 1950s is revealing in three particular respects.

First, the process of modernization and the modernistic attitude are directly tied to processes of change and moving forward out of the constraints and confines of tradition through innovation—modernism means updating and progressive change. It is also an ongoing, recurring process. Kallan's discussion of art demonstrates his conception of modernism clearly.

Modern art, Kallan notes, must be distinguished from classicism, on the one hand, and from modernist art, on the other. Following the French Revolution of 1789, the revolutionary government appointed Jacques-Louis David to govern art in the new republic. Schooled in the classical tradition of Rome, David imposed that style on French art. "Rome became the pictorial hieroglyph of the republic of France, events in Roman history, of events in the revolutionary history of France" (Kallan 1957:566). David's massive six-by-nine-metre painting—the *Consecration of the Emperor Napoleon I and Coronation of the Empress Josephine*—typifies the classical style that reigned supreme during the Napoleonic Empire.

Following the fall of Napoleon and the 1814 restoration of the Bourbon king Louis XVIII, there was a reaction to the Enlightenment rationalism that lay behind the French Revolution. Consistent with the restoration of the Bourbons as well as with the emotional turmoil that spanned the period from the Revolution and the ensuing Reign of Terror through the Napoleonic period, a Romantic style emerged within French art. The new style accentuated colour, passion (rather than reason), and realism (rather than a contrived classicism). Théodore Géricault's 1819 *The Raft of the Medusa* and Eugène Delacroix's 1830 *Liberty Leading the People* epitomize this new form.

Even though romanticism, as a reaction against the overwhelming emphasis and central importance that Enlightenment thinkers placed upon human reason, was grounded in the recent past, the new art form was termed modern because it represented a definitive break from the classical forms that European artists had inherited from ancient Greece and Rome. The realist focus and the use of colour and line to evoke emotion firmly located this new art form in the modern world—hence the adjective "modern" and the term "modern art."

The invention of the camera, which could capture real images with a reproductive accuracy no artist could rival, stimulated the rise of a new modernist approach to painting. Continuing to use colour to create an emotional response in the viewer, painters moved away from the realism of romanticist (modern) art and experimented with different techniques. As a result, artists like Camille Pissarro, Paul Cézanne, Claude Monet, Pierre-Auguste Renoir, and Armand Guillaumin forged a new modernist style that experimented with colour and brush techniques to express form, atmosphere, depth, and action to generate an internal, emotional experience for the viewer. Monet's *Impression, soleil levant* (*Impression, sunrise*) of 1873 gave the new style its perfect, descriptive identification—impressionism.

The impressionists, in turn, were challenged by other modernists—the post-impressionists, Vorticists, cubists, futurists, and Dadaists. These developments represented a rejection of the romanticists' refusal to engage with science and technology and, instead, tried to reconcile science and machinery with the creativity of art. Art in the impressionist and post-impressionist periods rejected all traditional art forms as well as the mechanical forms of reproduction ushered in by the camera; modernist art attempted to capture the creativity of humanity in an increasingly mechanical, technological world. Science and art, technical and emotional, innovation and tradition were drawn together in the various expressions of modernist art.

Viewed in this fashion, the unfolding history of art shows us innovation rejecting established notions—and this is the second important point to note about Kallan's idea of modernism. Kallan describes the forward movement inherent in modernism—tradition is replaced by modernizing development.

Most important, however, is what is not emphasized in Kallan's description of modernism. Although Kallan notes that there is a reconciliation of art, culture, and various aspects of social life with the emerging influence and growing importance of science, that theme is clearly subordinated in his presentation. Modernism, in Kallan's 1957 entry, is largely associated with breaking from tradition. This is the third element of note in Kallan's conception of modernism.

Today, modernism is strongly associated not only with the dismissal or marginalization of tradition but also with an overriding belief in progress and an increasing reliance on the systematic use of human reason and scientific knowledge to create technologies and social arrangements that will permit greater human freedom and more precise control of the social and natural worlds that humankind inhabits. The contrast with Kallan's view of modernism is clear. The association of Enlightenment reason and science with modernist thought is central to most contemporary discussions but was marginal to Kallan's 1957 entry in the *Encyclopaedia of the Social Sciences*.

Modernization

"Modernity" does not appear in the *International Encyclopedia of the Social Sciences* either.[76] The closest entry is Daniel Lerner's (1968:386–95)

---

76 Like the 1957 encyclopaedia, the *International Encyclopedia* does not contain entries on postmodernism, postmodernity, or any other post- entity.

discussion of modernization. Lerner's entry is significant for two particular reasons. First, in his 1957 discussion of modernism, Kallan had identified the process of modernization, but he described it as a general process of change, progress, and the updating of things. By 1968, the importance of modernism as a concept and its use as the root term associated with modernity—the term of greatest significance and worthy of elaboration—had declined as the conceptualization of the process of modernization gained in importance in the social sciences. In about a decade, a subcategory had become the main concept, and "modernism," as a term denoting a general category of social change, had almost disappeared. Modernization mattered far more than modernism and the general processes it encompassed.

Second, "modernization" became the key term because the social processes that it described had risen to paramount importance politically and conceptually. Modernization as a political objective and modernization theory as a way of understanding social, political, and economic progress in the post–World War II period dominated all discussions of the contemporary, modern world by the late 1960s. The presence of a definition of modernization in the *International Encyclopedia* is, therefore, not at all surprising—it was consistent with the times. Similarly, modernism, as it was presented by Kallan, was pretty much past its "best-by" date.

"Modernization," according to Lerner (1968),

> is the current term for an old process—the process of social change whereby less developed societies acquire characteristics common to more developed societies. The process is activated by international, or intersocietal, communication. As Karl Marx noted over a century ago in the preface to *Das Kapital:* "The country that is more developed industrially only shows, to the less developed, the image of its own future." (P. 386)

Lerner's statements reveal two key aspects about how the term "modernization" was understood and used in the late 1960s. First, it was associated with processes that were clearly identified with development, and development was associated with increased industrialization. The nations that experienced industrialization first, the First World, represented, in the sixties, the most developed, highest form of social organization. Through modernization, underdeveloped or developing nations could reach the levels of development found in the First World, and this end point was considered desirable.

Second, the citation from Marx indicates two additional features of modernization as Lerner and other social scientists understood it. First is Lerner's obvious main point—the highly industrialized nations represent the future of the less industrialized. There is a strong sense of the inevitability of the progressive industrialized development of all societies around the globe. But Lerner's use of Marx is particularly interesting for a second reason.

Lerner omits the two sentences that precede the one from Marx that he quotes favourably, the two sentences expressing the idea of the inevitability of the "natural laws of capitalist production" and their inherent tendencies "working themselves out with iron necessity" (Marx [1867] 1983:12). The working out with iron necessity fits Lerner's conception of modernization, but the natural laws of capitalist production that Marx was writing about were the contradictory laws of capitalist production that would, ultimately, lead to severe economic crises and the revolutionary transformation of capitalist society into a socialist one. "Modernization," as the term was used by sociologists in the late 1960s, did not include this notion at all—on the contrary, modernization theory presented an image of progress in which capitalist societies had already moved beyond the potentially volatile phase examined by Marx. Academics of that time, at least those working outside the Marxian tradition, considered capitalist societies to have entered an era of ongoing progress, development, and stable growth (Aron 1961, 1962; Bell 1960a, 1973; Dahrendorf 1959; Goldthorpe 1968a, 1968b, 1969).

Lerner's (1968:386–7) discussion of modernization also notes that social development was once conceptualized in nationalist terms—the anglicization of India, the gallicization of Indochina, for example—and then in regional terms—the Europeanization of parts of the world and, in the post–World War II period, the Americanization of many parts of the globe, including Europe. But soon these terms were viewed as too parochial to describe the pattern of change that social scientists were seeing around the world—it was clear that the "regularly patterned social change" seen so widely throughout the globe "required a global referent." "In response to this need," according to Lerner (1968), "the new term 'modernization' evolved" (p. 387).

Economic development is the central element of modernization, for Lerner (1968), but it is also associated with a number of broader social changes and developments:

> Modernization, therefore, is the process of social change in which development is the economic component. Modernization produces the societal environment in which rising output per head is effectively incorporated. For effective incorporation, the heads that produce (and consume) rising output must understand and accept the new rules of the game deeply enough to improve their own productive behaviour and to diffuse it throughout their society. As Harold D. Lasswell (1965) has forcefully reminded us, this transformation in perceiving and achieving

wealth-oriented behaviour entails nothing less than the ultimate reshaping and resharing of all social values, such as power, respect, rectitude, affection, well-being, skill, and enlightenment. This view of continuous and increasing interaction between economic and non-economic factors in development produced a second step forward, namely, systematic efforts to conceptualize modernization as the contemporary mode of social change that is both general in validity and global in scope. (P. 387)

In short, Lerner (1968) believes that the convergence of different disciplinary ways of thinking—he identifies economics, sociology, political science, and psychology—upon "a general model of modernization" has established the idea that change is "the distinctive component of virtually every social system" (p. 389). Few traditional societies remain; change, development, and modernization are found everywhere; and the pace of change is accelerating.

The modernization process, Lerner (1968) argues, brings all modernizing societies around the globe closer to realizing the same main features of modernity, and he identifies these "salient characteristics of modernity" as

(1) a degree of self-sustaining growth in the economy—or at least growth sufficient to increase both production and consumption regularly; (2) a measure of public participation in the polity—or at least democratic representation in defining and choosing policy alternatives; (3) a diffusion of secular-rational norms in the culture—understood approximately in Weberian-Parsonian terms; (4) an increment of mobility in the society— understood as personal freedom of physical, social, and psychic movement; and (5) a corresponding transformation in the modal personality that equips individuals to function effectively in a social order that operates according to the foregoing characteristics—the personality transformation involving as a minimum an increment of self-things seeking, termed "striving" by Cantril (1966) and "need achievement" by McClelland (1961), and an increment of self-others seeking, termed "other-direction" by Riesman (1950) and "empathy" by Lerner (1958). (P. 387)

There are four important points to note about Lerner's discussion of modernization. First, the term has grown out of a general concept—modernism—and now accentuates the industrialization of economies around the world and the associated social impacts that such economic development has on societies throughout the globe.

Second, there is a very strong emphasis upon the First World leading the way for the rest of the globe. Modernization describes the process through which less developed parts of the world will come to be more similar, if not identical, to the industrialized nations of western Europe and North America.

Third, the process of modernization involves the functional development and integration of a wide variety of institutions in modernizing societies. One is reminded of Saint-Simon's or Comte's notions concerning the three stages of human history—with industrial societies representing the pinnacle of human development.

Finally, modernization, as it was understood in the late 1960s, was a global process in which certain essential features of the advanced societies of the world would work themselves out—that is, become manifest—in other parts of the globe. Modernization was a project that was unfolding towards an ultimate telos or higher goal.

Modernism, Modernization, and Post–World War II Sociology

The promise of modernism in the social sciences—the development of science, scientific insight, and empirically based theory to guide the rational development and progress of human societies—appeared to be coming to full fruition in the early postwar period. That era can be seen as the culmination of a particular approach to social science research, one that extended from Descartes to Saint-Simon and Comte and through Durkheim to the work of three of North America's most influential sociologists—Talcott Parsons, Robert Merton (1938, 1949, 1957), and Paul Lazarsfeld (1954, 1955).[77] Structural functionalist theory and positivist research techniques, as they culminated in the work of these three sociologists, became, in Giddens's words, "the orthodox consensus" in sociology during the late 1950s and early 1960s (Giddens 1984).

The structural functionalism of Parsons (1951) sought to give sociology a single encompassing theory that sociologists could use to analyse all types of social action and the institutions and societies arising from them. This theory follows all of the precepts of science—it moves, on the basis of empirical evidence, from the complexity of everyday life to the development of increasingly refined and abstract concepts, which combine into a general model that describes and explains a wide variety of different activities and social formations. It relies heavily on the scientific practices of biology, and Parsons employs a very overt organic analogy, conceiving of societies as systems that need to maintain themselves or die and disappear.

Societies, Parsons and other structural functionalists claim, operate like biological organisms fulfilling four system requisites (or requirements)

---

77 For more on the sociology and sociologists of this period, see Mongardini and Tabbon (1998), Rocher (1974), and Jeřábek (2001).

—adaptation, goal-attainment, integration, and pattern maintenance. Each requisite is related to a dominant "sub-system of action,"—the biological organism, the personality, the social system, and culture. Finally, each system requisite and sub-system can be linked to a particular social institution— the economy, the polity, the community, and the sites of individual social- ization, for example, the family, education, or religion (Rocher 1974:40–67).

Parsons argues that the energy in the system is most clearly evident in the activities of adaptation and goal-attainment, which take place at the level of the biological organism and within the personality sub-systems of action that, at the institutional level, pertain to the economy and the polity. This energy is less obvious at the higher levels of the system, the levels of soci- ety and culture. At the same time, control emanates downwards from the top of the system and is exerted most directly on the lower levels. In other words, the realm of culture (the area of pattern maintenance or system inte- gration) creates the values that are internalized, via socialization, by individ- ual people, and thus culture guides their everyday actions—guidance from above, action from below.

Merton (1949, 1957) moves more cautiously than Parsons from the sys- tematic interrogation of the empirical social world to the development of sweeping theoretical insights. Among Merton's most highly recognized con- tributions to the development of sociology as a scientific enterprise are his arguments in favour of what he calls "theories of middle range." In opposition to Parsons, but working within exactly the same scientific tradition, Merton maintains that the empirical information sociologists gather and study is suf- ficient for them to formulate qualified theoretical generalizations but not the sweeping theoretical edifice that Parsons had constructed. According to Merton, more empirical work is needed before sociologists can present well-substantiated theories beyond those of middle range.

Lazarsfeld's (1954, 1955) stature within the development of the emerging theoretical and methodological consensus in the 1950s and 1960s is far greater than many recognize. Lazarsfeld's major contributions centre on research techniques and questions in the philosophy of science, but Lazarsfeld is a sophisticated theorist as well. Lazarsfeld's primary objective as a sociologist was to establish an empirically based science that would draw upon the fun- damental principles of mathematics to determine, with increasing certainty, the knowledge claims sociologists could make with confidence.

The most significant promise of modernism, as it broke from the con- straints of theological knowledge, was that human inquiry would allow humankind to control its future development through increasingly precise and accurate knowledge. Saint-Simon, Comte, Durkheim, and, ultimately, Parsons, Merton, and Lazarsfeld worked to extend into the study of society the search for the "laws of nature." The goal of such work was to develop theoretical generalizations about social life that would assist in the improvement of social conditions for all. From the perspective of North America, modernism and modernization seemed self-evident truths in the postwar period. The economy grew throughout the 1950s and 1960s, per capita wealth in Canada and the United States rose, and consumer goods became increasingly plentiful—at least that was the dominant image and the feeling among those who prospered (see, for example, Cohen 2003).

But no sooner did the mainstream of sociology embrace the progressive and developmental conceptions of modernization theory, which emphasized the functional integration of social relations, than the reality of the modern world began to undermine many of these key premises and conclusions. Women, African Americans, French Canadians, descendants of the First Nations, first-generation immigrants, and members of the working class experienced modernism and modernization as less than liberating or progressive. Thus, even though modernism supported the quest for empirically based, comprehensive scientific theories and motivated many sociologists to try to establish a single, overarching theoretical explanation for the events of the modern world, the antagonistic dimensions of modernism and within the modern world remained. As a result, the intellectual foundations of modernization theory came under careful scrutiny and by the late 1970s, and a number of different perspectives began to assert themselves in opposition to the dominant tradition of the modernist-inspired and scientific structural functionalism of the 1940s, 1950s, and 1960s.

Postmodernism

The *Blackwell Encyclopedia of Sociology* is the most recent attempt to draw together a comprehensive presentation of sociology and of the sociological understanding of the past and present. Although there are still very strong modernist elements, entries, and discussions in the encyclopaedia, it is heavily influenced by postmodernist approaches to sociology. It contains entries on modernity, modernization, postmodernism, postmodern culture, and postmodern theory.[78] The entry that is most relevant here is the one on postmodernism by Julie Albright (2007).

---

78 The entry on modernization emphasizes many of the same themes that Lerner (1968) notes although Ronald Inglehart and Christian Welzel (2007) also review the key debates around the notion of modernization that took place from the 1970s to the present. In essence, Inglehart and Welzel (2007) write, "Modernization is an encompassing process of massive social changes that, once set in motion, tends to penetrate all domains of social life, from economic activities to social life to political institutions, in a self-reinforcing process. Modernization brings an intense awareness of change and innovation, linked with the idea that human societies are progressing."

Although modernism and modernist approaches dominated sociology in the post–World War II period, by the late 1970s, a growing number of social thinkers were arguing that modernism, as a frame of mind, prevented many sociologists from recognizing the full complexity of the societies in which they lived and that they studied. Modernism, as a metanarrative—as a particular framework or discourse—filtered and shaped how people understood the world. More attention, this group maintained, had to be directed at contemporary social formations from the perspective of various critical theories or from a completely different intellectual vantage point.

In one very succinct formulation, Gary Woller (1997) notes that modernism is the frame of mind that represents the "trinity of the Enlightenment—reason, nature, and progress" (p. 9). Postmodernism is the frame of mind that seeks to depose that trinity. Jean-François Lyotard (1984:3), in one of the most influential examinations of the postmodern condition, also argues that knowledge has changed, in terms of its status and nature. Knowledge has changed in three fundamental ways. First, knowledge—all knowledge, including science—is, according to Lyotard, a form of discourse. Second, in the digital age, knowledge, more than ever, is power. Finally, "by concerning itself with such things as undecidables, the limits of precise control, conflicts characterized by incomplete information, 'fracta,' catastrophes, and pragmatic paradoxes," postmodern science has changed the meaning of knowledge: "It is producing not the known, but the unknown" (Lyotard 1984:60).

> The postmodern ... [is] that which, in the modern, puts forward the unpresentable in presentation itself; ... that which searches for new presentations, not in order to enjoy them but in order to impart a stronger sense of the unpresentable. A postmodern artist or writer is in the position of a philosopher: the text he writes, the work he produces are not in principle governed by preestablished rules, and they cannot be judged according to a determining judgement, by applying familiar categories to the text or to the work. Those rules and categories are what the work of art itself is looking for. The artist and the writer, then, are working without rules in order to formulate the rules of what *will have been done*. (Lyotard 1984:60)

In the postmodern period, science—the formerly dominant almost unchallenged form of knowledge and certainty—now faces rivals that are rewriting the rules of how one can best interpret and understand the world.

In her *Blackwell Encyclopedia* entry, Albright (2007) writes that postmodernism embodies a shift in sensibility, particularly evidenced in the arts, music, and architecture. Changes include a shift from concern with form to a concern with artifice, from structure to surface, from purity to pastiche, and from substance to image or simulation. The shift from modernism to postmodernism is best exemplified by two quotations. The first is from the definitive modernist architect Ludwig Mies van der Rohe: "Less is more." This encompasses the modernist sensibility in architecture—form follows function, all is stripped to essences, and there is simplification and a lack of ornamentation. The second quotation, from postmodern architect Robert Venturi, is "Less is a bore." It captures the spirit of postmodern architecture and, indeed, of postmodernism itself—a spirit that revels in playfulness, irony, and ornamentation and produces a pastiche of styles.

Modernism, rooted in the razor of Enlightenment reason, strips away everything that is extraneous to get to the essence of things. Modernism emphasizes function over form. Postmodernity "problematizes" or puts into question these modernist assumptions.

Like modernism, postmodernism is also an attitude of mind. It is one that calls into question, on the basis of the people's life experiences in the contemporary period, the fundamental assumptions and outlook of modernism. Postmodernism, as it has developed within modernity, focuses on three particular outcomes.

First, postmodernists seek to make people aware that the basic assumptions, goals, and principles of the modern era are the result of one particular metanarrative (or intellectual framework)—the Enlightenment worldview. The quest for scientific truths, postmodernists maintain, is not a quest for some eternal truths or for a set of underlying natural laws but merely an aspiration that arose from the particular social conditions existing in Europe during the Age of Reason and the Enlightenment.

Second, to establish the argument that human history is shaped by grand narratives or specific metanarratives, postmodernists focus on how events in the contemporary period have apparently exhausted the dominant Enlightenment perspective. Rather than moving towards more precise knowledge and enduring truths about nature or the social worlds in which people live, postmodernists point to the way in which the polarities that Enlightenment thought identified as mutually exclusive now exist simultaneously in the contemporary period. Postmodernists argue that relationships that should be, according to mainstream social thought, totally incompatible with one another have now collapsed into one another—apparently opposing conditions exist simultaneously, in proximity to each other. For example, postmodernists argue that colonialism has declined, yet there is increased globalization. The modern world established and was then centred on secular values, material interests, and consumerist practices, but one now sees a resurgence of religious beliefs and a dramatic growth in religious fundamentalism. As evangelists of various types preach about the evils of carnal pleasure to larger and larger live television and Internet audiences around the globe, sexual liberation continues to grow and a variety of sexualities flourish.

Instantaneous global communication through the Internet and digital technologies has ushered in a new information age that seems to promise to expand the exchange of ideas and to increase social freedom. At the same time, postmodernists note, there is greater surveillance, increased suspicion, and the suspension of basic human rights through legislation such as the American Patriot Act of 2001. The fall of the Berlin Wall and the breakup of the Union of Soviet Socialist Republics resulted in the end of the Cold War and the creation of a number of new, independent states. But there are new global power blocs, a growing fear of the proliferation of nuclear weapons, and the return to a siege mentality among some of the world's most powerful nations.

Finally, the presence of these collapsed polarities, postmodernists maintain, indicates that the dominant canon of Western thought is no longer adequate, can no longer help us understand or explain this increasingly complex world.[79] Arguing that many cultures have achieved sophisticated accomplishments in art, literature, and social and political theory, as well as knowledge of the natural world, postmodernists maintain that the Western canon comprised of the great works of Western societies—a body of writing that includes, for example, Plato, Aristotle, Jane Austen, Francis Bacon, Honoré de Balzac, Geoffrey Chaucer, Descartes, Goethe, Elizabeth Gaskell, Niccolò Machiavelli, Newton, Rousseau, Shakespeare, Mary Wollstonecraft Shelley, Adam Smith, Henry David Thoreau, Leonardo da Vinci, and Voltaire (Bloom 1987:243–312)—is too restrictive and limiting.[80] By focusing critically on the way in which Enlightenment metanarratives shaped how people in the modern era have interpreted the world and then demonstrating the weaknesses of that discourse, postmodernists seek to establish the view that all of human history has been shaped by particular metanarratives (worldviews or discourses).

As much as humans might wish for a discoverable underlying order in the natural and social worlds, this promise of the Enlightenment, most

---

79 Canon has two meanings and both are implied in the phrase "canon of Western thought." A canon is a standard, a norm, or a principle. A canon is also a catalogue or a list. The canon of Western thought suggests there is a list of great works and great thinkers whose contributions to Western culture represent the highest standards of cultural and intellectual achievement. The canon of Western thought is the list of works demonstrating the standards of excellence and the insights that thinkers in Western societies have achieved.

80 Former Harvard President Charles Elliot's 51-volume *Harvard Classics* is a useful guide to what many people consider the Western canon.

postmodernists argue, will always remain unfulfilled. Postmodernists main-tain that people must still attempt to understand the world around them, but they do not believe that it is possible or even desirable for people to seek grand, overarching theories about the natural or social world. Instead, peo-ple need to examine nature or social life in much more specific terms. The world is infinitely complex, postmodernists argue, and the best that research-ers can do is develop conceptual "theorizations" that enlighten people about the complexity. These understandings, however, will not and cannot pro-duce universally applicable theories of the social or natural worlds. Every theory—every theorization—is simply a conceptual understanding of the world—a social construction that is based on a set of specific assumptions. If one rejects an assumption, then the understanding is no longer valid; post-modernists argue that the way people now understand the world shows that the basic assumptions in science are open to question.

POSTMODERNITY AS AN ART FORM

Modernity, by the end of the twentieth century, was a concept related to what had proven to be an extremely complex world of social formations. Consequently, new frameworks were needed so that complexity could be grasped and consumed by the human mind without eliminating the inner tensions and intricacy of the world under scrutiny. Postmodernists attempt to make this utter complexity fathomable for at least a moment, so one can focus upon that tension-riddled totality and know what needs to be addressed if one wants to make change. It is the challenge of making the infi-nite—and thus really the unknowable—known for the moment.

Although Pablo Picasso and the surrealists predate postmodernism, their techniques convey the postmodernist quest to capture the infinite complex-ity of the world in images that are more faithful to reality than realist art could ever be. Surrealism is the reality of reality—realism plus. The world in which we live is never static; it is always in motion, and what is perceived in one instant is not the same the next. To be genuinely realistic, then, art has to capture this dynamism—it requires techniques beyond realism—realism plus. Art, according to the surrealists, has to connect the viewer to the *surré-alisme* of actual life. Yves Tanguy's 1942 work *Indefinite Divisibility* is just one example of a surrealist piece that captures the postmodernist dimensions of the surrealist movement.

In *Indefinite Divisibility*, the right foreground is dominated by a number of objects, mostly metal, that are clamped or connected together into an apparently meaningless structure that rises upwards towards the top of the piece. The shadow cast by this chaotic collection of things is that of a micro-scope. In front of the collection is another assemblage of objects that gives a platform some slight elevation—it too casts a small shadow, although this one is ambiguous and can be interpreted as a drafting table, a machine, or an object from the world of science fiction. The foreground is grey. It could be sand, but it also has a lunar appearance, and, as one's eyes move to the hori-zon, the colour shifts from light gray to darker gray to blue blending into a horizon that is not really defined but appears to be a cloudy sky on a bright day. The blue colours that transition from the land to the clouds of the sky have an almost aqueous appearance. Finally, adding to the apparent lunar effect of the foreground and middle ground are certain circular objects that, upon close inspection, show a regular, repeating pattern as the eye follows them into the horizon. In the distance, they look somewhat like the craters on the moon, although those in the foreground clearly are not. The work is eerie in many ways, breathtaking in others, and certainly open to an infinite number of interpretations.

As the eye moves around the canvas, the total image changes. The atten-tion of the viewer is drawn back to parts of the painting he or she has already studied, and the same thing is seen in a different context and way—a new image is present, is created. The eye cannot rest anywhere on the canvas; rest only comes by looking away—through a withdrawal from reality.

Picasso's work went through a number of phases, one of which was genu-inely surrealist, but there are many aspects of his work as a whole that make it postmodernist. Picasso's 1930 *The Acrobat*, for example, presents an image of a head, two legs, two arms, and no torso—the right foot is flat on the ground, the fingertips of the left hand are touching the ground while the right hand and the left foot are in the air. These limbs could never actually be in these positions at the same time except in this artistic rendering of the flexibil-ity, creativity, and mesmerising movement of an acrobat captured in time. One "sees" the acrobat as either a simultaneous viewing from different posi-tions or angles of vision or as the presentation of different movements and moments in time brought together into the same instant—or as both. As a painting, *The Acrobat* embodies a postmodernist attitude because it presents the viewer with a graphic capturing of motion, dynamism, and complexity through a "reality-plus" composition. At the same time, Picasso simultane-ously captures the acrobat from several vantage points or as a series of move-ments collapsed into one moment in time.

The postmodernist concern for artifice over form, surface rather than structure, pastiche more than purity, and simulation or image over substance is clearly found in a number of Picasso's works completed during the 1920s and 1930s, when he experimented with the presentation of form. *The Sculptor*,

Two Ladies, Reading, Woman with a Flower, Girl on a Pillow, and Picasso's portraits of his young lover Marie-Thérèse Walter, painted during the early to middle 1930s, feature disassembled bodies and forms that are reassembled in a pastiche that combines roughly hewn shapes, which appear like chiselled stone and convey the tactile dimensions of sculpture, with flamboyant colour to produce provocative images.

Girl Before a Mirror takes an everyday, tranquil moment of contemplation and jarringly brings it to life in all of its contradictions. The image presents the girl as simultaneously clothed and naked and as studying herself but also fixated on some other; her innermost being is known by her and also revealed to the viewer. The intense imagery is filled with sexual symbolism—one moment is here captured from a myriad of perspectives, views, and interpretive understandings through a technique that abandons early modern art and scientific ways of knowing and seeing.

These artistic images predate postmodernist conceptions of the world. They arose within one of the more volatile periods of the modern era, and they capture the tensions of modernity as it was giving way to postmodernism. Within the postmodern period, postmodernists, sociologists, literary critics, and cultural theorists would draw upon artistic motifs to describe the world. In many ways, Tanguy's *Indefinite Divisibility* and Picasso's *The Acrobat*, and *Girl Before a Mirror* give us the opening images of the postmodern world.

From Modernism to Postmodernism

The modern world, which began to emerge with the challenge to feudal society, gave rise to the hypothetico-deductive approach to understanding the natural and social worlds. This emergent scientific perspective seemed to represent the fundamental key to understanding the underlying laws of nature; it was considered the source of all that humanity needed to comprehend nature fully, so humankind could control it and human interactions with it rationally. The success and power of the scientific worldview held out the promise that the social world could also be understood, controlled, and shaped in a similar manner.

A belief in the power of science to enable humankind to act upon nature and create changes advancing the interests of humanity became a central feature of modernism—the frame of mind that progressively spread from the Renaissance to the Enlightenment and on into the nineteenth century. By the mid-nineteenth century, the industrializing societies of western Europe were characterized by increasingly rapid change, as modernity, in all of its complexity, began to come fully into being. During the next 100 years, the scope and pace of social change widened and accelerated; transportation expanded, and people, goods, and ideas moved around the globe with increased speed and deeper penetration into all areas of the world. These changes, in turn, made people aware of the vast cultural diversity existing in a wide variety of different social formations. As well, they came to appreciate the productive power of market societies, the technologies they produce, and the extent to which Western rationalism can revolutionize the way people carry out all aspects of their daily lives.

By the last quarter of the twentieth century, the heightened pace of change, the increasing use of ever-evolving information technologies, the shrinking of space and time, and the increasingly dense interconnections of the global economy all suggested that the promise of modernity was turning into reality. At the same time, however, the negative impacts of each of modernity's so-called advances, the legacy of two world wars, and an increasing sense that instrumental reason was enslaving humanity rather than liberating it brought modernism, as a frame of mind, and scientific reason, as the only way of achieving "true" knowledge, under closer and closer scrutiny.

Modernity, the actual experience of social and economic modernization in which "all that is solid melts into air," provided the impetus for some sociologists and cultural critics to question whether modernism was the only frame of mind for grasping the social and natural worlds. Enlightenment rationality was a powerful way for organizing one's understanding, but did it really represent the only way, the best way, or the single best way for understanding, or was it simply one possible way, one particular discourse?

As soon as scholars stepped outside the scientific worldview, other possibilities became apparent, and postmodernism, as a new attitude of mind, enabled them to focus upon the different metanarratives humans used to organize their daily activities, their understanding of nature, and their interaction with the natural and social world. And, according to postmodern thinkers, the variety of these metanarratives poses a challenge to modernist claims about objective and scientific knowledge. The condition of knowledge among the most developed societies of the world, Lyotard (1984) argues, demonstrates how much human understandings are shaped historically by metanarratives and why no single metanarrative can have greater absolute truth or value than another. Postmodernism, then, opens up a totally different way of thinking about the unity of science, the nature of the natural world, and the way knowledge or power channels people's understandings and actions within a relatively narrow set of options.

Yet despite the swirling world of change, the growing impact of cyber reality, and the increasing sense of humanity's limited knowledge, is it wise for sociologists to abandon the classical tradition? Sensitivity to a more artistic, a more craft-like approach to knowledge (to use Mills's imagery) is certainly required, but the task and promise of sociology will still remain essentially the same no matter how it is dressed up in different metanarratives. The best sociology will continue to explore critically the intersection of personal biography with the history of social structure, which means that Weber's sociology will remain relevant—indeed, critical—to understanding the postmodern world.

WEBER AND A VOCABULARY FOR CLEAR SOCIAL REFLECTION

What key concept or term can Weber's work add to the vocabulary required for clear social reflection? Although there are several possibilities, if one were restricted to a single term, then it would be "interpretive understanding." Interpretive understanding is a good choice for several reasons.

First, Weber, like Durkheim, argues that sociology has to be an observationally based undertaking, but his commitment to the empirical foundation of sociological investigation differs significantly from that made by Durkheim. Weber wants sociology to become a comprehensive science of social action. By this phrase, he means two things. By comprehensive, he means that sociology should be an all-encompassing undertaking; sociology should deal with the full extent of social life and social action. In addition, sociology should be comprehensive in the sense that the sociologist should interpret, grasp, or *comprehend* the meaning of social action.

Second, the term "interpretive understanding" also reminds us that Weber's conception of social action is directly tied to meaning—action is social "when its intended meaning takes account of the behaviour of *others* and is thereby oriented in its unfolding," he maintains (Weber 1956:1, 1968a:3). As a result, the interpretive perspective—the *verstehende Ansatz*—is critical to Weber's work.

Third, Weber's major substantive contributions to sociology address frames of mind and the role that ideas—particularly religious ideas and value systems—play in shaping social life. His essay *The Protestant Ethic and the Spirit of Capitalism* is just one example of Weber's goal to integrate the impact of particular frames of mind with the economic structure of society and the dominant forms of social action within a particular social formation. Through interpretive understanding, Weber attempts to establish general levels of understanding while also focusing on the specific aspects of each social formation he analyses.

Fourth, the general trends that Weber's work tracks—the rise of goal-rational action, the growth of bureaucracy, the structure of social power, and forms of domination—all centre on how particular forms of meaningful action shape and contour the way people understand, or *interpret*, the world in which they live. As some interpretive frameworks become dominant, others recede or disappear, leaving the range of human action limited because "other ways of doing things" do not come to mind.

Finally, interpretive understanding—*verstehende Soziologie*—is a critical term that differentiates Weber's conception of sociology from that of Durkheim or Marx. With respect to Durkheim, although the *conscience collective* is a central concept in Durkheim's work and involves both consciousness as well as the conscience and although Durkheim is sensitive to the importance of history in the study of society, his methodology, as set out in *The Rules of Sociological Method* and put into practice in *Suicide*, draws heavily from the positivist tradition extending from Descartes through Saint-Simon to Comte. Sociology, for Durkheim, has to strive to become a social science and must share, as much as possible, the methodological premises and tools of positivist natural science.

Weber's emphasis on the interpretive position, on the other hand, draws a stark line between the methods of the natural sciences and those of the humanities and social "sciences." The objects of study in sociology are, for Weber, radically different than the objects of study in the natural world; meaning is critically important in the human sciences or *Geisteswissenschaften* (the humanities and social sciences); as a result, the methodological approach has to be different. And the term "interpretive understanding" encapsulates the methodology Weber recommends and reminds us how different Weber and Durkheim are in their particular approach to the systematic study of social life.

The term "interpretive understanding" also captures the fundamental division between Marx and Weber, and it does so in two ways. First, Marx's materialist position begins with the central importance of labour (or the process of production), and, even though Marx sees labour as a creative, mediating process through which humankind externalizes its ideas, plans, and objectives, Marx's approach identifies the social relations of production that emerge over the course of history as the key departure point for analysis. Weber's sociology is closely associated with Marx's image of social history; Weber's concerns over the growing dominance of goal-rational action and legal-rational authority along with his deep engagement with various aspects of economic history show shared concerns and focal points of investigation. In the final analysis, however, it is meaningful action and an unwavering emphasis upon interpretive understanding that characterize Weber's sociology and separate him from even the most Hegelianized Marx. The term "interpretive understanding" brings to mind not only the similarities that Durkheim and Weber, on the one hand, and Marx and Weber, on the other, share in their work as sociologists but also the fundamental differences between Weber's sociology and that of either Durkheim or Marx.

PART THREE

SOCIOLOGY AND CONTEMPORARY CULTURE

9   THE FEAR OF MASS CULTURE

"Nowadays men often feel that their private lives are a series of traps," Mills notes in the opening sentence of *The Sociological Imagination*. People experience feelings "of *uneasiness*, of anxiety, which, if it is total enough, becomes a deadly unspecified malaise" (Mills 1959:3, 11). Although Mills's description applied to the 1950s, even at the end of the twentieth century, according to Bloom (1987:21), people lived in a world of chronic uncertainty. To escape that condition, Bloom argues, they must obey the command of the Delphic oracle: "Know thyself." To do that, he continues, they must wrestle with this question: "What is humankind?" But Bloom believes that only "the liberally educated" are properly prepared to address these challenges genuinely because they can "resist the easy and preferred answers" and draw upon other worthy alternatives.

The sentiment is certainly not a new one. As the age of modernity began to demonstrate its full impact upon social life, Arnold expressed these same concerns. He maintained that, to solve the problems people faced—problems similar to those Mills and Bloom identify—they had to turn to culture. In the pursuit of sweetness and light, people could draw upon "the best which has been thought and said in the world" (Arnold [1868] 1932:6).

Nineteenth-century Germany did not escape these problems either, despite military victory over its arch-enemy, France, and the unification of its separate independent states into a powerful single nation in 1871. Friedrich Nietzsche, for one, was also concerned about the future. In his "untimely meditations"—untimely because he asks the difficult questions most people want to avoid—Nietzsche ([1873] 1983) relates a simple anecdote that demonstrates his concern:

> A traveller who had seen many lands and peoples and several of the earth's continents was asked what quality in men he had discovered everywhere he had gone. He replied: "They have a tendency to laziness." He is right: men are even lazier than they are timid, and fear most of all the inconveniences with which unconditional honesty and nakedness would burden them. ... When the great thinker despises mankind, he despises its laziness: for it is on account of their laziness that men seem like factory products, things of no consequence and unworthy to be associated with or instructed. The man who does not wish to belong to the mass needs only to cease taking himself easily; let him follow his conscience, which calls to him: "Be your self! All you are now doing, thinking, desiring, is not you yourself." (P. 127)

Sixteen years and a dozen books later, Nietzsche had not altered his view. As the author of *The Antichrist*, one who has discovered happiness and found "the exit out of the labyrinth of thousands of years," Nietzsche ([1895] 1954) asks if "modern man" has found happiness but concludes that in the modern era "everything has got lost" (p. 569).

Nietzsche ([1886] 1968) argues that humanity has yielded to the "instinct of the herd" (p. 305); it has abandoned the desire for freedom and action.[81] Europeans, he believes, have succumbed to "the greed of the money-makers," "the greed of the state," and the superficial and ever-changing nature of popular taste (Nietzsche [1873] 1983:164–9). Consequently, Nietzsche ([1908] 1968:782) sees his task as standing "in opposition to the mendaciousness of millennia" and, like Arnold, he views culture as the solution to industrial society's problems. "Culture is liberation," Nietzsche ([1873] 1983:130) exclaims.

> [C]ulture is the child of each individual's self-knowledge and dissatisfaction with himself. Anyone who believes in culture is thereby saying: "I see above me something higher and more human than I am; let everyone help me to attain it, as I will help everyone who knows and suffers as I do: so that at last the man may appear who feels himself perfect and boundless in knowledge and love, perception and power, and who in his

---

81 Nietzsche ([1886] 1968) later identified *Beyond Good and Evil*, from which the quotation is taken, as "in all essentials, a *critique of modernity*" (p. 766; see also Nietzsche [1889] 1954:532, 543–51).

completeness is at one with nature, the judge and evaluator of things."
(Nietzsche [1873] 1983:162–3)

Nietzsche ([1889] 1954) argues that humanity must rediscover its active and creative Dionysian[82] capacity. He holds up Johann Wolfgang von Goethe[83] as a model of the free, highly educated, well-rounded, and self-affirming person to whom people should aspire.[84] From mid-nineteenth century through to the contemporary period, from Arnold and Nietzsche to Mills and Bloom, social reformers, essayists, and scholars have expressed deep concerns about the prospects of humanity as culture is progressively overwhelmed by the forces of the market and reduced to a popular, simplified commodity that is passively consumed by a mass public.

This chapter will draw upon the insights of the classical tradition and upon Mills's sociological imagination to explore the question of culture. It will focus on one specific question: Has culture in contemporary life become debased, shallow, and hollow, or does it still retain deep, layered complexity that stops one short and encourages one to consider and explore the tensions, contradictions, and dialectical dynamics of the social world? In short, has contemporary culture lost its Dionysian capacity?

Culture and Society

"Culture," Raymond Williams (1983) argues, "is one of the two or three most complicated words in the English language" (p. 87). His work *Culture and Society, 1780–1950* was instrumental in reshaping how sociologists and other scholars thought about the word and the phenomenon (actually phenomena) designated by the complicated word "culture."

"In the last decades of the eighteenth century, and in the first half of the nineteenth century," Williams (1961) writes, "a number of words, which are now of capital importance, came for the first time into common English use, or, where they had already been generally used in the language, acquired new and important meanings" (p. 13).[85] He argues that the general pattern

---

82 In Greek mythology, Dionysus is one of the many sons of the Greek god Zeus; he is the god of wine who represents the intoxicating and liberating power of wine and music. For Nietzsche, this god's most important quality is his ability to free people from normal life.

83 Johann Wolfgang von Goethe (1749–1832) was and remains a towering figure in German literature. Goethe's work spanned and dominated poetry, drama, literature, humanism, theology, and science. His presence in German intellectual life almost forced the great thinkers who came after him, such as Hegel, Friedrich Schelling, Arthur Schopenhauer, Ludwig Feuerbach, Marx, and Nietzsche, into realms of thought other than literature—largely into philosophy and critical social inquiry—because Goethe seemed to have exhausted what humanity could achieve in every other area (Hollingdale 1970:9–10).

84 See also Nietzsche ([1908] 1968:761–2).

85 Williams (1961) indicates that because he cannot include in *Culture and Society* "any detailed accounts of the changes in [these] words and meanings," he will publish the "supporting evidence, later, in a

of change in those words serves as "a special kind of map" that makes it possible to examine the "wider changes in life and thought to which the changes
in language evidently refer" (Williams 1961:13).

Williams identifies five key words for the map—"*industry, democracy,
class, art,* and *culture.*" Although culture had previously meant "the 'tending
of natural growth,' and then, by analogy, a process of human training," in the
eighteenth and early nineteenth centuries, Williams contends, its meaning
changed "to *culture* as such, a thing in itself":[86]

> It [culture] came to mean, first, "a general state or habit of the mind," hav-
> ing close relations with the idea of human perfection. Second, it came
> to mean "the general state of intellectual development, in a society as a
> whole." Third, it came to mean "the general body of the arts." Fourth, later
> in the century, it came to mean "a whole way of life, material, intellectual,
> and spiritual." It came also, as we know, to be a word which often pro-
> voked either hostility or embarrassment. (Williams 1961:16)

This shift in meaning, which took the term "culture" from its basic, material, and agricultural roots to its emerging and then dominant connotation
of a somewhat complex intellectual entity, arose in association with social
changes that began in the eighteenth century, were firmly established by
the mid-nineteenth century, and have remained a major force in constituting social relations and relationships into the present.

One response to the driving social and material forces of Europe as it
industrialized and became increasingly market based was the perceived need,
among governing elites, to create a separation between certain moral and
intellectual activities and the very material forces that now constituted the
foundation of society. At the same time, these moral and intellectual activities served as a court of human appeal that would trump the basic, practical processes of the market economy. In other words, the base of everyday
practical activity was seen in opposition to the loftier, cerebral judgements
concerning the qualities and potentials of humanity. Finally, the growth of
culture as an abstraction and a position from which one could make cerebral judgements served as a rallying alternative for those whose power was

---

specialist paper on *Changes in English during the Industrial Revolution*" (p. 11). Williams did even better,
producing an extensive account in *Keywords: A Vocabulary of Culture and Society* (Williams 1983).

86 In *Keywords,* Williams adds the word "nature" into his "record of inquiry into a *vocabulary*"—a collection of words that are "virtually forced on … attention" because their meanings are inextricably
bound to key debates and issues (Williams 1983:15). Nature, Williams (1983) notes "is perhaps the
most complicated word" (p. 219). "Any full sense of nature" he writes, "would be a history of a large
part of human thought," and then he directs readers to consult Lovejoy's *Essays in the History of Ideas*
(Williams 1983:220).

slipping away to the new capitalist class. There had to be a moral reference point for human action, and, cultural advocates maintained, industry, industrial production, the capitalist market, or the values associated with market behaviour and the cash nexus could not fulfil that task (Williams 1983:87–93).

However, culture's new meaning and role were more than just reactions against modernization. Williams (1961:17) maintains that the emerging conception of culture was a response to significant changes in the social and political world. Culture must be understood within the context of industrialization and the formation of a new class structure.

Three major points are worth noting.

First, the word "culture" has taken on different meanings at different points in time. Because it has changed under different social circumstances, the meaning of culture can clearly be studied sociologically. One can use the sociological imagination to grasp the term more fully and meaningfully.

Second, each of the four meanings Williams identifies as dominant in the late twentieth century continues to prevail. The term "culture" is used to represent a state of mind, and it implies or inspires the idea of human perfection. Arnold, Nietzsche, and Bloom all write of culture in this sense.

"Culture" is used to refer to the level of intellectual development within a society as a whole. Used in this way, the term permits one to rank societies or civilizations on the basis of their culture or cultural achievements.

The level of culture attained by a society or its cultural status is closely associated with the third meaning—"culture" as "the arts." Societies with cultures judged to be "advanced" or "high" demonstrate their development and achievement through abstract, intellectual pursuits that show the sophistication of the society's leading minds. The arts—literature, painting, sculpture, drama, dance, and other art forms—embody and project a society's cultured development and achievements.

"Culture" also refers to a way of life—one can think of Canadian culture in contrast to American or British; one can differentiate between French Canadian and English Canadian culture or between Texan and New England culture. When using the word "culture" in this sense, people often think of one dominant culture and of other subcultures competing for influence or status or simply coexisting within this overarching and predominant culture.

The final main point is the most important one. Williams demonstrates that, to grasp culture, one must link the term's meaning to the social activities from which it has arisen. The notion of culture was originally associated with "the tending *of* something, basically crops or animals" (Williams 1983:87). It had a very direct, material, physical, and active basis and point of origin—it involved physical work. The word "culture" comes from production—"to cultivate" is the transitive verb from which the noun arises. The labour of cultivation produces the agricultural—or cultured—products.

As the term's meaning expanded to involve cultivating minds, the material and labour-related basis of cultural production began to fade, as did the idea that culture is linked to social and economic relations. The relationship between people within a set of social relationships producing agricultural products is obviously linked to their material situation. However, the cultivation of the mind, the cultivation of ideas does not seem to be tied as closely to people's social circumstances. But it is, as Williams demonstrates. This insight is his fundamental contribution to the study of culture and is central to the material presented in this chapter. Culture—even intellectual culture—is produced by people living in specific social circumstances who actively cultivate things, people, and ideas. Culture is a *social* product and can be best understood sociologically.

The sociological study of culture must tie the meaning of the term to people's lived experiences. To do so, one must identify the social processes of cultural production as well as the cultural practices that come into existence. Finally, the sociologist must, once again, link those practices and their effects to the processes of cultural production. Culture is produced or constituted through specific social practices; once constituted, those practices play a role in the constitution and reconstitution of the original social practices themselves. This abstract conception will become clear when it is applied to the study of Bob Dylan's music, lyrics, and particular ideas about entertainment. Before turning to Dylan, however, we must situate more fully the various concerns that people have expressed over culture, especially popular culture, in contemporary society.

CULTURE VERSUS MASS CULTURE

From the early days of the emergence of capitalist society through the rise of the Industrial Revolution and the birth of modernity, many different people—educationalists, public intellectuals, educated lay persons and scholars—have expressed serious and deepening concerns over the effects that the prevailing reality and tenor of the times have had upon culture. Social commentators as diverse as Nietzsche ([1872] 1968, [1873] 1983, [1889] 1954, [1895] 1954), Arnold ([1868] 1932), F.R. Leavis and Denys Thompson (1933), Theodor Adorno and Max Horkheimer (1972), Herbert Marcuse (1964), Lukács (1963), Walter Benjamin (1968a, 1968b, 1978), Richard Hoggart (1957, 1970), Williams (1961), Herbert Schiller (1973, 1989), John Fiske (1989), Stuart Hall (1964), Neil Postman (1985, 1988), and Neal Gabler (1998) have expressed different concerns about the state of culture, its meaning, its nature, and, most significantly, its impact upon social life.

Today, one rarely sees "culture" as an unmodified noun—the term is almost always qualified with one of its many, sometimes hyphenated, modifiers: classical culture, modern culture, high culture, mass culture, popular culture, middlebrow culture, lowbrow culture, plastic culture, authentic culture, or e-culture, for example. But, to earlier commentators such as Arnold ([1868] 1932), culture did not require a modifier; it was simply "the pursuit of our [humanity's] total perfection by means of getting to know, on all matters which most concern us, the best which has been thought and said in the world" (p. 6). Through this knowledge, humanity could turn "a stream of fresh and free thought upon our stock notions and habits," allowing people to escape entrenched, narrowing thoughts, ideas, and actions. "Culture, which is the study of perfection," according to Arnold ([1868] 1932), will lead humankind "to conceive true human perfection as a *harmonious* perfection, developing all sides of our humanity" and "as a *general* perfection, developing all parts of our society" (p. 11).

Leavis and Thompson also lament the passing of culture, although their perspective is quite different from Arnold's.[87] Leavis and Thompson (1933) are concerned with the demise of English literary culture, arguing that it was being overwhelmed by a growing number of simple and simplifying forms of entertainment and information such as films, newspapers, advertising, "indeed the whole world outside the classroom" (p. 1). They felt that the organic community that sustains a living, thriving culture was being lost. According to them, works such as *Pilgrim's Progress*—"the supreme expression of the old English people"—*Change in the Village*, or *The Wheelwright's Shop* remain as testaments that "the English people did once have a culture (so nearly forgotten now that the educated often find it hard to grasp what the assertion means)"; however, as the rural and agricultural world was supplanted by the urban and industrial one, English culture was cut adrift from its roots (Leavis and Thompson 1933:2–3). In the place of an authentic, centuries-long tie to the natural rhythms of agricultural life was a mech-

---

87 Like Hoggart and Williams, Leavis and Thompson were involved in adult education. And they wrote *Culture and Environment* to help teachers train students in critical awareness: "This book, though designed for school use, was not designed for that alone. Its range of application is wide and varied and its methods flexible. The earlier the age at which the kind of work it deals with is begun the better; but all its topics are capable of subtlety and a depth of development demanding the maturest approach. It invites an unlimited number of applications at the university level. And in particular the need for teachers of some training on these lines will appeal to directors of Teachers' Training Colleges. Those interested in adult education, too, may recognize here something that will help to solve some of their most difficult problems. Indeed one of the incitements to writing this book was experience of work under the W.E.A. [Workers' Educational Association]" (Leavis and Thompson 1933:vii).

anized, industrialized world that responded only to the superficial needs of the market economy, Leavis and Thompson argue:

> The great agent of change, and, from our point of view, destruction, has of course been the machine—applied power. The machine has brought us many advantages, but it has destroyed the old ways of life, the old forms, and by reason of the continual rapid change it involves, prevented the growth of new. Moreover, the advantage it brings us in mass-production has turned out to involve standardization and levelling-down outside the realm of mere material goods. Those who in school are offered (perhaps) the beginnings of education in taste are exposed, out of school, to the competing exploitation of the cheapest emotional responses; films, newspapers, publicity [advertising] in all its forms, commercially-catered fiction—all offer satisfaction at the lowest level, and inculcate the choosing of the most immediate pleasures, got with the least effort. (Leavis and Thompson 1933:3)

Here we see the split between "popular culture" and "high culture," as some might label these two concepts, tied to industrialization and urbanization. Other scholars also address these themes. Hoggart's (1957) *The Uses of Literacy: Aspects of Working-class Life with Special Reference to Publications and Entertainment* builds directly on the Leavis and Thompson work while also confronting it critically. Hoggart (1958:3–14) quickly sketches a tentative profile of "the working class" to examine more meaningfully the impact of print and mass circulation publications on the lives of real working-class people and on their understanding of the world in which they lived. He uses the experiences of his family and of his ancestors to tell the story.

Hoggart's grandparents and the working people of their generation lived a rural existence, but the generation of his parents, aunts, and uncles, who were also from the working class, only retained a few rural habits, largely out of nostalgia. Hoggart (1958) and his generation were urbanites, fully at home with mass transit, chain stores, and the pace and feel of city life; the country or seaside had become merely places one might visit. The deep personal connection of earlier generations to the natural world was gone.

In the wake of this separation from the land, working class youth engaged with the "modern mass media of communication"; for example, young people went to "the picture-palaces," which were optical fairylands, often housed in grand buildings with spacious foyers and balconies placing patrons inside an arcade of mesmerising images and sounds. However, according to *The Uses of Literacy*, the second or third generation of the working class in England did not passively internalize a bland, commercialized culture. Hoggart presents a more nuanced examination of the effects of industrialization and urbanization on culture than do Leavis and Thompson. Nevertheless, despite the working class resistance to being subsumed by a banal, commercial culture—a resistance Hoggart describes with such respect and care—he is left with some serious reservations and concerns. Hoggart (1958:286) recognizes that many are familiar with the rise of mass culture and its potential consequences, but he feels that, although they "know all the arguments," they do not really understand how profoundly mass culture penetrates into people's everyday lives, limits their horizons, and seduces them into accepting banal entertainment. It is possible "to live in a sort of clever man's paradise" without really recognizing the assault of mass culture on human sensibility, he argues.

Hoggart's concern raises one of the most pressing and preoccupying questions of the twentieth century, which saw the initial seizure of power and then the defeat of Fascism at horrendous cost as well as an increasingly totalitarian Soviet Union—the question of freedom or of freedom's limits:

> [T]o define the limits of freedom ... is ... extremely difficult. But many
> of us seem so anxious to avoid the charge of authoritarianism that we will
> think hardly at all about the problem of definition. Meanwhile, the free-
> dom from official interference enjoyed in this kind of society, coupled
> with the tolerance we ourselves are so happy to show, seems to be allow-
> ing cultural developments as dangerous in their own way as those we are
> shocked at in totalitarian societies. (Hoggart 1958:286–7)

Hoggart fears that, without a conscious intervention into the commercial dynamic that is increasingly dominating and shaping culture, the substantial freedom provided by a complex, varied culture will be lost in the levelling down of the market as it appeals to the greatest mass of consumers. When that freedom is lost, Hoggart (1958) concludes, "the great new class would be unlikely to know it: its members would still regard themselves as free and be told that they were free" (p. 287).[88]

Hoggart addresses the problem of culture and literature from a different perspective a few years later in order to make the same points regarding the decline of both in the post–World War II era. First, he describes the benefits of what he terms "live literature":

> I value literature because of the way,—the peculiar way—in which it
> explores, re-creates and seeks for the meanings in human experience;

---

88 Note that a Huxleyan theme runs through a number of these critiques of mass culture (Huxley 1932). For more on Huxley, see the discussion that follows in this chapter.

because it explores the diversity, complexity and strangeness of that experience (of individual men or of men in groups or of men in relation to the
natural world); because it re-creates the texture of that experience; and
because it pursues its explorations with a disinterested passion (not woo-
ing nor apologizing nor bullying). I value literature because in it men
look at life with all the vulnerability, honesty and penetration they can
command ... and dramatize their insights by means of a unique relationship with language and form. (Hoggart 1970:11)

But this is literature at its best—literature as a cultural rather than a commercial production. Not all writing has this impact.

Conventional literature merely reinforces the existing way of seeing the
world while live literature, properly read, may disturb us, lead us to reflect,
and even "subvert our view of life" (Hoggart 1970:12). Echoing Leavis and
Thompson, Hoggart maintains that live literature seeks "to articulate something of the 'mass and majesty' of experience." But most people tend to narrow their focus; they "ignore embarrassing qualifications and complexities"
so that the world remains comfortable. But live literature prevents us from
slipping into such complacency as it "bring us up short," and stops "the
moulds from setting firm." It "habitually seeks to break the two-dimensional
frame of fixed 'being' which we just as habitually try to put round others; it
keeps us responsive and alert, extending our humanity and understanding
of the world" (Hoggart 1970:16). Hoggart, like Leavis and Thompson, jux-
taposes two cultural categories: one that is creative, exploratory, and complex and another that reinforces convention, ignores complexity, and seeks
to comfort, entertain, and give instant and easy pleasure. Hoggart continues
his argument by noting that what is true of individuals applies to societies as
a whole. A society in which literature is becoming increasingly conventional
loses its capacity to inspire people to consider and explore the full potential
of human life. "Things can never be quite the same," Hoggart (1970) concludes, "after we have read—really read—a good book" (p. 18).

Hoggart, like Leavis and Thompson, share Nietzsche's concerns about
humanity in the modern era following the "herd instinct" and losing its
Dionysian or creative and generative capacities. Although Leavis and
Thompson link their concerns to the industrialization of Europe, Hoggart
focuses on the growing impact of the market economy and the declining
standards in literature, which result in increasingly simplified entertainment
being sold to more and more consumers in the emerging mass society.

Although their backgrounds differ significantly from those of Arnold,
Leavis, Thompson, and Hoggart, members of the Frankfurt school—Adorno,
Horkheimer, and Marcuse—express similar concerns over the growth of

what they term "the totally administered society," which they associate with the increasing power of capitalism over social life. This power, they argue, had led to the rise and predominance of "one-dimensional man" (Marcuse's term) and to a modern world in which cultural forms are being continually levelled down by what they identify as "the culture industries." Horkheimer and Adorno, whose work is deeply rooted in the traditions of great classical music, art, and literature, were also influenced by Marx's critique of capitalist society, Weber's analyses of the growth of legal-rational domination in the increasingly bureaucratic world of the early twentieth century, and the rise of Fascism in Germany. According to them, the Enlightenment (and the process of becoming "enlightened" in the modern era), the growth of science, and the spread of technical, instrumental reason had significant negative consequences that remained insufficiently explored (Horkheimer 1974; Habermas 1970).[89]

In their 1944 essay "The Culture Industry: Enlightenment as Mass Deception," Horkheimer and Adorno (1972:120) argue that the culture industries—films, radio, and magazines—impress the same stamp on everything. Every aspect of modern society is dominated by technical efficiency, mass production techniques, and standardization—automobiles, bombs, and movies are subjugated to the same system of instrumental rationality (the most effective means of producing a mass product that is sold to mass publics) and totally integrated with culture subordinate to capital.

Horkheimer and Adorno draw attention to the manner in which industries that might appear at first sight to be separate and independent—broadcasters, the banks, the film industry, and utilities producers—are all tightly interwoven economically. Indeed, they argue, the integration is so complete that one can actually ignore any features that might demarcate different firms or branches of industry. They then focus the argument and their attention on "the culture industry" in a manner that is even more pessimistic than the perspectives of Arnold, Leavis, Thompson, or Hoggart. The gap between high and mass culture is replaced, in the outline provided by Horkheimer and Adorno, by the careful, calculated differentiation of consumers and their tastes, and "the culture industry" then churns out mass produced goods to

---

89 Horkheimer and Adorno took advantage of the ambiguity of the German language to convey a double meaning with respect to the word "enlightenment." In German, nouns are always preceded by an article, and they are always capitalized; as a result, *die Aufklärung* can mean "the Enlightenment" or simply "enlightenment." A central focus of Horkheimer and Adorno's critique of modern society centres on the rise of science and the associated domination of technical, instrumental rationality, which took place during the Enlightenment and has become the basis for what is perceived of as real knowledge—or true enlightenment; the dual meaning of *die Aufklärung*, then, allows them to develop their critique at several levels simultaneously.

suit consumer groups, but these are "mechanically differentiated products" that "prove to be all alike in the end" (Horkheimer and Adorno 1972:123).

Horkheimer and Adorno's assessment of entertainment and culture in mass society is scathing and relentless. All cultural products—music, film, art, literature—are reduced to standardized formulae wherein every consumer can predict, from the outset, what will come next and anticipate the conclusion. Mass culture comforts and even flatters the consumer even though its banality is so obvious. The "dialectic of enlightenment" turns out to be the negation of learning and of expanding one's horizons, as the producers of mass culture lower the intellectual depth of art, music, film, and literature to meet the manufactured wants of mass market consumers.

The most troubling theme within "The Culture Industry" is the extent to which Horkheimer and Adorno see the entertainment industry as the vehicle for what ultimately amounts to mass deception. "The fusion of culture and entertainment that is taking place today leads not only to a depravation of culture, but inevitably to an intellectualization of amusement" (Horkheimer and Adorno 1972:143). The intellectual energies of those working in the production of mass culture are focused on perfecting the techniques that will entertain and amuse rather than challenge and stop people short. The formula for success revolves around the production and reproduction of easily and then passively consumed entertainment. "The less the culture industry has to promise, the less it can offer a meaningful explanation of life, and the emptier is the ideology it disseminates" (Horkheimer and Adorno 1972:147).

It is within this context that Horkheimer and Adorno begin to draw parallels between the culture industry of North America and the Fascists' control of the media and their calculated manipulation of the masses in Hitler's Germany. The culture industry and advertising merge since the assembly-line nature of the culture industry and the indistinguishable hollow products it offers are perfectly suited to the world of advertising. And advertising is barely a short step away from propaganda as it offers half-truths and illusions to a public looking for simple solutions to its media constructed wants. The freedom to choose, they note, turns out to be simply the freedom to choose what is always the same.

Building on Horkheimer and Adorno's *Dialectic of Enlightenment* and the concept of the administered society, Marcuse's *One-Dimensional Man: Studies in the Ideology of Advanced Industrial Society* is an extended examination of "the paralysis of criticism" in the postwar Western world—a "society without opposition."[90] Echoing central themes from George Orwell's

---

90 Marcuse (1958) was equally critical of the Soviet Union: "No matter how high the level of technological progress and material culture, of labor productivity and efficiency, the change from socialist necessity to socialist freedom can only be the result of conscious effort and decision. The maintenance

(1949) *Nineteen Eighty-Four,* Marcuse (1964) begins his study provocatively: "Does not the threat of an atomic catastrophe which could wipe out the human race also serve to protect the very forces which perpetuate this danger?" (p. ix). Due to the potentially apocalyptic consequences of an East-West confrontation in the Cold War era, the public is almost immobilized by fear, Marcuse argues, and fails to search for ways that such a catastrophe could be prevented or the threat of it eliminated. More important, if people did begin to search for solutions to the postwar geopolitical situation, they would soon see that the dangerous state of affairs in which they find themselves actually benefits some very powerful vested interests in advanced industrial societies. Echoing Horkheimer and Adorno, Marcuse notes that the media have no problem in presenting these particular vested interests as "those of all sensible men," and, as a result, the apparent needs of society as a whole are accepted as individual needs and aspirations, the satisfaction of which is for the common good and seems to be completely rational (Marcuse 1964:12).

However, Marcuse maintains, the entire structure of the administered society is irrational: its productivity is destructive of the free and full development of human needs and faculties, peace is maintained by the constant threat of war, and growth depends upon the repression of the real possibilities for pacifying the struggle for existence. Most problematic of all, the "productive apparatus and the goods and services which it produces 'sell' or impose the social system as a whole" (Marcuse 1964:11-12).

> If the individuals are satisfied to the point of happiness with the goods and services handed down to them by the administration, why should they insist on different institutions for a different production of different goods and services? And if the individuals are pre-conditioned so that the satisfying goods also include thoughts, feelings, aspirations, why should they wish to think, feel, and imagine for themselves? True, the material and mental commodities offered may be bad, wasteful, rubbish—but *Geist* and knowledge are no telling arguments against the satisfaction of needs. (Marcuse 1964:50)

---

of repressive production relations, enables the Soviet state, with the instrumentalities of universal control, to regiment the consciousness of the underlying population. ... Left without a conceptual level for the 'determinate negation' of the established system, for comprehending and realizing its arrested potentialities, the ruled tend not only to submit to the rulers but also to reproduce themselves in their subordination. Again, this process is not specific to Soviet society" (Marcuse 1958:190). *One-Dimensional Man* takes up these themes, focusing particularly on repression through production relations and on the need for "determinate negation" of the established system, which Marcuse begins to call the "great refusal" of forms of modern domination.

Like Horkheimer and Adorno, Marcuse focuses on the commodification of all that humans produce, even thoughts, feelings, and cultural works. He describes how "mass communications blend together harmoniously, and often unnoticeably, art, politics, religion, and philosophy with commercials, they bring these realms of culture to their common denominator—the commodity form" (Marcuse 1964:57). High culture becomes material culture and, in that transformation, loses its critical tension and impetus to challenge the status quo. "The spectre that has haunted artistic consciousness since Mallarmé—the impossibility of speaking a non-reified language—has ceased to be a spectre" Marcuse (1964:68) laments.[91]

The expressing of concerns about the decline of culture from the 1930s through to the 1970s did not abate in the latter part of the twentieth century. Neil Postman, for example, shifted the focus from print culture to television. In *Amusing Ourselves to Death: Public Discourse in the Age of Show Business*, he writes,

> To say it, then, as plainly as I can, this book is an inquiry into and lamentation about the most significant American cultural fact of the second half of the twentieth century: the decline of the Age of Typography and the ascendancy of the Age of Television. This change-over has dramatically and irreversibly shifted the content and meaning of public discourse, since two media so vastly different cannot accommodate the same ideas. (Postman 1985:8)

Postman (1985:30–63) develops his argument by exploring the cultural power and possibilities of typography as a medium and the mindset it facilitates—what he terms "the Age of Exposition":

> Exposition is a mode of thought, a method of learning, and a means of expression. Almost all of the characteristics we associate with mature discourse were amplified by typography, which has the strongest possible bias toward exposition: a sophisticated ability to think conceptually, deductively, and sequentially; a high valuation of reason and order; an abhorrence of contradiction; a large capacity for detachment and objectivity; and a tolerance for delayed response. (Postman 1985:63)

---

91 Stéphane Mallarmé (1842–98) was a French symbolist poet who used the sound of the spoken word to bring different levels of meaning to his poetry. He believed that poetry was independent of the world and should be read with a focus on the music of its words rather than on referential meaning. The Tuesday night salons Mallarmé hosted were at the centre of the Parisian avant-garde's intellectual life in the 1890s.

Although typography and exposition dominated Canadian and American culture throughout the eighteenth and nineteenth centuries, their impact began to decline with the rise of what Postman calls "the Age of Show Business" (Postman 1985:64–98). In this age, which he argues North America has entered, history, politics, religion, and education have become forms of entertainment, and Canadians and Americans have become less able to cope with complexity, nuance, ambiguity, and uncertainty (Postman 1985, 1988, 1995). If Irving Berlin had changed one word in his great Broadway hit, Postman (1985) notes, he would have been prophetic—today, "There's No Business *But* Show Business" (p. 98).

One illustration demonstrates Postman's concerns regarding the dominance of the entertainment culture and the way in which this culture has subverted meaning, cohesive thought, and analysis—the nightly news (the source of most people's information about the world).[92] News, Postman (1985) argues, has become reduced to "Now ... this."

> "Now ... this" is commonly used on radio and television newscasts to indicate that what one has just heard or seen has no relevance to what one is about to hear or see, or possibly to anything one is ever likely to hear or see. The phrase is a means of acknowledging the fact that the world as mapped by the speeded-up electronic media has no order or meaning and is not to be taken seriously. There is no murder so brutal, no earthquake so devastating, no political blunder so costly—for that matter, no ball score so tantalizing or weather report so threatening—that it cannot be erased from our minds by a newscaster saying, "Now ... this." The newscaster means that you have thought long enough on the previous matter (approximately forty-five seconds), that you must not be morbidly preoccupied with it (let us say, for ninety seconds), and that you must now give your attention to another fragment of news or a commercial. (P. 99)

In the age of show business, then, events and circumstances are presented as disconnected, almost random events in which one is equally as important as the next. The "Now ... this" format obliterates history, ignores social context, and keeps the viewer watching through the constant flow of images, stories, and superficial information, which is paced to permit only passive attention; there is never the time or depth of coverage that would stimulate real reflection. The news captures and entertains viewers enough to keep them staying tuned from one set of commercials to the next.

---

92 Postman (1985:114–54) also describes the impact of the electronic media, particularly television, and show business culture on religion, politics, and education.

In the conclusion of *Amusing Ourselves to Death*, Postman (1985) argues that there are two ways in which "the spirit of a culture may be shrivelled" (p. 155). The first is Orwellian—culture becomes a prison. The citizens of Oceania in Orwell's (1949) *Nineteen Eighty-Four* are imprisoned in a world where the Ministry of Truth controls culture through "prolefeed," which consists of newspapers reporting almost nothing but crime, sport, and astrology; sensational novelettes; overly sexed films; and sentimental songs mechanically produced by the "versificator." Thought is limited and distorted as Oldspeak is replaced by the ever-shrinking vocabulary of Newspeak and "doublethink." And there is the ever-present threat of the pain that the Ministry of Love inflicts on dissidents. The second way culture dies is Huxleyan—the state controls through pleasure and entertainment. In Huxley's (1932) *Brave New World*, citizens are conditioned to consume, everything from the ubiquitous drug soma, which offers hangover-free "holidays" and eliminates the need for religion by replicating religious experiences, to recreational sex.[93] In this world, what matters is "happiness rather than truth and beauty." No doubt Postman would argue that we now live in a world in which life is replicating art.

Gabler's (1998) more recent analysis of the extent to which entertainment has conquered reality echoes many of Postman's concerns. "While an entertainment-driven, celebrity-oriented society is not necessarily one that destroys all moral value," Gabler (1998) writes, "it *is* one in which the standard of value is whether or not something can grab and then hold the public's attention" (p. 8). Serious ideas, serious literature, "serious anything" is marginalized. In such a society, Gabler notes, "*Homo sapiens* ["man" the thinker] is rapidly becoming *Homo scaenicus*—man the entertainer"(Gabler 1998:8).

Gabler's position differs from Postman's insofar as Postman placed a heavier burden on television for the decline in culture and the blunting of sensitivity; Gabler (1998), on the other hand, argues that, although television may well be what Postman calls "the command center of the new epistemology [basis for knowledge]," entertainment "was the cosmology that had governed American life with increasing vigour since at least the turn of the century" (p. 56). Today, the argument goes, entertainment has become the universe—the cosmos—within which television, radio, print media, the

---

93 Huxley wrote *Brave New World* following a trip to the United States during which he was repulsed by American youth culture, sexual promiscuity, and what he perceived as an artificial, commercially driven cheeriness in American interaction. The sex-hormone chewing gum was a parody of the ubiquitous chewing gum of US teens. But the book is more than a critique of American culture and is based on more than a fear of the Americanization of Europe—it was also a critical response to the utopian literature that followed H.G. Wells's *The World Set Free: A Story of Mankind* (1914) and *Men Like Gods: A Novel* (1923) and George Bernard Shaw's (1889, 1912) various pieces supporting socialism.

World Wide Web, iPods, iPhones, and e-culture orbit, operate, and exert their influence.

By the end of the twentieth century, according to Gabler, the great cultural debate had shifted from considering the differences between high culture and mass culture to one in which the key tension was between a culture of reality versus one of entertainment. (Note that Gabler uses the same *Brave New World* imagery as Postman.) The debate became one between "the realists who believed that a clear-eyed appreciation of the human condition was necessary to *be* human and the postrealists who believed that glossing reality and even transforming it into a movie were perfectly acceptable strategies if these made us happier" (Gabler 1998:243). "Is reality," Gabler asks, "as it was traditionally construed, morally, aesthetically and epistemologically preferable to postreality?" In other words, is life, "as traditionally construed, preferable to the movie version of life?"

From Arnold to Gabler: The Critique of Mass Culture

The foregoing demonstrates important continuity along with significant change in the study of culture and its fate in the modern period. Arnold's notion that culture is "the best which has been thought and said in the world" and that it can foster "true human perfection as a *harmonious* perfection" represents a key reference point for all ensuing analyses of culture and its degradation.

When Leavis and Thompson lament the separation of English culture or English literature from its premodern roots, they are really mourning the extent to which the demands of the emerging market, rather than the careful reflections of thoughtful members of a community, began to standardize, level down, and speed up the production of ideas, perceptions, and tastes. The break from the organic community and the rise of a machine-driven culture are their central concerns. Their position is simply a specific instance of Arnold's larger concern.

Hoggart is critical of the extent to which Leavis, Thompson, and others accepted the notion that the organic community was lost. True, it was no longer a rural community, according to Hoggart, but the working class—the real people who made up the 1950s working class—still constituted and still had a community, and, even though they were exposed to an increasingly commercialized culture, they filtered it and resisted it on the basis of values they developed from their own real experiences. But Hoggart is also well aware of the power of the "modern mass media of communication" and of the diminishing quality of their products—he understood "cultural debasement" and "the force of the assault outside."

Hoggart's concern links to Arnold's—although Hoggart does not neces-sarily celebrate culture with a capital "C," culture as that which contains the best that has been thought in human history, he values culture that "explores the diversity, complexity, and strangeness" of human experience—one that looks "at life with all the vulnerability, honesty, and penetration" that an indi-vidual can command and that dramatizes those insights so as to break out of conventional understanding or wisdom. Hoggart wants to ensure a lively engagement with the complexity of the human condition as it is translated through various cultural forms. Hoggart seeks to maintain cultural forms that explore the diversity and rich texture of life, so people do not narrow their focus and "ignore embarrassing qualifications and complexities"; cul-tural forms must exist, he believes, which "bring us up short [and] stop the moulds from setting firm." For him, critical issues were at stake—the notion of "freedom," what constitutes it, and how it is defined. People had to be able to recognize whether real freedom was slipping away and being incremen-tally replaced by an ever-tightening velvet straitjacket of comfortable and comforting entertainment.

Horkheimer, Adorno, and Marcuse, in the wake of their flight from Fascist Germany in the 1930s, were centrally concerned with Hoggart's question of freedom as well. What they saw in the United States were cultural indus-tries that emphasized technical efficiency, mass production, and standard-ization at the level of the lowest common denominator. Everything—from cars and appliances to music and motion pictures—was imprinted with the same stamp through the commodification of everyday life. Like Huxley before them, they saw the stamp of Henry Ford and Fordism everywhere—and most significantly, they believed standardization was rampant in the world of cultural production. They saw the dialectic of enlightenment, as it was being manifested in America, as a slippery slope that began with under-mining the complexity of culture through assembly-line production for mass audiences. Next came advertising strategies that homogenized consumers into undifferentiated audiences, and, finally, near the end of the path, came propaganda techniques and strategies similar to those of Nazi Germany, as choices narrowed, information was simplified, and consumers were bom-barded with the idea of choice when no real choice existed at all and free-dom had slipped away with hardly a stir.

Marcuse's *One-Dimensional Man* directly reflects some of Orwell's cen-tral themes in *Nineteen Eighty-Four*—peace is maintained by the constant threat of war, the threat of atomic catastrophe is tempered by the produc-tion of more and more atomic bombs, and the interests of particular individ-uals are purchased by mass publics as their own general interests. Switching dystopias, Marcuse notes that, in the one-dimensional, advanced industrial societies, individuals are able to buy the goods that will satisfy not only their physical needs but also their thoughts, feelings, and aspirations—satiated, there is no need to wish, think, feel, or imagine for oneself. Marcuse, like Horkheimer and Adorno, lamented the levelling of market-based culture and the loss of a culture of complexity—a culture of critique that could result in "the great refusal," his name for the proper response to the irrational repression of one-dimensional society.

Poster and Gabler revisit many of the same themes—the decline of the "Age of Typography" as the "Age of Television" came to dominate, and the end of the "Age of Exposition" as the West entered the "Age of Show Business." Both scholars, in their own way, lament the rise of a Huxleyan world of control through banal entertainment and the shift to a post-realist perspective in which the clear-eyed appreciation of the human condition is replaced by one in which glossing reality and transforming it into a movie is preferable because it keeps people happy.

All of these critics describe culture as having been replaced by a newly modified variant, and that variant—mass culture, popular culture, entertainment culture, one-dimensional culture, industrial culture, market culture—threatens fundamental aspects of Western civilization, they argue. But, as Williams notes, culture is a very complex word—it can be held aloft as a standard that humanity is failing to maintain and embody, or it can be seen as something people produce and then experience and resist, as something we humans adapt to and modify while, at the same time, powerful, entrenched social forces seek to mould us and produce conformity. Culture is something over which people struggle, and it is this perspective that merits some exploration.

MODIFIED CULTURES AND MODIFYING CULTURES

Four points are critical in moving beyond the standard rejection of market-based culture. The first centres on the best modifier or modifiers for the term "culture."

In the nineteenth century, Arnold used the term "culture" (without any modifier) to refer to an ideal of human refinement. Many now use the term "high culture" to express this meaning; the evaluative modifier "high" sets this culture apart from other cultural forms. Before exploring the rationale behind using "high," however, we must establish what type of culture "high culture" is above—is the binary "low culture," "mass culture," or even "uncultured"? Typically the binaries are high versus low or elite versus mass, although high culture and mass culture are also posed opposite one another.

The term mass culture, Herbert Gans (1974:9–10) notes, arose from two German terms—*Masse* and *Kultur.* The term *Masse* first came into usage in the late eighteenth century as a term that designated and labelled the non-aristocratic, uneducated portions of European society. By the nineteenth and twentieth centuries, *Masse* identified the lower-middle class, the working class, and the poor. The *Masse* was viewed with suspicion and sometimes fear by the privileged classes. Following the revolutionary uprisings of 1789 and 1848 and the Paris Commune of 1871, there was an ongoing, latent concern that the masses might be mobilized as a revolutionary force by a unifying ideology or a charismatic leader. At the same time, there was also the belief that the *Masse* was easily manipulated and satisfied—the elites of industrializing Europe, well-educated in classical history, knew about the bread and circuses practices of Rome. In short, the *Masse* was a group that upper-class Europeans looked down upon with suspicion, and, as an adjective linked to culture, the word "mass" remained a negative, dismissive, belittling, pejorative modifier.

Kultur refers to the cultural pastimes consumed and enjoyed by the well-educated elite of European society. *Kultur* includes art, music, literature, and other refined activities or objects. It also refers to the styles, modes of thought and expression, and sentiments expressed by the elite that prefers objects of *Kultur. Kultur*, then, is synonymous with being cultured. *Kultur* translates into English as "culture," and it has a meaning comparable to the one described by Arnold. Consequently, to ensure that the true meaning of *Kultur* was maintained in English as other forms of culture began to gain expression and influence, the word "culture"—which was never a proper noun and thus not capitalized in correct speech—was increasingly modified by "high" and occasionally by "elite."

As a result, "mass culture" has a negative meaning—it represents all the unrefined styles, modes of thought, expressions, sentiments, objects of consumption, and activities of the uneducated, lower orders of European society. Juxtaposing culture and mass culture or high culture and mass culture establishes, through the use of adjectives, what quickly appears to be a vast, evaluative gulf between two apparently readily identifiable cultures. But, if instead of positing mass culture opposite high culture one uses the word "popular" and speaks of popular culture versus culture, then much of the definitional distinction may vanish—a different adjective modifies one's conception of "not-high culture"; popular culture is widely consumed, openly embraced, and admired among its many consumers, adherents, supporters, and perhaps even producers. Whereas mass culture may carry a stronger sense of "bread and circuses" entertainment for an uneducated and potentially unruly mob, popular culture has a less negative connotation, even though it still suggests cultural products that are broadly and generally appealing. Thus, the first point is that the adjective modifying culture carries with it tremendous definitional power and needs to be thought about critically.

Second, defenders of high culture such as Arnold stress its humanist origins within the Renaissance and the high value this sort of culture places upon human creativity, aesthetically pleasing composition, and the artistic rendering of complexity in a form that gives immediate satisfaction yet draws one into deeper, evermore revealing contemplation and insight. They also point to the enduring value of the object, score, or manuscript—the creative legacy of high culture. At the same time, high culture celebrates an elitism that began to emerge in the Renaissance but ultimately served the bourgeoisie as an important mechanism for elevating its social status commensurate with the economic power it was establishing throughout the eighteenth century.

Pre-industrial European societies were culturally divided into high and folk cultures. "The latter," Gans (1974) notes, "was sparse, homemade, and, because peasants lived in isolated villages, largely invisible" (p. 52). High culture, supported by the nobility, the priesthood, and affluent merchants—people who had the time, resources, and educational background to consume and consider the cultural productions of talented and highly trained artists—created a system of patronage that distinguished the elite from the masses. Because these key aspects—the humanist origins of cultural values, the contemplative space required to enjoy the complexity of cultural works, the educational attainments needed for creation and appreciation within this culture, and elite social status—were so tightly bound together, the defenders of high culture ruled out, virtually by definition, the possibility that folk, mass, or popular culture would be considered equally creative, complex, aesthetically refined, captivating, and intellectually fulfilling. But popularity and widespread appeal do not automatically rule out depth or substance. On the contrary, cultural products that are widely available and popular among many people can gain that popularity from their artistry, complexity, and ability to stimulate reflection and ongoing analysis. Similarly, the invisible folk cultures that high culture obscured also contained elements that were as artistic as the objects celebrated by high culture. In fact, historically, it is the depth and eternal qualities of folk culture that frequently became the focal points of literature, sculpture, painting, and other traditional forms of high cultural production. Finally, it is the refined artistry of folk art that makes it sought after by cultural connoisseurs in the contemporary period. As a result, one must carefully resist the definitional link between high culture and complex, deeply meaningful artistic production—popular and folk cultures can entail equally compelling symbolic meaning and artistry.

The third main point that moves us beyond the standard rejection of market-based culture centres on where and how high cultural productions were originally produced. High culture was originally associated with the king's court and supported by the nobility, aristocracy, and *haute bourgeoisie*. As a result, cultural production was undertaken by genuine, highly skilled craftsmen—people with specialized knowledge, lengthy experience, talent, access to scarce resources, and some independence from by-the-clock production. High culture—then and now—centres on masterpieces; it was intimately linked to the work of master craftsmen working in tightly controlled crafts guilds.

The growth of the market challenged and ultimately undermined the tight control that the guilds exercised over all forms of production. Guild production soon competed with cottage industries and small workshops. Master craftsmen lost their monopoly control or the tight rein they once exercised over production, over the training of apprentices, and over quality.

While the growth of the market increased all forms of production, it necessarily created new opportunities for cultural production and expanded the range of cultural products. The very best art and literature remained the property of the wealthy, but larger audiences and a growing consumer base provided the opportunity for more writers, artists, and musicians to contribute to an increasingly diversifying world of cultural production. The market and modernity also created a demand for copies of masterpieces or the mass production of quickly made, inexpensive works.

This broadening range of cultural production is of the greatest concern to supporters of high culture—cheap knock-offs, lower quality works, mass-produced images, simplified presentations with broader appeal all represent a dilution of culture, and they spark the desire to differentiate "real" culture from mass culture. But there are two problems with this position.

First, it assumes that all cultural production in the premodern period was of the highest quality. It ignores the fact that, although the best Renaissance art, for example, has survived, thousands and thousands of pieces of lower aesthetic quality, artistry, or craftsmanship were cast aside long ago. The cultural production that high culture treasures was the tip of a proverbial iceberg of works of varying quality. Time ultimately determines what endures and what will become defined as high culture. Contemporary critique is important, but time is the ultimate judge of what is regarded as art and what falls by the wayside. What is more, two hundred years from now, some of the objects currently denigrated as the kitsch of mass culture might also be absorbed into the pantheon of high art.

Second, the argument also assumes that artists today are simply assembly-line producers churning out mass culture through mass production techniques. The artistry and craft of cultural production is easily glossed over in short-term immediate assessments. The full appreciation of an artist's craft may take time, and the taste for an innovative form may not develop until decades have passed. Avant-garde art forms necessarily challenge the status quo and are almost always met with resistance and rejection by the cultural establishment (King 2006). Only after a full appreciation for their artistry develops are new forms—often mass forms of art—incorporated into the realm of high cultural production.

This leads to the last point of importance—the existence of what Gans (1974:69–118) calls "taste cultures." Gans (1974) notes that there are a number of popular cultures, and "they, as well as high culture, are all *taste cultures* which function to entertain, inform, and beautify life" (p. 10). These different taste cultures also "express values and standards of taste and aesthetics." Most important, when various taste cultures are compared to high culture, they turn out to be very similar to each other in many ways:

> Taste cultures, as I define them, consist of values and the cultural forms which express these values: music, art, design, literature, drama, comedy, poetry, criticism, news, and the media in which these are expressed— books, magazines, newspapers, records, films, and television programs, paintings and sculpture, architecture, and, insofar as ordinary consumer goods also express aesthetic values or functions, furnishings, clothes, appliances, and automobiles as well. (Gans 1974:10-11)

Gans also argues that taste cultures are lived cultures—they cannot be abstracted from the social contexts within which they are created and consumed. In fact, it is this direct link to real individuals, acting within specific social relationships, that ensures that taste cultures are a vibrant dimension to people's social lives.

Gans's discussion shows that, in a stable and homogenous society, cultural expression is relatively consistent and narrow; in diverse societies, however, there is a wide range of cultural expression and a number of tastes to which different taste cultures appeal. One of the dominant features of the contemporary period is the extent to which social life is diversified, and it is not surprising that new cultural forms emerge and existing ones are modified or reinterpreted and appreciated either anew or from a different perspective.

Gans (1974:70) also notes that a number of variables will influence a person's interest in a particular taste culture—class, religion, ethnic and racial background, regional origin, place of residency, age, and gender—although he emphasizes that class and education are the critical factors in this determination. Gans's position on class and education rests on the material and experiential circumstances associated with both variables. The greater the resources and the larger the set of intellectual tools that a person has to draw upon to enjoy, interact with, and interrogate different taste cultures, the wider the range of taste cultures that person can find attractive and interesting.

Gans's ultimate argument is twofold. On the one hand, he supports the position that there is a hierarchy of taste cultures and a hierarchy of "taste publics" in twentieth-century America. He identifies the different taste cultures and taste publics as high culture, upper-middle culture, lower-middle culture, low culture, and quasi-folk low culture (Gans 1974:71), and he argues that high culture is "better or at least more comprehensive and more informative than the lower ones [taste cultures]" (Gans 1974:125).

At the same time—and this is the second aspect of his argument—Gans states that the lower taste cultures serve important purposes in the cultural mosaic of contemporary society. Until social leaders, policy makers, and cultural producers have found a way of ensuring "the cultural mobility that would allow people to have the educational and socioeconomic background prerequisite to choosing the higher taste cultures," Gans (1974:129) strongly supports a multilayered set of taste cultures to meet the needs of various taste publics. Thus, although Gans (1974) argues that higher taste cultures have greater value in comparison to lower taste cultures, he maintains that all taste cultures are "of equal worth when considered in relation to their taste publics" (p. 128). Gans's position is reflected in the following policy statement:

> American society should pursue policies that would maximize educational and other opportunities for all so as to permit everyone to choose from higher taste cultures. Until such opportunities are available, however, it would be wrong to expect a society with a median educational level of twelve years to choose only from taste cultures requiring a college education, or for that matter, to support through public policies the welfare of the higher cultures at the expense of the lower ones. Moreover, it would be wrong to criticize people for holding and applying aesthetic standards that are related to their educational background, and for participating in taste cultures reflecting this background. (Gans 1974:128)

Gans's position moderates elitism with a commitment to democracy and a respect for diversity, but it still marginalizes popular culture.

There is, however, a different way of building on Gans's work. One of his points is that high culture "differs from all other taste cultures in that it is dominated by creators—and critics—and that many of its users accept the standards and perspectives of creators" (Gans 1974:75). This circumstance aptly describes the higher taste culture of classical music, which accepts as

benchmarks of excellence the work of Bach, Beethoven, or Chopin, for example. But it can also be applied in other taste cultures—to the musical standards derived from the work of jazz greats such as Duke Ellington, Count
Basie, or John Coltrane or of hip-hop artists such as 2Pac, 50 Cent, or The
Original 50 Cent. Although some might argue that hip hop hardly compares
to opera, a person really knowledgeable about either will be able to determine when a new composition fails to meet the standards or to fit within the
overall perspective of either musical form. More important, people deeply
embedded within a specific taste culture experience a far greater symbolic
meaning and cultural richness when confronting a cultural product from that
taste culture than do outsiders or those simply sampling. Before determining
whether a particular cultural product belongs in a taste culture that is high,
low, or even quasi-folk, though, one needs to understand more about the
intersection between cultural products and the way the social distribution
of cultural resources influences the production, dissemination, and appreciation of all forms of culture. That is the first focal point in the next chapter.

10 THE DIALECTICS OF POPULAR CULTURE

The explosion of popular cultural forms in the latter half of the twentieth century did not occur in a vacuum—it began in the sparse soil of hardship, in the period between 1910 and 1939, when folk, jazz, and blues gave different expression to the heavy sighs of individuals and families eking out their existence (see, for example, Agee and Evans 1941; Dos Passos 1932, 1936, 1937; Steinbeck 1937, 1939, 1952). Those sounds blended with the optimistic flights of hope and the bright tapestry of cultural experience that waves of European immigrants brought to Canada and the United States as they sought to forge new lives and lay the foundation for the next generation's prosperity.

World War I, the Great Depression, Franklin Delano Roosevelt's New Deal, William Lyon Mackenzie King's programs in industrial reconstruction in Canada, and World War II mixed sombre tones with the unyielding belief that rewards would come to those who committed themselves to an unselfish, collective effort against foes that would be overcome. Long before Barack Obama campaigned on "Yes we can!" Canadians and Americans believed that, through national mobilization, they could overcome economic depression and war. And, as each crisis was met and endured, Canadians and Americans reaffirmed their belief in the promise of social renewal through steadfast faith and commitment to the cause. Regular people found themselves involved in extraordinary struggles, and they rose to the challenge. Common people displayed heroic achievement in ways that demanded celebration and cultural recognition. There was a fundamental democratization of hardship, but also leadership, commitment, recognition, and reward; significant cultural transformation was underway.

When Fascism was finally pushed back into Hitler's bunker beneath the Reich Chancellery, the sounds of war gave way to those of reconstruction, and North Americans soon found themselves in the midst of what Lizabeth Cohen (2003) has termed "the landscape of mass consumption." This landscape included new limited-access highways that bypassed the slower established commercial routes, and along those highways "suburban settlements sprouted on what had been fields of corn, celery, spinach, and cabbage." Shopping centres "became the new centers of community life, providing a place to spend a Saturday, to attend an evening concert, to take the children to visit Santa Claus, [and] to see candidates campaign" (Cohen 2003:6). Cohen describes this new landscape as being filled with children and with products especially designed for their consumption:

> Like many in my baby boomer generation, I grew up in a world of kids—
> on the block, in overflowing schools, and on television, where so many
> programs and advertisements seemed to have been made just for us, from
> *Captain Kangaroo, Romper Room,* and the *Howdy Doody Show* when we
> were young to *Rin Tin Tin, Lassie,* and *American Bandstand* as we grew
> older. (Cohen 2003:6)

Cohen's description contrasts starkly with the images Norman Rockwell used in 1943 to illustrate President Roosevelt's promise of "four freedoms"— freedom of speech and expression, freedom of religion, freedom from want, and freedom from fear. Rockwell's *Saturday Evening Post* covers capture the world of rural self-sufficiency and local community, and they present an apparently shared consensus of values and worldview. Cohen and the rest of her generation were born into a dramatically different and changing world— an urban world of asphalt, concrete, construction, burgeoning commerce, mass production, mass advertising, and mass consumption. It was also a world that categorized people into separate and distinct market groups based on gender, race, and social status. In many ways, if the transition from rural, agrarian (even feudal) society to urban, industrializing, capitalist society represents the first great transformation, then the dramatic shifts that took place in the first half of the twentieth century represent a second great transformation in the life experiences and life chances of people in Canada, the United States, and western Europe.

Although, during the war years, Canadian and American families had saved, lived on rations, and bought war bonds to support the war effort, at the end of World War II, businesses lost little time in telling people what to do with those savings. "WHAT THIS WAR IS ALL ABOUT," a Royal type-writer ad described by Cohen notes, is the right to "once more walk into any store in the land and buy anything you want":

> Likewise, a public service ad placed by Macy's in the *New York Daily News* in September 1943 to promote the Third War Loan Drive said it all. Under the headline "What We're Fighting For ..." came a short paragraph with the expected orthodoxies—"defending Democracy," "battling for a better world". ... But thereafter the ad was devoted to a long list "of little things" "we're fighting for": "a steak for every frying pan," permission "to take a taxi to Brooklyn," "the right to have cuffs on our pants," "the return of those lively golf balls that'll go a mile," to name just a few. (Cohen 2003:71–3)

"As the war dragged on," Cohen (2003) continues, "the return to normalcy increasingly referred to a lifestyle that purchaser consumers would soon be able to buy" (p. 73). After total war, then, Canadians and Americans looked forward to total living.

Mass consumption in postwar North America was not regarded as an indulgence; it was viewed as a civic responsibility that would ensure full employment, the expansion of the economy, and a thriving society that would contrast with, confront, and quash Soviet aspirations to spread communism across the globe. Film, the popular press, business leaders, and academics drew links between the benefits of mass production, mass consumption, an expanding economy, the *embourgeoisement* of blue-collar workers through their increased purchasing power, and the strengthening of democratic nations with the same shared values (Aron 1961, 1962; Bell 1960a, 1973; Dahrendorf 1959, 1967; Giddens 1973; Goldthorpe 1968a, 1968b, 1969).

The link between consumerism, democracy, and claims of North American superiority was best captured in the famous 1959 "kitchen debate" between then Vice-President Richard Nixon and Soviet Premier Nikita Khrushchev. The debate was one of several pointed and difficult exchanges between Nixon and Khrushchev during Nixon's visit to a US trade and cultural fair in Sokolniki in the USSR. Outside a model US kitchen set up at the fair—hence the moniker "kitchen debate"—Nixon boasted about the superiority of American over Soviet life by focusing on the mass consumer goods featured in the display. He emphasized the affordability of American housing, US superiority in the television industry, the variety of dishwashers from which a housewife could choose, and American innovation in the production of goods, such as self-activated floor sweepers and other household gadgets. Khrushchev dismissed Nixon's claims by noting that, unlike the durable products of the Soviet Union, American gadgets were easily broken and quickly became obsolete. At the end of the exchange, Nixon and Khrushchev re-established a modicum of conviviality by toasting one another with glasses of Pepsi ("Kitchen Debate" 1959; Universal International News 1959). To the American home market, however, there was no question about which nation was serving its citizens best or how far ahead the United States was in everything from consumer goods and rocket production to freedom of speech and freedom from need.

"Faith in a mass consumption postwar economy," Cohen (2003) writes, "came to mean much more than the ready availability of goods to buy":

> Rather, it stood for an elaborate, integrated ideal of economic abundance and democratic political freedom, both equitably distributed, that became almost a national civil religion from the late 1950s into the 1970s. As ever present as this paradigm was, however, it bore no specific label at the time, so for convenience sake I will dub it the Consumers' Republic. For at least a quarter century, the ideal of the Consumers' Republic provided the blueprint for American [and Canadian] economic, social, and political maturation, as well as for export around the globe. (P. 127)

This consumers' republic was the foundation for popular cultural forms that would dwarf even the worst nightmares of Arnold and Nietzsche, and, although the expansion of consumer goods was manna for some, it was a cause for concern among many. Moreover, although the vast array of popular culture forms suggested a growing diversity in tastes and cultural products to consume, much of popular culture was homogenous irrespective of the cultural medium (music, art, literature, drama, television, or movies). That homogeneity is best understood by looking at the intersection of the history of the social structure with the development of cultural forms and production.

From 78s to 45s and LPs: The Growth of Cultural Diversity

The consumers' republic provided the overall framework and context for the rise to dominance of mass cultural forms, an eventuality that Hoggart, Adorno, Horkheimer, Marcuse, Postman, and Gabler feared. However, by going inside that republic, one begins to appreciate why the monolithic banality they dreaded did not exist for long. What emerged in its place were numerous vibrant forms of popular culture. The record industry provides some insight into this development.

"Why 1955?" Richard Peterson (1990) asks. In the brief span between 1954 and 1956, he maintains, there was a major aesthetic revolution as rock replaced jazz in American popular music. "Frank Sinatra, Tommy Dorsey, Patty Page, Perry Como, Nat King Cole, Tony Bennett, Kay Starr, Les Paul, Eddie Fisher, Jo Stafford, Frankie Lane, Johnnie Ray and Doris Day," Peterson (1990) writes, "gave way to Elvis Presley, Chuck Berry, The Platters, Bill Haley, Buddy Holly, Little Richard, Carl Perkins and the growing legion of rockers" (p. 97). The reasons for the change were complex and involved far more than the birth of the Baby Boomers (the oldest of whom would have been only nine in 1955).

Peterson's argument focuses on copyright law, patent law, the regulatory practices of the Federal Communications Commission in the United States, technological development, changes in the broadcast and record industry, and changes in the organizational structure of radio stations, phonograph record producing firms, and television studios. Peterson also considers the way careers changed in the recording industry and on radio, as well as the segmentation of the consumer market in the wake of all these other changes.

In 1909, copyright law in the United States provided protection, for the first time, to the owners of musical compositions. Prior to that time, American sheet music printer-publishers had maintained themselves by reprinting standard favourites and appropriating the work of European composers, who were not protected by US copyright. The change in copyright law meant that sheet music writers and publishers could now invest in the development and promotion of new songs because others could not legally reproduce their work without paying royalties.

One problem remained, however. The new law did not provide a mechanism for the writers and publishers to collect the royalties they were due under the new law from all of the numerous places where their music was played. As a result, a number of them banded together in 1914 to form the American Society of Composers, Authors, and Publishers (ASCAP). By the 1930s, ASCAP was not only collecting royalties on behalf of its membership and delivering music to musicians, radio stations, musical theatre, and the film industry, for example, but also protecting its members' interests by influencing what music was played. "It did this," Peterson (1990) writes, "by, in effect, mandating that only ASCAP licensed music could be played in Broadway musicals, performed on the radio, and incorporated into movies" (p. 99). As late as 1950, an oligopoly of only 18 publishers controlled the music that the public heard (Ryan 1985). Songs such as "Tea for Two," "Stardust," and "Always" are representative of the music the group favoured—well-crafted, abstract love themes with strong melodies and muted jazz rhythms and harmonies. "The work of black musicians in the blues, jazz, r&b, and what later came to be called soul genres was systematically excluded, as were the songs in the developing Latin and country music traditions" (Peterson 1990:99–100).

The copyright law modification and the establishment of ASCAP are significant because they represent the forces leading to the homogenization of the music industry in the pre–World War II period, a homogenization that encouraged the increasingly banal, levelled-down cultural production that Leavis, Thompson, Hoggart, Adorno, Horkheimer, and Marcuse criticized so heavily and feared would dominate the realm of culture well into the future. The tension between a simplified mass culture and a vibrant, sophisticated popular culture boils down to a struggle between the monopoly or oligopoly interests of big businesses, on the one hand, and the pursuit of diversity and innovation by small independent artists and producers, on the other. That struggle took place in a number of locations within the different culture industries.

In response to the oligopoly control that ASCAP exercised over the production and performance of music, a number of radio networks formed a rival licensing agency in 1939—Broadcast Music Incorporated (BMI). BMI signed its own stable of music publishers and songwriters including those whom ASCAP had excluded (Ryan 1985). The BMI challenge to ASCAP's control of the music industry began to broaden the type of music that reached the public and created new taste publics for previously excluded musical forms. But this did not open the door to rock—it would take much more than a shift in who wrote the music and an increase in the venues from which it could be played.

A second key ingredient was the phonographic record. By the 1930s, the 10-inch, 78 revolutions per minute (rpm) shellac disk was the standard record in the industry. These 78s had their limitations; the quality of sound reproduction was not particularly high—the constant low-level hissing and scratching sound in the background that one associates with 1930s and 1940s records was due to the limited sound quality of the 78—and they were quite fragile.

Following World War II, Columbia Records wanted to produce a high-fidelity record that could hold more music than the standard 78. In 1948, Columbia released a stunning, technological breakthrough—the 12-inch, $33\frac{1}{3}$ rpm, long-playing record (the LP). Columbia offered to share the technology with its larger arch-rival RCA to establish a common industry standard, but RCA refused the offer. RCA brought out its own alternative to the 78— the 7-inch, 45 rpm vinyl record with the large hole in the middle (the 45).

By 1952, the 78 had almost disappeared, the 12-inch LP was the predominant medium for classical music, and 45 singles dominated popular music and were played on the radio and in jukeboxes and stores.[94] The 45 was key to the development of rock for two reasons.

First, like free music downloading from the Internet today, jukeboxes became a platform that a wide variety of musicians could use to get needed exposure. With respect to rock, jukeboxes put this new music form into the soda shops, restaurants, and hangouts where young consumers could play and replay and replay a record at minimal cost. Jukebox 45s helped build the taste culture for an emerging style of music.

Second, compared to the brittle 78s, the vinyl 45s were almost unbreakable. This durability allowed major record companies to send 45s to radio stations and wholesale distributors through the mail rather than through the expensive private distribution systems that the fragile 78s required. At the same time, small record companies could also distribute their songs at an affordable cost, which allowed them to compete with the big corporations. The 45 helped break down the oligopolistic control that the major record producers had once enjoyed as a consequence of the cost of distribution being prohibitive for the small independents.

Although the oligopoly on taste was loosened by the creation of BMI and by the opportunity for record producers, both large and small, to ship 45s around the continent, another step in broadening consumer taste was necessary to lay the foundation for the birth of rock and roll. This step involved increasing the number of broadcasting stations that could play the 45s. During the 1930s, the Federal Communications Commission (FCC) had restricted the number of stations across the United States. Each market had only three to five stations—NBC, CBS, and MBS (Mutual Broadcasting System) were always present, which left room for one or two independents. Leading up to World War II, a number of groups, in the public interest, applied for radio broadcast licences, but the FCC held off on its decisions until after 1945. By then, the advent of television reduced the resistance of the three major networks, which regarded television, and not radio, as the wave of the future. The number of independent radio stations soared. The oligopoly in radio came to a quick end, as the major broadcasting stations shifted to television and left radio to a number of new, energetic and innovative entrepreneurs.

Television may have been the most visible technological change that encouraged the proliferation of radio stations and thus increased the demand for music of varying types, but the tiny transistor that replaced the large

---

94 The reason for the large hole in the centre of the 45 was the primitive technology of the jukebox. The mechanism that selected the record and then placed it on the turntable was not precise enough to always line the pin in the turntable with the standard, smaller hole of a 78; the larger hole allowed for greater error in the system and ensured that the automated system worked time after time after time.

power-consuming, heat-generating, and cumbersome vacuum tubes was the revolutionary innovation that put those radio stations into the hands of teenagers and young adults across the nation. Lightweight, pocketbook-sized, relatively inexpensive, made-in-Japan transistor radios, complete with earphones, became almost as ubiquitous among teenagers in the late 1950s as the iPod is today. The transistor radio made music more than portable, however—it also allowed it to be personal.

Prior to the transistor radio, most homes had one large cabinet radio-record player in the household. The cabinet housed the radio and record player and provided storage space for 78s, LPs, and 45s—it was a standard piece of household furniture, and, depending on its quality and appearance, it conferred status on the family. Because the cabinet was located centrally in the house, parents controlled the selection of radio stations and records. The inexpensive transistor radio allowed households to have more radios and loosened parental control over what was heard. For teenagers, the portable transistor and the quickly popular portable record player gave unprecedented freedom of choice when it came to music.

Peterson's (1990:103–8) analysis of the rise of rock music presents a useful contrast between the 1948 and the 1958 radio and recording industries, and the key intervening variable is television. Prior to the advent of television, radio was the dominant form of home entertainment, and the three major networks competed for an increased slice of the listening public. Because of the comparable strength and market positions of these major networks, each was risk averse, so, rather than introduce radically different programming, they produced daily and weekly schedules that were virtually identical. Here is Peterson's description of the evening radio schedule in 1948:

> On weekend evenings, each of the radio networks featured the major dance bands of the era broadcast *live* from one of the many large dance halls or elegant hotels around the country. The popular hits of the day were also played on the air by studio orchestras as part of the mix of the comedy and variety shows hosted by the likes of Bob Hope and Jack Benny. There was a programme called "Your Hit Parade" that featured the top ten selling records of the week. But the *records* were not played! Rather, the studio band and its male or female singer, as appropriate, performed each of the songs in turn. Since the hit songs of 1948 were written, arranged and recorded by professionals to fit widely understood swing era conventions, it was easy for the studio band to faithfully reproduce the sound of the record. (Peterson 1990:103)

The major networks did not play records on their national programs in the 1940s, but, Peterson (1990:104) notes, several local affiliates did—although the format was telling. Martin Block's *Make Believe Ballroom*, first broadcast over New York's WNEW, virtually duplicated, through his introductions, the sequencing of songs, and the pseudo-interviews with band leaders, the live broadcasts of the majors.

There was a similar concentration of control in the record industry in 1948; RCA, Columbia (CBS), Capitol, and American Decca (MCA) released 80 per cent of the songs that reached the top ten hit list, and eight firms released 95 per cent of all the hits (Peterson and Berger 1975). The major record companies ensured their dominance by signing the best creative people to long-term contracts and investing in the promotion of their work. The majors also enjoyed near monopoly control over the distribution of their music to radio stations, and they kept in close contact with the national networks to ensure that their music played (while other music did not). They were equally successful, Peterson (1990) notes, "in controlling the songs that reached the public ear via Broadway musicals and movies" (p. 104).

By 1958, television had led to the total transformation of the radio broadcast industry. The networks that had fought each other so fiercely for a slice of radio's listening public, so they could sell that audience to advertisers, now turned the bulk of their time, energy, and resources to the battle for television audiences (Jhally 1990; Smythe 1977). At the same time, hundreds of local radio outlets came on stream: "[W]hat had been one single national market with four contending networks, became upwards of one hundred autonomous local markets each with eight to a dozen or more radio stations competing with each other" (Peterson 1990:105).

The resources that had once supported live radio programming collapsed amid the competition for advertising revenue and the shift of network funds to television. Radio stations, large and small, were virtually forced to turn to records to fill their programming needs. Radio and the record industry were now inexorably bound together: "Radio depended on the music industry for programming material, and record-makers, finding that radio airplay increased rather than depressed the demand for a record, quickly came to depend on radio to, in effect, advertise and promote their new releases" (Peterson 1990:105).

The increased play of records on radio profoundly influenced the record industry in three ways. First, the growth of local radio networks ended the near monopoly control of radio by the majors, and the large number of competing stations forced each one to pursue a particular niche in the market. A radio station would seek out a specific market segment and appeal to its tastes—and form those tastes—with the music the station played.

RCA, Columbia, Capital, and Decca were slow to adapt to the concomitant broadening of musical taste, so smaller, more flexible producers—Sun Records, Atlantic Records, Stax, King, Chess, Vee Jay, Dot, Coral, and Imperial, for example—filled the void with a wider range of music. The niche marketing techniques of the numerous radio networks undermined the control of the major record producers, opening the way for new labels and new opportunities.

Second, as the number of record producers grew, the opportunities for recording artists with different talents increased until even the big four began to lose some of their artists to higher paying competitors. These talented artists, who had often been forced to the margins by the oligopolistic control of the major producers, brought high-quality music, from a broader range of musical styles, to the listening and consuming public. The homogeneity of the 1940s was rapidly disappearing on radio and in the record industry itself.

Third, the shift of attention and resources to television by the major networks had a significant impact on all of radio. The budgets of the national network outlets fell as resources went to television. As budgets fell, the size of the crew decreased, and greater programming responsibility fell on the shoulders of fewer and fewer people. Disk Jockeys (DJs) quickly enjoyed greater latitude, and they also became the focal point for their increasingly specialized audiences. Although the television series WKRP in Cincinnati parodied some aspects of radio in the rock and roll era, the show's portrayal of the importance of celebrity DJs was accurate; radio stars (like the show's Dr. Johnny Fever and Venus Flytrap) determined the sound and personality of radio stations in the 1950s and 1960s. Real DJs, such as Wolfman Jack (Robert Weston Smith) of XERB-AM in the Tijuana area, Cousin Brucie (Bruce Morrow) of 77 WABC in New York, and Al Boliska of 1050 CHUM in Toronto, became vital forces in capturing audiences, promoting specific styles of music, and generating revenue for themselves, their stations, the record companies, and the artists whose music they played.

The emerging diversity in music had an important spillover into the record industry. During the oligopoly years of the 1930s and 1940s, songwriters had "one specialized job in the 'tune factory' that regularly turned out new records at the major record companies" (Peterson 1990:110). These writers did not write on the basis of their own personal experience or inspiration—"they wrote well-crafted songs much like those that were hits at the time or were tailored to satisfy the demands of the person commissioning the song" (Peterson 1990: 110). By the mid-1950s, artists such as Chuck Berry, Buddy Holly, and Little Richard began to appeal to certain audiences, and, although not all of their songs were popular, those that did succeed were sensations. The recording industry, in response, shifted away from compositions written by corporate "tune factory" songwriters to music written by or for an emerging cadre of high-profile artists.

By the end of the 1950s, the stage was set for a second revolution in music as popular culture—a genuine flowering in the diversity of music, lyrics, and styles. Much of the homogeneity and monopoly control had been left behind. A growing number of independent radio stations and record producers were drawing in an increasingly diversified talent pool of DJs, writers, and performers—all of whom created a broader range of taste cultures and an expanding audience. And, by the end of the 1950s, the Baby Boomers were entering their teens as full-fledged members of the consumers' republic, eager to be a part of the growing *American Bandstand*.

In terms of this discussion of the dialectics of popular culture, an interesting set of somewhat contradictory forces created or enabled significant change. As the major broadcast corporations shifted their interest and resources from radio to television, the risk-averse practices that had kept music production and the shaping of popular taste within fairly narrow parameters were removed. With fewer resources, radio stations had to restructure themselves, and this restructuring had two significant outcomes. First, stations began to compete for niche markets that they could maintain on relatively low budget operations. Second, as the cost of launching an independent radio station fell, the number of stations, also looking for niche markets, grew. This expansion meant that each station wanting to reach a particular target audience had to provide content that would appeal. Taken as a whole, these factors resulted in a major diversification of styles and sounds on radio.

But several critical questions remain. Did these diverse musical forms make significant contributions to culture, to the way humans understood themselves and the social world? Did they have aesthetic and intrinsic value, or did they provide only a broader range of "bread and circus" entertainment for the indiscriminating masses? To answer these questions, we need to look more closely at the music traditions out of which some of these new styles developed and at the substance of post-1950s music as it reached wider audiences over the next few decades.

DYLAN: THE REAL THING OR SIMULACRUM?

There are a number of figures one could use to examine whether popular cultural forms have the complexity, aesthetic quality, meaningfulness, artistry, craftsmanship, and apparent genius of established art, music, literature, and poetry—of the creations categorized under the label "high culture." None, however, is more appropriate than Bob Dylan. In Dylan's work, the layers of artistry seem to be endless, and each one leads to a renewed perspective and a deeper level of appreciation. Moving deeper into Dylan's work also explodes some cherished myths and sometimes shatters illusions. Dylan, the artist, to say nothing of Dylan the person, is a genuinely tension-filled, dialectically unstable, dynamic totality. But Dylan—the artist, person, cultural icon, or, most important, producer of popular culture—cannot be appreciated fully without examining the intersection of his personal biography with the history of social structure.

Almost everyone interested in Dylan or in Dylan's place in popular culture—in twentieth and twenty-first century culture—wants to know the answer to one simple yet almost perversely enigmatic question: Who is Dylan? That question quickly brings out two more: Is he the real thing? Or is he simply a simulacrum?

But, as surely as one question leads to two and then to three, the questions keep coming: Of what would Dylan be the real thing? A real revolutionary—in what revolution? A real entertainer—in what sense of the word "entertainment": entertainment as satisfaction, as expanding, or as provoking? Was he the voice and consciousness of a generation, or just another Beat poet who used a guitar and harmonica rather than bongos? And what does one mean by Dylan: the person, the artist, or the entertainer (or are they really parts of some whole)?

Then there is the question of simulacra. What does one mean by the term? A simulacrum is, at one level, a likeness, something that shares a likeness with another thing. Its early usage was positive: a painting captured the likeness of its subject—the term "simulacra" conveyed identity. By the late nineteenth century, however, "simulacra" became a negative term: the simulacrum was simply a copy of the original and thus inferior because it lacked the substance, quality, and unique artistry of the original. So, if Dylan is a simulacrum, in which sense of the term?

Despite its enigmatic dimensions, the Dylan conundrum is the perfect vehicle for exploring the rich diversity and artistry of popular culture—mostly because Dylan, himself recognizes that meaning, art, and culture are multilayered: "I don't know whether to do a serious interview or carry on in that absurdist way we talked last night," Paul Robbins says at the beginning of a 1965 interview with Dylan. "It'll be the same thing anyway, man," Dylan (2006d:37) replies.

Even during the early days of his fame, Dylan challenged anyone who felt capable of reading deeper meaning into his work and his accomplishments; he dismissed such a pursuit as futile, meaningless, and senseless. Joan Baez recounts Dylan reading some of his lyrics to her and asking if she thought she knew what they meant. She said no, and Dylan replied, in a dismissive tone, that he was not sure he did either, but, he mused, people would some-day try to analyse and interpret his lyrics anyway (Scorsese 2005). Was Dylan really dismissing the notion that his work had a deeper meaning, or did he really want people to study and dissect his work?

During his first brushes with the music industry, Dylan certainly pre-sented himself as a mystery whose true depth had to be plumbed. John Hammond of Columbia Records signed Bob Dylan to his first recording contract in October 1961; he quickly introduced Dylan to Lou Levy, the head of Leeds Music, a music publishing company for whom Dylan would become a prolific songwriter (Dylan 2004:288–91). After a quick tour of the facilities, Levy called in Billy James, the head of publicity, to put together some promo-tional material. In his biography *Chronicles: Volume One*, Dylan (2004:7–8) recounts the meeting. As he strolled into James's office, Dylan started to provide flippant answers to the background questions James asked. Dylan implied he had been a drifter, working dozens of different jobs, estranged from his family and riding the rails in search of his fortune.

In 1961, when Dylan first met Izzy Young, the owner of the Folklore Center—"the citadel of American folk music"—he gave a similar account (Scorsese 2005). In a WBAI radio interview with Cynthia Gooding a year later, Dylan claimed that he had been a "carnie" doing everything from run-ning the Ferris wheel to cleaning up (Dylan 2006g:3–4, 24–5).

Dylan's 1963 poem "My Life in a Stolen Moment" notes that Dylan was born in Duluth and moved to Hibbing, Minnesota, and it goes on to describe Hibbing as a quintessentially small town in America with churches and a store-lined main drag that teens cruised up and down in their hot rods—all of which was true (Dylan 1963e). But Dylan continually embellishes his relationship to Hibbing, claiming, for example, to have run away seven times when he was between the ages of 10 and 18—and to have been brought back on six of those occasions (Dylan 2004:8, 230–304; Dylan 2006h:8–9, 2006a:20–2).[95]

In actual fact, Bob Dylan—born Robert Zimmerman in Duluth, Minnesota, on May 24, 1941—did spend the bulk of his childhood in Hibbing, Minnesota. He tuned in to blues and country radio stations broad-casting from Shreveport, Louisiana, and later to early rock 'n roll stations, where he found inspiration and a sound with which he could identify in the work of Chuck Berry, Elvis Presley, and Buddy Holly (Dylan 2006e:433). As

---

95 In 1964, Dylan (2006a:24–5) gives another variation of his story. He places the tale of running away within the context of being free, saying that he ran away from home so often in his youth because he was not free—his parents' expectations confined him. In this version, Dylan blends together running away, travelling with the carnival, and finally breaking away for New York City.

rock became bland during the 1950s, Dylan was drawn to folk by the sound of the Kingston Trio and later Odetta,[96] Lead Belly,[97] and then Woody Guthrie.

In 1959, Zimmerman enrolled at the University of Minnesota, but, as his poem indicates, he hardly ever went to classes (Dylan 1963e). Instead, his focus centred on folk music, partly because he could perform it on his own, as all he needed was a guitar and a repertoire of songs (Dylan 2006f:56). Dylan began playing at the Ten O'clock Scholar, a coffee house near campus, and he became involved in the folk music circuit of Dinkytown, an area within the Marcy Holmes neighbourhood of Minneapolis that had restaurants, diners, cafés, coffee shops, bars, and student housing (Dylan 2004:234–44). It was then that he began to introduce himself as Bob Dylan.

At the end of his freshman year, Dylan dropped out of university, and, in January 1961—at the age of 20, not 18—he headed for New York City. He did not hop a freight train to New York; Dylan (2004:8–9) admits in his autobiography that he made up this story. He hitchhiked across the Midwest, arriving in midwinter in a city he describes as "too intricate to understand," and he certainly was not going to try.

Dylan went to New York to find singers such as Dave Van Ronk, Peggy Seeger, Ed McCurdy, Brownie McGhee and Sonny Terry, Josh White, the New Lost City Ramblers, and Reverend Gary Davis, but he went there "most of all to find Woody Guthrie" (Dylan 2004:9). Why them and why Guthrie in particular? Before exploring Dylan's frenetic first few months in Greenwich Village in 1961, we should take a step back into the larger context within which he planned to immerse himself. Like every aspect of Dylan and his contributions to culture, mass culture, popular culture, and specific taste cultures, the relationships between Dylan, the interests that led him to New York, and where these interests take him are more than what first meets the eye; to understand them requires linking his biography with the history of social structure.

Woody Guthrie, Pete Seeger, and the Folk Movement

Although New York City seems an odd place for the centre of the folk movement, especially since folk's roots are deeply rural, this music thrived in Washington Square Park and Greenwich Village, in the clubs and coffee houses around the intersection of Bleecker Street and Macdougal during the 1940s, fifties, and early sixties.[98] Folk music flourished as singers and

---

96 Odetta Holmes, known as Odetta, sang folk, blues, jazz, and spirituals; she is frequently called "The voice of the civil rights movement."

97 Huddie William Ledbetter (1888–1949) was a virtuoso on the 12-string guitar; his vocals, too, had a clear, forceful blues and folk sound. Ledbetter adopted the stage name "Lead Belly," and, although some of his recordings list him as "Leadbelly," he always spelled it "Lead Belly."

98 New York was not the only place where folk was vibrant—Toronto's Yorkdale was the bohemian centre of folk life in the 1950s and 1960s. There were similar satellite communities in Cambridge (Massachusetts), Berkeley, Los Angeles, Chicago, and Vancouver.

instrumentalists played for the intrinsic rewards of sharing their music with others; they consequently became part of a long-standing tradition—carrying a message and tying into the temper of the times through song and lyric. Folk was non-commercial—it came from the heart, spoke to the soul, and nourished a spiritual community. Folk singers, songwriters, Beat poets, and street philosophers along Macdougal and Bleecker streets created their own subculture and community amid the concrete, glass, skyscrapers, and grey flannel suits of mainstream urban life.

Folk originated, however, "in the backwoods of Appalachia, where families would gather to sing in their homes, in their fields, on their porches, and in their churches," according to Unterberger (2002:22). The music endured, "despite severe poverty and repression, among the descendants of African slaves in the deep South, where the form known as blues began to prosper," he continues (Unterberger 2002:22). But folk music also includes cowboys' ballads and lamentations, as well as music with the rhythms, melodies, and lyrics that new immigrants brought from Europe. By the 1920s, folk found its way on to records, although sales were small and fell with the Great Depression.

The Depression and "the dirty thirties" revitalized folk and guided its themes towards contemporary political and social circumstances. This new thematic focus can be seen clearly in the works of Woody Guthrie as they arose from the intersection of his personal biography with the contemporary public issues of social structure. Born and raised in the Oklahoma wheat belt, which became known as the "Dust Bowl" in the 1930s, Guthrie travelled by boxcar, thumb, and on foot across the United States listening to, remembering, writing down, adding to, and recording the music of the people, especially of the marginalized and the dispossessed. Guthrie captures the spirit of his quest and his legacy in the opening paragraphs of his autobiography:

> I could see men of all colors bouncing along in the boxcar. We stood up.
> We laid down. We piled around on each other. We used each other for
> pillows. I could smell the sour and bitter sweat soaking through my own
> khaki shirt and britches, and the work clothes, overhauls and saggy, dirty
> suits of the other guys. ... We looked like a gang of lost corpses heading back to the boneyard. Hot in the September heat, tired, mean and
> mad, cussing and sweating, raving and preaching ... About all I could
> hear above the raving and cussing and the roar of the car was the jingle
> and clink on the under side every time the wheels went over a rail joint. I
> guess ten or fifteen of us guys was singing:
> This train don't carry no gamblers,
> Liars, thieves and big-shot ramblers;
> This train is bound for glory,
> This train! (Guthrie 1943:19)

"Like Scotland's Robert Burns and the Ukraine's Taras Shevchenko," Pete Seeger (1971:viii) writes, "Woody was a national folk poet." His talent ultimately brought him to New York City, where he was "lionized by the literati ... from whom he declared his independence and remained his own profane, radical, ornery self" (Seeger 1971:viii). During the Depression, Guthrie "developed a religious view of Christ the Great Revolutionary"; he sided with labour and worked for social justice. As Seeger (1971:viii), himself a victim of the McCarthy blacklist, notes, "it may come as a surprise to some ... to know that the author of *This Land is Your Land* was in 1940 a columnist for the small newspaper he euphemistically called *The Sabbath Employee*"— *The Sunday Worker*, the weekend edition of the Communist *Daily Worker*.

Although Guthrie and Seeger were instrumental in popularizing folk music because they tapped deeply into its roots and kept them alive, it was the recording industry that made the folk archive permanent and allowed its sound to spread into the cities and reach audiences it would otherwise never have touched. During the thirties, for example, one of America's most influential blues artists, Robert Johnson, recorded all his works, which helped preserve the blues and spread its influence well beyond the stingy soil in which it first found life. Similarly, Bill Monroe, one of the key originators of bluegrass, cut his first record in 1936. The Delmore Brothers' tight harmonies laid the groundwork for rockabilly and set the table for the Everly Brothers' sound of the 1950s and 1960s, and Bob Wills mixed swing jazz, blues, country, and pop into a unique western swing sound (Unterberger 2002). Records not only made the otherwise invisible music of folk culture visible but also spread its reach and brought innovative collaboration into the mix.

Part of that collaboration took place in New York City, where urban intellectuals and political activists absorbed the folk culture and soon became some of folk music's most important producers. New York had long been a centre of intellectual ferment. In the postwar period, the city had at least 20 institutions of higher learning, and these spanned the spectrum from Columbia University, an Ivy League institution founded by royal charter in 1754, through to City College, which began as the Free Academy of the City of New York in 1847 and became a noted hotbed of left-wing radicalism from the 1930s through to the 1950s (Hook 1987; Wald 1987). Lee Hays of the Weavers; Sis Cunningham and Gordon Friesen, who later founded the folk magazine *Broadside*; and Guthrie all lived in Greenwich Village in the 1940s, as did folk song collector John Lomax (Cohen 2002).[99] When Lomax and his son discovered that blues and folk legend Lead Belly was in a

---

99 *Broadside* took its name from the tradition extending back to the sixteenth century of printing, on a single sheet of cheap paper, music, rhymes, or news so this material could be circulated quickly and widely among the people. Balladeers would often sell broadsides at fairs or have them distributed

Louisiana prison, they gained his release—or thought they had—and Lead Belly joined them in New York.[100]

Seeger, who dropped out of Harvard in 1938 when his political activism began to hurt his grades, was instrumental in cementing an enduring link between folk and progressive politics. Seeger first formed a group called the Almanac Singers. It featured himself, Hays, Guthrie, Burl Ives, and others, and it promoted union causes, racial integration, and religious freedom. The group used, in Unterberger's words, "the best of folk traditions, while crafting rousing lyrics pertinent to burning social issues of the day" (Unterberger 2002:24). In 1942, after American entry into World War II, however, the Almanac musicians had to weather difficult times; the anti-draft stance of one of the group's earlier (and now repudiated) albums caused members to lie low. But these folk musicians resurfaced in 1945 as Seeger launched the People's Songs, an organization committed to reviving the folk tradition and carrying it forward.

In January 1946, writing in *The Daily Worker,* Mike Gold reported that "a group of Almanac Singers, plus others concerned with labor music, started to organize something again the day before New Year. Songs, songs of, by, and for the people." He continues, "The spirit has not died, it has only been unemployed" (quoted in Cohen 2002:43). The first issue of the *People's Songs* newsletter exuded a new, postwar optimism:

> The people are on the march and must have songs to sing. Now, in 1946, the truth must reassert itself in many singing voices ... it is clear that there must be an organization to make and send songs of labor and the American people through the land. (Cohen 2002:43)

All of the above coalesces in the following key points about Bob Dylan and popular culture. First, the music and styles of Lead Belly, Guthrie, Seeger, Hays, Ives, and others constitute an informal standard by which all music claiming to be folk can be measured. Key elements in the "folk sound" are acoustic instrumentation and well-crafted lyrics focused on issues of conscience and social relevance; both are supported by harmonies of care, hope, and the struggle for change.

---

ahead of performances to attract audiences. Seeger, the folk traditionalist, named *Broadside* in honour of that tradition because he intended the periodical to spread modern folk music more broadly.

100 While the Lomaxes thought their intervention had freed Lead Belly from prison, it seems that he was really released because he had served the minimum time on the assault conviction that had landed him there. No matter what the reason, Lead Belly was happy to find a new home in New York among folkie friends.

Second, during the Great Depression and World War II, the folk tradition began to shift from its early roots. Although folk has always been socially conscious and has reflected the realities of America's poor, it began to lean more explicitly to the left during the thirties and forties, as singers and their ballads were tied ever closer to the labour movement and linked directly and indirectly to socialist and communist political groups and to issues such as religious freedom and racial integration. Folk was no longer simply, to paraphrase Marx ([1844] 1968, [1844] 1975), "the sigh of the oppressed creature, the heart of a heartless world"; it was becoming an increasingly political and politicized sound and movement that not only "interpreted the world in various ways" but also sought "to change it" (Marx 1932a, 1939).[101]

Third, despite folk's rural roots, the growth of New York City as the centre of the first folk revival meant that this music would become urbanized and modernized. Part of that change centres on the spread of folk through radio and record sales. Folk changed from something people shared among friends and sang on their porches or in churches to something people listened to on the radio or by playing phonographs in the privacy of their own homes or heard live at small clubs, coffee houses, or college hootenannies. By the 1960s, folk had become "cool"—it had become, in fact, an urban cool:

> Those raised in subsequent generations of sensory overload may find it hard to comprehend that quiet acoustic folk, which sounds so tame to many twenty-first century listeners, was once considered *the* counter-cultural music. In part that was because, beneath the layer of the Kingston Trio and the like, folk was still fairly underground, and in-the-making bohemians are always attracted to movements in which the mere discovery of obscure records and books helps set one apart from the mainstream. In part it was also because of its lingering associations with egalitarian activism, which was implicit (and sometimes explicit) in the humane concerns voiced by many of the songs, whether traditional or newly penned. With anti-Communist hysteria dying down as the 1950s turned to the 1960s, there wasn't as much real or imagined danger in hanging around with the likes of Pete Seeger, who was continuing to tirelessly advocate social justice. He did not allow his political agenda to get in the way of his music, which directly inspired many musicians—network ban be damned—via a busy concert schedule. (Unterberger 2002:32)[102]

---

101 Many themes of the music of the 1960s have their roots in the songs that Seeger, Guthrie, and others wrote in the thirties and forties. The idea of "A Better World A-Comin'"—a dominant refrain in the sixties—comes directly from the title of a Guthrie composition of the forties.

102 Because Seeger had been placed on the black list of "communists and fellow travellers" by Senator Joe McCarthy and the House Un-American Activities Committee (HUAC) in 1955, no television network

This background serves as the primer for the raw canvas upon which the popular cultural artistry of Dylan will begin to take shape. The base coat to the unfinished work is Guthrie—with sketching, colour, texture, and continual refining and experimentation to follow.

Dylan, Guthrie, and Folk

Dylan's relationship to Guthrie provides one set of insights into Dylan's work as a cultural producer. In Hibbing and on the Dinkytown folk circuit in Minneapolis, Dylan wanted to be a folk singer. It was Flo Castner, a friend from a coffee house, who first introduced Dylan to Guthrie's sound and power. Picking up a set of 12 double-sided Guthrie 78s, Dylan placed one on the turntable. "When the needle dropped, I was stunned—didn't know if I was stoned or straight." The sound made him gasp—"it was like the land parted"—Guthrie was "so poetic and tough and rhythmic," it was an epiphany (Dylan 2004:242–43).[103]

Studs Terkel, famous for his unique poetic revelations of the most intimate thoughts of the common men and women of America in works like *Division Street: America* (1967), *Hard Times: An Oral History of the Great Depression* (1970), and *Working* (1974), asked Dylan in 1963 about Guthrie's influence:

> Studs Terkel: Woody Guthrie, is he a factor in your life?
>
> Dylan: Oh yeah. Woody's a big factor. I feel lucky just to know Woody. I'd heard of Woody, I knew of Woody. I saw Woody once, a long, long time ago in Burbank, California, when I was a little boy. I don't even remember seeing him, but I heard him play.
>
> Studs Terkel: What was it that stuck in your mind?
>
> Dylan: It stuck in my mind that he was Woody, and everybody else I could see around me was everybody else." (Dylan 2006h:5–6)

In another interview a year later, Dylan (2006a) notes that Guthrie "was the main reason I came East. He was an idol to me" (p. 25).

In his autobiography, Dylan (2004) writes that the song that brought him to the attention of Leeds Music's John Hammond in the first place was "an

---

would allow him to appear on any programs, despite his central place in folk music. A number of folk singers, such as Joan Baez, were asked to perform on various folk shows during the 1960s, but they refused until the networks lifted their ban on Seeger. The ban was lifted in the mid-1960s.

103 Some of the reverence and tender care Dylan had for Guthrie comes across in Dylan's account of his visits with Woody at the Greystone Hospital in Morristown, New Jersey, where Guthrie was hospitalized as his Huntington's disease advanced (Dylan 2004:98–100).

homage in lyric and melody to the man who'd pointed out the starting place for my identity and destiny—the great Woody Guthrie" (p. 229). Dylan also notes that, when he first heard Guthrie in the 1950s, "it was like a million megaton bomb had dropped" (Dylan 2004:229).

"Woody turned me on romantically," Dylan (2006f:90) commented five years after arriving in New York. He admired how Guthrie had dedicated himself to building the genealogy of American folk music and then added his own unique voice to the tradition. Guthrie's influence, however, "was never in inflection or in voice," according to Dylan: "What drew me to him was that hearing his voice I could tell that he [Guthrie] was very lonesome, very alone, and lost in his time. That's why I dug him" (Dylan 2006f:90). For Dylan, Guthrie was "the true voice of the American spirit" (Dylan 2004:99).

Thirty-eight years later, Dylan is more expansive. Following an April 2004 interview with Dylan, Robert Hilburn of the *Los Angeles Times* summarizes Dylan's attitude in this way: "Even after all these years, his [Dylan's] eyes still light up at the mention of Guthrie, the 'Dust Bowl' poet, whose best songs, such as 'This Land is Your Land,' spoke so eloquently about the gulf Guthrie saw between America's ideals and its practices" (Dylan 2006e:430). "To me, Woody Guthrie was the be-all and end-all," Dylan tells Hilburn in the interview:

> Woody's songs were about everything at the same time. They were about rich and poor, black and white, the highs and lows of life, contradictions between what they were teaching in school and what was really happening. He was saying everything in his songs that I felt but didn't know how to. (Dylan 2006e:430)

As mentioned, according to Dylan (2004), his first song of any substantial importance was a tribute to Woody Guthrie—"Song to Woody." Written in the early 1960s, the song pays homage to Guthrie and his travels over vast geographic distances, as well as to the broad spectrum of humanity that he embraced. In it, Dylan captures Guthrie's own perceptions of a world that is tired and torn, filled with the hungry and sick, and, some would lament, coming to an end. But, for Guthrie, this world is only at the beginning—with the future of a newborn child lying ahead.[104]

---

104 See also Dylan's (1963d) "Last Thoughts on Woody Guthrie," a Whitman-like, free flowing poem that Dylan read on April 12, 1963, at the end of a concert at the New York Town Hall. After capturing in Guthriesque images all the ways people feel uncertain about life, Dylan indicates that it's possible to solve these problems by going to church or making your way to the Brooklyn State Hospital. In one, you will find God, and, in the other, you will find Woody Guthrie—a poignant lament for a great humanitarian who would soon be lost to Huntington's.

Upon arriving in New York for the first time, Dylan explored the coffee-house scene and hung around Café Wha?, but he soon began frequenting the Folklore Center (Dylan 2004:18). Located on Macdougal between Bleecker and Third, up one flight of stairs, "it was like an ancient chapel, like a shoe-box sized institute" run by Izzy Young, a long-time folk aficionado who was as much a fixture and character as the archive of folk treasures that he collected, sold, and cherished (Dylan 2004:18–19).

In the back room, by the potbellied stove, Young had a treasure trove of old records, sheet music, and scrolls. Dylan sat back there playing Young's disks on the record player, ignoring the modern world and all its complications, and reflecting on John Henry driving steel, the sinking of the Titanic, the Galveston flood, or "the desperate John Hardy shooting a man on the West Virginia line" (Dylan 2004:20).

Amid the records and conversation, Dylan told Young tall tales about his background while Young introduced the neophyte singer-songwriter to the history of folk and began Dylan's journey forward by taking him back into the lore of folk and its genuine roots.

Dylan was comfortable with Young, and the young musician revealed to the older man some important aspects of his personality, aspirations, and motivations. Talking about his maternal grandmother one day, Dylan (2004) recounted a telling story to Young: "She ... told me once that happiness isn't on the road to anything. That happiness is the road" (p. 20). Throughout his career, Dylan fans have seen him "arrive" at a place—a place where they were happy and they thought he should be happy—but, for Dylan, there never was and never will be such a place. Happiness is the journey.

In his early club and coffee-house days, Dylan sang so much from Guthrie's repertoire that he was dubbed a "Woody Guthrie jukebox." When he discovered that Ramblin' Jack Elliott was doing exactly the same thing, Dylan was stopped short. But he soon realized that what set him apart was his ability to write songs. Writing songs and explaining how one writes them are, however, two very different things. The first came easily to Dylan; the latter he has always presented as something of a mystery.

Becoming a songwriter, Dylan (2004) maintains, happens by degrees. It might begin when a singer wants to do something a little different, turning "something that exists into something that didn't yet":

Sometimes you just want to do things your way, want to see for your-self what lies behind a misty curtain. It's not like you see songs approach-ing and invite them in. It's not that easy. You want to write songs that are bigger than life. You want to say things about strange things that have happened to you, strange things you've seen. You have to know and

understand something and then go past the vernacular. The chilling precision that these old-timers used in coming up with their songs was no
small thing. Sometimes you could hear a song and your mind jumps
ahead. You see similar patterns in the ways you were thinking about
things. (Dylan 2004:51–2)

Dylan often uses the notion of turning something upside down or inside
out. The best songs unveil a side of people that they never knew was there
(Dylan 2004:54).

Writing is a craft that Dylan began to learn about and fully appreciate
in the musty archives of the Folklore Center. "You can't just copy somebody," however, Dylan (2006e) emphasizes: "If you like someone's work,
the important thing is to be exposed to everything that person has been
exposed to" (p. 429). One has to listen to as much folk music as possible
and study its form and structure right back to its origins 100 years ago. "I go
back to Stephen Foster," Dylan offers.[105]

Steeped in the history and craft of folk music and in the folk tales of the
misty past, Dylan (2006e) notes that, in writing a song—especially a multilayered one such as "Like a Rolling Stone," he thinks about much more than
lyrical content: "I'm not thinking about what I want to say, I'm just thinking
'Is this OK for the meter?'" And, at the same time, composing has an element
of mystery: "It's like a ghost is writing a song like that," Dylan continues. The
ghost gives you the song, and it goes away: "You don't know what it means.
Except the ghost picked me to write the song" (p. 432).

Does the music or do the words come first? Dylan (2006e:437) claims
that, for him, the music is already there. He is not a melodist; his music
springs from old Protestant hymns, Carter Family songs, or variations of the
blues. Dylan says that he starts with some song playing in his head—medi-
tating on it—until he reaches the point at which the words begin to change
and a new song emerges (Dylan 2006e:438; Dylan 2004:228–9). He wrote
"Blowin' in the Wind" in 10 minutes by putting new words to the old spiritual "No More Auction Block," which he probably learned from listening
to Odetta. "The Times They Are A-Changin'" has its inspiration in Irish and
Scottish folk songs, Dylan once admitted (Crowe 1985).

Dylan's songs and their impact stem from his unique blend of folk music
and its traditions; his compressed, high-speed apprenticeship in New York

---

105 Stephen Foster (1826–64) is frequently referred to as "the father of American music." His songs "Oh!
Susanna," "Old Black Joe," "My Old Kentucky Home," "Old Dog Tray," and "Beautiful Dreamer"
are learned and sung generation after generation. Foster's music combines the intricacies of classical music, the politeness of parlour music, and the spirited freedom of minstrel songs and carnival
entertainment.

City, which was conducted in coffee houses, jam sessions, and conversations with Young, Guthrie, Seeger, and others; his distinct and changing vocal sound; and his unique talent with words. "Dylan's admirers have come to accept and even delight in the harshness [of his voice]" Hentoff (Dylan 2006a) writes in 1964, "because of the vitality and wit at its core. And they point out that in intimate ballads he is capable of a fragile lyricism that does not slip into bathos" (p. 22).

> It's Dylan's work as a composer, however, that has won him a wider audience than his singing alone might have. Whether concerned with cosmic spectres or personal conundrums, Dylan's lyrics are pungently idiomatic. He has a superb ear for speech rhythms, a generally astute sense of selective detail, and a natural storyteller's command of narrative pacing. His songs sound as if they were being created out of oral street history rather than carefully written in tranquillity. On a stage, Dylan performs his songs as if he had an urgent story to tell. In his work there is little of the polished grace of such carefully trained contemporary minstrels as Richard Dyer-Bennet. Nor, on the other hand, do Dylan's performances reflect the calculated showmanship of Harry Belafonte or of Peter, Paul and Mary. Dylan off the stage is very much the same as Dylan the performer—restless, insatiably hungry for experience, idealistic, but sceptical of neatly defined causes. (Dylan 2006a:22-3)

At that very time Hentoff was writing, however, Dylan was already moving on. After writing in the liner notes of a Joan Baez album that beauty could be defined as "the crackin', shakin', breakin' sounds," Dylan decided to give up on definitions; he was taking things as they were. "That's why I like Hemingway," Dylan noted that same year. "He didn't have to use adjectives. He didn't really have to define what he was saying. He just said it. I can't do that yet, but that's what I want to be able to do" (Dylan 2006a:25).

Five points are significant at this juncture. First, Dylan really began in folk—Odetta, Lead Belly, and Guthrie provided the first hook; Young and the Folklore Center took him deep into its roots; and the New York coffee-house scene brought folk music out of him for the first time. Those roots were inescapable; they shaped his work from 1961 through to the present, but in ways that were unexpected. Rather than generating a simple easy-to-grasp and easy-to-assimilate product for popular culture, folk music and the depth of the folk experience provided a pivotal foundation for the complex artistry found in Dylan's work.

Second, those who thought Dylan was folk and would remain a singer-songwriter in the folk tradition did not understand Dylan's own folk roots properly. Even in 1962, Dylan didn't think of himself as a folk singer:

> I really don't think of myself as a folksinger thing. ... I'm not on the circuit or anything. ... I play a little, once in a while. But I like more than just folk music too ... yeah, I like folk music ... like Hobart Smith's stuff. (Dylan 2006g:2)

Dylan knew folk—genuine, hardscrabble folk—and he knew what "folk" meant in the late 1950s and early 1960s. He was closer to the traditions of the former and always distanced himself from (and was dismissive of) the latter.

But it was always more than being "a folksinger thing"; for Dylan, folk was a road—not a destination. This too is critical for understanding Dylan as a cultural producer. Art and artist journeyed, grew, developed, and changed directions as different colours and new techniques were integrated into the canvas. Scorsese (2005) captures this aspect of Dylan in titling his documentary *No Direction Home*.

Third, rooted in the true using-what-is-handed-down tradition of folk artists such as Lead Belly, Guthrie, and Seeger, Dylan's music sprang from the urban landscape of mid-twentieth century America. Many of Dylan's songs have an eternal quality, but they emerged from the texture of contemporary life and spoke most powerfully to the present moment. Dylan's songs completed the shift from the folk traditions of Appalachia, the dirty thirties, and Guthrie to those located at the centre of the largest metropolis in the United States and reflective of postwar America, the Beats, and a newly emerging critical spirit (Dylan 2004:82). New York City was indefinable—everything was in flux. And it was there that Dylan's folk for the industrialized, urban world found its inspiration (Dylan 1962b).

One of Dylan's earliest compositions—"Hard Times in New York Town"—epitomizes this aspect of his work, his relation to folk, and his habit of using what is handed down. Written 11 months after Dylan first arrived in New York, the song tells of Dylan's troubles getting established in the world's premier metropolis, but the song's first two lines, its tune, and its verse structure come from an old standard among poor white Southern farmers, "Down on Penny's Farm" (Dylan 1961; Glazer 1972:90–2). Drawing upon this old folk standard, Dylan uses comparable lyrics and inflection to capture the sounds of a naïve neophyte experiencing hard times in New York. He explores the search for work, the contrasts of rich and poor, and the physical demands of surviving in the metropolis. Despite the hardship it describes, the song ends defiantly—no matter how hard people try to beat and keep him down, he will leave New York City standing on his feet.

Beat poet Allan Ginsberg captures two aspects of Dylan's work that constitute the fourth point. Commenting on the impact that "A Hard Rain's A-Gonna Fall" had on him, Ginsberg says that he was knocked out by its eloquence—"particularly 'I'll know my song well before I start singin' and the images of biblical prophecy the song conveyed" (Scorsese 2005). Dylan's power, according to Ginsberg, stems from the imagery Dylan creates with words and from the unusual combinations of words and angles of observation he presents—there is a powerful eloquent grandeur to Dylan's work.

At the same time, Ginsberg explains, Dylan's words "are empowered and make your hair stand on end," and his descriptions turn something into a subjective truth that also has an "objective reality to it because somebody has realized it" (Scorsese 2005). The words come first, and, as Ginsberg notes, words that achieve those ends are later called poetry.

Irish folk singer Liam Clancy completes Ginsberg's insight. Dylan, Clancy notes, never was, never had to be, and never really could be a single, definitive person—"He was a receiver; he was possessed. And he articulated what the rest of us wanted to say but couldn't" (Scorsese 2005).

Finally, no matter how much people want to tie Dylan to a position, a cause, or a movement, he is always a rolling stone. Commenting on the civil rights movement, Dylan (2006a:26) notes that, although he agrees with everything going on within the movement, he is certainly not part of it. If he were in the movement, it would define him. So he is not because he cannot accept others setting rules and expectations for him.

Dylan is not just spouting rhetoric here. In December 1963, the Emergency Civil Liberties Committee, a group that he and Joan Baez had helped in some small fundraising events, presented him with a Tom Paine Award (Spitz 1989:240).[106] The presentation of this award was the centrepiece of the committee's main fundraising endeavour, a dinner held in the grand ballroom of the American Hotel in New York.

As Dylan (2006a:26) looked around the room that evening, he could not see anyone who was his age, connected with his politics, or tied into his value system. The room was filled with members of the Old Left, who were now supporting civil rights drives. But Dylan felt no connection to them. He began to leave but was told he had to stay to receive the award. Dylan complied, but his speech was not like anything the group expected.

---

106 The Tom Paine Award, named for the radical author and intellectual Thomas Paine (1737–1809), was given to honour a nonconformist who cried out for justice (Spitz 1989:240).

During the dinner, people around Dylan had been talking about Kennedy's assassination, the deaths of Bill Moore and civil rights leader Medgar Evers, and Buddhist monks setting themselves aflame to protest Vietnam.[107] Upon receiving the award, as Dylan began to speak, he could not get his focus off Kennedy's alleged assassin—Lee Harvey Oswald. Dylan told the audience that he had read a lot about Oswald, how uptight he was, and Dylan said that he had experienced those feelings too. "I saw a lot of myself in Oswald, I said, and I saw in him a lot of the time we're all living in" (Dylan 2006a:26–7). Members of the audience thought Dylan saw something positive in Oswald killing Kennedy, "that's how far out they were":

> I was talking about Oswald. And then I started talking about friends of mine in Harlem—some of them junkies, all of them poor. And I said they need freedom as much as anybody else, and what's anybody doing for them?... Now, what I was supposed to be was a nice cat. I was supposed to say "I appreciate your award ... and I'll support your cause." But I didn't, and so I wasn't accepted that night. That's the cause of a lot of those chains I was talking about—people wanting to be accepted, people not wanting to be alone. But, after all, what is it to be alone? I've been alone sometimes in front of three thousand people. I was alone that night. (Dylan 2006a:27)[108]

The irony of this situation is reflected in Dylan's legacy; he is "the voice of a generation" because he speaks only for himself—and from the position of an outsider. Because he sits at the margins or alone at the centre of so much, Dylan is able to produce his art. Some of that art is consumed as popular culture, but much in those very same songs remains multilayered—they are avant-garde compositions that withhold some meaning while laying bare truths of the moment.

---

107 William Lewis Moore (1927–63) was a postal carrier and member of the Congress on Racial Equality. Moore staged one man protests against segregation by walking to key capital cities and hand delivering letters of protest to civic leaders. He was murdered on April 23, 1963, as he walked towards Jackson, Mississippi, carrying a letter and wearing a sandwich board declaring "Equal Rights for All" on one side and "Mississippi or Bust" on the other. Medgar Evers was a civil rights activist who was denied acceptance to law school at the University of Mississippi, leading to the National Association for the Advancement of Colored People's campaign to desegregate the school. Evers was assassinated in the driveway of his home in June 1963.

108 In 2004, Dylan once again discussed his orientation to politics: "I never set out to write politics. I didn't want to be a political moralist. There were people who just did that. Phil Ochs focused on political things, but there are many sides to us, and I wanted to follow them all. We can feel very generous one day and very selfish the next hour" (Dylan 2006e:435).

DYLAN AND AVANT-GARDE CULTURE

The best way to appreciate Dylan as an artist producing complex popular culture is to focus on his first four frenetic years in New York City and on his first four LPs (Lerner 2007).

Dylan's first album, *Bob Dylan*, released in March 1962, was a quickly produced collection derived from Dylan's performances in various coffee houses. At that time, his repertoire consisted mainly of traditional folk and blues tunes interspersed with some of his own material. Even the two original songs on the album—"Talkin' New York Blues" and "Song to Woody"—directly reflect Guthrie's impact on Dylan as he began to emerge as a singer-songwriter as well as Dylan's roots in folk and blues.

Dylan has claimed that, at the time, he did not want to reveal too much of himself, but that claim is highly misleading on two counts. First, in 1962, Dylan was still an insecure fledgling artist who, despite undergoing a rapid maturation process within the New York coffee-house scene, was still looking to find his own footing.

Second, at this time, Dylan was a great imitator, a sponge, a living jukebox, a receiver, a collector and an amalgam of all that he had been hearing, encountering, and absorbing since his immersion in the New York world of folk music and Beat poetry. His version of "The House of the Rising Sun" is a good example. The song was an old folk standard—Lead Belly had sung it; Lead Belly, Guthrie, and Seeger had performed it together; and Odetta had her own searching and disturbing interpretation. But the version Dylan cut on *Bob Dylan* features the chording that he had heard Dave Van Ronk use in New York. Without thinking to ask, Dylan cut that version—one that the Animals would later duplicate but express, to greater acclaim, electrically rather than acoustically—to bring new life to the song.[109] Despite the LP, Dylan was still apprenticing to become an artist.

The Freewheelin' Bob Dylan appeared in May 1963 and coincided with Dylan's involvement with the civil rights movement, in particular, and with "the protest movement" more broadly. The link between Dylan and the civil rights movement is intimately tied, in several ways, to his lyrics for "Blowin' in the Wind"—the first cut on the album.

---

109 Van Ronk would laugh years later when recounting the story (Scorsese 2005). After Dylan cut "The House," whenever Van Ronk played it people said "Hey that's Dylan's song." But, once the Animals released a version—essentially Van Ronk's chording used by Dylan and then the Animals—whenever Dylan sang the song people responded with "Oh yeah, that's the Animals' song." So Dylan too, like Van Ronk before him, dropped it from his repertoire. Revitalized by Van Ronk, Dylan, and the Animals, "The House of the Rising Sun" became a blues standard in the 1960s and was sung by the Beatles, Hendrix, the Stones, the Doors, and Led Zeppelin, to name just a few.

Dylan first published the lyrics in May 1962 in *Broadside,* a magazine devoted to topical songs. The melody was taken from or inspired by the "Negro spiritual" entitled "No More Auction Block," which originated in Canada among former slaves who had left the United States for the British colony after England abolished slavery in 1833. That is the first strand connecting Dylan, "Blowin' in the Wind," and the civil rights movement.[110]

Dylan's manager at the time, Albert Grossman, also managed Peter, Paul, and Mary, and they were the first to record "Blowin' in the Wind." In the first week of its release, it sold 300,000 copies—an unheard of sale for a folk song at that time—and reached number two on *Billboard* magazine's pop chart (which ranked songs on a composite statistic based on air play and sales and was the gold standard ranking for the industry). The fine harmony of Peter, Paul, and Mary and, later, the sweet inspirational power of Joan Baez's voice quickly turned "Blowin' in the Wind" into one of the anthems of the civil rights movement.

In Scorsese's *No Direction Home* (2005), blues and gospel singer Mavis Staples recounts that, upon hearing "Blowin' in the Wind," she experienced initial incredulity that a white man could write something to capture the spirit and frustrations of blacks. However, she says that she quickly recognized the enduring power of the lyrics and melody.

Dylan's link to the civil rights movement and the centrality of "Blowin' in the Wind" to that movement were cemented further with the 1963 march on Washington, the occasion of Martin Luther King Jr.'s "I Have a Dream" speech. Baez and Dylan sang the song in front of the thousands gathered by the Washington Monument, galvanizing the crowd and connecting Dylan and the song to social protest.

Finally, "Blowin' in the Wind," as music critic Andy Gill (1998:23) notes, represents a crucial shift in emphasis in Dylan's work. His focus moved from the particular—see his earlier songs "Talkin' Bear Mountain," "Rambling, Gambling Willie," or "Who Killed Davey Moore"—to the more abstract and general; Dylan's musical poetry took on a more timeless quality.

Freewheelin' also included some surrealist, talking blues pieces—"Masters of War" and "Talkin' World War III Blues"—which would soon link Dylan's music to the anti-Vietnam War movement in the mid-1960s. But those pieces stood alongside some finely crafted, bittersweet love songs, such as "Don't Think Twice, It's Alright," and "Girl of the North Country."

However, the most complex and compelling song on *Freewheelin'* was "A Hard Rain's A-Gonna Fall." Dylan wrote this song during the most

---

110 Bauldie (1991) notes that Dylan may have heard the song on Odetta's 1960 Carnegie Hall concert LP. And he performed the song live at New York's Gaslight Cafe in October 1962, forging a second link to traditional folk and the civil rights movement.

threatening confrontation between the United States and the Soviet Union—
the Cuban missile crisis of October 1962 (Dylan 2006h:6). American recon-
naissance flights reported the construction of missile launching sites in Cuba.
In response, Kennedy addressed an international television audience in
October 1962 and indicated that any nuclear missile launched from Cuba
against any nation in the western hemisphere would be regarded as an attack
on the United States and would result in a full retaliatory response against
the Soviet Union. Kennedy also established "a strict quarantine"—avoiding
the term "blockade," which is a term of war—of all offensive military equip-
ment destined for Cuba.

People around the globe held their breath as Soviet ships headed towards
Cuba, carrying material for the ongoing construction of the missile sites. Up
to the moment Khrushchev finally blinked in this game of "nuclear chicken"
and ordered the ships to turn back to the USSR, the media and public discourse were filled with fears of nuclear attack, the ensuing nuclear fallout,
nuclear rain, and nuclear winter. But Dylan always insisted that "Hard Rain"
had nothing to do with the Cuban crisis.

In one interview, Studs Terkel comments that he thinks "Hard Rain" will
become a classic—"Even though it may have come out of your feelings about
atomic rain" (Dylan 2006h:7). Dylan responds emphatically: "No, no, it
wasn't atomic rain. Somebody else thought that too. It's not atomic rain, it's
just a hard rain. It's not the fallout rain, it isn't that at all" (Dylan 2006h:7).

Hilburn (Dylan 2006e) describes the song as an "apocalyptic tale of a
society being torn apart on many levels" and its lyrics as "rich and poetic
enough to defy age" (p. 436). At the time, Dylan's imagery and wordsmithery
were being influenced by many artists, from blues musician Robert Johnson
to French symbolist poet Arthur Rimbaud. When he read one of Rimbaud's
letters, the one entitled "I is somebody else," Dylan (2004:288) reports that
he could hear the bells going off everywhere—suddenly everything was in
transition, and Dylan's view of the world changed dramatically.

Terkel describes "Hard Rain" as a great tapestry. Dylan agrees, explaining why. Every line, he notes, is "really another song":

> Every line ... could be used as a whole song. ... I wrote that when I didn't
> know how many other songs I could write. ... I wanted to get the most
> down that I knew about into one song. It was during the Cuba trouble ...
> I was a little worried, maybe that's the word. (Dylan 2006h:7)

The song opens like so many folk tunes with a simple question for a
rambling son—Where has he been?—but the lyrics quickly shift to a mesmerising avalanche of places, images, and metaphors that follow one after

the other: from mountains and highways to forests, oceans, and graveyards (Dylan 1963a). The next three verses explore, in the same imagery and style, questions about what the boy had seen and heard and whom he had met on his travels—before the song asks about what will come next. The answer is desperate but defiant: the son will return to the depths of the forest— an apparently desolate place where people are hungry, water is poisoned, there are prisons and executioners, and souls perish alone and neglected— a bleak, black, empty world. But the boy will capture the harsh truth of it all and, like a hard rain that everyone feels as it falls from the mountain, this truth will create at least the potential for rebirth and growth as he struggles against drowning in the sea of sorrow surrounding him. In one of the more profound images, Dylan notes that the boy's experiences will mean he knows his song well even before he starts singing—the words, images, and cadence will spring from lived experience and a commitment to lay the truth bare.

At the same time, however, *Freewheelin'* expresses Dylan's irreverence and symbolizes his refusal to be what others think he is or should become. The final cut is entitled "I Shall be Free," and, within the context of the times and the album itself, this title suggests that the track is a "protest song." But really this song speaks for nobody but Dylan. "I Shall be Free" is an extended, sur-realist, and personal commentary on the consumers' republic (Dylan 1963c). Far from the world of high culture, the song explores the way that a drunk eases his mind and escapes in fantasies that really leave him trapped in the past and present—anything but free.

Dylan's third album—*The Times They Are A-Changin'*—hit the record stores eight months after the release of *The Freewheelin' Bob Dylan*. Dylan intentionally wrote the album's lead song, "The Times They Are A-Changin'," to be an anthem for the times. It was, in his words, a song with a purpose, influenced by Irish and Scottish ballads such as "Come All Ye Bold Highway Men" and "Come All Ye Tender Hearted Maidens," tunes that he had absorbed listening to the Clancy Brothers. "I wanted to write a big song," Dylan notes, "with short concise verses that piled up on each other in a hypnotic way," and "The Times" certainly met that objective (Crowe 1985).

The song opens with some of Dylan's (1963b) most familiar lyrics, but it is their cadence that is most remarkable, striking, and engrossing. "The Times They Are A-Changin'" begins by invoking classical and biblical imagery— the people gather around a prophet as the swelling flood waters of change grow and what feels like an impending doom looms. This first verse provides a timeless background for the next three verses, which focus on the imme- diate and contemporary. Writers and critics, congressmen and senators, and mothers and fathers across the land are faced with a world they do not under- stand—a world that is rapidly changing. They are told to get out of the way if they cannot lend a hand. Dylan returns, however, to timeless imagery to close the song and bring it full circle. Echoing the Sermon on the Mount and the eight beatitudes, Dylan notes that the slow will be fast, the first shall be last, and the old order is fading as generational change pushes forward.

The album, as a whole, remains classic Dylan insofar as he combines his anthem for the times with some cynical, bleak, tormenting, and melancholy material. The opening cut is followed by a number of pieces that challenge the anthem—material that accentuates the tensions and contradictions inherent in change: that change is a necessary and inevitable natural occurrence, that change is resisted by established powers and legal structures, and that struggles, won and lost, create change.

For many, The Times represents a politicized Dylan, but the reality is that it represents a Dylan grounded in the events of his time, capturing and chronicling them but in a manner that presents those events in the upside-down, inside-out, distorted manner Dylan was perfecting—a style that stops the listener short and, to use Hoggart's (1970:16) expression, keeps the moulds from setting. Nothing in The Times is cliché. There is no hint of a levelling-down formula of interchangeable parts in these songs. They are probing and disturbing, and the more one reflects upon the lyrics and locates the potential sources for their inspiration, the more complex each song and the album as a whole becomes. After listening to The Times, really listening to it, we find that things are never quite the same—to place Hoggart's (1970:18) notion in a different context.

The second song on the album describes an extremely troubling murder-suicide that leaves a wife, five children, and a destitute South Dakota farmer dead—the "Ballad of Hollis Brown" (Dylan 1963b). "With God on Our Side" follows—a song of cynicism and change (Dylan 1963g). With God on its side, the education system teaches people what to believe—even as those lessons change with time and circumstance. Death and destruction and hatred—whether pursued in the expropriation of First Nations' lands or during the Spanish-American War, the American Civil War, the world wars, or the Cold War—can be justified, with God on one's side. In the last verse, Dylan raises his level of cynicism further by noting that, despite their recognition of how education and popular prejudice shape people's knowledge and beliefs, even those who begin to see through the distortions cannot break away fully—God remains as the best hope for preventing more war.

"Only a Pawn in Their Game"—the sixth song on the LP—puts Dylan's comments at the Tom Paine Award dinner into an interesting perspective. The award dinner was in December 1963, and, although The Times was released in February 1964, it was produced in August 1963. Obviously, then, the song is not a direct commentary on the events of the dinner, which it proceeded. Nevertheless, "Only a Pawn" does indicate that issues related to Dylan's uncomfortable ruminations on Oswald had been on his mind a good many months before the December 1963 dinner. "Only a Pawn" does not focus on the murder of activist Medgar Evers as much as it centres on the poor white man who shot him. It is the quintessential inside-out, upside-down perspective as Dylan (1963g) constructs the event from the assassin's perspective. Most important, the drawn out, throbbing cadence of the beat and the lyrics and imagery capture the way in which beliefs and prejudices are driven, through constant and ongoing repetition, deep into one's mind where they shape and motivate one's actions. "Only a Pawn" challenges the opening anthem to the LP. Time may pass but are the times really changing?

In the final cut, "Restless Farewell," Dylan (1963f) returns to his Guthrie roots to symbolically bid adieu to the civil rights movement and to the constraining expectations that were growing up around him as a "folkie." The sound is deeply wistful and melancholy, but it reflects the realization that he cannot stay. Ironically, perhaps, there is an overriding sense of inevitability that seems to contradict the opening anthem of the album. Or perhaps Dylan places one element of the dialectic of freedom and determination at either end of the album and the dynamic tensions involved in the human struggle for meaning in the cuts in between.

Dylan's fourth album—released just three months later—is aptly entitled *Another Side of Bob Dylan*, and one does encounter a very different Dylan here. "All I Really Want to Do" sets the dominant tone for the album. "Spanish Harlem Incident," "To Ramona," "Ballad in Plain D," and "I Don't Believe You" show a sensitive, deeply emotional side of the songwriter—one responding to love and love lost. Dylan's flippant surrealism is still there in "I Shall be Free #10" and "Motorpsycho Nightmare," but the two critical songs in terms of Dylan's artistic development are "The Chimes of Freedom," with, as Ginsberg enthuses, its "chains of flashing images," and "My Back Pages" (Scorsese 2005). Both of these cuts are deeply metaphorical, conjuring powerful images; they evince the new maturity that enters Dylan's work from this point on—a maturity that is captured in the ironic refrain of "My Back Pages," which speaks of his escape from age and tradition into a "younger" and freer self: "Ah, but I was so much older then, / I'm younger than that now" (Dylan 1964).

POPULAR CULTURE AND THE SOCIOLOGICAL IMAGINATION

Perhaps one of the most significant ironies of the culture wars is that one of the icons of contemporary popular culture—Bob Dylan—is as critical of mass culture as he is a master at using it to present his audiences with some of the twentieth century's most probing analyses of the modern world and the human condition.

If, for example, one returns to Arnold and his notions of turning "a stream of fresh and free thought upon our stock notions and habits" or his goal of pursuing humanity's "total perfection by means of getting to know, on all matters which most concern us, the best which has been thought and said in the world," then Dylan's popular cultural productions cannot be over-looked. Similarly, the intrinsic value that Leavis and Thompson as well as Hoggart (1970) discover in a grounded culture or a sophisticated literature that "explores, re-creates and seeks for the meanings in human experience" runs through Dylan's work from his earliest pieces in 1961 to his latest pro-ductions in 2009 (p. 11).

Far from the Huxleyan-Marcusean world of simplified satisfactions and one-dimensionality, Dylan's cultural production is disturbing, layered, and challenging. Dylan's restlessness dominates his work, and no listener can "chill" to his sound and its accompanying imagery—sometimes impres-sionist, sometimes surrealist or Dadaist—with all of its dialectical contra-dictions and dynamism.

Postman may be correct that television represents a different epistemol-ogy than typography, but the age of exposition did not necessarily die with the age of show business. Dylan has taken Berlin's "There's no business like show business" and turned it inside out and upside down by using show busi-ness to stop audiences short—forcing them to see themselves, in a single phrase, as they never have before—to take them from entertainment back to the realities they have missed or ignored. Postman is correct: one can shrivel the spirit of a culture through Orwellian or Huxleyan techniques, but one can also expand the spirit of a culture by capturing the popular imagination and taking it on rides it has never previously experienced.

Dylan's work might not surpass Beethoven's Fifth Symphony but, taken as a whole, his songs are popular cultural productions that aspire to the heights of Beethoven's genius. To ignore "The Times They Are A-Changin'" or con-sider it a simple anthem of the 1960s misses the mark. One must recognize that it is the opening prelude to an entire symphony that runs through "The Ballad of Hollis Brown," "With God on Our Side," "Only a Pawn in Their Game," "The Lonesome Death of Hattie Carroll," "Restless Farewell," and "Boots of Spanish Leather"—a symphony that both provokes thought and provides soothing balm to counteract the harsh realities of the modern world.

Dylan is an artist of enormous talent, but the substance of his artistry, as this chapter has documented at some length, comes from the intersec-tion of his own personal biography with the history of the social structure.

Moreover, Dylan's artistry is sophisticated, multilayered, and critically insightful because it explores that intersection from a number of different perspectives and vantage points. Dylan's lyrics capture the malaise of the times and force the listener to think beyond the moment into the roots of anomie, alienation, and social dissatisfaction. Regardless of whether Dylan ever read Mills or Mills ever listened to Dylan, they both tapped into some of the deepest issues in people's lives during the latter half of the twentieth century, and their work continues to stimulate critical reflection on social life today.

THE PROMISE OF SOCIOLOGY

This text has introduced students to sociology by focusing on its classical tradition, on three of sociology's most significant thinkers, and on the manner in which C. Wright Mills draws the tradition's key elements together in his concept "the sociological imagination." In the final analysis, Mills (1959) argues, sociologists working in the classical tradition examine "history and biography and the relations between the two within society" (p. 6). This, Mills maintains, constitutes sociology's task and promise.

Mills's (1959) neat formulation and the three sets of questions that he proposed to guide a sociologist's work are necessary for any study "to complete its intellectual journey" (p. 6). They also bring a helpful unity to what is, in fact, a complex and internally divided tradition. Although this unifying formulation is helpful, it is also important to understand where the differences, tensions, and divisions lie so that one can use the classical tradition critically and perceptively—fully aware of many of the classical tradition's strengths, limitations, contradictions, and prospects for further development. To this end, this book has overviewed the work and thought of three key founders of sociology—Karl Marx, Émile Durkheim, and Max Weber—and indicated how their work arose from within earlier currents of thought and contributed to the formation of the classical tradition in sociology.

The classical tradition has two different interrelated yet also somewhat antagonistic strands running through it. Both strands were shaped by the social and intellectual currents of Renaissance and Enlightenment Europe;

both share a fundamental belief in the power of human reason and the idea that there is an underlying order or rationality to the natural and social worlds.

The strand running from Bacon, Galileo, and Descartes to Montesquieu, Saint-Simon, and Comte emphasizes the central importance of observation and observationally based knowledge in the quest for knowing the underlying, law-like order of the natural and social worlds. This strand is tightly tied to the growing significance of the systematic observation of the empirical world that developed within the natural sciences, and its proponents sought to distance their analyses from the metaphysical debates and premises of classical philosophy and medieval theology. The ultimate reference point for this strand is the controlled methodology of experimental science. Although the human mind would, on the basis of precisely directed observation, seek to explain the law-like interconnections of the disparate parts of the natural or social worlds, for thinkers within this strand, the role of the mind was secondary to the status of empirical facts gained by dispassionate, objective observation and the interrelationships that could be observed and that others could replicate and verify.

Thinkers within the second strand that shaped the classical tradition include Descartes, Hume, Kant, Schelling, and Hegel. Before they would commit to trying to understand the empirical world, they wrestled with the fundamental question of metaphysics—what could the human mind really know? According to proponents of this strand, the mind plays a significant role in interpreting—in moving knowledge from a superficial understanding to one that grasps the natural and social worlds as a complex, integrated totality. Their view is that knowledge must be based upon fully developed reason. Below the level of appearance (reality), which one can observe, they argue, lies a deeper actuality or essence that the mind has to construct interpretively. The thorough theorization of the world, then, is centrally important because it is only through theory that one can know what to observe, what those observations mean, and how they fit together into the totality and full actuality of the natural or social world.

The first strand directly influenced Durkheim's image of sociology as a positive science and his approach to sociology, although he was also swayed by the German intellectual tradition. One of Durkheim's most important contributions to sociology—the concept *conscience collective*—is a theoretical construction. The *conscience collective* arose as a concept from an empirically based understanding of how societies held together, and it served as a guide for which social facts Durkheim would focus upon in later studies. However, the construct is also deeply tied to a theoretical, systematic conception of society as a *sui generis* entity. Nevertheless, despite the fundamental infusion of theory within his sociology, Durkheim advocated openly and passionately for the empirical nature of sociology. For him, the *conscience collective* was an existing social fact for which there were various observable indicators, and one could know it indirectly through those indicators. Durkheim considered the *conscience collective* a *real, existing social fact* (with each word emphasized separately and together as a whole). In the end, although Durkheim was fully aware of the role that theory plays in guiding observation, he believed that, in the last instance, sociology had to be—and should strive to become—an empirical, observationally based, positive science.

Marx began his intellectual development thoroughly immersed in the German idealist tradition—particularly in the work of Hegel—but he ultimately tried to move beyond idealism into an empirically informed analysis and understanding of different social formations. Marx's materialism centres on the intellectual construction of a holistic grasp of the dialectical complexity of capitalist society. Marx's critique of capitalism, however, stems from observation and the systematic study of the social world. Still, this examination took place within—and added to—a rationally constructed, theoretical comprehension of the underlying actuality of the social world. Drawing upon Saint-Simon and political economy, Marx turns Hegel's focus on the active mind into one that emphasizes the full creative capacities of human labour, and he uses this new conception of the dialectics of labour as the ontological foundation for understanding the complex totality of the social world and for changing it.

Weber's sociology rejects what I have described as part of the first strand of the classical tradition; Weber does not seek to understand the social world using an approach rooted in the natural sciences. Instead, heavily influenced by Kant, Rickert, and Dilthey, Weber draws a sharp distinction between the methodology and objectives of the natural sciences (*Naturwissenschaften*) and the humanities and social sciences (*Geisteswissenschaften*). For Weber, sociology is the comprehensive study of social action and rests upon an interpretive approach to social life. Like Durkheim, Weber recognizes and emphasizes the importance of dominant frames of mind in the ordering and structuring of different social formations. Weber differs from Durkheim, however, regarding how one can best grasp the dominant frame of mind or *conscience collective* and concerning the prospects for the future given the rise of goal-rational action to such prominence in modernity.

Nevertheless, although Weber rejects any notion of the unity of the sciences, he shares Durkheim's fundamental concerns about developing sociology as an observationally based undertaking that requires a complete commitment to the canons of science—the highest standards of dispassionate observation. Both agree—as does Marx—that one can only change the world when it has been correctly grasped, although all three have different standards concerning what is involved in fully comprehending the world.

In addition to presenting the key aspects of the classical tradition, this text explores the complex concept of culture—once in the context of the Millennials and their heavy reliance upon e-culture and later in a case study of how one might apply the sociological imagination to a particular social phenomenon.

Culture is, as Williams notes, one of the most complex words in the English language. Part of the analysis in the introduction and in Chapters 9 and 10 underscores why culture is such a complex concept. At the same time, the analysis of culture—particularly in Chapter 10—indicates that, despite its complexity, one can critically assess culture and evaluate how it contributes to the quality of social life.

Culture, like the *conscience collective,* a dominant ideology, or goal-rational action as the dominant and predominant dimension of social action, arises from human interaction with the material world within which human agents live. It is tied to the social relationships that shape people's indirect, mediated relationship with the natural world. At the same time, culture serves as a filter through which people view the social and natural worlds, and it influences their understandings and actions in their daily lives. It is for these reasons that thinkers as diverse as Marx, Durkheim, Weber, Arnold, Nietzsche, Leavis, Thompson, Adorno, Horkheimer, Marcuse, Hoggart, Williams, Gans, Postman, and Gabler have all expressed different concerns about the social determination of culture. If culture becomes increasingly one dimensional, to use Marcuse's term, then people begin to lose the capacity to assess critically the society in which they live—they may be left with a sense of malaise and discontent, but they remain unsure of how to take those feelings further or of how to act upon and change their social circumstances.

Drawing its inspiration from the classical tradition in sociology, the sociological imagination helps people recognize that their personal troubles of milieu are tied to broader, public issues of social structure. The sociological perspective that develops from the intersection of personal biography and the history of social structure provides a more encompassing vantage point to assess the way forward critically.

The discussion of culture is tied to one more theme discussed in this text—the social world today that many term postmodern. The postmodern world and its associated postmodernist perspectives are, on the one hand, very different from modernity and the modernist perspective represented by the classical tradition. There are some who would reject all traces of modernist social thought in favour of thoroughly postmodernist approaches. This decision may ultimately prove correct, but it is not one that a sociologist should make without first fully exploring the critical and analytical power of sociology's centuries-old classical tradition. Understood properly, especially within the context of the public issues that exist in an increasingly globalized world, the classical tradition still offers penetrating insight into social concerns and social relationships. It is also the foundation upon which postmodernist theories developed, so those recent theories assume a detailed understanding of the various strands of social thought that are woven into sociology's classical tradition.

There is one more point to note about this text. In *Images of Man: The Classic Tradition in Sociological Thinking*—the companion volume to *The Sociological Imagination* (Mills 2000:136)—Mills (1960) notes that the sociological frame of reference can begin with "the acquisition of a vocabulary that is adequate for clear social reflection" (p. 17). Such a vocabulary requires "only some twenty or so pivotal terms" (Mills 1960:17). In reading *The Promise of Sociology*, students have had the opportunity to start to build that vocabulary. Five terms that one might include in such a vocabulary are "the sociological imagination" and "intellectual craftsmanship" (from Mills), "class struggle" (from Marx), "*conscience collective*" or "collective conscience/consciousness" (from Durkheim), and "interpretive understanding" (from Weber).

Each of these terms is a shorthand—or rich symbol—for some of the central concerns of each thinker. Each term becomes useful as one draws upon the complex ideas that surround it and make it so central to the work of Mills, Marx, Durkheim, or Weber.

Students who have completed this book are now ready to take these terms and use them to explore some of sociology's main areas of concern—work, social inequality, deviant behaviour, war, and social movements, for example. Drawing upon an emerging language for critical reflection and the power of the sociological imagination, students can expand their vocabularies further while learning more about the social world in which they live. That is the promise of sociology now lying ahead.

BIBLIOGRAPHY

Adoratsky, V., ed. 1934. *Karl Marx: Chronik seines Lebens in Einzeldaten* (*Karl Marx: A Chronology of His Life in Single Dates*). Moscow: Marx-Engels-Verlag.

Agee, James and Walker Evans. 1941. *Let Us Now Praise Famous Men*. Boston: Houghton Mifflin.

Adorno, Theodor and Max Horkheimer. 1972. *Dialectic of Enlightenment*. Translated by John Cumming. New York: Herder and Herder.

Albright, Julie. 2007. "Postmodernism." *Blackwell Encyclopedia of Sociology,* edited by George Ritzer. Retrieved December 16, 2009 (http://www.blackwellreference. com/).

Alexander, Jeffrey. 1986. "Rethinking Durkheim's Intellectual Development I: 'Marxism' and the Anxiety of Being Misunderstood." *International Sociology* 1:91–107.

Althusser, Louis. 1977a. "The '1844 Manuscripts' of Karl Marx." Pp. 153–60 in *For Marx,* translated by Ben Brewster. London: New Left Books.

———. 1977b. "On the Materialist Dialectic." Pp. 161–218 in *For Marx,* translated by Ben Brewster. London: New Left Books.

———. 1977c. "On the Young Marx." Pp. 49–86 in *For Marx,* translated by Ben Brewster. London: New Left Books.

Andréas, Bert. 1963. *Le Manifeste Communiste de Marx et Engels: Histoire et bibliographie, 1848–1918* (*The Communist Manifesto of Marx and Engels: History and Bibliography, 1848–1918*). Milan: Feltrinelli.

Aptheker, Herbert. 1965. *Marxism and Alienation: A Symposium*. New York: Humanities Press.

Are You Smarter Than a 5th Grader? 2007–present. Fox and syndicated networks.

Arnold, Matthew. [1868] 1932. *Culture and Anarchy: An Essay in Political and Social Criticism*. Cambridge: Cambridge University Press.

Aron, Raymond. 1961. *Sociologie des societes industrielles: Esquisse d'une theorie des regimes politiques* (*Sociology of Industrial Societies: Outline of a Theory of Political Regimes*). Paris: Centre de documentation universitaire.

———. 1962. *Dix-huit leçons sur la société industrielle* (*Eighteen Lectures on Industrial Society*). Paris: Gallimard.

———. 1964. *German Sociology*. Translated by Mary and Thomas Bottomore. New York: The Free Press of Glencoe.

———. 1965. *Main Currents in Sociological Thought*. Vol. 1, *Montesquieu, Comte, Marx, de Tocqueville, the Sociologists and the Revolution of 1848*. Translated by R. Howard and H. Weaver. New York: Basic Books.

———. 1967. *Main Currents in Sociological Thought*. Vol. 2, *Durkheim, Pareto, Weber*. Translated by R. Howard and H. Weaver. New York: Basic Books.

Aronowitz, Stanley. 1974. *Food, Shelter, and the American Dream*. New York: Seabury Press.

Avineri, Shlomo. 1967. "From Hoax to Dogma: A Footnote on Marx and Darwin." *Encounter* 28:30–2.

Bacon, Francis. 1864. *The Physical and Metaphysical Works of Lord Bacon, Including His Dignity and Advancement of Learning and His Novum Organum; Or, Precepts for the Interpretation of Nature*, edited by Joseph Devey. London: H.G. Bohn.

Bauldie, John. 1991. "Liner Notes." *Bob Dylan: The Bootleg Series*. Vols. 1–3, *Rare & Unreleased, 1961–1991*. New York: Sony Music Entertainment Inc.

Beamish, Rob. 1992. *Marx, Method, and the Division of Labor*. Chicago: University of Illinois Press.

———. 1998. "The Making of the Manifesto." *Socialist Register* 34:218–39.

Beamish, Rob and Ian Ritchie. 2006. *Highest, Fastest, Strongest: A Critique of High-Performance Sport*. New York: Routledge.

Beloit College. 2008. "The Beloit College Mindset List." Retrieved May 15, 2008 (http://www.beloit.edu/~pubaff/mindset/).

Beloit College. 2009. "Mindset List for the Class of 2013." Retrieved December 9, 2009 (http://www.beloit.edu/mindset/2013.php).

Bell, Daniel. 1960a. *The End of Ideology: On the Exhaustion of Political Ideas in the Fifties*. Glencoe, IL: Free Press.

———. 1960b. "Two Roads from Marx." Pp. 335–68 in *The End of Ideology: On the Exhaustion of Political Ideas in the Fifties*. Glencoe, IL: Free Press.

———. 1973. *The Coming of Post-Industrial Society: A Venture in Social Forecasting*. New York: Basic Books.

———. 1976. *The Cultural Contradictions of Capitalism*. New York: Basic Books.

Benjamin, Walter. 1968a. *Illuminations: Essays and Reflections*. Edited by Hannah Arendt, translated by H. Zohn. New York: Schocken Books.

———. 1968b. "The Work of Art in the Age of Mechanical Reproduction." Pp. 217–52 in *Illuminations: Essays and Reflections*, edited by Hannah Arendt. New York: Schocken Books.

———. 1978. *Reflections: Essays, Aphorisms, Autobiographical Writings*. Edited by P. Demetz, translated by E. Jephcott. New York: Schoken Books.

———. 2002. *The Arcades Project*. Edited by H. Eiland, translated by K. McLaughlin and R. Tiedemann. Cambridge, MA: Belknap Press.

Bensaïd, Daniel. 2002. *Marx for Our Times*. Translated by Gregory Elliott. New York: Verso Books.

Bentham, Jeremy. 1948. *Fragment on Government and an Introduction to the Principles of Morals and Legislation*. Oxford: Blackwell Books. (Written in 1776 and 1789 respectively.)

Berger, Peter. 1963. *Invitation to Sociology*. New York: Anchor Books.

Berman, Marshall. 1988. *All That is Solid Melts Into Air: The Experience of Modernity*. Markham: Penguin Books.

Bernstein, Eduard. [1899] 1909. *Evolutionary Socialism: A Criticism and Affirmation*. Translated by Edith Harvey. London: Independent Labour Party.

———. [1899] 1969. *Die Voraustezungen des Sozialismus und die Aufgaben der Sozialdemokratie* (*The Presuppositions of Socialism and the Task of Social Democracy*). Edited by Günther Hillmann. Hamburg: Rowohlt Verlag.

Bloom, Allan. 1987. *The Closing of the American Mind: How Higher Education Has Failed Democracy and Impoverished the Souls of Today's Students*. Toronto: Simon and Schuster.

Böhm-Bawerk, Eugen. 1949. *Karl Marx and the Close of His System*. New York: Augustus M. Kelley.

Bottomore, Tom and Maximilien Rubel, eds. 1956. *Karl Marx: Selected Writings in Sociology and Social Philosophy*. London: Watts and Co.

Bumstead, J.F. 1841. *The Blackboard in the Primary Schools*. Boston: Perkins & Marvin.

Cantril, Hadley. 1966. *The Pattern of Human Concerns*. New Brunswick, NJ: Rutgers University Press.

Carr, Edward. 1961. *What is History?* New York: St. Martin's Press.

Carver, Terrell. 1998. *The Postmodern Marx*. Manchester: Manchester University Press.

Cheung, Edward. 2007. *Baby Boomers, Generation X, and Social Cycles*. Toronto: Longwave Press.

Cohen, Gerald. 1978. *Karl Marx's Theory of History: A Defence*. New York: Oxford University Press.

Cohen, Lizabeth. 2003. *A Consumers' Republic: The Politics of Mass Consumption in Postwar America*. New York: Knopf.

Cohen, Ronald. 2002. *Rainbow Quest: The Folk Music Revival in America, 1940–1970*. Amherst: University of Massachusetts Press.

Cohler, Anne. 1989. "Introduction." Pp. xi–xxviii in *The Spirit of the Laws*, edited by A. Cohler, B. Miller, and H. Stone. Cambridge: Cambridge University Press.

Cole, G.D.H. 1934. *What Marx Really Meant*. London: Victor Gollancz.

———. 1954. *Socialist Thought: Marxism and Anarchism, 1850–1890*. London: Macmillan & Co. Ltd.

Collingwood, R.G. 1962. *The Idea of History*. Oxford: Clarendon Press.

Comte, Auguste. N.d. *Cours de philosophie positive: Discours sur l'esprit positif* (*Course of Positive Philosophy: A Discourse on the Positivist Spirit*). 2 vols. Paris: Librarie Garnier.

———. 1974. *The Essential Comte: Selected from Cours de philosophie positive*. Edited by Stanislav Andreski. New York: Barnes and Noble.

Côté, James and Anton Allahar. 2007. *Ivory Tower Blues: A University System in Crisis.* Toronto: University of Toronto Press.

Coupland, Douglas. 1991. *Generation X: Tales for an Accelerated Culture.* New York: St. Martin's Press.

Crowe, Cameron. 1985. "Liner Notes and Text for *Biograph.*" *Bob Dylan: Biograph* [CD recording]. New York: Columbia.

D'Souza, Dinesh. 1992. *Illiberal Education.* New York: Vintage Books.

Dahrendorf, Ralf. 1959. *Class and Class Conflict in Industrial Society.* Stanford, CA: Stanford University Press.

———. 1967. *Society and Democracy in Germany.* Garden City, NY: Doubleday.

Delanty, Gerard. 2007. "Modernity." *Blackwell Encyclopedia of Sociology,* edited by George Ritzer. Retrieved October 2, 2007 (http://www.blackwellreference.com/).

Derrida, Jacques. 1994. *Specters of Marx.* Translated by Peggy Kamuf. London: Routledge.

Descartes, René. [1637] 1966. *Discours de la méthode.* Paris: Garnier Flammarion.

———. 1911. *The Philosophical Works of Descartes.* Vol. 1. Translated by E.S. Haldane and G.R.T. Ross. Cambridge: Cambridge University Press.

Deutscher, Isaac. "Discovering *Das Kapital.*" Pp. 255–64 in *Marxism in Our Time,* edited by Tamara Deutscher. San Francisco: Ramparts Press.

Dobb, Maurice. 1947. *Studies in the Development of Capitalism.* New York: International Publishers.

Dos Passos, John. 1932. *Nineteen Nineteen.* London: Constable.

———. 1936. *Big Money.* New York: Harcourt, Brace.

———. 1937. *U.S.A.* New York: Modern Library.

Durkheim, Émile. [1893] 1902. *De la division du travail social (The Division of Social Labour).* Paris: F. Alcan.

———. [1893] 1933. *The Division of Labor in Society.* Translated by G. Simpson. New York: The Free Press of Glencoe.

———. [1895] 1912. *Les régles de la methode sociologique (The Rules of Sociological Method).* 6th ed. Paris: F. Alcan.

———. [1895] 1938. *Rules of Sociological Method.* Translated by Sarah A. Solovay and John H. Mueller. New York: The Free Press of Glencoe.

———. [1897] 1951. *Suicide: A Study in Sociology.* Translated by J. Spaulding and G. Simpson. New York: The Free Press of Glencoe.

———. [1897] 1983a. *Le suicide: Étude de sociologie (Suicide: A Study in Sociology).* Paris: Presses universitaires de France.

———. 1912. *Les formes élémentaire de la vie religieuse (The Elementary Forms of Religious Life).* Paris: F. Alcan.

———. [1912] 1915. *The Elementary Forms of the Religious Life: A Study in Religious Sociology.* Translated by Joseph Swain. New York: The Macmillan Company.

———. [1924] 1953. *Sociology and Philosophy.* Translated by D.F. Pocock. London: Cohen & West.

———. [1924] 1969. *Sociologie et philosophie (Sociology and Philosophy).* Paris: Presses universitaires de France.

———. 1925. *L'éducation morale (Moral Education).* Paris: F. Alcan.

———. [1928] 1958. *Socialism and Saint-Simon*. Edited by Marcel Mauss, translated by Charlotte Sattler. Yellow Springs, OH: The Antioch Press.

———. [1928] 1971. *Le socialisme: Sa définition, ses debuts, la doctrine saint-simonienne* (*Socialism: Its Definition, Goals, and the Doctrine of Saint-Simon*). Paris: Presses universitaires de France.

———. [1938] 1969. *L'évolution pédagogique en France* (*The Evolution of Educational Thought in France*). 2nd ed. Paris: Presses universitaires de France.

———. [1938] 1977. *The Evolution of Educational Thought: Lectures on the Formation and Development of Secondary Education in France*. Boston: Routledge & Kegan Paul.

———. 1950. *Leçons de sociologie: Physique des moeurs et du droit* (*Sociology Lessons: The Physics of Morals and the Law*). Paris: Presses universitaires de France. (Unpublished lectures delivered at Bordeaux between 1896 and 1900 and at the Sorbonne in Paris between 1902 and 1915.)

———. 1955. *Pragmatisme et sociologie* (*Pragmatism and Sociology*). Paris: J. Vrin. (Lectures delivered at the Sorbonne between 1913 and 1914.)

——— . [1955] 1983. *Pragmatism and Sociology*. New York: Cambridge University Press.

———. 1958. *Professional Ethics and Civic Morals*. Translated by Cornelia Brookfield. London: Routledge & Kegan Paul.

———. 1960. *Montesquieu and Rousseau: Forerunners of Sociology*. Translated by R. Manheim. Ann Arbor: University of Michigan Press.

———. 1966. *Montesquieu et Rousseau: Precurseurs de la sociologie* (*Montesquieu and Rousseau: Forerunners of Sociology*). Paris: M. Riviere.

———. 1972. *Emile Durkheim: Selected Writings*. Edited by Anthony Giddens. Cambridge: Cambridge University Press.

———. 2004. *Durkheim's Philosophy Lectures*. Edited and translated by Neil Gross and Robert Alun Jones. Cambridge: Cambridge University Press.

Dylan, Bob. 1961. "Hard Times in New York Town." Retrieved March 8, 2009 (http://www.bobdylanlyrics.net/hatimeny.html).

———. 1962a. "Song to Woody." Retrieved March 7, 2009 (http://www.bobdylanlyrics.net/songwoody.html).

———. 1962b. "Talking New York Blues." Retrieved March 8, 2009 (http://orad.dent.kyushu-u.ac.jp/dylan/talkinny.html).

———. 1963a. "A Hard Rain's A-Gonna Fall." Retrieved March 8, 2009 (http://orad.dent.kyushu-u.ac.jp/dylan/hardrain.html).

———. 1963b. "Ballad of Hollis Brown." Retrieved March 11, 2009 (http://orad.dent.kyushu-u.ac.jp/dylan/balladhb.html).

———. 1963c. "I Shall be Free." Retrieved March 8, 2009 (http://orad.dent.kyushu-u.ac.jp/dylan/ishalfre.html).

———. 1963d. "Last Thoughts on Woody Guthrie." Retrieved March 8, 2009 (http://www.bobdylanlyrics.net/lasthowg.html).

———. 1963e. "My Life in a Stolen Moment." Retrieved March 5, 2009 (http://homepage.mac.com/danielmartin/Dylan/html/songs/M/MyLifeInAStolenMoment.html).

———. 1963f. "Restless Farewell." Retrieved March 11, 2009 (http://orad.dent.kyushu-u.ac.jp/dylan/reslessf.html).

———. 1963g. "With God on Our Side." Retrieved March 11, 2009 (http://orad.dent. kyushu-u.ac.jp/dylan/withgods.html).

———. 1964. "My Back Pages." Retrieved March 11, 2009 (http://orad.dent.kyushu-u. ac.jp/dylan/mybackpa.html).

———. 2004. *Chronicles: Volume One.* Toronto: Simon & Schuster Paperbacks.

———. 2006a. "The Crackin', Shakin', Breakin' Sounds" [Interview by Nat Hentoff of *The New Yorker,* October 24, 1964]. Pp. 13–28 in *Dylan on Dylan: The Essential Interviews,* edited by Jonathan Cott. London: Hodder & Stoughton.

———. 2006b. "Interview with Joseph Haas, *Chicago Daily News,* November 27, 1965." Pp. 55–61 in *Dylan on Dylan: The Essential Interviews,* edited by Jonathan Cott. London: Hodder & Stoughton.

———. 2006c. "Interview with Nat Hentoff, *Playboy,* March 1966." Pp. 93–111 in *Dylan on Dylan: The Essential Interviews,* edited by Jonathan Cott. London: Hodder & Stoughton.

———. 2006d. "Interview with Paul Robins, *L.A. Free Press,* March 1965." Pp. 37–46 in *Dylan on Dylan: The Essential Interviews,* edited by Jonathan Cott. London: Hodder & Stoughton.

———. 2006e. "Interview with Robert Hilburn, *Los Angeles Times,* April, 2004." Pp. 429–38 in *Dylan on Dylan: The Essential Interviews,* edited by Jonathan Cott. London: Hodder & Stoughton.

———. 2006f. "Interview with Robert Shelton, from *No Direction Home,* March 1966." Pp. 81–91 in *Dylan on Dylan: The Essential Interviews,* edited by Jonathan Cott. London: Hodder & Stoughton.

———. 2006g. "Radio Interview with Cynthia Gooding, WBAI (New York), 1962." Pp. 1–4 in *Dylan on Dylan: The Essential Interviews,* edited by Jonathan Cott. London: Hodder & Stoughton.

———. 2006h. "Radio Interview with Studs Terkel, WFMT (Chicago) May, 1963." Pp. 5–12 in *Dylan on Dylan: The Essential Interviews,* edited by Jonathan Cott. London: Hodder & Stoughton.

Elliot, Charles, ed. 1909–17. *Harvard Classics.* 51 vols. New York: P.F. Collier & Son.

Emberley, Peter and Waller Newell. 1994. *Bankrupt Education: The Decline of Liberal Education in Canada.* Toronto: University of Toronto Press.

Engels, Frederick. [1844] 1975. *Outlines of a Critique of Political Economy.* Pp. 418–34 in *Karl Marx and Frederick Engels: Collected Works.* Vol. 3. New York: International Publishers.

———. [1845] 1975. *The Condition of the Working-Class in England.* Translated by Florence Kelly-Wischnewetzky. Pp. 295–596 in *Karl Marx and Frederick Engels: Collected Works.* Vol. 4. New York: International Publishers.

———. [1878] 1939. *Anti-Dühring: Herr Eugen Dühring's Revolution in Science.* Edited by Clemens Dutt, translated by Emile Burns, . New York: International Publishers. (First published in serial form in *Vorwärts* in 1877–78.)

———. [1883] 1958. "Speech at the Graveside of Karl Marx." Pp. 167–9 in *Karl Marx and Frederick Engels: Selected Works.* Vol. 2. Moscow: Foreign Languages Publishing House.

———. [1883] 1962. "Das Begräbnis von Karl Marx" (Eulogy at Marx's Graveside). Pp. 335–39 in *Werke (Collected Works).* Vol. 19. Berlin: Dietz Verlag.

————. [1886] 1935. *Socialism: Utopian and Scientific*. Translated by Edward Aveling. New York: International Publishers.

————. [1888] 1941. *Ludwig Feuerbach and the Outcome of Classical German Philosophy*. Edited by Clemens Dutt. New York: International Publishers. (First published in two instalments in *Die Neue Zeit* in 1886 but revised and published as a monograph in 1888.)

————. 1935. *Dialektik der Natur* (*Dialectics of Nature*). Pp. 481–716 in *Marx-Engels Gesamtausgabe* (*Marx-Engels Complete Works*), edited by V. Adoratsky. Moscow: Marx-Engels Verlag. (Written between 1873 and 1883.)

————. 1940. *Dialectics of Nature*. Translated and edited by Clemens Dutt. New York: International Publishers. (Written between 1873 and 1883.)

Fay, Margaret. 1978. "Did Marx Offer to Dedicate Capital to Darwin? A Reassessment of the Evidence." *Journal of the History of Ideas* 39:133–46.

Ferguson, Adam. [1767] 1971. *An Essay on the History of Civil Society*. New York: Garland Publishers.

Ferguson, Niall. 2001. *The Cash Nexus: Money and Power in the Modern World, 1700–2000*. New York: Basic Books.

Fetscher, Iring. 1985. *Karl Marx und der Marxismus: Von der Ökonomiekritik zur Weltanschauung* (*Karl Marx and Marxism: From the Critique of Political Economy to Worldview*). 4th ed. Munich: Piper Verlag.

Fichte, Johann Gottlieb. 1834–46. *Sämmtliche Werke* (Collected Works). 11 vols. Berlin: Veit und Comp.

Fiske, John. 1989. *Reading the Popular*. Boston: Unwin Hyman.

Fitch, Sir Joshua Girling. 1898. *Thomas and Matthew Arnold and Their Influence on English Education*. New York: Scribner's Sons.

Foot, David. 1996. *Boom, Bust & Echo: How to Profit from the Coming Demographic Shift*. Toronto: Macfarlane, Walter & Ross.

Foucault, Michel. 1970. *The Order of Things: An Archaeology of the Human Sciences*. New York: Random House.

————. 1972. *The Archaeology of Knowledge*. Translated by A.M. Sheridan Smith. New York: Harper & Row. (First published in French in 1969.)

————. 1988. *The History of Sexuality*. Vol. 3, *The Care of the Self*. Translated by Robert Hurley. New York: Vintage Books. (First published in French in 1984.)

————. 1990a. *The History of Sexuality*. Vol. 1, *An Introduction*. Translated by Robert Hurley. New York: Vintage Books. (First published in French in 1976.)

————. 1990b. *The History of Sexuality*. Vol. 2, *The Use of Pleasure*. Translated by Robert Hurley. New York: Vintage Books. (First published in French in 1984.)

————. 1995. *Discipline and Punish: The Birth of the Prison*. Translated by Alan Sheridan. New York: Vintage Books. (First published in French in 1975.)

————. 2008. *The Birth of Biopolitics*. Edited by Michel Senellart, translated by Graham Burchell. New York: Palgrave Macmillan. (Lectures given at the Collège de France, 1978–79.)

Friedan, Betty. 1963. *The Feminine Mystique*. New York: Norton.

Frieden, Jeffry. 2006. *Global Capitalism: Its Fall and Rise in the Twentieth Century*. New York: W.W. Norton & Company.

Fromm, Erich. 1961. *Marx's Concept of Man*. New York: Frederick Ungar Publishing Co.

————, ed. 1965. *Socialist Humanism: An International Symposium.* New York: Doubleday.

Gabler, Neal. 1998. *Life: The Movie—How Entertainment Conquered Reality.* New York: Vintage Books.

Galilei, Galileo. 1967. *Dialogue Concerning the Two Chief World Systems: Ptolemaic and Copernican.* Translated by Stillman Drake. Berkeley: University of California Press.

Gans, Herbert. 1974. *Popular Culture and High Culture: An Analysis and Evaluation of Taste.* New York: Basic Books.

Geary, Daniel. 2009. *Radical Ambition: C. Wright Mills, the Left, and American Social Thought.* Berkeley: University of California Press.

Giddens, Anthony. 1971. *Capitalism and Modern Social Theory: An Analysis of the Writings of Marx, Durkheim, and Max Weber.* New York: Cambridge University Press.

————. 1972. "Introduction: Durkheim's Writings in Sociology and Social Philosophy." Pp. 1–50 in *Emile Durkheim: Selected Writings,* edited by Anthony Giddens. New York: Cambridge University Press.

————. 1973. *The Class Structure of the Advanced Societies.* London: Hutchinson.

————. 1976. "Classical Social Theory and the Origins of Modern Sociology." *American Journal of Sociology* 81:703–29.

————. 1984. *The Constitution of Society.* Berkeley: University of California Press.

Gill, Andy. 1998. *My Back Pages: Classic Bob Dylan, 1962–69.* London: Carleton Books.

Glazer, Tom, ed. 1972. *Songs of Peace, Freedom & Protest.* New York: David McKay.

Goldthorpe, John. 1968a. *The Affluent Worker: Industrial Attitudes and Behaviour.* London: Cambridge University Press.

————. 1968b. *The Affluent Worker: Political Attitudes and Behaviour.* London: Cambridge University Press.

————. 1969. *The Affluent Worker in the Class Structure.* London: Cambridge University Press.

Google. N.d. "Google Books Library Project—An Enhanced Card Catalog of the World's Books." Retrieved April 29, 2009 (http://books.google.com/googlebooks/library.html).

Gouldner, Alvin. 1958. "Introduction." Pp. v–xxvii in *Socialism and Saint-Simon,* by Émile Durkheim, edited by Marcel Mauss. Yellow Springs, OH: The Antioch Press.

————. 1970. *The Coming Crisis of Western Sociology.* New York: Basic Books.

Grossmann, Henryk. 1929. *Das Akkumulations- und Zusammenbruchsgesetz des kapitalistischen Systems (The Law of Accumulation and Collapse of the Capitalist System).* Leipzig: Verlag von C.L. Hirschfeld.

Guizot, François. 1997. *The History of Civilization in Europe.* Translated by William Hazlitt. Toronto: Penguin Books.

Guthrie, Woody. 1943. *Bound for Glory.* New York: E.P. Dutton.

————. 1971. *Bound for Glory.* New York: Penguin Books.

Habermas, Jürgen. 1970. "Technology and Science as 'Ideology.'" Pp. 81–122 in *Toward a Rational Society,* translated by Jeremy Shapiro. Boston: Beacon Press.

Hall, Donald, ed. 1994. *Muscular Christianity: Embodying the Victorian Age.* New York: Cambridge University Press.

Hall, Stuart. 1964. *The Popular Arts.* London: Hutchinson Educational Books.

Harrington, Michael. 1965. *The Accidental Century.* Baltimore: Penguin Books.

Harvey, David. 2005. *A Brief History of Neoliberalism.* New York: Oxford University Press.

Haupt, Georges. 1982. "Marx and Marxism." Pp. 265–89 in *The History of Marxism: Marxism in Marx's Day,* edited by Eric Hobsbawm. Bloomington: Indiana University Press.

Hayek, Friedrich von. 1931. *Prices and Production.* London: G. Routledge and Sons.

———. 1934. *Monetary Theory and the Trade Cycle.* London: Cape Editions.

Hegel, Georg Wilhelm Friedrich. 1807. *Phänomenologie des Geistes (Phenomenology of Spirit).* Hamburg: Goebhardt.

———. [1830] 1983. *Enzyklopädie der philosophischen Wissenschaften (Encyclopaedia of Philosophical Sciences).* 3rd ed. 3 vols. Frankfurt: Suhrkamp.

———. 1840. *Georg Wilhelm Friedrich Hegel's Vorlesungen über die Geschichte der Philosophie (Hegel's Lectures on the History of Philosophy).* Vol. 1. Edited by Carl Michelet. Berlin: Duncker and Humbolt.

——— —. 1841. *Wissenschaft der Logik (The Science of Logic).* 2nd ed. Berlin: Duncker.

———. 1844. *Georg Wilhelm Friedrich Hegel's Vorlesungen über die Geschichte der Philosophie (Hegel's Lectures on the History of Philosophy).* Vol. 2. Edited by Carl Michelet. Berlin: Duncker and Humbolt.

———. 1892–96. *Hegel's Lectures on the History of Philosophy.* 3 vols. Translated by Elizabeth Haldane and Frances Simson. London: K. Paul, Trench, Truebner, and Co.

———. 1977. *The Phenomenology of Spirit.* Translated by A.V. Miller. Oxford: Clarendon Press. (Translation of the 5th edition published in 1952; work first published in German in 1807.)

———. 1983. "Introduction to the History of Philosophy." Pp. 67–142 in *Hegel's Idea of Philosophy,* translated and introduced by Quentin Lauer. New York: Fordham University Press.

Hilferding, Rudolf. 1949. *Böhm-Bawerk's Criticism of Marx.* New York: Augustus M. Kelley. (First published in 1904 in the first issue of the journal *Marx Studien.*)

Hitchcock, Alfred (Director). 1960. *Psycho* [DVD]. Los Angeles: Universal Studios.

Hobbes, Thomas. [1651] 1968. *Leviathan.* Edited by C.B. Macpherson. Toronto: Penguin Books.

Hobsbawm, Eric. 1964. *Labouring Men: Studies in the History of Labour.* London: Weidenfeld and Nicolson.

———. 1994. *The Age of Extremes: The Short Twentieth Century, 1914–1991.* London: Michael Joseph.

———. 1999. *Industry and Empire: The Birth of the Industrial Revolution.* New York: The New Press.

Hoggart, Richard. 1957. *The Uses of Literacy: Aspects of Working-Class Life, With Special Reference to Publications and Entertainment.* London: Chatto and Windus.

———. 1958. *The Uses of Literacy: Aspects of Working-Class Life, With Special Reference to Publications and Entertainment.* Harmondsworth: Pelican Books.

———. 1970. "Why I Value Literature." Pp. 11–18 in *Speaking to Each Other,* by Richard Hoggart. Vol. 2. Harmondsworth: Penguin Books.

Hollingdale, Reginald. 1970. "Introduction." Pp. 9–38 in *Schopenhauer: Essays and Aphorisms,* translated and edited by Reginald Hollingdale. Markham, ON: Penguin Books.

Hook, Sidney. 1987. *Out of Step: An Unquiet Life in the 20th Century.* New York: Harper and Row.

Horkheimer, Max. 1947. *Eclipse of Reason.* New York: Oxford University Press.

———. 1974. *The Critique of Instrumental Reason.* Translated by Matthew O'Connell. New York: Seabury Press.

Horkheimer, Max and Theodor Adorno. 1972. *Dialectic of Enlightenment.* Translated by John Cumming. New York: Seabury Press.

Horowitz, Irving Louis, ed. 1965. *The New Sociology: Essays in Social Science and Social Theory in Honor of C. Wright Mills.* New York: Oxford University Press.

———. 1983. *C. Wright Mills: An American Utopian.* New York: Free Press.

Howe, Neil and William Strauss. 2000. *Millennials Rising: The Next Great Generation.* New York: Vintage Books.

Hughes, Thomas. 1857. *Tom Brown's Schooldays.* London: George Routledge.

Hume, David. [1739–40] 1941. *A Treatise on Human Nature.* 3 vols. Edited by L.A. Selby-Bigge. Oxford: The Clarendon Press.

———. [1748] 1966. *Enquiry Concerning Human Understanding.* La Salle, IL: Open Court Classics.

Huxley, Aldous. 1932. *Brave New World.* Garden City, NY: Garden City Publishing Company.

Inglehart, Ronald and Christian Welzel. 2007. "Modernization." *Blackwell Encyclopedia of Sociology,* edited by George Ritzer. Retrieved October 2, 2007 (http://www.blackwellreference.com).

Jeřábek, Hynek. 2001. "Paul Lazarsfeld—the Founder of Modern Empirical Sociology: A Research Biography." *International Journal of Public Opinion Research* 13:229–44.

Jhally, Sut. 1990. *The Codes of Advertising.* New York: Routledge.

Jones, Garth Stedman. 1982. "Engels and the History of Marxism." Pp. 290–326 in *The History of Marxism: Marxism in Marx's Day,* edited by Eric Hobsbawm. Bloomington: Indiana University Press.

Kaiser, Bruno. 1967. *Ex Libris Karl Marx und Friedrich Engels (From the Library of Karl Marx and Friedrich Engels).* Berlin: Dietz Verlag.

Kallan, Horace. 1957. "Modernism." Pp. 564–9 in *Encyclopaedia of the Social Sciences.* Vol. 10, edited by Edwin Seligman and Alvin Johnson. New York: The Macmillan Company.

Kant, Immanuel. [1783] 1968. *Prolegomena zu einer jeden künftigen Metaphysik die als Wissenschaft wird auftreten können (Prolegomena to any Future Metaphysics that can Qualify as a Science).* Pp. 113–264 in *Werke (Collected Works).* Vol. 5. Darmstadt: Wissenschaftlighe Buchgeselschaft.

Kautsky, Karl. 1887. *Karl Marx's Oekonomische Lehren* (Karl Marx's Economic Doctrines). Stuttgart: Verlag von J.H.W. Dietz.

———. 1898–1903. *Karl Kautsky Papers.* D XIV 123–8. International Institute for Social History, Amsterdam, Netherlands.

———. 1925. *The Economic Doctrines of Karl Marx.* Translated by H. J. Stenning. London: A. & C. Black.

———. 1927a. *Die materialistische Geschichtsaufassung (The Materialist Conception of History).* Bd. 1, *Natur und Gesellschaft* (Vol. 1, *Nature and Society*). Berlin: J.H.W. Dietz.

———. 1927b. *Die materialistische Geschichtsaufassung* (*The Materialist Conception of History*). Bd. 2, *Der Staat und die Entwicklung der Menscheit* (Vol. 2, *The State and the Development of Humankind*). Berlin: J.H.W. Dietz.

———. 1935. *Aus der Frühzeit des Marxismus: Engels' Briefwechsel mit Kautsky* (*From the Early Period of Marxism: Engels's Correspondence with Kautsky*), edited and elucidated by Karl Kautsky. Prague: Orbis Verlag.

Keynes, John Maynard. 1936. *The General Theory of Employment, Interest, and Money*. New York: Harcourt, Brace.

King, Ross. 2006. *The Judgment of Paris: The Revolutionary Decade That Gave the World Impressionism*. New York: Walker and Company.

"Kitchen Debate: An Exploration into Cold War Ideologies and Propaganda." 1959. Personal Homepage about the Khrushchev-Nixon Debate held on July 24, 1959. Retrieved February 20, 2009 (http://www3.sympatico.ca/robsab/debate.html).

Kolakowski, Lezek. 1972. *Positivist Philosophy from Hume to the Vienna Circle*. Translated by Norbert Guterman. Harmondsworth: Penguin Books.

Korsch, Karl. 1922. *Kernpunkte der materialistischen Geschichtsauffassung* (*Principles of the Materialist Conception of History*). Leipzig: C.L. Hirschfeld.

——— . 1923. *Marxismus und Philosophie* (*Marxism and Philosophy*). Leipzig: C.L. Hirschfeld.

———. 1929. *Die materialistische Geschichtsauffassung: Eine Auseinandersetzung mit Karl Kautsky* (*The Materialist Conception of History: A Dispute with Karl Kautsky*). Leipzig: C.L. Hirschfeld.

———. 1970. *Marxism and Philosophy*. Translated by Fred Halliday. London: New Left Books. (First published in German in 1923.)

———. 1971. *Die materialistische Geschichtsauffasung und andere Schriften* (*The Materialist Conception of History and Other Writings*), edited by Erich Gerlach. Frankfurt: Europäische Verlagsanstalt.

Külow, Volker and André Jaroslawski, eds. 1993. *David Rjasanow: Marx-Engels-Forscher, Humanist, Dissident* (*David Ryazanov: Marx-Engels Scholar, Humanist, Dissident*). Berlin: Dietz Verlag.

Labriola, Antonio. 1904. "Historical Materialism." Pp. 95–246 in *Essays on the Materialistic Conception of History*, translated by Charles H. Kerr. New York: Charles H. Kerr.

Lasswell, Harold. 1965. "The Policy Sciences of Development." *World Politics* 17:286-309.

Lazarsfeld, Paul. 1954. *Mathematical Thinking in the Social Sciences*. Glencoe, IL: The Free Press.

Lazarsfeld, Paul and Morris Rosenberg, eds. 1955. *The Language of Social Research: A Reader in the Methodology of Social Research*. Glencoe, IL: The Free Press.

Leavis, F.R. and Denys Thompson. 1933. *Culture and Environment: The Training of Critical Awareness*. London: Chatto & Windus.

Lenin, Vladimir. 1927. *Materialism and Empirio-Criticism*. New York: International Publishers.

———. 1943. "The Proletarian Revolution and the Renegade Kautsky." Pp. 113–217 in *V. I. Lenin Selected Works*. Vol. 7. New York: International Publishers. (First published in *Pravda* on 11 October 1918.)

———. 1972. *Philosophical Notebooks*. London: Lawrence and Wishart. (Written between 1895 and 1916 with the bulk written between 1915–16.)

Lerner, Daniel. 1958. *The Passing of Traditional Society: Modernizing the Middle East*. Glencoe, IL: The Free Press.

———. 1968. "Modernization." Pp. 386–95 in *International Encyclopedia of the Social Sciences*. Vol. 10, edited by David Sills. New York: Crowell Collier and Macmillan.

Lerner, Murray (Producer). 2007. *The Other Side of the Mirror: Bob Dylan Live at Newport Folk Festival 1963–1965*. New York: Columbia.

Levine, Melvin. 2005. *Ready or Not, Here Life Comes*. New York: Simon & Schuster.

Lewis, Clive Staples. 2001. *Mere Christianity*. New York: HarperCollins.

Lichtheim, George. 1965. *Marxism: An Historical and Critical Study*. New York: Frederick A. Praeger.

Lichtman, Richard. 1979. *An Outline of Marxism*. Toronto: Coles Publishing.

Lilienfeld, Paul von. 1873. *Die menschliche Gesellschaft als Realer Organismus* (*Human Society as a Real Organism*). Hamburg: E. Behre Verlag.

Locke, John. [1694] 1967. *Two Treatises on Government*. London: Cambridge University Press.

Lovejoy, Arthur. 1948. *Essays in the History of Ideas*. Baltimore: Johns Hopkins Press.

Lukács, Georg. 1923. *Geschichte und Kalssenbewusstsein* (*History and Class Consciousness*). Berlin: Malik Verlag.

———. 1963. *The Historical Novel*. Translated by Hannah and Stanley Mitchell. Boston: Beacon Press.

———. 1970. *History and Class Consciousness*. Translated by Rodney Livingstone. London: Merlin Books.

Lukes, Stephen. 1973. *Emile Durkheim, His Life and Work: An Historical and Critical Study*. New York: Harper and Row.

Luxemburg, Rosa. 1951. *The Accumulation of Capital*. Translated by Agnes Schwarzschild. London: Routledge and Kegan Paul.

Lyotard, Jean-François. 1984. *The Postmodern Condition: A Report on Knowledge*. Translated by Geoff Bennington and Brian Massumi. Minneapolis: University of Minnesota Press.

Maguire, John. 1971. *Marx's Paris Writings*. Dublin: Gill and Macmillan.

Malthus, Thomas. 1827. *Definitions in Political Economy*. London: Murray.

Marcuse, Herbert. 1932. "Neue Quellen zur Grundlegung des Historischen Materialismus" (New Sources in the Foundation of Historical Materialism). *Die Gesellschaft* 9:136–74.

———. 1954. *Reason and Revolution: Hegel and the Rise of Social Theory*. New York: Humanities Press.

———. 1955. *Eros and Civilization*. Boston: The Beacon Press.

———. 1958. *Soviet Marxism: A Critical Analysis*. London: Routledge and Kegan Paul.

———. 1964. *One-Dimensional Man: Studies in the Ideology of Advanced Industrial Society*. Boston: Beacon Press.

Markham, Felix. 1964. "Introduction." Pp. xxxiii–xliv in *Social Organization, The Science of Man, and Other Writings*, by Henri de Saint-Simon. Edited and translated by F. Markham. New York: Harper Torchbooks.

Marx, Karl. [1843] 1927. "Zur Kritik der Hegelschen Rechtsphilosophie" (Towards
the Critique of the Hegelian Philosophy of Law). Pp. 607–21 in *Historisch-kritische
Gesamtausgabe* (*Historical and Critical Complete Works*). Pt. I, vol. 1.1, edited by D.
Ryazanov. Frankfurt: Marx-Engels-Archiv Verlagsgesellschaft M.B.H.

———. [1844] 1968. "Zur Kritik der Hegelschen Rechtsphilosophie: Einlietung"
(Towards the Critique of Hegel's Philosophy of Right: Introduction). Pp. 378–91 in
Werke (*Collected Works*). Vol. 1. Berlin: Dietz Verlag.

———. [1844] 1975. "Contribution to the Critique of Hegel's Philosophy of Law:
Introduction." Pp. 175–86 in *Collected Works*. Vol. 3. New York: International
Publishers.

———. [1847] 1950. *Misère de la Philosophie en Réponse à la Philosophie de la Misère de
M. Proudhon* (*The Poverty of Philosophy: A Response to the Philosophy of Poverty by
Proudhon*). Paris: Alfred Costes.

———. [1849] 1933. *Wage-Labour and Capital; Value, Price, and Profit*. New York:
International Publishers.

———. [1852] 1937. *The Eighteenth Brumaire of Louis Bonaparte*. Edited by Clemens Dutt.
New York: International Publishers.

———. [1859] 1980. *Zur Kritik der politischen Ökonomie* (*Towards the Critique of Political
Economy*). Pp. 95–245 in *Gesamtausgabe* (*Complete Works*). Part II, vol. 2. Berlin:
Dietz Verlag.

———. [1859] 2005. "Preface to *Towards the Critique of Political Economy*." Pp. 55–66
in *Intersections: Readings in Sociology's Task and Promise*, edited by Rob Beamish.
Boston: Pearson Custom Publishing.

———. [1860] 1982. *Herr Vogt: A Spy in the Workers' Movement*. Translated by
R.A. Archer. London: New Park Publications.

———. [1867] 1983. *Das Kapital* (*Capital*). 1st ed. Vol. 1. Pp. 1–651 in *Gesamtausgabe*
(*Complete Works*). Part II, vol. 5. Berlin: Dietz Verlag.

———. [1872] 1932. *Das Kapital* (*Capital*). 2nd ed. Vol. 1. Berlin: Gustav Kiepenheuer
Verlag.

———. [1872] 1987. *Das Kapital* (*Capital*). 2nd ed. Vol. 1. Pp. 57–719 in *Gesamtausgabe*
(*Complete Works*). Part II, vol. 6. Berlin: Dietz Verlag.

———. [1875] 1989. *Le capital* (*Capital*). Vol. 1. Pp. 1–699 in *Gesamtausgabe* (Complete
Works). Part II, vol. 7. Berlin: Dietz Verlag.

———. [1881] 1962. "Randglossen zu Adolph Wagner's *Lehrbuch der politischen
Ökonomie*" (Marginal Notes to Adolph Wagner's *Textbook on Political Economy*). Pp.
355–84 in *Werke* (*Collected Works*). Vol. 19. Berlin: Dietz Verlag.

———. [1881] 1975. "Marx's Notes (1879–1880) on Adolph Wagner." Pp. 161–219 in *Karl
Marx: Texts on Method*, translated by Terrell Carver. Oxford: Basil Blackwell.

———. [1890] 1976. *Capital*. 4th ed. Vol. 1. Translated by Ben Fowkes. Markham:
Penguin Books.

———. 1914. *Das Kapital: Kritik der politischen Ökonomie* (*Capital: Critique of Political
Economy*). Vol. 1. Edited by Karl Kautsky. Berlin: J.H.W. Dietz.

———. 1921a. *Theorien über den Mehrwert* (*Theories of Surplus Value*). Vol. 1. Edited by
Karl Kautsky. Stuttgart: Verlag von J.H. Dietz. (Written between 1861 and 1863.)

———. 1921b. *Theorien über den Mehrwert* (*Theories of Surplus Value*). Vol. 2,
pt. 1. Edited by Karl Kautsky. Stuttgart: Verlag von J.H. Dietz. (Written between 1861
and 1863.)

————. 1921c. *Theorien über den Mehrwert* (*Theories of Surplus Value*). Vol. 2, pt. 2. Edited by Karl Kautsky. Stuttgart: Verlag von J.H. Dietz. (Written between 1861 and 1863.)

————. 1921d. *Theorien über den Mehrwert* (*Theories of Surplus Value*). Vol. 3. Edited by Karl Kautsky. Stuttgart: Verlag von J.H. Dietz. (Written between 1861 and 1863.)

————. 1926. *Das Kapital: Kritik der politischen Ökonomie* (*Capital: Critique of Political Economy*). Vol. 2. Arranged by Karl Kautsky with the assistance of Benedikt Kautsky. Berlin: J.H.W. Dietz.

————. 1929a. *Das Kapital: Kritik der politischen Ökonomie* (*Capital: Critique of Political Economy*). Vol. 3, pt. 1. Arranged by Benedikt Kautsky with the assistance of Karl Kautsky. Berlin: J.H.W. Dietz.

————. 1929b. *Das Kapital: Kritik der politischen Ökonomie* (*Capital: Critique of Political Economy*). Vol. 3, pt. 2. Arranged by Benedikt Kautsky with the assistance of Karl Kautsky. Berlin: J.H.W. Dietz.

————. 1932a. *Ökonomisch-philosophische Manuskripte aus dem Jahre 1844* (*Economic and Philosophical Manuscripts of 1844*). Pp. 29–172 in *Historisch-kritische Gesamtausgabe* (*Historical and Critical Complete Works*). Pt. I, vol. 3, edited by V. Adoratsky. Berlin: Marx-Engels Verlag. (Written in 1844.)

————. 1932b. "*Nationalökonomie und Philosophie*" (Political Economy and Philosophy). Pp. 283–375 in *Der historische Materialismus: Die Frühschriften* (*Historical Materialism: Early Writings*), edited by Siegfried Landshut and Jacob Mayer. Leipzig: Alfred Kröner Verlag. (Written in 1844.)

————. 1935. *Class Struggles in France*. Edited by Clemens Dutt. New York: International Publishers. (First published in a periodical in 1850.)

————. 1939. *Grundrisse der Kritik der politischen Ökonomie: Rohentwurf* (*Foundations for the Critique of Political Economy: Rough Draft*). Moscow: Verlag für fremdsprachige Literatur. (Written between 1857 and 1858.)

————. 1941. *Grundrisse der Kritik der politischen Ökonomie: Anhang* (*Outlines of the Critique of Political Economy: Appendix*). Moscow: Verlag für fremdsprachige Literatur. (Written in 1858.)

————. 1950. *Nationalökonomie und Philosophie* (*Political Economy and Philosophy*). Berlin: Verlag Gustav Kiepenheuer GmbH. (Written in 1844.)

————. 1953. *Grundrisse der Kritik der politischen Ökonomie: Rohentwurf* (*Foundations for the Critique of Political Economy: Rough Draft*). Berlin: Dietz Verlag. (Written between 1857–58).

————. 1959. *Economic and Philosophic Manuscripts*. Translated by Martin Milligan. London: Lawrence and Wishart. (Written in 1844).

————. 1962. *Manuscrits de 1844: Économie politique et philosophie* (*Manuscripts of 1844: Political Economy and Philosophy*). Translated by Emile Bottigelli. Paris: Editions Sociales. (Written in 1844.)

————. 1963. "Economic and Philosophic Manuscripts." Pp. 61–220 in *Karl Marx: Early Writings*, translated and edited by Tom Bottomore. London: C.A. Watts. (Written in 1844.)

————. 1968a. "Ökonomisch-philosophische Manuskripte aus dem Jahre 1844" (Economic and Philosophical Manuscripts of 1844). Pp. 467–588 in *Werke* (*Collected Works*). Supplementary volume, pt. 1. Berlin: Dietz Verlag. (Written in 1844.)

————. 1968b. "Kritik der Hegelschen Staatsrechts §§ 261–313" (Critique of Hegel's Code of Law §§ 261–313). Pp. 203–436 in *Werke* (*Collected Works*). Vol. 1. Berlin: Dietz Verlag. (Written in 1843.)

————. 1968c. "Differenz der demokritischen und epikureischen Naturphilosophie nebst einem Anhange von Karl Heinrich Marx, Doktor der Philosophie" (The Difference between the Democritean and Epicurean Philosophy of Nature with an Appendix by Karl Marx, Doctor of Philosophy). Pp. 257–308 in *Werke* (*Collected Works*). Supplementary volume, pt. 1. Berlin: Dietz Verlag. (Written in 1841 as Marx's doctoral dissertation.)

————. 1975. "Economic and Philosophical Manuscripts." Pp. 279–400 in *Karl Marx: Early Writings,* translated by Rodney Livingstone. Markham: Penguin Books Canada. (Written in 1844.)

Marx, Karl and Friedrich Engels. [1845] 1975. *The Holy Family.* Pp. 1–211 in *Collected Works.* Vol. 4. New York: International Publishers.

————. 1848. *Manifest der kommunistischen Partei* (*Manifesto of the Communist Party*). London: Bildungs-Gesellschaft für Arbeiter.

————. [1848] 1932. *Manifest der Kommunistischen Partei* (*Manifesto of the Communist Party*). Pp. 525–60 in *Historisch-kritische Gesamtausgabe* (*Historical and Critical Complete Works*). Pt. I, vol. 6, edited by V. Adoratsky. Berlin: Marx-Engels-Verlag.

————. [1848] 1934. *Manifesto of the Communist Party.* London: Martin Lawrence.

————. 1932. *Die deutsche Ideologie* (*The German Ideology*). Pp. 1–528 in *Historisch-kritische Gesamtausgabe* (*Historical and Critical Complete Works*). Pt. I, vol. 5, edited by V. Adoratsky. Berlin: Marx-Engels Verlag. (Unpublished draft manuscript written in 1845.)

————. 1939. *The German Ideology.* Edited by R. Pascal. New York: International Publishers. (Written in 1845.)

————. 1955. *Selected Correspondence.* Moscow: Progress Publishers.

————. 1957. *Werke* (*Collected Works*). Vol. 2. Berlin: Dietz Verlag.

————. 1958. *Werke* (*Collected Works*). Vol. 3. Berlin: Dietz Verlag.

————. 1960. *Werke* (*Collected Works*). Vol. 8. Berlin: Dietz Verlag.

————. 1962a. *Werke* (*Collected Works*). Vol. 19. Berlin: Dietz Verlag.

————. 1962b. *Werke* (*Collected Works*). Vol. 23. Berlin: Dietz Verlag.

————. 1963a. *Werke* (*Collected Works*). Vol. 16. Berlin: Dietz Verlag.

————. 1963b. *Werke* (*Collected Works*). Vol. 24. Berlin: Dietz Verlag.

————. 1964a. *Werke* (*Collected Works*). Vol. 20. Berlin: Dietz Verlag.

————. 1964b. *Werke* (*Collected Works*). Vol. 25. Berlin: Dietz Verlag.

————. 1965a. *Werke* (*Collected Works*). Vol. 26.1. Berlin: Dietz Verlag.

————. 1965b. *Werke* (*Collected Works*). Vol. 31. Berlin: Dietz Verlag.

————. 1965c. *Werke* (*Collected Works*). Vol. 32. Berlin: Dietz Verlag.

————. 1966. *Werke* (*Collected Works*). Vol. 6. Berlin: Dietz Verlag.

————. 1967a. *Werke* (*Collected Works*). Vol. 26.2. Berlin: Dietz Verlag.

————. 1967b. *Werke* (*Collected Works*). Vol. 37. Berlin: Dietz Verlag.

————. 1968. *Werke* (*Collected Works*). Vol. 26.3. Berlin: Dietz Verlag.

————. 1969. *Die deutsche Ideologie* (*The German Ideology*). Pp. 9–529 in *Werke* (*Collected Works*). Vol. 3. Berlin: Dietz Verlag. (Unpublished draft manuscript written in 1845.)

———. 1975. *Gesamtausgabe (Complete Works)*. Pt. 3, vol. 1. Berlin: Dietz Verlag.

———. 1976. *The German Ideology*. Pp. 19–539 in *Collected Works*. Vol. 5. New York: International Publishers. (Unpublished draft manuscript written in 1845.)

———. 1976–91. *Gesamtausgabe (Complete Works)*. Pt. IV. Berlin: Dietz Verlag.

———. 1978. *Werke (Collected Works)*. Vol. 29. Berlin: Dietz Verlag.

———. 1982. *Gesamtausgabe (Complete Works)*. Pt. I, vol. 2. Berlin: Dietz Verlag.

———. 1985. *Collected Works*. Vol. 38. New York: International Publishers.

———. 1990. *Gesamtausgabe (Complete Works)*. Pt. III, vol. 8. Berlin: Dietz Verlag.

———. 1992–2005. *Gesamtausgabe (Complete Works)*. Pt. IV. Berlin: Akademie Verlag.

———. 1999. *Gesamtausgabe (Complete Works)*. Pt. IV, vol. 32. Berlin: Akademie Verlag.

M*A*S*H*. 1972–83. New York: CBS.

McCarty, John and Brian Kelleher. 1985. *Alfred Hitchcock Presents: An Illustrated Guide to the Ten-Year Television Career of the Master of Suspense*. New York: St. Martin's Press.

mclainlove. 2009. "A Vision of Clark College Students Today." Retrieved December 24, 2009 (http://www.youtube.com/watch?v=xZKYM2WhZj4).

McClelland, David. 1961. *The Achieving Society*. Princeton, NJ: Van Nostrand.

McLellan, David. 1973. *Karl Marx: His Life and Thought*. London: Macmillan.

McLuhan, Marshall. N.d. "Marshall McLuhan Quotes/Quotations." Retrieved May 1, 2009 (http://www.icelebz.com/quotes/marshall_mcluhan/).

McLuhan, Marshall. 1964. *Understanding Media: The Extensions of Man*. New York: Mentor.

Merton, Robert. 1938. "Social Structure and Anomie." *American Sociological Review* 3:672–82.

———. 1949. *Social Theory and Social Structure: Toward the Codification of Theory and Research*. Glencoe, IL: The Free Press.

———. 1957. *Social Theory and Social Structure*. Rev. ed. New York: The Free Press of Glencoe.

Meštrović, Stjepan. 1988. *Emile Durkheim and the Reformation of Sociology*. Totawa, NJ: Rowman & Littlefield.

Mészáros, István. 1970. *Marx's Theory of Alienation*. London: Merlin Press.

———. 1975. *Marx's Theory of Alienation*. 4th ed. London: Merlin Press.

Meyer, Eduard. 1902. *Zur Theorie und Methodik der Geschichte (On Theory and Methods in History)*. Halle: S.M. Niemeyer.

Miliband, Ralph. 1968. "C. Wright Mills." Pp. 3–11 in *C. Wright Mills and the Power Elite*, edited by William Domhoff and Hoyt Ballard. Boston: Beacon Press.

Mill, James. [1821] 1844. *Elements of Political Economy*. London: Henry G. Bohn.

Mill, John Stuart. 1848. *Principles of Political Economy, With Some of Their Applications to Social Philosophy*. London: J.W. Parker.

Millett, Kate. 1970. *Sexual Politics*. New York: Doubleday.

Mills, C. Wright. 1948. *New Men of Power: America's Labor Leaders*. New York: Harcourt Brace.

———. 1951. *White Collar: The American Middle Classes*. New York: Oxford University Press.

———. 1956. *The Power Elite*. New York: Oxford University Press.

————. 1958. *The Causes of World War Three*. New York: Ballantine Books.

————. 1959. *The Sociological Imagination*. New York: Oxford University Press.

————. 1960. *Images of Man: The Classic Tradition in Sociological Thinking*. New York: George Braziller.

————. 1962. *The Marxists*. New York: Dell Publishing.

————. 1963. *Power, Politics, and People: The Collected Essays of C. Wright Mills*. Edited by Irving Louis Horowitz. New York: Ballantine Books.

————. 2000. *C. Wright Mills: Letters and Autobiographical Writings*. Edited by Kathryn Mills with Pamela Mills. Berkeley: University of California Press.

Mills, Kathryn. 2000. "Remembrance." Pp. xvii–xx in *C. Wright Mills: Letters and Autobiographical Writings*, edited by Kathryn Mills with Pamela Mills. Berkeley: University of California Press.

Mills, Pamela. 2000. "My Father Haunts Me." Pp. xxi–xxiv in *C. Wright Mills: Letters and Autobiographical Writings*, edited by Kathryn Mills with Pamela Mills. Berkeley: University of California Press.

Mises, Ludwig von. 1934. *The Theory of Money and Credit*. London: Cape Editions.

Mongardini, Carlo and Simonetta Tabboni, eds. 1998. *Robert K. Merton and Contemporary Sociology*. New Brunswick, NJ: Transaction Publishers.

Montchréstien, Antoine de. [1615] 1889. *Traicté de l'économie politique, dédié au Roy et à la Reyne mère du Roy* (*Treatise on Political Economy, dedicated in 1615 to the King and the Queen Mother*). Paris: Plon.

Montesquieu, Charles de Secondat, baron de. [1721] 1975. *Lettres persanes* (*Persian Letters*). Paris: Garnier.

————. [1734] 1968. *Considerations on the Causes of the Greatness of the Romans and Their Decline*. Translated by David Lowenthal. Ithaca: Cornell University Press.

————. [1748] 1750. *De l'esprit des loix: Nouvelle édition, avec les dernières corrections & illustrations de l'auteur* (*The Spirit of the Laws: New Edition with the Author's Final Corrections and Illustrations*). Edinbourg [sic]: G. Hamilton & J. Balfour.

————. [1748] 1989. *The Spirit of the Laws*. Translated and edited by A.M. Cohler, B.C. Miller, and H.S. Stone. Cambridge: Cambridge University Press.

————. 1898. *Considérations sur les causes de la grandeur des Romains, et de leur décadence* (*Considerations on the Causes of the Greatness of the Romans and Their Decline*). Paris: Hachette et Cie.

Musto, Marcello, ed. 2008. *Karl Marx's Grundrisse: Foundations of the Critique of Political Economy 150 Years Later*. London: Routledge.

Newton, Isaac. 1953. *Newton's Philosophy of Nature: Selections from His Writings*. Edited by H.S. Thayer. New York: Hafner Press.

Nietzsche, Friedrich. [1872] 1968. *The Birth of Tragedy or: Hellenism and Pessimism*. Pp. 3–144 in *Basic Writings of Nietzsche*, translated and edited by Walter Kaufmann. New York: The Modern Library.

————. [1873] 1983. *Untimely Meditations*. Translated by R.J. Hollingdale. Cambridge: Cambridge University Press.

————. [1882] 1974. *The Gay Science*. Translated by Walter Kaufmann. New York: Vintage Books.

————. [1886] 1968. *Beyond Good and Evil*. Pp. 181–438 in *Basic Writings of Nietzsche*, translated and edited by Walter Kaufmann. New York: The Modern Library.

———. [1889] 1954. *Twilight of the Idols: How One Philosophizes with a Hammer.* Pp. 465–563 in *The Portable Nietzsche,* translated and edited by Walter Kaufmann. New York: The Viking Press.

———. [1895] 1954. *The Antichrist.* Pp. 568–656 in *The Portable Nietzsche,* translated and edited by Walter Kaufmann. New York: The Viking Press.

———. [1908] 1968. *Ecce Homo.* Pp. 657–781 in *Basic Writings of Nietzsche,* translated and edited by Walter Kaufmann. New York: The Modern Library.

Oberg, Jamie. 2007. "YouTube is a Hit in K-State Classroom, World." *49 News.* KTKA 49 ABC. Retrieved May 17, 2008 (http://www.ktka.com/news/2007/feb/15/kstate_professor_goes_hightech_instill_appreciatio/).

Ollman, Bertell. 1971. *Alienation: Marx's Conception of Man in Capitalist Society.* Cambridge: Cambridge University Press.

Orwell, George. 1949. *Nineteen Eighty-Four.* New York: Harcourt, Brace.

Owen, Robert. [1814] 1927. *A New View of Society and Other Writings.* Toronto: J.M. Dent & Sons.

———. 1927. *Report on the County of Lanark.* Toronto: J.M. Dent & Sons.

Pappenheim, Fritz. 1959. *The Alienation of Modern Man.* New York: Monthly Review Press.

Parsons, Talcott. 1949. *The Structure of Social Action.* 2nd ed. Glencoe, IL: The Free Press.

———. 1951. *The Social System.* Glencoe, IL: The Free Press.

———. 1968. "Emile Durkheim." Pp. 311–20 in *International Encyclopedia of the Social Sciences,* edited by David Sills. New York: Macmillan Publishing.

Perlman, Freddy. 1970. *The Incoherence of the Intellectual: C. Wright Mills's Struggle to Unite Knowledge and Action.* Detroit: Black and Red.

Peterson, Richard. 1990. "Why 1955? Explaining the Advent of Rock Music." *Popular Music* 9:97–116.

Peterson, Richard and David Berger. 1975. "Cycles in Symbol Production: The Case of Popular Music." *American Sociological Review* 40:158–73.

Peyre, Henri. 1960. "Foreward." Pp. v–xvi in *Montesquieu and Rousseau: Forerunners of Sociology,* translated by Ralph Mannheim. Ann Arbor: University of Michigan Press.

Polanyi, Karl. 1944. *The Great Transformation.* Toronto: Farrar and Rinehart.

Popitz, Heinrich. 1967. *Der entfremdete Mensch: Zeitkritik und Geschichtsphilosophie des jungen Marx (Alienated Man: Critique of the Era and Philosophy of History in the Young Marx).* Frankfurt: Europäische Verlagsanstalt.

Postman, Neil. 1985. *Amusing Ourselves to Death: Public Discourse in the Age of Show Business.* New York: Viking Press.

———. 1988. *Conscientious Objections: Stirring up Trouble about Language, Technology, and Education.* New York: Knopf.

———. 1995. *The End of Education: Redefining the Value of School.* New York: Vintage Books.

Presnell, Don and Marty McGee. 1998. *A Critical History of Television's The Twilight Zone.* Jefferson, NC: McFarland.

Project Gutenberg. N.d. "About Project Gutenberg." Retrieved April 29, 2009 (http://www.gutenberg.org/wiki/Gutenberg:About).

Rebello, Stephen. 1990. *Alfred Hitchcock and the Making of Psycho.* New York: Dembner Books.

Ricardo, David. [1817] 1891. *Principles of Political Economy and Taxation.* London: G. Bell and Sons.

Riesman, David. 1950. *The Lonely Crowd: A Study of Changing American Character.* New Haven: Yale University Press.

Ritzer, George, ed. 2007. *Blackwell Encyclopedia of Sociology.* 11 vols. Oxford: Blackwell.

Rius. 1976. *Marx for Beginners.* Translated by Richard Appignanesi. New York: Pantheon Books.

Rocher, Guy. 1974. *Talcott Parsons and American Sociology.* Translated by Barbara and Stephen Mennell. London: Nelson.

Rojahn, Jürgen. 1983. "Marxismus—Marx—Geschichtswissenschaft: Der Fall der sog 'Ökonomisch-philosophischen Manuskripte aus dem Jahre 1844'" (Marxism—Marx—Knowledge of History: The Case of the So-called "Economic and Philosophical Manuscripts of 1844"). *International Review of Social History* 28:2–49.

———. 1985. "Die Marxschen Manuskripte aus dem Jahre 1844 in der neuen Marx-Engels-Gesamtausgabe" (Marx's Manuscripts from 1844 in the *New Marx-Engels Complete Works*). *Archiv für Sozialgeschichte* 25:647–63.

———. 1998. "Publishing Marx and Engels after 1989: The Fate of the MEGA." *Critique* 31:196–207.

Rosdolsky, Roman. 1977. *The Making of Marx's 'Capital.'* Translated by Pete Burgess. London: Pluto Press.

Rousseau, Jean-Jacques. [1762] 1963. *The Social Contract and Discourses.* Translated by G. D. H. Cole. New York: Dutton.

Rubel, Maximilien. 1957. *Karl Marx: Essai de biographie intellectuelle* (Karl Marx: Towards an Intellectual Biography). Paris: Librairie Marcel Rivière et Cie.

———. 1968. "Introduction." Pp. xvii-cxxxii in *Karl Marx Oeuvres Économique* (*Karl Marx, Economic Works*). Vol. 2. Paris: Gallimard.

———. 1974. *Marx critique du marxisme* (*Marx and the Critique of Marxism*). Paris: Payot & Rivages.

———. 1981a. "A History of Marx's 'Economics.'" Pp. 82–189 in *Rubel on Marx: Five Essays,* edited by Joseph O'Malley and Keith Algozin. New York: Cambridge University Press.

———. 1981b. "The 'Marx Legend,' or Engels, Founder of Marxism." Pp. 15–25 in *Rubel on Marx: Five Essays,* edited by Joseph O'Malley and Keith Algozin. New York: Cambridge University Press.

———. 1981c. "The Plan and Method of the 'Economics.'" Pp. 190–229 in *Rubel on Marx: Five Essays,* edited by Joseph O'Malley and Keith Algozin. New York: Cambridge University Press.

Rubel, Maximilien and Margaret Manale. 1975. *Marx Without Myth.* Oxford: Basil Blackwell.

Ryan, John. 1985. *The Production of Culture in the Music Industry: The ASCAP-BMI Controversy.* Lanham, MD: University Press of America.

Ryazanov, David. 1925. "Neueste Mitteilungen über der literarischen Nachlaß von Karl Marx und Friedrich Engels" (The Latest Information on the Marx-Engels Literary Estate). *Archiv für die Geschichte des Sozialismus und der Arbeiterbewegung* (*Archive for the History of Socialism and the Workers' Movement*) 11:385–400.

―――. 1930. "Siebzig Jahre *Zur Kritik der politischen Ökonomie*" (On the 70th Anniversary of *Towards the Critique of Political Economy*). *Archiv für die Geschichte des Sozialismus und der Arbeiterbewegung* (*Archive for the History of Socialism and the Workers' Movement*) 15:1–31.

Saint-Simon, Henri. [1825] 1964. *Social Organization, The Science of Man, and Other Writings.* Edited and translated by F. Markham. New York: Harper Torchbooks.

―――. 1975. *Selected Writings on Science, Industry, and Social Organization.* Translated and edited by K. Taylor. New York: Holmes and Meier Publishers.

Say, Jean-Baptiste. 1817. *Traité d'économie politique* (*Treatise on Political Economy*). 3rd ed. Paris: Déterville.

Schacht, Richard. 1970. *Alienation.* Garden City: Doubleday.

Schäffle, Albert. 1896. *Bau und Leben des Socialen Körpers* (*The Structure and Life of the Social Body*). 2nd ed. Tubingen: Verlag der H. Laupp'schen Buchhandlung.

Schelling, Friedrich von. 1856–61. *Sämmtliche Werke* (*Collected Works*). Stuttgart: Cota Verlag.

Schiller, Herbert. 1973. *Mind Managers.* Boston: Beacon Press.

―――. 1989. *Culture Inc.: The Corporate Takeover of Public Expression.* New York: Oxford University Press.

Schmidt, Alfred. 1971. *The Concept of Nature in Marx.* Translated by Ben Fowkes. London: New Left Books.

―――. 1972. "Henri Lefèbvre and Contemporary Interpretations of Marx." Pp. 322–41 in *The Unknown Dimension: European Marxism Since Lenin*, edited by Dick Howard and Karl Klare. New York: Basic Books.

Schouls, Peter. 1989. *Descartes and the Enlightenment.* Montreal: McGill-Queen's University Press.

Schutz, Alfred. 1973. *The Structures of the Life-World.* Evanston, IL: Northwestern University Press.

Scorsese, Martin (Director). 2005. *No Direction Home: Bob Dylan.* Hollywood, CA: Paramount.

Seeger, Pete. 1971. "So Long, Woody, It's Been Good to Know Ya." Pp. vii–ix in *Bound for Glory.* New York: Penguin Books.

Seinfeld. 1989–98. New York: NBC.

Seligman, Edwin and Alvin Johnson, eds. 1957. *Encyclopaedia of the Social Sciences.* 15 vols. New York: The Macmillan Company.

Sesame Street. 1969–70. New York: National Educational Television (NET).

Sesame Street. 1970–present. Arlington, VA: PBS.

Shaw, George Bernard. 1889. *Fabian Essays on Socialism.* London: The Fabian Society.

―――. 1912. *The Intelligent Woman's Guide to Socialism and Capitalism.* London: Constable and Company.

Sills, David, ed. 1968. *International Encyclopedia of the Social Sciences.* 17 vols. New York: Crowell Collier and Macmillan.

Simmel, Georg. 1955. *Conflict and the Web of Group Affiliations.* Translated by Kurt Wolff and Reinhard Bendix. Glencoe, IL: The Free Press.

Sismondi, Simonde de. [1815] 1966. *Political Economy.* New York: Augustus M. Kelley.

Smith, Adam. [1776] 1976. *An Inquiry into the Nature and Causes of the Wealth of Nations.*
2 vols. Edited by R.H. Campbell and A.S. Skinner. Indianapolis: Liberty Press.

Smith, David and Phil Evans. 1982. *Marx's Kapital for Beginners.* New York: Pantheon
Books.

Smythe, Dallas. 1977. "Communications: Blindspot of Western Marxism." *Canadian
Journal of Political and Social Theory* 1:1–27.

Snyder, Timothy. 1997. *Nationalism, Marxism, and Modern Central Europe. A Biography of
Kazimierz Kelles-Krauz (1872–1905).* Cambridge, MA: Harvard University Press.

Sombart, Werner. 1991. *The Economics and Sociology of Capitalism.* Edited by Richard
Swedberg. Princeton, NJ: Princeton University Press.

SparkNotes Editors. 2007. *Karl Marx, 1818–1883.* SparkNotes Philosophy Guide.
Retrieved December 14, 2009 (http://www.sparknotes.com/philosophy/marx).

Spencer, Herbert. 1876. *The Principles of Sociology.* Vol. 1. London: Williams and Norgate.

———. 1893. *The Principles of Sociology.* Vol. 2. London: Williams and Norgate.

———. 1896. *The Principles of Sociology.* Vol. 3. London: Williams and Norgate.

Spielberg, Stephen. 1993. *Jurassic Park.* Los Angeles: Universal Studios.

Spitz, Bob. 1989. *Dylan: A Biography.* New York: McGraw-Hill.

Stammler, Rudolf. [1894] 1924. *Wirtschaft und Recht nach der materialistischen
Geschichtsauffassung: eine sozialphilosophische Untersuchung (Economy and Law
According to the Materialist Conception of History: A Socio-Philosophical Investigation).*
Berlin: de Gruyter.

Star Trek. 1966–69. New York: NBC.

Star Trek: The Next Generation. 1987–94. Syndicated Networks.

Statistics Canada. 1996. "1996 Census: Nation Tables." Retrieved October 6, 2005
(http://www.statcan.ca/english/census96/may12/source.htm).

———. 2005. "University Degrees, Diplomas, and Certificates (2003)." *The Daily,*
October 11. Retrieved June 11, 2007 (http://www.statcan.ca/Daily/English/051011/
d051011d.htm).

Steinbeck, John. 1937. *Of Mice and Men.* New York: Covici.

———. 1939. *The Grapes of Wrath.* New York: Viking Press.

———. 1952. *East of Eden.* New York: Viking Press.

Stewart, James. [1770] 1776. *An Inquiry into the Principles of Political Oeconomy: Being
an Essay on the Science of Domestic Policy in Free Nations, In Which are Particularly
Considered Population, Agriculture, Trade, Industry, Money.* 2 vols. London: A. Millar
and T. Cadell.

Stewart, Dugald. 1968. *Lectures on Political Economy.* New York: A.M. Kelley.

Summers, John. 2008. *The Politics of Truth: Selected Writings of C. Wright Mills.* New York:
Oxford University Press.

Taylor, Keith. 1975. "Introduction." Pp. 13-61 in *Henri Saint-Simon (1760–1825).* Translated
and edited by K. Taylor. New York: Holmes and Meier Publishers.

Terkel, Studs. 1967. *Division Street: America.* New York: Pantheon Books.

———. 1970. *Hard Times: An Oral History of the Great Depression.* New York: Pantheon
Books.

———. 1974. *Working: People Talk About What They Do All Day and How They Feel About
What They Do.* New York: Pantheon Books.

The Muppet Show. 1976–81. London, UK: Associated Television (ATV) Network.

The Simpsons. 1989–present. Los Angeles: Fox Broadcasting Company.

Thompson, E.P. 1970. *The Making of the English Working Class.* Markham: Penguin Books Canada.

Tindal, Gerald, Jan Hasbrouck, and Christopher Jones. 2005. *Oral Reading Fluency: 90 Years of Measurement.* Eugene, OR: Behavioural Research and Teaching.

Tönnies, Ferdinand. 1887. *Gemeinschaft und Gesellschaft: Grundbegriffe der reinen Soziologie* (*Community and Society: Fundamental Concepts for a Pure Sociology*). Leipzig: Fues Verlag.

———. [1887] 1957. *Community and Society.* East Lansing: Michigan State University Press.

Universal International News. 1959. "Nixon in U.S.S.R.—Opening U.S. Fair, Clashes with Mr. K." Retrieved February 21, 2009 (http://www.youtube.com/watch?v=PIJ1S9wAGbA).

Unterberger, Richie. 2002. *Turn! Turn! Turn! The '60's Folk-Rock Revolution.* San Francisco: Backbeat Books.

Wakefield, Dan. 2000. "Introduction." Pp. 1–18 in *C. Wright Mills: Letters and Autobiographical Writings,* edited by Kathryn Mills with Pamela Mills. Berkeley: University of California Press.

Wald, Alan. 1987. *The New York Intellectuals: The Rise and Decline of the Anti-Stalinist Left from the 1930s to the 1980s.* Chapel Hill: The University of North Carolina Press.

Weber, Max. [1891] 1966. *Die Römische Agrargeschichte in ihrer Bedeutung für das Statts- und Privatrecht* (*Roman Agrarian History and Its Significance for State and Private Right*). Amsterdam: Verlag P. Schippers.

———. 1922. *Gesammelte Aufsätze zur Religionssoziologie* (*Collected Essays on the Sociology of Religion*). Vol. 1. Tübingen: Verlag J.C.B. Mohr.

———. 1923a. *Gesammelte Aufsätze zur Religionssoziologie* (*Collected Essays on the Sociology of Religion*). Vol. 2. Tübingen: Verlag J.C.B. Mohr.

———. 1923b. *Gesammelte Aufsätze zur Religionssoziologie* (*Collected Essays on the Sociology of Religion*) Vol. 3. Tübingen: Verlag J.C.B. Mohr.

———. [1923] 1958. *Wirtschaftsgeschichte: Abriß der universalen Sozial- und Wirtschaftsgeschichte* (*Economic History: Overview of Social and Economic History*). Berlin: Duncker & Humbolt.

———. 1927. *General Economic History.* Translated by Frank Knight. Glencoe, IL: The Free Press. (Published in German in 1923.)

———. [1930] 1958. *The Protestant Ethic and the Spirit of Capitalism.* Translated by Talcott Parsons. New York: Charles Scribner's Sons.

———. [1930] 1969. *Die protestantische Ethik I* (*The Protestant Ethic I*), edited by Johannes Winckelmann. Munich: Siebenstern-Taschenbuch.

———. 1946a. "Politics as a Vocation." Pp. 77–128 in *From Max Weber: Essays in Sociology,* translated and edited by Hans Gerth and C. Wright Mills. New York: Oxford University Press. (Originally given as a lecture on 28 January 1919.)

———. 1946b. "Science as a Vocation." Pp. 129–58 in *From Max Weber: Essays in Sociology,* translated and edited by Hans Gerth and C. Wright Mills. New York: Oxford University Press. (Originally given as a lecture in January 1919.)

————. 1949a. "Critical Studies in the Logic of the Cultural Sciences: A Critique of Eduard Meyer's Methodological Views." Pp. 113–88 in *The Methodology of the Social Sciences*, translated and edited by Edward Shils and Henry Finch. New York: The Free Press. (Written in 1905.)

————. 1949b. *The Methodology of the Social Sciences*. Translated and edited by Edward Shils and Henry Finch. New York: The Free Press.

————. 1956. *Wirtschaft und Gesellschaft: Grundriss der verstehenden Soziologie (Economy and Society: An Outline of Interpretive Sociology)*. 2 vols. Tübingen: J.C.B. Mohr.

————. 1958. *Politik als Beruf (Politics as a Vocation)*. Pp. 396–450 in *Gesammelte politische Schriften (Collected Essays in Politics)*, edited by Johannes Winckelmann. Tübingen: J.C.B. Mohr. (Originally given as a lecture on 28 January 1919).

————. 1968a. *Economy and Society: An Outline of Interpretive Sociology*. 3 vols. Translated by Gunether Roth and Claus Wittich. New York: Bedminster Press.

————. 1968b. *Gesammelte Aufsätze zur Wissenschaftslehre von Max Weber (Collected Essays in the Philosophy of Science)*. Edited by Johannes Winckelmann. Tübingen: J.C.B. Mohr.

————. 1968c. "R. Stammlers 'Überwindung' der materialistischen Geschichtsauffasung" (R. Stammler's "Refutation" of the Materialist Conception of History). Pp. 291–359 in *Gesammelte Aufsätze zur Wissenschaftslehre von Max Weber (Max Weber's Collected Essays in the Philosophy of Science)*, edited by Johannes Winckelmann. Tübingen: J.C.B. Mohr. (Written in 1907.)

————. 1968d. "Roscher und Knies und die logischen Probleme der historischen Nationalökonomie" (Roscher and Knies and the Logical Problems of Historical Political Economy). Pp. 1–145 in *Gesammelte Aufsätze zur Wissenschaftslehre von Max Weber (Max Weber's Collected Essays in the Philosophy of Science)*, edited by Johannes Winckelmann. Tübingen: J.C.B. Mohr. (These essays were first published in 1903, 1905, and 1906 and then gathered together in this 1968 publication.)

————. 1968e. *Wissenschaft als Beruf (Science as a Vocation)*. Pp. 582–613 in *Gesammelte Aufsätze zur Wissenschaftslehre von Max Weber (Max Weber's Collected Essays in the Philosophy of Science)*, edited by Johannes Winckelmann. Tübingen: J.C.B. Mohr. (Originally given as a lecture in January 1919.)

————. 1968f. "Zur Auseinandersetzung mit Eduard Meyer" (A Dispute with Eduard Meyer). Pp. 215–65 in *Gesammelte Aufsätze zur Wissenschaftslehre von Max Weber (Max Weber's Collected Essays in the Philosophy of Science)*, edited by Johannes Winckelmann. Tübingen: J.C.B. Mohr. (Written in 1905 and published in the *Archiv*.)

————. 1975. *Roscher and Knies: The Logical Problems of Historical Economics*. Translated by Guy Oakes. New York: The Free Press. (Essays first published in 1903, 1905, and 1906.)

————. 1976. *The Agrarian Sociology of Ancient Civilizations*. Translated by R.I. Frank. London: New Left Books.

————. 1977. *Critique of Stammler*. Translated by Guy Oakes. New York: The Free Press. (Written in 1907.)

Wells, Herbert George. 1914. *The World Set Free: A Story of Mankind*. New York: E.P. Dutton & Company.

————. 1923. *Men Like Gods: A Novel*. New York: The Macmillan Company.

Wesch, Michael. 2007a. "A Vision of Students Today." Retrieved May 17, 2008 (http://www.youtube.com/watch?v=dGCJ46vyR9o).

———. 2007b. "Information R/evolution." Retrieved May 17, 2008 (http://www.youtube.com/watch?v=-4CV05HyAbM).

———. 2007c. "The Machine is Us/ing Us (Final Version)." Retrieved May 17, 2008 (http://www.youtube.com/watch?v=NLlGopyXT_g).

———. 2008a. "Anti-Teaching: Confronting the Crisis of Significance." *Education Canada* 48(2):4–7. Retrieved May 21, 2008 (http://www.cea-ace.ca/media/en/AntiTeaching_Spring08.pdf).

———. 2008b. "Michael Wesch Homepage, Kansas State University, Anthropology Program." Retrieved May 17, 2008 (http://www.ksu.edu/sasw/anthro/wesch.htm).

Whyte, William. 1956. *The Organization Man.* Garden City, NY: Doubleday & Company.

Williams, Raymond. 1961. *Culture and Society, 1780–1950.* Harmondsworth: Penguin Books.

———. 1983. *Keywords: A Vocabulary of Culture and Society.* 2nd ed. London: Fontana Paperbacks.

Wilson, Sloan. 1955. *The Man in the Gray Flannel Suit.* New York: Simon and Schuster.

Woller, Gary. 1997. "Public Administration and Postmodernism: Editor's Introduction." *American Behavioral Scientist* 41:9–11.

Zamiatin, Eugene. [1924] 1952. *We.* Translated by Gregory Ziboorg. New York: E.P. Dutton.

Zeitlin, Irving. *Ideology and the Development of Sociological Theory.* Englewood Cliffs, NJ: Prentice-Hall.

Zemeckis, Robert (Director). 1994. *Forrest Gump* [Film]. Hollywood, CA: Paramount Pictures.

Zicree, Marc. 1982. *The Twilight Zone Companion.* Toronto: Bantam Books.

INDEX